HONOURING AGE

STUDIES IN CHRISTIANITY AND JUDAISM
Series editor: Richard S. Ascough

The Studies in Christianity and Judaism series publishes volumes dealing with Christianity and Judaism in their formative periods, with special interest in studies of the relationships between them and of the cultural and social contexts within which they developed.

The series is sponsored by the Canadian Corporation for Studies in Religion whose constituent societies include the Canadian Society of Biblical Studies, Canadian Society for the Study of Religion, Canadian Society of Patristic Studies, Canadian Theological Society, Société canadienne de théologie, and Société québécoise pour l'étude de la religion.

1 Sacred Ritual, Profane Space
  The Roman House as Early Christian Meeting Place
  Jenn Cianca

2 The Christian Moses
  Vision, Authority, and the Limits of Humanity in the New Testament and Early Christianity
  Jaeda Calaway

3 Recovering an Undomesticated Apostle
  Essays on the Legacy of Paul
  Edited by Christopher B. Zeichmann and John A. Egger

4 Honouring Age
  The Social Dynamics of Age Structure in 1 Timothy
  Mona Tokarek LaFosse

HONOURING AGE

The Social Dynamics of Age Structure in 1 Timothy

MONA TOKAREK LAFOSSE

McGill-Queen's University Press
Montreal & Kingston • London • Chicago

© McGill-Queen's University Press 2023

ISBN 978-0-2280-1934-3 (cloth)
ISBN 978-0-2280-1935-0 (paper)
ISBN 978-0-2280-1973-2 (ePDF)

Legal deposit fourth quarter 2023
Bibliothèque nationale du Québec

Printed in Canada on acid-free paper that is 100% ancient forest free (100% post-consumer recycled), processed chlorine free

This book has been published with the help of a grant from the Canadian Federation for the Humanities and Social Sciences, through the Awards to Scholarly Publications Program, using funds provided by the Social Sciences and Humanities Research Council of Canada.

We acknowledge the support of the Canada Council for the Arts.
Nous remercions le Conseil des arts du Canada de son soutien.

McGill-Queen's University Press in Montreal is on land which long served as a site of meeting and exchange amongst Indigenous Peoples, including the Haudenosaunee and Anishinabeg nations. In Kingston it is situated on the territory of the Haudenosaunee and Anishinaabek. We acknowledge and thank the diverse Indigenous Peoples whose footsteps have marked these territories on which peoples of the world now gather.

Library and Archives Canada Cataloguing in Publication

Title: Honouring age : the social dynamics of age structure in 1 Timothy / Mona Tokarek LaFosse.
Names: LaFosse, Mona Tokarek, author.
Series: Studies in Christianity and Judaism ; 4.
Description: Series statement: Studies in Christianity and Judaism ; 4 | Includes bibliographical references and index.
Identifiers: Canadiana (print) 20230482120 | Canadiana (ebook) 20230482198 | ISBN 9780228019343 (cloth) | ISBN 9780228019350 (paper) | ISBN 9780228019732 (ePDF)
Subjects: LCSH: Bible. Timothy, 1st—Criticism, interpretation, etc. | LCSH: Age groups—Mediterranean Region—History.
Classification: LCC BS2745.52.L34 2024 | DDC 227/.83—dc23

This book was typeset in 10.5/13 Sabon Pro.

For Garrett
and my *familia*

Contents

Table and Figures ix
Acknowledgments xi
A Note on Ancient Sources xv

1 Why Study Age in 1 Timothy? 3
2 Mediterranean Dynamics of Age Structure and 1 Timothy 19
3 One Letter, Two Stories: Rhetoric and Crisis 53
4 Ideal Behaviour in the "Household of God" (1 Tim. 5:1–2) 80
5 Categorizing Widows: Definitions and Responsibilities 93
6 Why Sixty? 113
7 Younger Widows and Age Hierarchy among Women 148
8 A Believing Woman 176
9 Elders 198
10 Intergenerational Conflict in 1 Timothy: The Big Picture 225
11 The Visibility of Age 245

Notes 265
References 341
Index 369

Table and Figures

TABLE

6.1 A comparison of overseer, *diakonos*, and sixty+ widow   122

FIGURES

1.1 Funerary altar of Caltilius and Caltilia (100–125 CE). Unknown (Roman). Digital image courtesy of Getty's Open Content Program. The J. Paul Getty Museum, Villa Collection, Malibu, California, Gift of Achille Moretti, 83.AA.209.   8
2.1 The generational cycle   29
2.2 A model of age status and the generational cycle   37
2.3 A model of Mediterranean generational stability and social change   50
3.1 Grave stele with the busts of a father and son (mid-second century CE). Unknown (Roman). Digital image courtesy of Getty's Open Content Program. The J. Paul Getty Museum, Villa Collection, Malibu, California, 71.AA.282.   73
4.1 Grave naiskos of a woman named Sime honoured by her husband and grown children (about 320 BCE). Unknown (Greek; Attic). Digital image courtesy of Getty's Open Content Program. The J. Paul Getty Museum, Villa Collection, Malibu, California, 77.AA.89.   84

7.1 The typical contrast between 60+ widows (5:9) and younger widows (5:11) 152
7.2 A contrast between real widows (5:3) and younger widows (5:11) 153
7.3 Cameo set in a modern ring (100–1 BCE). Unknown (Roman). Digital image courtesy of Getty's Open Content Program. The J. Paul Getty Museum, Villa Collection, Malibu, California, 2001.28.10. 164
8.1 Statue of a Roman woman (third century CE). Unknown (Roman). Digital image courtesy of Getty's Open Content Program. The J. Paul Getty Museum, Villa Collection, Malibu, California, 72.AA.153.b. 193
9.1 Portrait of a bearded man (about 150 BCE). Unknown (Greek). Digital image courtesy of Getty's Open Content Program. The J. Paul Getty Museum, Villa Collection, Malibu, California, 91.AA.14. 208

Acknowledgments

We all age. I am keenly aware of this reality as I put this project (which I began nearly twenty years ago) out into the world. Originally crafted as my doctoral dissertation, it has aged, morphed, and matured alongside me.

The prospect of trying to thank everyone who has encouraged me along the way, let alone provided feedback in one way or another, is daunting indeed. To all who have chatted with me about this project, interacted with related conference papers, and/or said you looked forward to reading it – thank you. These conversations have motivated me to keep working toward this publication.

This book has been published with the help of a grant from the Federation for the Humanities and Social Sciences, through the Awards to Scholarly Publications Program, using funds provided by the Social Sciences and Humanities Research Council of Canada. It is a revised version of my doctoral dissertation, completed in the Department for the Study of Religion at the University of Toronto and funded by a four-year Social Sciences and Humanities Research Council of Canada Doctoral Fellowship.

I am grateful to have had remarkable mentors along the way. John Kloppenborg's careful guidance and supervision in the dissertation phase formed the foundation for the major shape and argument, along with many details, of the book. As a doctoral committee member and former editor of this series, Studies in Christianity and Judaism, Terry Donaldson has read through several versions of this project; his suggestions and reassurance along the way have been vital. Margaret Y. MacDonald's comments as external examiner and her continued encouragement have been invaluable. For introducing me to the critical study of the letters to Timothy and Titus, I thank Peter Richardson. Harriet Lyons, my mentor in (armchair) cultural anthropology, graciously served on my doctoral committee. For my knowledge of the field of anthropology, I am also indebted to professors Robert Park, Dorothy Counts, Anne Zeller, and Thomas Abler (University of Waterloo), Mathias Guenther and Laird Christie (Wilfrid Laurier University), and Janice Boddy (University of Toronto).

I wish to honour three scholars who knew that I would one day publish this book but passed away before it came to print: Abraham Malherbe, whose encouragement and agreement with many of my ideas was thrilling and humbling; my mentor, Harold Remus, who immersed me in critical scholarship and asked the big questions; and my Greek teacher, Gary Yamasaki, who had faith in me from the beginning (and taught me diagramming!).

Many friends, colleagues, and students have cheered me on along this long road: colleagues associated with the Canadian Society of Patristic Studies/Association canadienne des études patristiques, the Canadian Society of Biblical Studies, the Canadian Corporation for Studies in Religion, the Context Group, and colleagues and students at Huron University College, Wilfrid Laurier University, Martin Luther University College, and Emmanuel College (Victoria University, University of Toronto). I offer special thanks to Debbie Lou Ludolph, Kate Harper, Olena Darewych, Daniel Maoz, Maria Dasios, Pamela McCarroll, HyeRan Kim-Cragg, and Allen Jorgenson. Allen generously read and commented on every chapter of an earlier (and longer) version of the manuscript. Paul Karalus, a Laurier student, kindly volunteered to update my research on ancient demography. Emmanuel student Jaemin Lee assisted me with the index, with funding from Emmanuel College.

For the latter stages of the project, I am grateful to Richard Ascough (series editor) and the wonderful staff at McGill-Queen's University Press, with special thanks to Kyla Madden (senior editor), whose patience, enthusiasm, and availability have been critical, and to Kate Merriman for her astute copyediting skills. I am indebted especially to the reviewers for their careful reading and assessment, and to Alistair Stewart, whose wise counsel helped make this a better book. I am only too aware, however, that its weaknesses, errors, and omissions rest squarely on me.

I owe special thanks to faithful friends who have shared many joys and challenges in this part of the life course, particularly Lori Kantymir, Sarah J. King, Heather Landells, Sesheeni Joud Selvaratnam, and Andrzej and Dorota Mlynarz.

My greatest debt of gratitude goes to my *familia*. It takes a lot of time and energy to write and revise a book, and it happens in the midst of real family life, day-to-day and year-to-year. In the early years of this project, several family members gave me time to work on it by spending time with my children: Carol (my mother-in-law), and nieces Candice and Rachel (who now have their own children!). Thank you to my mom and dad, Ben and Reta (the generation before me), for raising me, supporting me, encouraging me to pursue my interests, instilling in me a deep respect for history and the importance of humility. To my children, Carter and Summer (the generation after me), thank you for your inspiration and bringing me balance and joy. You have literally waited your whole lives to see the completion of "the book"! And to Garrett, my partner, husband, and best friend, who has walked alongside me the whole way: the words aren't nearly adequate, but thank you for your love, support, persistence, endurance, humour, and unfaltering loyalty.

A Note on Ancient Sources

Within academic disciplines that use ancient Roman and Greek sources, there is a standard system for identifying sources, authors, and passages. Unless the author is quoting from a particular translation, a particular edition is not normally identified. A comprehensive list of Greek and Roman writers can be found in *The Oxford Classical Dictionary* (Hornblower and Spawforth, 2003).

Many of the other ancient sources referenced in this book can be found in series or on databases through an internet search engine, though some can only be readily accessed through subscription, such as the Loeb Classical Library (university libraries often subscribe to such volumes and databases). For sources related to early Christianity, translations in the public domain can be found on the Early Christian Writings website: https://www.earlychristianwritings.com/.

Names of books found in the Christian Bible are abbreviated according to *The Chicago Manual of Style* (17th ed.).

THE APOSTOLIC FATHERS

All references to the following authors and works are found in *The Apostolic Fathers* (AF), volumes 1 and 2, edited by Bart D. Ehrman (2003). These are noncanonical, early Christian texts written in the late first century CE and early to mid-second century CE.

First Clement – *1 Clem.*
Ignatius
  Eph. – *Letter to the Ephesians*
  Mag. – *Letter to the Magnesians*

Poly. – *Letter to Polycarp*
Rom. – *Letter to the Romans*
Smyr. – *Letter to the Smyrnaeans*
Trall. – *Letter to the Trallians*
Polycarp, Phil. – *Letter to the Philippians*
Didache
The Martyrdom of Polycarp
Papias
Epistle to Diognetus
Shepherd of Hermas

ANCIENT INSCRIPTIONS AND PAPYRI

The following sources include two kinds of written evidence from ancient Roman and Greek cultures. (1) Inscriptions (also known as epigraphy) include memorials for those who have died, voluntary association rules, and lists of honoured people. They were written on stone (or similar material), found in Greek (IG, SEG), Latin (CIL), and other languages. (2) Papyri include letters, wills, and legal documents written on an ancient form of paper that is often fragmentary due to its delicate nature. Both sources are associated with people from a range of social statuses and positions, including non-elite persons, and thus are often readily comparable to early Christ followers.

AM	*Mitteilungen des Deutschen Archäologischen Instituts, Athenische Abteilung*
CIL	*Corpus Inscriptiorum Latinorum*
IG	*Inscriptiones Graecae*
P.Köln	*Papyrus Köln*
P.Mich	*Michigan Papyri*
P.Mil.Vogl	*Papiri Milanesi*, ed. A. Vogliano
P.Oxy.	*The Oxyrhynchus Papyri*
SEG	*Supplementum Epigraphicum Graecum*
Sel.Pap.	*Select Papyri*, 3 volumes. Loeb Classical Library

HONOURING AGE

1

Why Study Age in 1 Timothy?

We all age. This is a truism, to be sure, but it is far from a simple concept. Aging is an embodied reality. It is a fundamental part of social identity. And it is a human experience that is truly universal, yet entirely individual at the same time. Each of us observes the effects of age in our individual experience of the life course, the progression from birth to death. Our bodies age. We watch our loved ones grow up and grow older. A person's age is an important part of their familial, peer, and other social roles. Indeed, age is an integral part of social interaction – and always has been.

Despite its vital importance in human experience, age has been largely overlooked in early Christian studies. One likely reason is that age, unlike gender or social status, is not often explicit in early Christian texts.[1] Age is also a more elusive social category than gender or social status (which were relatively stable in the cultural context of the ancient Mediterranean): no one stays the same age for long. And yet, in the ancient Mediterranean, age was always part of negotiating social relationships and thus critical to an understanding of social interactions and expectations.

First Timothy is particularly rich with references to age: Timothy is clearly young (4:12), intergenerational relationships are highlighted (3:4, 12), and older and younger women and men are the subject of an extended section (5:1–25). *Honouring Age* applies a culturally sensitive view of age to 1 Timothy, thereby revealing a fresh interpretation of this letter, challenging some long-held views, and reconceptualizing the situation surrounding the widows (5:3–16) and elders (5:17–25), as well as the rhetoric of the letter as a whole.

After all, the author places his directives in the form of written correspondence from an older Paul to an explicitly younger Timothy (1:2, 18; 4:12; 5:1-2).

Paul and Timothy are familiar figures for this late first-century audience, revered for their roles in the origins of the movement. Using the voice of Paul, the author offers, ostensibly to Timothy, a set of strong directives for a troubled community beset with teachings the author vehemently opposes. In the author's estimation, these teachings are upsetting social order and threatening the community's reputation. His solution is to embrace traditional hierarchical structure as found in the household. Gender hierarchy is obvious: women are to learn in silence and should not be allowed to teach or have authority over men (2:9-15); overseers and deacons are specifically men (3:2, 12; but see 3:11); and young women are to find their place by getting married, bearing children, and running a household (5:14). However, arguably even more critical to the author was *age hierarchy*: younger people were to respect and care for older people (5:1-4, 8; see chapters 4 and 5); older women were to be proper mentors and models to younger women (5:9-16; see chapters 6, 7, and 8); and younger men were to be deferential to their elders (4:14; 5:1, 19-22; see chapters 3, 9, and 10). These actions reflect honourable behaviour that, for the author of 1 Timothy, would combat the problematic teachings. Thwarting these social expectations and obligations, on the other hand, is a denial of faith and display of behaviour that is worse than that of an unbeliever (5:8). The author declares that restoring the social order to reflect the "household of God" (3:15) would save Timothy and his hearers (4:16), but more importantly, it would save his real audience.

I pause here with a note for non-specialist readers (who may not be familiar with early Christian scholarship): I recommend starting with the summary in chapter 10 in order to get a sense of the "big picture" before proceeding to the specific details of the argument.

WHY STUDY AGE?

While aging is a universal experience, how one experiences the life course depends on many factors and makes studying age complex. At a basic level, in order to understand age dynamics within early Christ groups like the one represented by 1 Timothy,[2] an informed awareness of Roman demography is essential. Indeed, classicists

Claire Holleran and April Pudsey argue that "historical demography is important precisely because a wide range of responses to social and economic change can be observed through the study of a population's demographic dynamics. Demographic dynamics should, therefore, be central to any socio-economic analysis of the ancient world" (2016, 2).

Broadly speaking, demography is the study of the structure and development of human populations, as well as trends in populations over time. Demographers use quantitative data related to three factors: mortality, fertility, and migration (Holleran and Pudsey 2016, 1; Hin 2013, 6; Scheidel 2012, 101). *Mortality* refers to the rate at which people are dying within a population; *fertility* is the rate at which babies are being born into the population (Parkin 1992, 72); and *migration* is the rate at which people are leaving or entering the population (not through death or birth). In the modern Western world,[3] this data is relatively easy to obtain from census collection, but not enough reliable quantitative data is available from the ancient Mediterranean world for accurate calculations of any of these factors (Scheidel 2001a, 13). The complex and controversial nature of the data available makes the particulars of studying Roman demography challenging but important to grasp.[4]

Demographic trends in the Roman world were radically different from those of the modern West. There were comparatively few old people, a significantly higher proportion of children, high rates of mortality for infants and children, and much greater fatality from infectious diseases that affected all ages. It is difficult for someone (like me) growing up in the dominating culture of the modern Western world to imagine how this age distribution – especially what I would consider "untimely" deaths among children and younger adults – would affect one's view of the life course and one's relationships. Yet this was the reality of the early Christ followers.

Infant mortality, fertility, and disease are all factors that affect life expectancy.[5] *Life expectancy* refers to the average number of years one expects to live from a certain point in the life course. For example, one might discuss life expectancy *at birth*, life expectancy *at age fifteen*, life expectancy *at sixty*, and so on. Life expectancy is variable, depending on socio-cultural and environmental factors, including climate, nutrition, exposure to disease, immunity, dangerous activity, socio-economic level, and genetics. However, for the pre-modern world, *where* one lived (e.g., crowded urban area or rural area; coastal area or inland) and how prevalent certain diseases were (like malaria) affected life expectancy as well.[6]

Demographers generally agree that the average life expectancy at birth in the ancient Roman world (ca 200 BCE to 200 CE) was somewhere between the early twenties and early thirties.[7] Anthropologist Kenneth M. Weiss makes the important point that "average life expectancy" is misleading because very few people die at the "average" age (1981, 51). This is particularly true with respect to "average life expectancy at birth." Thus, a life expectancy at birth of approximately twenty-five to thirty years does not point to droves of people in their twenties and thirties dying; rather, the average is affected by high infant and child mortality rates in a culture with high fertility (Gowland 2007, 156). That is, the relatively high number of deaths among infants and young children, when combined with the ages of those who die later in life, tends to skew the average downward. About one-fifth of all infants died before their first birthday, and more than a third of all children died before they reached sexual maturity.[8] If a person survived the precarious childhood years, they had a reasonable chance of living into later adulthood. According to Tim G. Parkin, at age five, a person could expect, on average, to live to the age of forty-five (1992, 92; 2003, 280). At age twenty, a person might expect to live to fifty-one years on average (Parkin 2003, 280), and thirty-nine out of one hundred people who reached age fifteen could expect to live to sixty (292).[9] After the age of sixty or so, there was a significant rise in mortality; those who were over sixty likely made up 5 to 10 per cent of the total population (49–50, 224).

Given these numbers, it should be clear that *average* life expectancy at birth does not reflect a *typical* life experience (Saller 1994, 12). The reality of a low life expectancy at birth does not mean that people in ancient Roman society aged at a substantially accelerated rate. As Parkin notes, "Romans did not necessarily or typically become old at a significantly younger age than we do today" (2003, 25).[10] Thus, they did not grow "old" by age thirty. In fact, some ancient Roman authors saw thirty as the time when a man was just emerging from his youth![11]

Moreover, people did not expect to die in early adulthood (Parkin 2003, 36–7, 44–5, 48–51). The anthropological literature confirms that in many pre-industrial cultures, people expect to grow old, even if many do not live to old age because of disease, infection, or accident, and even if the elderly make up a minority of the population

(Cowgill and Holmes 1972, 322).¹² Indeed, Parkin remarks, "The chances of surviving to the age of (say) 60 in the ancient world were not so slim as to make people of advanced age so unusual or remarkable" (2003, 56). This sentiment is articulated by Aristotle, who stated, "For the young the future is long, the past short; for in the morning of life it is not possible for them to remember anything, but they have everything to hope" (2020, 245, 2.12.8 [Bekker's numbering, 1389A]). Likewise, Cicero recounts a common sentiment: "the young man hopes that he will live for a long time and this hope the old man cannot have" (1923, 81, *On Old Age* 19 [Falconer's numbering, 68],). Though Cicero considers this sentiment foolish, for a person can die at any age, it suggests that he *did not expect* people to die in the third or fourth decade of life (Parkin 2003, 36–7, 48–51).¹³ It is important to note that because life expectancy is about averages, life expectancy ratios do not dictate age distribution in the population at any given time (Scheidel 2001b, 1; Woods 2007). That is, life expectancy averages allow us a broad picture but cannot be used to dictate specifics about the composition of a particular population at a particular time. Despite the generalized picture, life expectancy patterns in the ancient Mediterranean identify an important facet of the lived experience of the early Christ followers.

If it is true that "age structure is instrumental in framing and shaping expectations and experiences" of private and public life (Scheidel 2001b, 1), it is helpful to illustrate how demography may have shaped family life. To this end, on the basis of model life tables, Richard P. Saller developed a simulation of the "kin universe" of men and women – a notion of what a person's kinship connections through their lifetime might look like (1994, 48–65). The simulation is strictly meant to sketch broad generalizations. For example, it was probably common for a young adult to have only one or possibly no living parents. According to Saller's calculations, at age twenty, half of all men could expect to have lost their fathers, and half of all men between the ages of twenty-five and thirty could expect their mothers to have died. By age forty, only about one in ten men still might have a living father, and approximately one-quarter might have mothers who were still alive. These numbers must be understood as general trends that are illustrative and not as specific statistics,¹⁴ but they do speak to how many gaps a person might have in their familial and kin networks due to low average life expectancy. Also, age at first marriage has implications for the life course. In the ancient

Figure 1.1 | Funerary altar of Caltilius and Caltilia (100–125 CE), a Roman married couple. The husband is clearly five to ten years older than his wife. Digital image courtesy of Getty's Open Content Program.

Roman world, most women likely married in their late teens (Shaw 1987:30–46; see also Lelis, Percy, and Verstraete 2003; Evans-Grubbs 2007). Men were typically five to ten years older than their wives when they first married (figure 1.1). This resulted in significant age gaps between fathers and children and a higher likelihood of widowhood for women.[15]

Although the demographic evidence suggests an experience quite different from a typical modern Western experience of the life course, the fact that the physical, generational, and contextual experience of age and aging is common to all human experience may serve to bridge a personal gap between us (as readers) and the historical people in and behind the text (see Minois 1989; Johnson and Thane 1998). While this book is a historical study, it calls for an acknowledgment of the reader's own assumptions about age and an implicit comparison with the reader's concepts of age and aging with what we observe in 1 Timothy and its late first-century context.

This implicit comparison has a basis in certain aspects of age that are universal: *Each of us lives in an aging body.* How fast we age, how old we feel, and how age affects our physical functioning depend on our stage of life and state of health and ability. *Each of us experiences relationships with generations before and after us.* We are raised and guided by parents, guardians, grandparents, and/or their contemporaries (e.g., teachers, coaches). In turn, most of us who reach an age to do so have a sense of responsibility to raise, guide, and protect the generations after us, namely, children and grandchildren, our own or others'. We also have a sense of responsibility for our parents' and grandparents' generations, who often require support as they age. *Each of us belongs to a certain age cohort*, a group within a specific age range who "has shared a common historical experience [and] ... is defined by its interaction with the historical events that affect the subsequent life course development of that group" (Hareven 1994, 440–1).[16] Each age cohort encounters the opportunities and limitations within its period of social history, and those who belong to a particular age cohort face life transitions around the same time. Different age cohorts experience societal and global experiences in disparate ways because of their age and stage of life, and each remembers pivotal events in society (and on a smaller scale, events in social circles and family) in ways that shape their experience of aging. The differences shape and texture our social experiences of aging. For example, those who remember celebrating the end of the Second World War or who witnessed the original transmission of the first person walking on the moon are in age cohorts far removed from my own. Those who were in elementary school when the events of 11 September 2001 unfolded in New York City belong to the youngest age cohort to remember 9/11 and the first to grow up in a "post-9/11" world. My own age cohort grew up without cell phones or the internet, but my children's exposure to these ubiquitous forms of technology is shaping the lives of their age cohort in profound ways. The recent global pandemic of COVID-19 and intensified climate change, which we have all experienced, will have long-term age cohort effects that have not yet manifested.

All people everywhere feel the physical, intergenerational, and cohort effects of aging, but a person ages within a specific historical timeframe and cultural context. *How a person frames* their experiences of aging is structured by cultural norms and expectations. That is, every culture structures age differently. *Age structure* refers to the roles, responsibilities, and expectations assigned to a person in each stage of the life course. For example, the expected roles and responsibilities of a ten-year-old child differ significantly from those of her mother or father or grandparents. Those evolving roles and expectations over the life course depend on culture. In Canada, children are legally bound to attend school from the age of four or five until they reach their late teens; in other times and cultures, children in this age range have been expected to work (often depending on social class and familial need). The duration and nature of the stages of the life course – childhood, youth, adulthood, elder years – are also culturally determined. The expected age of marriage, whether marriage and/or remarriage is necessary, what kind of marriage partner is suitable, and whether and when a couple is expected to have children are all culturally determined. Crucial to the present study, age structure determines how younger and older generations interact, cooperate, and deal with conflict, for such interactions are closely tied to cultural norms (Foner 1984).

How an individual progresses through the stages of the life course is largely determined by their circumstances. This includes social class and status, familial relationships, societal values and expectations (such as mandatory military duty), or significant losses (such as bankruptcy or widowhood). However, the extent to which individual choices affect one's life course is also dependent on cultural context. In general, in modern Western cultures, the individual is largely encouraged to make decisions on the basis of their own desires (e.g., career choice, choice of marriage or not, choice of romantic partner), whereas in many other cultures, one's family and community have a much greater influence on life course decisions (traditionally, this may mean doing the same work as one's parents or expecting an arranged marriage).

An exploration of age structure and the experience of aging for early Christ followers in the ancient Mediterranean offers us a fresh view of 1 Timothy, and also demonstrates that age was a crucial aspect of early Christian identity and experience in general. I hope to convey that, in the study of Christ groups and early Christian communities, age matters.

CONTEXTUALIZING 1 TIMOTHY

Within the Pauline corpus, 1 Timothy is not a particularly popular text to study, not least because it is difficult to place into a particular historical setting. Its authorship and date are long-standing, contentious issues. Nevertheless, by focusing on the rhetoric of the letter, aspects of the social setting become clearer, including the problem of opponents who promoted behaviour that threatened the reputation of the community in a time of profound social change (chapter 3). I argue that, in response to his perception of the problems facing the community, the author of 1 Timothy strongly advocates reaffirming age hierarchy as a way of contending with these.

Authorship of 1 Timothy

As should already be evident, along with the majority of critical scholars, I posit that 1 Timothy was not written by Paul, but by an author writing at a later time. While Luke Timothy Johnson and Philip H. Towner rightly point out that scholarship has become complacent in assuming Paul did not write this letter (along with Titus and 2 Timothy), I remain convinced Paul did not write it.[17] The vocabulary and style are significantly different from the undisputed Pauline letters (e.g., Harrison 1921). First Timothy has the largest proportion of unique words among the letters attributed to Paul (LaFosse 2001, 77). Typical Pauline concepts such as the redemptive metaphor of the cross of Christ (e.g., 1 Cor. 1:17–18, Gal. 6:12,14;

Phil. 3:18) and the phrase "in Christ" (ἐν Χριστῷ; e.g., Rom. 8:1, 12:5; 1 Cor. 1:30, 4:15; Gal. 3:28; Phil. 1:13, 2:1) are missing from this letter. Concepts such as εὐσέβεια ("duty and devotion"; 1 Tim. 2:2, 3:16, 4:8, 6:5-6, 6:11, cf. 1:9; see chapter 5), ὑγιανούσῃ διδακαλίᾳ ("healthy teaching," 1 Tim. 1:10; also "healthy words [λόγοι]," 6:3), and καθαρᾶ συνειδήσις ("clean conscience," 1 Tim. 3:9) or συνειδήσις ἀγαθή ("good conscience," 1 Tim. 1:5, 19) are not found in Paul's undisputed letters. "The gospel" (τὸ εὐαγγέλιον; e.g., Rom. 1:16, 1 Cor. 9:23; 2 Cor. 4:3; Gal. 1:7; Phil. 1:7, 5, 12; Philem. 13) seems to have been replaced by "the faith" (ἡ πίστις, 1 Tim. 4:1, 6; 5:8), "the truth" (ἡ ἀλήθεια, 1 Tim. 4:3), and the deposit to be guarded (τὴν παραθήκην φύλαξον; 1 Tim. 6:20). Whereas the "good news" of the gospel reflects Paul's enthusiasm of a new revelation, "the faith" and "the truth" are concepts that suggest a more developed definition of what constitutes the Jesus tradition, both as a philosophical notion and as part of communal identity.

Furthermore, the letter is not easily placed within the timeframe of Paul's known mission and travels. While it is possible that Paul could have written 2 Timothy during his Roman imprisonment as outlined in Acts 28, 1 Timothy and Titus are both much more difficult to situate. For this reason, some advocates of Pauline authorship have created a "fourth" missionary journey followed by a second imprisonment in Rome (e.g., Knight 1992, 15–20) or suggest that, although these letters may not fit into what is known from extant literature, they could *provide* data otherwise unknown to us (Johnson 2001, 67–8). It is notable that these explanations better account for Titus and 2 Timothy being written in Paul's lifetime than for 1 Timothy (67).

Perhaps the most convincing evidence that Paul did not write the letter is that the social structure is strikingly different from what we see in Paul's letters. For example, whereas Paul focuses on the community's unity in his analogy of a body with many members (1 Cor. 12:12), the author of 1 Timothy clearly and strongly advocates hierarchical structure: particular men as overseers and *diakonoi* (1 Tim. 3),[18] women as relegated to household duties and child rearing (2:15; 5:14), and slaves as obedient to their masters (6:1-2).

Though 1 Timothy is normally referred to as a "pseudonymous" letter (written under a "false" name), we might consider using the term "heteronymous" (written under an "other" name, from the

Greek word ἕτερος), which has fewer negative connotations.[19] It is said to have been written to a Christian community in Ephesus (1:3). Though the heteronymous nature of the letter prevents certainty,[20] I assume that it is associated with Asia Minor, perhaps Ephesus itself, as the letter indicates an association with Ephesus (1:3; Treblico 2004, 205–6). The date is also uncertain, but given the apparent social situation, it was likely several decades after Paul's death (which occurred circa 65 CE) toward the end of the first century (perhaps between 90 and 100 CE).[21]

First Timothy on Its Own Terms

Beginning with F.C. Baur in 1835 (Herzer 2008, 548–9), scholars have tended to read the so-called "Pastoral Epistles" (1 Timothy, 2 Timothy, and Titus) as one text. This assumes that all three letters are written about the same situation and people. Indeed, with respect to age, the letters to Timothy and Titus all reveal particular interest in issues of age structure, especially intergenerational relationships. For example, Timothy is said to have received instruction from his mother and grandmother in 2 Tim. 1:5. Various age groups are admonished in Titus 2:2–7.

These letters have some important linguistic, thematic, and perhaps situational connections, and form a kind of a corpus, and there is a literary connection of some kind among them. Similar phrasing in the three letters is unique among the letters attributed to Paul, such as ὑγιαινούσῃ διδακαλία ("healthy teaching"; 1 Tim. 1:10, 2 Tim. 4:3, Titus 1:9, 2:1) or ὑγιαίνοντες λόγοι ("healthy words"; 1 Tim. 6:3, 2 Tim. 1:3; cf. Titus 1:13, 2:2). However, they are often read *as if they are one letter*. For instance, Martin Dibelius and Hans Conzelmann state that "the Pastoral Epistles, taken together, are all three expressions of the one and same concept" (1972, 8). I find this claim methodologically problematic, and it has been questioned in recent study of these letters.[22] The three are distinct letters in their own right and have different purposes, goals, and tone. Assumptions of unity have conflated issues present in all three letters such as the nature and identity of the opposing teachers (e.g., Treblico 2004, 209; see chapter 3). Instead of a complete picture of the opponents (Dibelius and Conzelmann 1972, 65), the blending of the three letters may provide an erroneous, fabricated picture of opponents that does not reflect any one letter accurately (Gourgues 2010, 41). For example, they are characterized as Judeans/Jews (or possibly circumcised Gentiles) who taught Torah (1 Tim. 1:7) and advanced Judean myths (Titus 1:14).²³ While the opponents in Titus are specified as being "of the circumcision" (1:10, NRSV) and promoting "Jewish myths" (1:14, NRSV), it does not necessarily follow that the νομοδιδάσκαλοι ("teachers of the νόμος [law]") in 1 Tim. 1:7 are teachers of Judean Torah (see chapter 3).²⁴

Thus, whether all three are authored by the same person or around the same time is debatable. Advocating for Pauline authorship, Towner recognizes "the letters to Timothy and Titus" (2006, 88–9) as separate texts, stating, "An intentional corpus reading of the letters is unwarranted. First, there are no internal clues to suggest that they originated from the same place or time, or that they are to be read as a single literary unit. From a general perspective, the letters read as separate messages, and where language and themes overlap, each letter nevertheless employs them to achieve unique literary objectives" (28). William A. Richards posits three separate authors writing at different times: Titus written first (65–80 CE) to a community that did not know Paul (2002, 220); 2 Timothy written later to a divided community in need of encouragement (80–100 CE; 228); and 1 Timothy reshaping the first two letters (100–130 CE), addressing new social situations (regarding women, slaves, the wealthy, etc.; 237–8). While these specific conclusions are debatable, Richards's attempt to examine each letter on its own terms is worth further consideration. Jens Herzer suggests that examining the letters separately problematizes widely held notions about the letters as a corpus, but also "we are better able to understand the Pastoral Epistles if we receive them as distinct writings that are related to each other, but differ in their theological, historical, and social setting" (2008, 566). Furthermore, by studying the letters as separate entities, we may find better arguments for how the three *are* related (566).²⁵

For this study, I suspend a conclusion on how the situations, settings, and audiences of the three letters are related. I favour the immediate context of 1 Timothy on its own terms. This focus on 1 Timothy highlights the author's sensitivity to outsiders' opinions and the crisis of communal identity he perceives. A significant aspect of his solution to the problems he addresses is to affirm age hierarchy.

"One Letter, Two Stories" (and Age)

The first letter to Timothy is actually "doubly" heteronymous, meaning that Paul himself did not write it, nor was Timothy the original recipient. Although Timothy ostensibly receives instructions he is to pass along to his (fictive) community, the actual audience (the true recipients of the instructions in the late first century) did not receive them from Timothy himself, but from the fictive letter, imbued with the authority of Paul. The author wrote the letter with this real audience in mind (rather than the historical Timothy's situation). The author had two main purposes: to have his audience apply the specific instructions to their own situation, and to have them label certain teachings and teachers as deviant.[26]

John W. Marshall's view of double heteronymity in Titus is helpful for conceptualizing the situation for 1 Timothy: we might say that as the original audience "listened" to Paul's conversation with Timothy, they "overheard" Paul's assessment and advice about situations that resembled their own. Marshall describes the fiction in narrative terms: there is "one letter, two stories" (2008, 784). Rather than having "Paul" address the actual audience directly, the author fabricated the characters of "Paul" and "Timothy" (on the basis, of course, of the historical figures who were known to the community through stories about them, and perhaps Paul's own letters). The author may have been so rhetorically successful in creating a narrative of the two characters that the actual original audience believed it to be a letter from Paul (Marshall 2008, 799–800), or at least they played along with the fiction. In other words, the "story" in 1 Timothy involves the fictive Paul exhorting his beloved, younger colleague Timothy in order to promote proper teaching and behaviour, as well as to name and reject what he deems deviant teaching and behaviour.[27]

By "overhearing" Paul's half of the conversation, the audience was meant to "insert" themselves into the narrative by applying his instructions to their own situation. That is, the original author of the fictive letter intended his actual audience to see their own situation in what he wrote. Like the directives for specific age groups in Titus 2:1–10 (Marshall 2008, 800), certain instructions in 1 Timothy were directed to the problems in the recipient community: how (and why) to demonstrate respect to governing authorities (2:1–2); how women and men were to behave in the community gathering

(2:8–15); how to choose appropriate leaders on the basis of honourable characteristics (3:1–13); how to treat older and younger members (5:1–2); how to solve problems associated with widows (5:3–16), elders (5:17–25), and slaves (6:1–4); and how to direct those who were materially wealthy (6:17–19). In these sections, we can gain an understanding of the author's view of the social situation of his real audience as he uses the medium of a fictive letter from Paul to Timothy.

In sum, the letter is a mix of fictive elements (e.g., Timothy's commission from Paul in Ephesus) and "real" elements (e.g., the problems with widows) in the guise of a fictive letter from Paul to Timothy, written to a particular community and addressing a particular social situation.[28] Though I often refer to "the author" and his real recipients, when I do refer to "Paul" and "Timothy" in the letter of 1 Timothy, I am referring to the fictive characters rather than the historical figures (unless otherwise specified).

OUTLINE OF THE PROJECT

While I began my work on age by thinking about old age, I soon realized that I needed to take a step back and view age structure within the ancient Mediterranean context more broadly, to consider the nature of the life course, demographic realities, and how intergenerational relationships functioned within this cultural context. Thus, I begin by sketching two related models that help a non-ancient Mediterranean audience to conceptualize norms and expectations around age-related social roles, intergenerational relationships, and the life course in the ancient Mediterranean. I first present a simple model of *age status and the generational cycle*. Further considerations of social complexities result in the model of *generational stability and social change* (chapter 2). To develop these models, I study the ethnographic data of cultural anthropologists working with traditional Mediterranean culture groups in the twentieth century. These studies provide informative analogies to be tested against evidence from ancient Roman sources, which help to disconfirm, confirm, or expand insights derived from ethnographies. Illustrative ethnographic and ancient evidence is woven through the subsequent chapters. I also interact with early Christian scholarship on relevant topics, such as elders, parent-child relationships, and certain aspects of social hierarchy in Pauline and post-Pauline communities. But in contrast to most of those studies, I make age my primary focus. By reading early Christian texts with cultural sensitivity to issues of age, this crucial aspect of social identity yields new and (I hope) helpful insights about the letter to 1 Timothy and about Christ groups and early Christian experience more generally.

For the remainder of the book, I view 1 Timothy through insights and models derived from ethnographies. As I apply the models, I consider how the context of social change and age in the late first- and early second-century Roman world relates to 1 Timothy (chapter 3). Faced with profound social change, the author of 1 Timothy focuses on what he deems to be proper behaviour in the "household of God" (3:15) – his designation for this community – as a way to quell the suspicions of outsiders as well as to combat the opposing teachers. This includes proper behaviour according to the norms of age structure (5:1–2; chapter 4). Proper and honourable behaviour in the ancient world included care for one's parents (filial piety). The author admonishes some of his readers for neglecting their duty and the devotion (εὐσέβεια) due to family in older generations, especially older widows who are mothers and grandmothers (5:4, 8). Such neglect would reflect badly not only on those members, but on the community as a whole (chapter 5).

As I explore categories of widows in 5:3–16, I do not equate the "real widows" (5:3, 5, 16) with the widows in 5:9. The precise age designation for the widows in 5:9, who are "not less than sixty," correlates with what it means for these exemplary widows to be put on a list (καταλέγω) as a means of highlighting their honourable behaviour (chapter 6). Applying ideas of age hierarchy among women to the problem of the younger widows in 5:11–16, I suggest that some of the enigmatic challenges of the whole of 5:3–16 are best read as admonitions to middle-aged women in the community who are neglecting their duties toward younger widows (chapters 7 and 8). This unique reading of the situation of the various widows and women makes clearer sense of the text than previous interpretations have.

The next section (5:17–25) deals with elders and age hierarchies among men, especially appropriate public behaviour between older and younger men. A culturally sensitive reading of this section suggests that the author wants to emphasize the subordination of young men who were making unfounded accusations against their elders, especially since their behaviour affected the public reputation of the community (chapter 9).

Finally, I place 1 Tim. 5 within the letter as whole, exploring how the rhetoric of 1 Timothy reflects problematic intergenerational relationships in the author's community (chapter 10). This close reading of 1 Timothy suggests a larger conclusion about an important aspect of age structure in early Christian communities: age became more visible in the texts produced by and for early Christian communities around the end of the first century (see chapter 11).

As I consider how age dynamics illuminate 1 Timothy, I am also convinced of the importance of age in early Christ groups more generally. Age was always a crucial part of social identity and dynamics among these communities, even if it only became more visible in the extant texts written in the late first century. Alongside identity markers such as gender and social status, age was a critical part of the social dynamics in Christ groups and early Christian communities.

2

Mediterranean Dynamics of Age Structure and 1 Timothy

As a historian, I am curious about the everyday experiences of the early Christ followers in their ancient Mediterranean contexts. With regard to age, the universal aspects of human aging on the one hand and the demographic realities of low life expectancy at birth on the other are a good starting point. However, in order to discern the culturally specific concepts of age, as well as functions of age structure, that are relevant in 1 Timothy (and early Christ groups and Christian communities more generally), a more complex approach is needed. To that end, I develop two related models of age structure in Mediterranean cultures on the basis of my own comparison of ethnographic data, set alongside anthropological theories of aging.[1] Since we are examining the same geographical region over time, with due caution we can hypothesize some elements of cultural continuity from the ancient to the contemporary Mediterranean world when we discuss values and traditional worldviews related to age-related roles, responsibilities, and expectations. The models derived from this data can then be tested and corroborated (or challenged) with ancient data. The models challenge modern Western ethnocentric and anachronistic ideas about age, especially what constituted proper conduct, norms of behaviour, and deviations from the norm, but also mechanisms for social change related to intergenerational exchange.

DEVELOPING MODELS: METHODOLOGICAL CONSIDERATIONS

Many modern Western values (in all their variety) are largely driven by elements foreign to the ancient Roman world: technological progress; surgical, pharmaceutical, and other medical advances; individualism; consumerism; multinational marketing; globalism; decolonizing movements; and rapid social change (to name a few). Thus, the study of early Christian texts in their ancient Roman context is not only a historical endeavour but a cross-cultural one as well.[2] This realization highlights my own "ethnocentric bias" (Dubisch 1986a, 8) in reading 1 Timothy and pushes me to read outside my own experience, with a goal of striving toward historical and cultural realism by observing, learning about, and respecting ways of thinking that differ from my own. Anthropological models provide a set of lenses through which we can observe the culture(s) of early Christian communities with some level of cultural sensitivity. Such lenses offer cultural context that renders the ancient data – especially New Testament texts that are often familiar as sacred texts – as "foreign," and then provide an interpretive tool to help understand their social and cultural dynamics (Malina 2001; MacDonald 1996, 15–20).

According to Bruce J. Malina, "models are generalizations or abstract descriptions of real-world experiences; they are approximate, simple representations of more complex forms, processes, and functions of physical and non-physical phenomena" (2001, 19).[3] A model is heuristic, providing a way of interpreting ancient data using recent data as an analogy (Carney 1975, xvi). Models are most useful if they are considered malleable rather than inflexible, being tested and revised as they are used. I am not "creating" data, however;[4] I am developing a conceptual framework and an informed imagination to help readers of today to see the ancient data through a cross-cultural lens. By exploring values and norms in contemporary traditional Mediterranean cultures, I can more accurately imagine similar situations in the ancient Mediterranean world. In other words, since we cannot observe or question our ancient informants, an informed imagination that employs Mediterranean ethnographic data sheds light on social dynamics in early Christian texts.

There are some important cautions to heed in this endeavour. One strength of using ethnographical data is that it emerges from the anthropologist's unique position as trained cross-cultural observer. However, the postmodern critique of anthropology as a discipline (for example, see Nash 2007) highlights the importance of recognizing that ethnography has a basis and bias in one researcher's observations and interpretations, sometimes with little reflection on the anthropologist's own role in the process, especially in earlier ethnographies. An ethnography is necessarily a translation of what the anthropologist observes, through their own personal and academic lens. Of course, the entire enterprise of cross-cultural study for an academic's own purposes is somewhat selfish and ethnocentric (hence the rise of applied anthropology – anthropology that endeavours to assist and partner with peoples who are marginalized rather than "study" them). Nevertheless, my attempt to view the ancient Christ groups and Christian communities on their own cultural terms is meant to convey respect for them and their cultural ways, as well as gain knowledge about them.

As we analyze the data, we cannot *assume* similarities or continuity across every region or community (see Abu-Lughod 1993, 13–16). The job of the historian is to evaluate the apparent similarities by finding suitable corroborating ancient evidence. We must also be cautious of circular reasoning. Despite the substantial cultural continuity that can inform us of the ancient Mediterranean prior to Christendom, the subsequent Christian and Muslim histories of the ethnographic communities should be kept in mind.[5] In addition, historians, who value apprehending (or surmising) the historical circumstances from a relative paucity of information, need to resist the temptation, on the one hand, to apply later developments back onto the earliest Christ followers, and on the other hand, the temptation to find their own values nestled in the text.[6]

A model can be a valuable tool for cultural insights that may be otherwise elusive, but, as noted, its use should be accompanied by constant readjustment as new data appear and re-evaluation of data is performed, both in the discipline of social-scientific criticism and in the anthropological work of today. Some social phenomena in the text may not be explicable in terms of general models or knowledge of cultural norms since these elements might be different from more recent cultures, or they might be anomalies. In addition, an important evaluation of cultural models should arise from the nature of culture itself: culture is never stagnant, as one might assume from reading some classic ethnographies (Dubisch 1986a, 8). In my historical work, I focus on a particular era in early Christian history that is situated in the midst of the evolution of the Roman Empire, and in the present study I focus on one text that represents a particular moment in a community with individuals at various stages of their own life courses. Thus, my study of 1 Timothy is necessarily synchronic – an attempt to understand this moment. And what I find in the text is a glimpse of the reality behind the words of the author, helped by the models that illuminate this glimpse. As part of this reality, I recognize, for example, that orality was the primary mode of communication in the ancient world (see, for example, Botha 2012; Hearon and Ruge-Jones 2009, and Hurtado 2014), and that the written text known as 1 Timothy captures only a thin slice of the complexity and vibrancy of the community through one privileged voice. Broader conclusions drawn from the particulars need to be understood as possibilities to be evaluated for other texts rather than certainties to be generalized.

USE OF ETHNOGRAPHIC EVIDENCE

Since a full survey of Mediterranean ethnography would be unwieldy, the models and other insights in this study are derived primarily from six ethnographies that explicitly include descriptions and discussions of age categories and intergenerational relationships from Sicily, Greece, Turkey, Iraq, and Egypt. Following anthropological convention, I tend to use the "ethnographic present" to distinguish this work from the ancient texts, but I recognize that these ethnographies present snapshots from several decades ago that may no longer reflect current realities.

These six ethnographies represent Mediterranean fieldwork done prior to major modernizing changes in these communities. In 1935, Charlotte Gower Chapman (1971) did fieldwork in Milocca, a small agricultural village in rural Sicily, before the arrival of electricity. Her manuscript was lost during the Second World War, but subsequently found, edited, and published nearly forty years later. Ernestine Friedl (1962) carried out her fieldwork in a Greek village called Vasilika in 1955–56, with follow-up fieldwork in 1959. J.K. Campbell (1964) wrote his ethnography on the basis of work he did in 1955–56 with the Sarakatsani people, semi-nomadic shepherds in rural Greece. Paul Stirling's (1965) ethnography was the first study of rural Turkey, based on his work in 1949–50 in two somewhat typical Turkish villages, Sakaltutan and Elbaşi (25). Elizabeth Warnock Fernea's (1965) first-person account of life within a traditional Iraqi village in the late 1950s offers insight into women's lives before the 1958 Iraqi Revolution. Lila Abu-Lughod did her initial fieldwork among the Bedouin of Egypt in 1978–79, resulting in the publication of her first book-length study (1986), followed by another more self-reflexive ethnography focused on the stories of Bedouin women (1993).

These ethnographies present a diversity of cultural practices and activities in different parts of the Mediterranean and at various times in the twentieth century.[7] Yet, what I find remarkable and useful for the present study is that within all of this variety, there are clearly broad patterns of continuity with regard to age structure. These patterns became the basis for the models presented below.

I make some important assumptions about these sources. I assume that pre-modern, traditional ways of life in Mediterranean ethnographies provide a useful analogy to hypothesize about cultural concepts in the ancient world in general, and in Christ groups in particular. I also assume that because they mostly predate modernization, the cultural values and behaviours recorded in these ethnographies of rural peoples still provide a better analogy to the ancient Mediterranean than contemporary observations of changes resulting from modernization might. Specifically, I assume that peasant, rural lifestyles exhibit cultural values similar to those found in the ancient Mediterranean, even in urban areas, because compared to today's urban areas, they are less affected by, and even critical of, modernization (Abu-Lughod 1986, 43–4).[8] However, ethnographic research on urban life and social change in the Mediterranean of the recent past may also give us some valuable clues about the ancient urban setting in which Christianity thrived in the first few centuries. Thus, I incorporate some studies from urban areas that demonstrate how cultural values can translate into lifestyles and living arrangements in the village and city.[9]

USE OF ANCIENT EVIDENCE

In the analysis of 1 Timothy in chapters 3 to 10, I formulate hypotheses about social dynamics using an informed imagination and modern data and models. I undertake to corroborate these hypotheses with ancient evidence. Here, too, I make some important assumptions.

I assume that the community represented by 1 Timothy in the late first century largely reflected the social norms of the surrounding polytheistic Roman culture during the early Roman empire.[10] I follow Keith R. Bradley in defining "Roman" as "any place and people imbued with Roman culture in a broad sense" and using it to describe a set of cultural values found in the regions conquered by the Romans in the late Republic and early Empire between 200 BCE and 200 CE (1991, 4).[11] For this study, when possible, I focus on Asia Minor, the region associated with Christ groups from the first century and thus with many early Christian texts from the first and early second centuries, including 1 Timothy.[12] Prior to Roman occupation, Asia Minor, especially the coastal region, was heavily influenced by Hellenism following Alexander the Great's conquest in the fourth century BCE. When the Romans conquered the area, starting in the late first century BCE, they established roads, military presence, taxation, urban administrative presence, and the emperor cult. This made the area "as much Roman as it was Anatolian" (Mitchell 2003, 191).[13] Augustus established benefactions to gain power and prestige, but he also brought stability to Greek cities of Asia Minor with consistent justice (including appeals to the emperor), roads, stable taxes, and secure local government. As they "romanized," cities began to look more alike.

Roman elite writings provide rich material to illuminate Roman culture, but I use these sources with some caution given that most were written from a male elite adult perspective and thus have limited applicability to women and children, and often the non-elite in general. Such texts exhibit ideas about age from a particular viewpoint, but they still provide evidence for how age structure was understood by some in the ancient Mediterranean; such understanding probably reflected male adult non-elite views at least to some extent.[14] For example, two important treatises that deal directly with old age are Cicero's *On Old Age* and Plutarch's *Whether an Old Man Should Engage in Public Affairs* (*Moralia* 10:783B–797F). Both confront negative aspects of old age, affirm that old men have important roles in society as public servants and as models for younger men, and admit that old men should take on fewer strenuous duties. Both offer an almost exclusively male elite perspective, but also some overall attitudes about old age in the ancient Mediterranean.[15] Moreover, the texts from early Christians, written from non-elite perspectives, are also written from male perspectives, so we might expect some continuity in this respect, despite the differences in social position and status. Comments about women in both types of sources reveal more about male perception of the female life course than the female life course itself, but piecing together women's lives from ancient sources is always a challenge.

Other sources, such as popular fiction (plays, novels, etc.), exhibit common attitudes about age. Their artistic liberty, namely, the exaggeration and stereotypes presented, must be taken into account, but they often reflected and influenced the non-elite, who attended theatrical productions (Winter 2003, 31).[16] We can also glean indirect clues about the non-elite perspective, as in the case of some legal documents. For example, Justinian's *Digest* contains references to legal rulings on proceedings brought by non-elite persons. Material culture, such as visual art, while not engaged to any great extent in this study, promises to provide evidence for future studies of age and aging among the non-elite. Visual art can also reveal or help confirm various aspects of age and intergenerational relationships. The Romans were known to create realistic portraits and sculptures, some of which depict old age and obvious age differences between spouses or brothers (Harlow and Laurence 2002, 2, 70, 83, 94; Cokayne 2003, 21; see for example figure 1.1). Another promising area of material study for aging is osteology, the study of human skeletal remains and surrounding contexts (e.g., Gowland 2007, 165–8; MacKinnon 2007). Epigraphy, namely, inscriptions on tombstones and monuments erected for voluntary associations, can contain useful information about age and intergenerational relationships of some non-elite people, though not all (see chapter 1, note 4). Likewise, the extant papyri largely represent non-elite interests and clues about age and family life in the form of wills, other documents related to inheritance, and personal letters related to one family over time.[17]

Honour and the Household

Before turning to the models themselves, it is necessary to outline two cultural factors critical to understanding age-related behaviour in the ancient and modern Mediterranean: honour and the household – two central concepts in 1 Timothy (most obvious in 3:15; 5:3, 17).

Honour undergirds most social relationships in Mediterranean cultures and is arguably the most important and enduring cultural value of the region. Though anthropologists generally recognize that honour (sometimes rendered "honour and shame"[18]) exists around the Mediterranean, the manifestations and nuances of meaning of honour vary according to culture and language (Herzfeld 1980; see also Gilmore 1986). Nevertheless, a broad definition of honour identifies cultural values that apply to Mediterranean cultures (and others), stretching from ancient times until today.

In general terms, honour is the social status, worth, and reputation a person has in the opinion of his or her peers. A person's honour is never only their own; it is also reflected onto and reflective of the person's group. One's "group" depends on context in the moment, but can be one's family, household, village, ethnic group, etc. Honour is maintained and/or gained through challenging the honour of others outside the group whose status is roughly equal to one's own. Such challenges promote a certain amount of in-group solidarity (particularly within the family) and distrust for outsiders. Honour is also maintained through the deferential behaviour of one's subordinates and dependents. This deferential behaviour, termed modesty or shame,[19] entails restraint, tentativeness, and prudence when interacting with or on behalf of a person of higher status. "Shame" is two-pronged, with both positive and negative connotations. On the one hand, it denotes sensitivity to what constitutes properly deferential behaviour (modesty). On the other hand, it names the negative consequences of a lack of proper honourable or modest behaviour (the opposite of honour). A woman's sexual chastity is a crucial manifestation of modest behaviour, reflecting the honour of her family. But modesty is not associated only with women's behaviour toward men;[20] it is also the behaviour befitting anyone with lower status such as a person of younger age or lower social position (such as a client toward his patron).[21] Modest behaviour affirms and maintains the honour of the person of higher status, as well as the group to which both belong.[22]

Honour is derived from public reputation within a specific context: public reputation arises from and is perpetuated by proper behaviour, or more accurately, others' *perceptions* of a person's or group's behaviour (Dubisch 1986b, 208–9). That is, honour depends on the opinions of others. Between families – especially men – it is competitive in nature. In Mediterranean cultures, the public face of honour is often associated with men who defend their own and their family's honour in the public realm. However, women also strive to maintain family honour. In public perception, they do this through preserving sexual modesty, which, if not preserved, can threaten family honour (Stirling 1965, 233; Dubisch 1986b, 208–9). Women also maintain honour through virtuous behaviour, such as cooperation and generosity, largely in the private sphere.

Honour is reflective of and reflected upon all family members because traditional Mediterranean relationships are "collective" or group-oriented, a value which contrasts with the contemporary Western value of individualism (Geertz 1976, 225–35). In group-oriented thinking, "one is a part of a network of mutually binding relationships where one is judged according to role specific and personal criteria" as opposed to "universal and abstract criteria" (Fry 1980, 9; see also Malina 2001, 58–80). Thus, a person is careful to maintain family honour through their own actions. Likewise, one's personal honour is derived from the moral character and behaviour of one's family, kin, and even ancestors (Abu-Lughod 1986, 87; Campbell 1964, 37). Honour is reproduced over generations as well.[23] Behaviour related to honour depends on social context, so that within a village, families are concerned for family reputation among neighbouring families, but in the presence of an outsider, they are concerned for the reputation of the whole village. Again, variation and nuances are important to consider. Honour is not expressed in uniform ways across cultures and time.[24]

Integral to family honour is the setting of the household. In ancient Roman times, the *paterfamilias* (head of the household) protected and ruled over his household, and the members of the household maintained virtue (positive shame or modesty), in order to maintain honour and prestige for the household. Cicero noted that because of reproduction, the husband-wife unit was the most important basis of the household (*On Duties* 1.17.54), but matters of generational continuity and inheritance suggest that the parent-child, especially the father-son, relationship was central (Moxnes 1997, 31; Lassen 1997, 111–12).[25] Children and wealth (which preserved social standing) ensured the survival of the household and the maintenance of its honour (Saller 1994, 86).

The Roman household was the central locus of honour as well as the "location of the life course" (Harlow and Laurence 2002, 20). The household formed the most basic level of a person's identity

(Osiek and Balch 1997, 215; Moxnes 1997, 20).[26] Although each individual had a unique life course, understanding the age-related roles within the household is critical for understanding a general *structure* of the life course in the ancient Mediterranean. The household provided the main social unit for age structure, stereotypes of age-related behaviour, life course stages, and the general age-related expectations within the culture, all of which were highly dependent on gender. Roles associated with age (and gender) were reflected in how one's life unfolded, but the stages of the life course also formed the basis for the experience of relationships between members of the household. In short, although the life course was experienced on an individual level, it was experienced within the context of a person's position in the household.[27]

Honourable behaviour in the "household of God" (1 Tim. 3:15) appears to be the central reason for the penning of the letter of 1 Timothy. The household and household language are prominent in Christ groups and early Christian literature.[28] Households were central to the early Christian movement. Christ followers assembled in house churches and often incorporated whole households into the community (e.g., Acts 16:15; 1 Cor. 1:16, 16:15; see Ascough 1998, 9; Osiek and Balch 1997, 33–4). From the earliest extant texts, "households" were evident. In Pauline communities, households are explicitly mentioned (e.g., 1 Cor. 1:16; Rom. 16:10, 11; see also 1 Tim. 3:4; Acts 11:14).[29] After Paul's time, the community invested in socializing children (MacDonald 2014), and entire households continued to join the movement (1 Tim. 3:4, 5, 12), but the communities were larger, more socially diversified, and presented more complex problems than in Paul's time (Lührmann 1981, 95). The physical structure of the household was also often the meeting place of the early Christ groups (Gehring 2004, 119–228; Cianca 2018), with all of the usual activity of an ancient household (Osiek and MacDonald 2006, 67; see also LaFosse 2017b, 387–92.).

One final note on honour and the ancient Roman household: as I consider the broad strokes of the life course, I focus on free persons who have status and reputation to be gained or lost. Aspects of the life course might be similar for slaves and free persons (Sigismund-Nielsen 2013), but since we cannot assume they would be the same, I do not address their life courses directly in this project.[30]

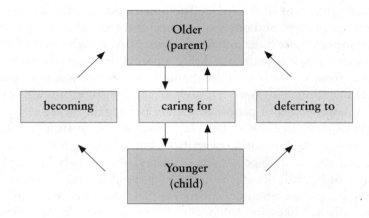

Figure 2.1 | The generational cycle

AGE STATUS AND THE GENERATIONAL CYCLE

With the background of honour and the household in mind, I now turn to age dynamics in modern Mediterranean cultures. Using ethnographic data, I summarize my observations of age status and the generational cycle in these cultures, with preliminary notes on how this cultural context informs my reading of 1 Timothy. *Age status* refers to social roles based on age which are defined by the age structure of a particular culture. People of different age statuses relate to one another in intergenerational relationships according to cultural norms (Foner 1984). The *generational cycle* refers to the cycle of young people growing old and replacing their elders in the social system as their children in turn fulfill the role of young adults (see figure 2.1).[31]

Elders: Preference, Seniority, and Honourable Behaviour

In modern Mediterranean cultures, age status generally governs behaviour between older and younger people within two realms: the household and the public. The focal point for traditional Mediterranean relationships is the household, and the household provides a consistent point of reference. The household always includes different age groups, and one's age status (and gender) dictates proper behaviour to those older and those younger. Although levels of affection may vary, it is understood that a parent deserves deference and respect from her or his children, and older siblings maintain precedence over younger ones.[32] Household relationships provide "natural" classifications of people in society (Chapman 1971, 229), and everyone recognizes his or her place with respect to social rank (on the basis of class, wealth, occupation, kin, and sometimes lineage), sex, and age, with expectations to behave accordingly (48, 67). In other words, seniority status in the household is closely tied to age. Young people are often dependent on their older kin, but older kin eventually are likewise dependent on younger people. Specifically, they need their labour, the benefits of their marriages (e.g., interfamily alliance, grandchildren), and the security of their care in old age (Foner 1984, 135–8).

Outside the family, behaviour is shaped by one's age in the public realm so that older people have precedence, and younger people display deference. It follows that ideal behaviour that is expected in the family is translated into honour through formal behaviour in public. For example, in rural Turkey, "relative age is always important since deference to elders is strictly enjoined at all age levels" (Stirling 1965, 224). This is true for both sexes. In Turkey, "both among men and women, seniority of generation and age confers authority and privilege, and divides, or in large households ranks, the household population. Girls are expected to be deferential to older women, to wait upon them, and to speak only when spoken to. Equally, boys and young men defer to and obey their male seniors" (Stirling 1965, 119). Likewise, among the Egyptian Bedouin, those who control resources and are responsible for dependents are usually older men, and they have precedence over those who are weaker, including women and younger men (Abu-Lughod 1986, 80–2). Abu-Lughod suggests that the structure of the family provides a prototype or analogy for other hierarchical relationships in society that tempers "the potential conflict in relations of inequality by suggesting something other than simple domination versus subordination" (1986, 81). The family analogy that governs hierarchy also includes the complementary roles of family members, including love, identity, and caring for weaker members (81–2).

It follows that seniority contributes significantly to social position. In Stirling's observation, for example, the senior men in Turkish villages sit in the central foremost position in the mosque because their "age and religious reputation count highly," even though all men are theoretically equal (1965, 235). He describes seniority this way: "An old, poor, and shameless man will be thought little of, but treated with respect for his age. A young man who has no senior kin and who commands ample resources will be listened to and given respect, but his youth will limit his standing in the village. Between those roughly equal in other ways seniority is of great importance" (235).

In rural Greece, anyone belonging to a younger age cohort treats those in older cohorts with "at least some of the deference with which all treat the elders," and those who are older treat younger people as subordinate, "with some of the peremptoriness with which the elders are entitled to treat all others" (Friedl 1962, 88). If an older man enters a guest room, he is seated quickly, given the best chair (near the fireplace in winter), and always served first unless visitors are present. He is allowed to lean against the stalls in church when others are not (Friedl 1962, 88). Similarly, in a Turkish village, men arrange themselves in a generally accepted scale with older men in preferred seats in guest rooms, wedding feasts, and mosques (Stirling 1965, 221-2, 224, 235). A similar pattern is evident among women in an Iraqi village. When women attend a religious gathering, they greet friends and kiss the older women with deference (Fernea 1965, 108). Old women also had places of honour near the bride at a wedding (137). In one instance, an old woman came to Fernea's home and took the best chair (132–5). She expected deference and cooperation from Fernea, assumedly because of her age.

In 1 Timothy, the rhetoric of Paul as an older man demonstrates his authority in providing guidance to the young Timothy, and thus to the community (1:1,16,18). In chapter 3, I argue that this rhetoric puts forward a traditional age structure similar to that sketched above. The author of 1 Timothy conceives of the community as a "household of God" (3:15), explicitly using familial language of father, mother, brother, and sister to promote age-appropriate behaviour among older and younger men and women (5:1–2; see chapter 4). Precedence due to seniority is also evident in the prominence of the overseer and *diakonoi* in 1 Tim. 3 (who appear to be household owners with grown children; 3:4, 12), as well as certain elders (5:17–19; see chapters 5 and 9). Recognizing the seniority of older women with authority over (and responsibility for) younger women helps to untangle the situation in 1 Tim. 5:3–16 (chapters 5–8).

Abu-Lughod observes, however, that among the Egyptian Bedouin, authority based on age is not guaranteed, just as greater wealth or male gender do not guarantee authority (1986, 86, 92). Age must be accompanied by honour in order for age to confer respect: "It is not age per se that entitles one to authority over others or to higher social standing, as the position of idiots and insane demonstrate. Age tends to go with increasing self-mastery as well as responsibility for others. Age also brings increasing freedom from those on whom one depends or who have authority over one, because as time passes they die. Wealth provides the means for *gadr* (power) in that it allows a person to be generous, to host lavishly, to reciprocate all gifts (hence, to meet all challenges), and finally, to support many dependents" (93). Abu-Lughod describes an old man in his sixties who squandered his wealth, chased women, and acted irresponsibly. His dishonourable behaviour meant that younger kin no longer respected him, for he no longer deserved their respect (93). The rights of age seem automatic, but they are actually ascribed if an older person has spent her or his lifetime gaining independence, control of property, and the respect of people who owe her or him deference.

The idea that seniority does not automatically convey honour but requires honourable behaviour relates to certain groups of older women and men in 1 Timothy. Regarding women, this may be why Timothy is admonished to honour the "real widow" (5:3), who appears to have little to offer because she is alone (5:5). She still deserves the respect (5:3) and care (5:16) due to an older woman, who should be treated like a mother (5:1), especially because she does contribute to the community through her prayers (5:5; see chapter 7). As for older men, the author is adamant that elders who are respectable and provide leadership should be honoured (5:17–18) and not accused without due process (5:19). This suggests to me that their accusers are questioning the elders' precedence and right to respect, and thus the accusers rather than the elders are in the wrong (5:20; see chapter 9).

The Young: Deference, Modesty, and Honourable Behaviour

As we have seen, younger people's deference is expected. Deference toward older people in Mediterranean cultures is similar to women's deference to men in that it has a basis in modesty or positive shame. In fact, anyone who is subordinate, weaker, and dependent is expected to act with modesty (shame) when in the company of their superiors (Abu-Lughod 1986, 80–2; Friedl 1962, 88).[33] Abu-Lughod describes modesty as "the honor of voluntary deference, which is the moral virtue of dependents in Egyptian Bedouin society" (1986, 165). Dependents gain honour and "escape moral stigma" through their willingness to choose deference in the presence of their superiors (i.e., those who deserve respect and have responsibility over them). "Women and other dependents are morally inferior because of their dependency (hence, lack of autonomy), but they can achieve honor by showing deference to those on whom they depend" (166). Younger men defer to their father and father's generation as well as older brothers; clients defer to their patron and anyone who shares the same status as the patron; women defer to some older women, especially older women in their husband's family, and to most older men (Abu-Lughod 1986, 112–13). Thus, they are not passive in maintaining honour but are important cultural actors: a subordinate person is held responsible for acting with modesty (117) and thus may wield a kind of power or influence (Dubisch 1986a; Abu-Lughod 1986; Osiek and MacDonald 2007; see below). Abu-Lughod points out that among the Egyptian Bedouin, wilfulness can be a positive quality, even for women or the young, as long as a person knows how to be deferential (and display generosity and honesty) in the right settings (109–11).

Age is also similar to gender in that "subordination or devaluation may exist in one context and not in another" (Dubisch 1986a, 15).[34] Abu-Lughod notes that although men typically have precedence over women, some women achieve more honour than men who are younger or of lower status. Some men are deferential to older women, or to women from an important family (1986, 118).[35]

These contextual nuances of embodying shame through deferential and modest behaviour may contribute to the complexity of the situation in 1 Timothy, with competing notions between what the author and the opponents thought constituted appropriate age-related behaviours in a time of social change (see chapter 4), including the expected influence and care of older women toward younger women (chapters 7–8) and the expected deference of younger men to their elders (chapter 9).

Typically, young Mediterranean men obey and respect their fathers in public, in accordance with formal social rules. They do not smoke, drink, play cards, engage in coarse talk, or talk about sex in front of their fathers. They do not speak in public without the father's permission and do not answer back (Friedl 1962, 88; Stirling 1965, 101; Fernea 1965, 100). Campbell suggests this is because these are activities of equals that demonstrate manliness, and thus are not appropriate for fathers to witness (1964, 160). Young Egyptian Bedouin men seem uncomfortable with older kin; they do not laugh or joke around them. They sit quietly and listen; they are ready to serve and seem to prefer the company of peers or female kin (Abu-Lughod 1986, 116). Other deferential behaviour may include avoidance and self-effacing gestures such as downcast eyes and exercising restraint in eating, talking, or relaxing (Abu-Lughod 1986, 165). Among the Sarakatsani in rural Greece, an ideal young man displays a "restrained manner towards his elders" (Campbell 1964, 279). Striking or insulting one's parent is considered a sin (Campbell 1964, 160–1, 324). In rural Greece, older people order their juniors to do small services for them, often with a loud, imperative exhortation, such as "*grigora!*" or "*gligora!*" (fast!). Such a term is never used by a younger person. Friedl notes that the tone of command and dismissal is the "most telling expression of a superordinate person's relation to a subordinate." A younger person will reply, "immediately" or "I have already arrived" (1962, 88).

In 1 Timothy, this norm among men reinforces the importance of Timothy as a younger man who is deferential to his elders (4:12–14) and is expected to follow Paul's advice for himself and his hearers (4:16). Kinship terms serve to define relations between older and younger men and women (5:1–2; see chapter 4), and kinship terminology establishes the kind of relationship Paul has with Timothy as his "child" (1:2, 16), namely, a child who is properly deferential to his elders (4:14; see chapter 3). On the basis of age-related behaviour among men in the modern Mediterranean (corroborated with ancient evidence), I challenge the conventional reading of 5:17–25 as constituting elders being chastised. I argue instead that younger men were the ones who "continued to sin" (5:20) by accusing their elders in a way that could compromise the community's reputation (5:19). Thus, Paul calls for the younger men to be disciplined before the community (5:20) and for Timothy not to join his peers in their wrongdoing (5:22; see chapter 9).

In the modern Mediterranean, kinship terminology confers respect for older persons who are not necessarily kin relations. In Greek, a title of courtesy for an older man might be "uncle" (*thiós*, or perhaps *bárbas*, which is more familiar) or "grandfather" (*papús*) and for an older woman "aunt" (*thía*) or "grandmother" (*yáya*),[36] depending on whether the elder is in one's parents' or grandparents' generation (Kenna 1976, 360).[37] Older people address younger people by their given names (Friedl 1962, 88; see also Abu-Lughod 1986, 63). Terms of respect for elders might be used when one is requesting a favour, as a reflection of reciprocity between close kin helping one another (so as not to imply they are requesting a handout). Such kinship terms may also be used to indicate the opposite sentiment. For instance, calling a non-kin older man "uncle" instead of "*kyrios*" (meaning "mister" or "sir") in Greece implies the old man does not command respect. Thus, terminology indicates a moral dimension to exchanges between people of different generations (Kenna 1976, 360–1). A similar ambivalence for older people can be found in the ancient Roman literature (see especially Cokayne 2003).

In addition to appropriate preference and deference, honour is expressed and retained through the fulfillment of obligations and reciprocity. For example, one behaves honourably by being hospitable and treating visitors or those with social standing with proper respect (Herzfeld 1980, 343). Since others can observe this action, its proper fulfillment is perceived as honourable behaviour. Similarly, caring for one's aging parents is a family obligation, and part of honourable, moral behaviour (Chapman 1971, 230; Brandes 1995, 1; Friedl 1962, 86). Hospitality and filial duty are both publicly visible actions; others judge how honourable a person and family are in accordance with such actions.

In modern urban areas of the Mediterranean, adult children still maintain an attitude of respect for their parents but may find ways to avoid the practical aspects of filial duty. For instance, Stanley Brandes observes that in Iberia, some parents and children will exploit one another for individual material gain. However, this exploitation is a private affair; it should never thwart the family's reputation. Maintaining honour includes taking care of elderly parents, though in practice this care is not necessarily automatically provided and may be motivated by anticipating an inheritance (1995, 14–15, 22–6). Public deference to elders is important, even if private activities of filial duty are not idyllic.

In 1 Timothy, the expectation for children and grandchildren to care for their widowed mothers and grandmothers (5:4) is an example of filial duty. Neglecting this duty was abhorrent (5:8), not least because such neglect would affect the community's reputation (see chapter 5). The importance of hospitality as a manifestation of respect for age may be behind the "double honour" that should be given to certain elders (5:17), which is likely referring to a double portion of food (see chapter 9).

Age Status and the Generational Cycle: Model 1

Figure 2.2 summarizes expected (and typical) roles and behaviour in Mediterranean cultures, helping to illuminate important dynamics of age hierarchy in 1 Timothy, including the realm of women and women's networks. On the one hand, the generational cycle (figure 2.1) represents the experience of an individual family member during her or his own life course, which is a good starting point since "aging and death occur individually, and not as a collective process" (Weiss 1981, 27). On the other hand, the generational cycle also applies to the ongoing process of family members in successive generations passing through the life course. Parent-child as well as other senior-junior roles are determined by cultural values, such as honour. In turn, parent-child roles specify the behaviour that reflects and reinforces cultural values. Age structure remains relatively stable over time because age-related roles, determined by cultural values, prescribe expected behaviour between older and younger generations. The behaviour reflects cultural values and also serves to reinforce them. Although an individual's age is constantly changing, and their age status shifts through the life course, the overall social order remains relatively stable. Specific behaviour associated with social roles, such as the role of the father, or how the young and old interact, is stable over time.

Unlike the largely immutable nature of gender (and social position, for the most part) in ancient and traditional Mediterranean thought,[38] age is a social category that shifts with the life stage of the individual. However, within the generational cycle, the young fulfill relatively consistent roles. Intergenerational relationships and

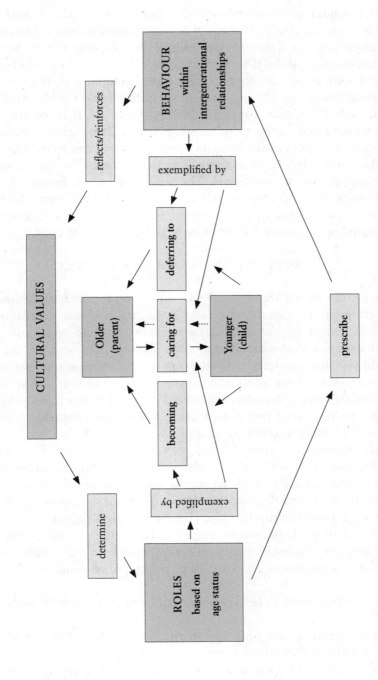

Figure 2.2 | A model of age status and the generational cycle

public behaviour of deference and preference are both focused on the household, family, and kin in Mediterranean cultures. The continuity of the age structure is a result of the solidarity of the family. Children are socialized to respect their elders, but they also learn that family members rely on each other throughout their lives for meeting needs and to keep each other accountable for honourable behaviour (Chapman 1971, 73; Stirling 1965, 99). It is the duty of kin to help and support one another; spend leisure time together; cooperate in work; help in small crises, such as unexpected guests, and in large crises, such as times of sickness, food shortage, or rites of passage (Stirling 1965, 148). The pivotal role of the family allows old people to find "repose and respect" in their children's homes (Fernea 1965, 185; see also Johnson 1983). Thus, the solidarity of the family promotes the continuity of the generational cycle.

AGE STRUCTURE AND SOCIAL CHANGE

The second model accounts for two other elements that affect intergenerational relationships: power dynamics between generations and the effect of historical circumstances on these relationships. Both are related to social change. In 1 Timothy, the author's use of traditional hierarchies to resist the opponents' teaching suggests that the opponents were advocating social change and that the author desired to control the rate and/or kind of social change. At the very least, his resistance points to tension within the community over ideas that challenged the status quo.

My ethnographic research suggests that possibilities for social change can occur within the family mechanism of young-old conflict and cooperation, for this is where the young test out the efficacy of cultural values, and their elders respond. External influences may precipitate potential cultural changes, but such changes begin to take root in the family or household context. This is because in Mediterranean cultures, the domestic realm generally provides a culturally sanctioned, safe social space to work out conflict and resentment.[39]

Power Dynamics in Intergenerational Cooperation and Conflict

The expectations we observed in the first model reflect an ideal but not the reality of relationships over time, for even within the stable age structure of Mediterranean cultures, the young and old have disagreements. In her cross-cultural study of intergenerational relationships, Nancy Foner notes that if intergenerational conflict is not overt, it can be mitigated in various forms of accommodating behaviour (1984, 124–55). One cultural norm that helps mitigate the power differential between old and young is the promise of future rewards as one progresses through the life course. That is, if a person is assured they will one day obtain power in their older years, they are less likely to rebel against their elders when they are young (Foner 1984, 130–2). In general, a Mediterranean father has rightful authority over his son, and the son respects and obeys his father, especially when his father is active and competent to conduct family affairs. In patrilineal Mediterranean cultures, a man usually inherits the headship of the household when his father dies. Thus, he occupies a liminal position from the time of marriage until his father's death. He does most of the heavy labour, yet his aging father retains authority to make decisions and control the money (Lisón-Tolosana 1976, 306; see also Chapman 1971, 79; Stirling 1965, 224; Campbell 1964, 159–63). But eventually (all things being equal) he will attain the power his father once had. That is, in the typical Mediterranean life course, individual roles and access to power change over time. "Every household and every relationship within it is changing all the time. As people grow older they move from one socially defined group to another, and the circumstances in which they have to play their rôles change constantly" (Stirling 1965, 98).

Formal behaviour, such as the proper honourable behaviour observed in Mediterranean cultures (e.g., maintaining silence in the presence of an elder and the use of respectful titles), is another form of accommodation that emphasizes familial relationships and cooperation (Foner 1984, 138–40). As we have seen, proper behaviour based on age status is a matter of family honour. All family members have a concern for and a stake in the honourable standing of the family. Since public behaviour reflects on and affects honour, proper behaviour according to age status, especially deference to older people – including filial duty and hospitality – is honourable and virtuous behaviour (Stirling 1965, 233; Fernea 1965, 150; Friedl 1962, 86). Moral behaviour in the public realm with regard to age stems from and contributes to a stable social structure. If younger people challenged their elders in public, they would compromise their family's reputation as well as their own, so they are compelled to maintain deference in the public domain. However, power between young and old may be negotiated in the private realm through interchanges that make room for cooperation and also have the potential to challenge the status quo within culturally appropriate venues.

Reputation was evidently important to the author of 1 Timothy (3:4–7, 5:14), and the importance of age hierarchy to the community's reputation is woven through 1 Tim. 5 (see chapters 5–9). Ideal *public* behaviour does not necessarily correlate with private conflict, and the author of 1 Timothy is concerned that private conflict not spill into public view (see especially chapters 4, 7, 9 and 10). But it may be in the private spaces that change was brewing in a way the author did not respect or approve of. Several examples of private conflict from the Mediterranean ethnographic data have potential resonance with 1 Timothy, hinting at ways that such challenges may have begun. These examples include offering opinions, folklore, marriage, and inheritance.

Opinions and Advice

The most forthright and benign challenge to age hierarchy involves younger people offering opinions to their elders. This is acceptable as long as the elders' place of precedence is maintained. In Milocca, Chapman observes that young people have a right to make suggestions or give advice to their elders, but the latter retain authority and responsibility (1971, 79). In the Greek village of Vasilika, during routine activities, expressing opinions is part of typical conversation, but very few of these opinions have any real effect. The older man has the final say (Friedl 1962, 81). On the other hand, Friedl notes that he will not usually choose a course of action that will anger his juniors (81, 88). Though it may appear the younger person has no real influence over his elder, the exchange may actually be a mechanism for cooperation and allaying conflict when it comes to larger issues. In 1 Timothy, this kind of negotiation between old and young might be reflected in the relationship dynamics that are assumed and modelled in Paul's fictive relationship with Timothy.

Folklore

Intergenerational conflict is also evident in less obvious ways in the realm of what I label "folklore," such as sayings, poems, songs, or stories. Different age groups may use folklore to mitigate conflict by expressing ambivalence or resentment without compromising family honour (Foner 1984, 147–8). This is evident in Miloccan sayings. On the one hand, they say, "Listen to old people, for they do not deceive you" and "The old hens make the best broth"; on the other hand, they say, "Have no faith in old people and strangers" and "The old flower stinks" (Chapman 1971, 47). Young Egyptian Bedouin men recite lyrical poetry among the women, both in mundane conversation and at weddings, as a way of expressing personal emotion (which is unacceptable for honourable behaviour) and as a means of resisting older men's control over their lives (Abu-Lughod 1990, 46–7). In rural Spain, where sons-in-law find themselves under the power of their wives' mothers, songs depict mothers-in-law in a negative light (recorded by Gilmore 1986). In Turkey, folksongs, folktales, and jokes about conflicts between mother-in-law and bride are plentiful (Kiray 1976, 264). The songs are a latent form of resistance on the part of younger people. On the other hand, the poems of older Egyptian Bedouin women (Abu-Lughod 1986) and laments of older Greek women (Caraveli 1986) can also be seen as an expression of resistance to social structure and authority.

One traditional Mediterranean folk tale demonstrates the anxiety older people might feel about their reliance on their children. The tale helps to reinforce the generational cycle of filial care as much as it articulates underlying fears of conflict and neglect. "The legend states that one day an old man was taken to Papa's Peak [a deserted mountain] by his son. About to suffer abandonment, the old man counseled the son to leave him only half a blanket and take the other half for himself when it was his turn. Startled and confused by his advice, the son asked whether he would also eventually die on the mountain. 'Well, what else?' responded the old man. 'I brought my father here, you bring me here, and your son will treat you the same.' Upon hearing this response, the son hurriedly put the old man back in the cart and carried him home" (translation from Portuguese in Brandes 1995, 13).[40] As Stanley Brandes notes, folklore echoes and reinforces aspects of social structure. In this case, the young person cares for his father for his own future self-preservation (13), but the old man is notably active in prolonging his life.[41]

In 1 Timothy, there are hints that folklore may have been a mechanism for power challenges because the author maligns its use and influence. He accuses the opponents of using myths and never-ending genealogies as a basis for their wayward teaching (1:4), promoting empty talk (1:6) and (by implication) "profane myths" (NRSV) associated with old women (4:7). The content of these myths is unclear, but the power they had to sway members of the community is evident. How much they were associated with particular age groups is also unknown, but it is noteworthy that some were connected to older women.

Marriage

Though it may not be an obvious way to question the authority of elders, by its very nature marriage changes the status quo. In Mediterranean societies, marriage is a pivotal part of honour and interfamilial relationships: "Both as an event and as a relationship marriage is at the centre of village society" (Stirling 1965, 178). In the face of competition between families, marriage negotiations require cooperation and trust between families that challenges the self-sufficiency and independence of a family (Campbell 1964, 39, 131, 137–8). But Abu-Lughod also observes that attitudes toward sexuality and marriage challenge the hierarchy between elders and juniors. Marriage gives a young Egyptian Bedouin man a chance to rule over his own domain, and Abu-Lughod observes senior men avoiding weddings, perhaps because of the implicit challenge to their authority (1986, 147). By focusing on marriage as the joining of two kin groups, senior men have control over who their adult children marry (149), and kinship bonds trump marriage bonds (148). The conformity and cooperation of the young bride and groom are required in order for the elders of the family to retain honour, especially since this union involves the carefully guarded female sexuality of the bride, representing the honour of her family. Thus, decisions involving marriage become moments in which younger people can have power.

In 1 Timothy, marriage is critical to the roles of the overseer (5:2) and the *diakonoi* (5:12). It is also essential for an exemplary old widow (5:9; see chapter 6). Marriage is apparently forbidden by the author's opponents (4:3), which is most likely why it plays such an important role in advice concerning widows, especially young widows who can still bear children (5:11–15). I argue in chapter 8 that power struggles resulting from teaching of the opponents are related to the role of older women in assisting with matchmaking. These elements at least point to complex dynamics at play in intergenerational relationships in the community involving marriage.

Inheritance

Finally, inheritance is an important and often contentious issue for intergenerational relations in the Mediterranean, particularly among men.[42] There are numerous variations of inheritance patterns,[43] but they are inevitably linked with care for parents in old age, and thus intergenerational negotiations: the reward of inheritance is exchanged for bearing the burden of caring for elderly parents (Lisón-Tolosana 1976, 310–11; Kenna 1976, 358; Brandes 1995, 16). Practices around the Mediterranean vary. Sons may resent the power and authority of their fathers and exert pressure on them to hand over economic control. In some areas, parents may retain control to ensure their own well-being into old age (Brandes 1995, 22–3). In the Turkish village, land is usually handed over to sons at the father's death, unless the father is senile. The land might be divided if the brothers do not get along (Stirling 1965, 94). In other cases, if the father is senile, the eldest son may control household affairs but still give formal respect to the father as nominal head of the household (103). If the father is not senile, however, he retains control of the household, and his grown sons rely on him, even for cash (95).[44] On the other hand, among the Sarakatsani, tension increases when an adult son with young children is waiting for his father to step down as active head of the family. It is thought a grown man should relieve his elderly father of duties or face ridicule for not doing so. The son may show disrespect to his father before he is assured of his inheritance, but not usually in public. A father's "retirement" resolves this tension (Campbell 1964, 69). In these cases, inheritance represents male economic control in the negotiation of power between old and younger generations.

Whether the mention of wealth in 1 Timothy 6:9–10 relates to this element of intergenerational power remains to be seen, but Timothy is clearly called to guard what was entrusted to him (6:20), a kind of spiritual inheritance embodied in Paul's message to the younger Timothy that affirms that author's values over those of his opponents (see chapter 10).

Inevitably, the relationships between young and old in Mediterranean societies involve power struggles. Those whose age and functionality make them dependent, and thus less powerful in the material realm, possess other kinds of power.[45] If power involves not only authority and prestige, but also influence, then people who are otherwise considered dependent and subordinate can also be said to have power, albeit perhaps "illegitimate" power, or latent power (such as when female behaviour determines the reputation of men; Dubisch 1986a, 19; see also MacDonald 1996). Jill Dubisch applies these ideas to men and women, but they can also apply to the old and the young. In a manner similar to the ways that women employ resistance to power, so the young (and the very old) employ resistance to challenge the power structure and ensure their needs are met.

Thus, intergenerational relationships may present publicly as ideal, but innate power struggles and conflict, as well as strategies for cooperation, between people of different ages, are simmering in the private realm. These negotiations represent a microcosm of the larger whole, as articulated by Muriel Dimen in her observations of rural Greece:

> The relationships of parents to children, of sibling to sibling, of adults of both genders to each other, of youngsters to elders, and of kin to kin and to strangers communicate to the young and to adults a comprehensive picture of how people are supposed to behave in these relationships and the cultural meaning of these bonds. In communicating intangible meaning and values, domestic relations also re-create invisible social structure, as well as the tangible persons organized by that structure. This is because domestic relations, like all social relations, are simultaneously behavioral and symbolic: they are what they are, as well as what they represent. They re-create not only the structure as it is supposed to be, but also its hidden contradictions; thus, what child and adult absorb from the domestic process of social reproduction is both social compliance and social criticism. (1986, 60)

Thus, people are socialized not only to uphold an ideal by behaving properly, but to test ideals for their efficacy and value. This is exemplified above in intergenerational interactions in the private realm, namely, giving advice, folklore, marriage, and inheritance.

In sum, the ethnographic data suggests that in traditional Mediterranean societies older people's authority is assumed but can be challenged. Intergenerational relationships within the family are the basic arena for age status conflict and resolution. Within the domestic sphere, younger and older people engage in power struggles. Those who are less powerful in the hierarchy have socially acceptable ways to challenge those who have authority over them and express a kind of latent form of power or influence, often within the context of the family or private sphere. Intergenerational conflict can then be acted upon and resolved within the family structure, and not publicly. In other words, in the private realm, the young can question or challenge the authority of their elders, and elders can negotiate their power in a sphere that does not dishonour the family. The designation "household of God" (3:15) in 1 Timothy is a means of curbing challenges to hierarchy by framing them as domestic, private, in-house issues. The rhetoric of Paul as an elder gives him negotiating power, with hopes of mitigating judgment from outsiders and maintaining honour.

LIFE COURSE APPROACH

So far our discussion of age has assumed a synchronic framework to situate age status within the relative stability of Mediterranean age structure. However, culture is never stagnant, and social structure can (and does) change over time (Stirling 1965, 99). Our investigation into intergenerational relationships in 1 Timothy assumes the letter was written in response to a particular community composed of older and younger people amidst particular historical circumstances. This leads us to consider age using the "life course approach."

The life course approach (also called the life course perspective) has been used in sociological, anthropological, and historical studies of age and aging (see for example, Hareven 1982). It is a "theoretical orientation" that offers a "holistic understanding of lives over time and across changing social contexts" (Elder, Johnson, and Crosnoe 2003, 15). This approach suggests that in order to study any stage in the human life span effectively, one must consider both cultural and social norms of the process of the whole life course (various roles, life decisions, and transitions), as well as the historical context of a person or age cohort. Cultural expectations related to social position, status, gender, and geographical location strongly guide the stages of a person's life course, but the life course is also an experience affected by personal decisions amid life circumstances (e.g., the death of a close family member). In other words, every culture has a normative framework for how a person progresses through life (Harlow and Laurence 2002, 3; see also Hareven 1982, 6–9),[46] but another crucial layer of the life course is the fact that people are affected by social change within the historical circumstances of their lifetime. The individual makes decisions within the opportunities available in a particular historical and social framework and within their familial context. Their life decisions affect the life courses of others in their family (Elder, Johnson, and Crosnoe 2003, 11–13). This is especially evident in later life. "A life-course perspective illuminates how problems, needs, and patterns of adaptation of older people were shaped by their earlier life experiences and by historical conditions affecting them" (Hareven 1996, 3).

Using the life course approach, a model of Mediterranean generational stability and social change helps us to consider the interplay between historical circumstances and life course decisions of individuals who act within the constraints and freedoms of their age, experience, cultural values, and close relationships. Early Christian texts generally offer few clues about life course decisions amid historical circumstances. However, this model helps us to glimpse something of the complexities of the life course within the historical and social contexts of those who are represented by these texts.

The most salient example of social change in many ethnographies involves the effects of modernization in the twentieth century, namely, changes brought about by the encroachment of modern Western dominating culture with its technological, economic, commercial, consumerist, and social influences. I argued earlier that I chose traditional Mediterranean ethnographies because they represented cultures with fewer effects of modernization, and thus more chance of offering suitable analogies for age structure in the ancient world. However, in ethnographies that present observations of cultures undergoing modernization, we find clues about the nature of social change in the Mediterranean suggesting that as the young grow older, they tend to return to the familiar patterns of their parents and elders. In other words, generational change may in fact promote cultural continuity much more than it promotes social change.[47]

Modernization arose under very specific historical circumstances. Comparison with the ancient world must attempt to identify and bracket ethnocentric bias and insensitivity to the ancient Mediterranean world view and way of life, which was "pre-clock, pre-monastic, pre-Newtonian, pre-Enlightenment, pre-Industrial Revolution and pre-Einsteinian" (Malina 1989, 9–10). Thus, though theories of age and modernization generally provide little guidance for this study of early Christians,[48] some anecdotal stories of social change due to modernization can provide possibilities for comparison with the ancient Mediterranean.

In the Greek village of Vasilika, Friedl observes that older people are "no less progressive" than younger ones, agreeing on important family goals and how to achieve them (1962, 89). For example, the older generation agreed that the use of chemicals and machinery was more efficient for agriculture (26). In general, these goals seem to include "enhancement of the honor and prestige of the family" (37) and transmitting wealth and property to the next generation, which is an "essential family obligation" (18). They ensure dowries for daughters, education for sons, and material improvement in the household (37–8). These examples are all economic, likely important to all generations in the aftermath of the Greek civil war. In fact, such ardent family solidarity may have been a reaction to the divisions within families that occurred during the civil war.

Among Egyptian Bedouin, with exposure to Western notions about weddings and marriage that focus on the newlywed couple rather than kin connections, young women ally themselves with young men in rebellion against older women (and thus their fathers and uncles as well). Young women buy lingerie, which draws attention to a woman's sexuality rather than her moral reputation, childbearing role, and ability to manage a household and help kin. Abu-Lughod interprets this kind of resistance as a way for young women to express their openness to change in response to external influences, but also their uncertainty that the traditional ways can adequately address the implications of these foreign influences. "Young women, in resisting for themselves the older women's coarseness by buying moisturizing creams and frilly nylon negligees are, it could be argued, chafing against expectations that do not take account of the new set of socio economic circumstances into which they are moving" (1990, 50; also 48, 52). The young are using an ambivalent, but important, Egyptian Bedouin value of assertiveness to express their consideration of what external change means for them as young people (110–11). In order to discipline the younger women within the female context, the older women complain that younger women have no modesty (78). It is quite possible that as these young people grow old, they will reinforce values and privileges similar to those they resist now.

In a study of Italian immigrants living in Syracuse, New York, Johnson observes that the family is the focal point of people's social relationships, characterized by the kind of solidarity and pursuit of family honour we find in traditional Mediterranean ethnographies. Even with the educational, occupational, and social status changes that occur between generations, children choose to live near their parents, promoting interdependence and constant social contact and support. Authority follows the lines of traditional Italian families where the old have power over the young, and men over women, reinforcing conformity to the family hierarchy and duties, even at the expense of personal interests. The family context provides an "escape valve" for frustrations and ambivalence of the young, caught between their personal interests (endorsed by the larger American culture) and their family's expectations for conformity. An emotional outburst within the family challenges the norms but is an acceptable way to vent feelings without compromising family honour. Frequent family contact continues to reinforce family solidarity and loyalty. Because of this continuity, the elderly retain their roles of authority in the family (1983, 94–102). Johnson's study demonstrates the enduring quality of the generational cycle common to Mediterranean cultures, even in the midst of tremendous change in the immigrant experience.

Finally, in rural Greece, Campbell emphasizes how older Sarakatsan men (over sixty) traditionally step down from their active control in the family, but he also notes that during his fieldwork in the 1950s, the older men were generally illiterate. The outside world was more accessible to their literate sons (1964, 161–2; see also Achebe 1959). One wonders if literacy and access to the outside world that was slowly infringing on the Sarakatsani exerted more influence on the timing and quality of male "retirement" than he accounts for. It is possible that the younger sons disregard their old fathers' views (163–4) because they no longer consider them relevant in changing times. It might be that Campbell was invested in describing traditional culture and/or typical generational changes in rural Greek culture and downplayed the influence of modernization. But, given the tenacious nature of age structure, what kind of power these literate young men have when they become old men is an interesting question. Foner argues that if social change challenges the age stratification system itself, older people's domination is questioned but may not be completely eradicated. "Young rebels, of course, often turn into respectable citizens and staunch upholders of customary ways when they become older." Furthermore, "cultural traditions, we know, often die hard, and age norms are no exception"; for example, in the Mediterranean, age deserves respect (1984, 225; see also Stirling 1965, 27).

Social change is not predictable, but the resilience of age structure may be a factor that delays or resists radical change in Mediterranean cultures. In chapter 3, I present examples from extant moments of social change in Greek and Roman history that demonstrate similar patterns, suggesting that historical circumstances (namely, a crisis of identity) factored into the motivation for the composition of 1 Timothy.

Generational Stability and Social Change: Model 2

These illustrations of power dynamics and conservative forces resisting change in the modern Mediterranean support a model of generational stability and social change. The stability and safety of the household provides for the possibility of social change (either through resistance of young people to their elders or cooperation between generations), as well as social continuity (because young people grow old and come into the power positions of their parents). This model builds on the generational cycle (figure 2.2), by considering diachronic and historical contexts (figure 2.3).

In this model, social relationships function in two connected and fluid realms: the private (household) and the public (larger society or community).[49] At the centre, the generational cycle confirms that age is important in familial roles, with parent and child (and all other familial) roles changing as each member moves through various transitions of the life course (figure 2.2). These roles provide a framework for stable age structure in the public realm: the young defer to the old, and the old maintain precedence over the young. At a societal level, a stable structure of relational norms based on age, gender, and social status helps maintain honour. At the same time, the family provides a context for both challenging and reinforcing the age hierarchy. It provides a safe space for working out conflict in various ways. Power struggles within the private sphere are rarely aired in public, as this would negatively affect family reputation, and with it the honour of all family members. Generations replicate similar behaviour with regard to age status, which contributes to social stability. But as historical circumstances change, the possibility for questioning age hierarchy in the family opens the potential

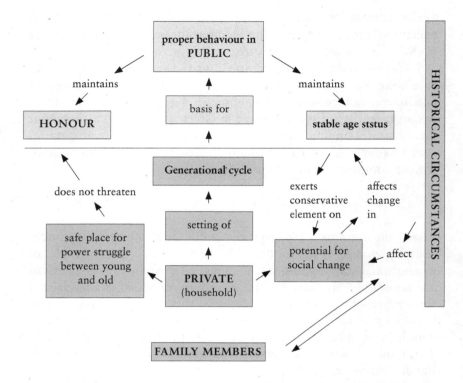

Figure 2.3 | A model of Mediterranean generational stability and social change

for changing the social structure as well. At the same time, one's familial identity provides a conservative element, for young family members grow into more powerful older adults. This generational cycle ultimately exerts a conservative pressure that largely maintains the social structure. In 1 Timothy, this conservative tendency helps to explain the author's proposed "solutions" that apply social hierarchy to the problems in the community.

CONCLUSION

A twenty-first-century Western cultural lens provides a relatively poor basis for a historical reading of 1 Timothy (and other early Christian texts) and is apt to render a reading that reflects more about its contemporary reader than about the text's original author and recipients. On the other hand, the application of insights from Mediterranean ethnographies illuminates aspects of social and cultural norms of the ancient Mediterranean that might otherwise remain elusive or obscure. Evidence for the non-elite (especially women) is sparse and/or biased. However, the evidence we do have can be better understood by viewing it through an anthropological lens that organizes Mediterranean ethnographic data in a way that provides a culturally sensitive lens with which to view the dynamics of age structure in the ancient Mediterranean. I attempt to do this through two interrelated models.

A model of age structure and the generational cycle illustrates the continuity of age-related Mediterranean cultural values: the young defer to their elders; the older generation cares for the younger generation until they grow old and need younger folk to care for them. The expected roles of older and younger members prescribe particular behaviours that both reflect and reinforce cultural values. This first model helps to illuminate the situation and advice in 1 Timothy regarding expectations of age-related roles. It represents an ideal. However, the people who fulfill these expected roles are also subject to historical circumstances and the possibility of social change.

Thus, the second model incorporates the generational cycle within an elaborated model of generational stability and social change. Using examples of social change in modern Mediterranean ethnographies, I argue that a family's (or group's) honour and reputation within community drives proper behaviour in the public realm, namely, deference and respect for elders, as well as care and support for weaker members (young and very old). Proper behaviour in turn maintains stable age status, which manifests in the expected roles found in the generational cycle. The author of 1 Timothy promotes proper behaviour and thus upholds the typical age structure. In spite of this, within the private space of the household – the setting of the generational cycle – the young and old find a safe place for negotiating power, including the potential for and reactions to social change, especially change associated with age-related roles. In general, family members and age cohorts can effect social change within their particular historical circumstances, but the stability of the generational cycle tends to apply conservative pressure on social change. In a time of crisis (see chapter 3), the author of 1 Timothy frames the community as a "household of God" (3:15) and seeks to apply the conservative pressure of the generational cycle to combat the opposing teachings.

These models provide lenses through which to view 1 Timothy within its own time and place, considering both the historical circumstances of that moment in early Christian community and the cultural norms and expectations of age that played a role in the author's proposed solutions to the community's problems. The remainder of this study examines 1 Timothy, especially 1 Tim. 5, through these lenses, alongside corroborating ancient evidence, with an eye to evaluating the efficacy of these models for examining age within texts associated with other early Christ followers within their social and cultural contexts.

3

One Letter, Two Stories: Rhetoric and Crisis

We begin our detailed study of 1 Timothy by considering the letter as whole, particularly its deliberate framework as an intergenerational interaction between an older Paul and younger Timothy. The fictional nature of the letter points to our encounter with two stories: on the one hand, a fictive story of an older Paul instructing his successor and heir, a younger Timothy, and, on the other hand, the situation of a real late first-century audience facing divergent teachings and public suspicion of their behaviour, framed by what the author considered problematic teachings (see chapter 1). The rhetoric of the letter, couched in the voice of Paul, and the implicit situation of the real audience can be difficult to untangle, but discerning the reasons for the author's choice of format, along with grammatical clues, illuminates the social dynamics that lie beneath the author's central concern, which is the effect the opposing teachings are having on the community.

In order to illuminate the situation that precipitated this letter, I apply the models developed in chapter 2 to 1 Timothy. With a focus on age and intergenerational relationships in Mediterranean cultural contexts, the *model of age status and the generational cycle* points us toward the rhetoric that reflects ideals of "proper behaviour" between old and young in this community, designated as the "household of God" (3:15). Pushing deeper, the ancient Mediterranean evidence from records of crisis and social change related to intergenerational upheaval suggests that generational stability tends to bring a sense of stasis, as the *model of generational stability and social change* suggests. This evidence persuades us to consider the historical circumstances that precipitated the writing of this letter. I propose that the real author and audience in their post-Pauline community in the late first century are dealing with a specific crisis of identity: the original community members were passing away, leaving the community without the "living memories" of the community's founders. This was not a sudden change, but rather a slowly emerging reality. Thus, from his conservative stance, the author of 1 Timothy insists on age hierarchy as a way to bring stability amid a crisis of identity.

PROPER BEHAVIOUR IN THE "HOUSEHOLD OF GOD"

The rhetoric in 1 Timothy has a basis in age hierarchy. Timothy is clearly young: "Let no one despise your youth [σου τῆς νεότητος], but set an example in speech and conduct, in love, in faith, in purity" (4:12, NRSV).[1] Paul is portrayed as an older man, addressing Timothy as "my child in the faith" (1:2; see also 1:18), thus assuming Paul's seniority or age, or both (see Malherbe 1994; 2008). Given the cultural value of age hierarchy in the ancient Mediterranean, this emphasis on an age differential is deliberate: the letter was a carefully constructed set of instructions from an older man to a younger man.

The rhetorical strategy was employed to direct the "real" audience toward proper behaviour. At times, the directions are couched in Paul's directives to Timothy, and at other times the grammatical constructions are more clearly meant for a real audience "overhearing" the letter.[2]

In the fictional narrative of the letter, Paul directs Timothy in two ways: to watch his own behaviour and to teach proper behaviour to others. Specifically, he exhorts Timothy to "fight the good fight" of the faith (1:18, 6:14; NRSV), to avoid "profane myths and old wives' tales" as well as "profane chatter" and false knowledge (4:6; 6:20; NRSV), to train himself in duty and devotion (εὐσέβεια, 4:7), and to live blamelessly (6:14). Paul also instructs Timothy to insist on and teach the behaviour outlined in the letter (4:11, 6:2b), to be an example to others, ensuring the sacred texts are read and taught in the community meetings (4:12–16), and to guard what was entrusted to him (6:20). In fact, his central purpose for the letter is presenting and encouraging proper behaviour: "I am writing you these things hoping to come to you soon; but if I delay [I am writing] in order that you might know *how one ought to behave in the household of God* [πῶς δεῖ ἐν οἴκῳ θεοῦ ἀναστρέφεσθαι], which is the assembly of the living God, a pillar and foundation of truth" (1 Tim. 3:15–16).³ The author expected the real audience to see themselves as members of the "household of God" and wanted to ensure they understood how they "ought to behave" in the community in the face of the conflict before them.

The author implicitly appeals to a code that is self-evident to his readers. For example, the author directs men and women to behave properly according to an unspecified set of expectations related to gender roles: men were to display concord with one another (2:8), and men suitable for leadership should teach and model proper behaviour (3:1–10, 12–13). Women were to marry and raise children (2:15, 5:14), not gossip (3:11), dress modestly, remain silent while learning, not participate in teaching, and not have authority over men (2:9–15). The author expected his readers to recognize these behaviours as proper, but *why this was proper* is not explained. Other behaviours are portrayed as self-evident as well. The author directs members to pray for governing authorities and seek a peaceable life (2:1–2); he expects proper behaviour of and toward different age groups (5:1–2), widows (5:3–16), elders (5:17–29), and younger men (5:20–22; see chapter 9); and he expects slaves to respect their masters (6:1–2). He does not state why this is the "right" way to behave.

On the other hand, the author does provide reasons for *why he recommends or condemns* these behaviours. Paul is concerned about a group of people who are promoting perspectives and behaviour that opposed his own: "Just as I exhorted you when I was going on to Macedonia, remain longer in Ephesus, so that you might direct certain people not to teach other [or different] things [ἑτεροδιδασκαλεῖν]" (1:3; see also 6:3). These "different" teachings are portrayed as being at the root of the problem in the community. These teachings are also defined as "whatever is opposed to healthy teaching" (τι ἕτερον τῇ ὑγιαινούσῃ διδασκαλίᾳ ἀντίκειται, 1:10; see Malherbe 1980). Those who promote these teachings "occupy themselves with myths and endless genealogies that promote speculations rather than the divine training [οἰκονομία] that is known by faith" (1:4, NRSV; also 4:7). These opponents[4] fancy themselves νομοδιδάσκαλοι, that is, "teachers of the νόμος," which the author argues they do not understand (1:7). The word νόμος is usually understood to mean the Judean "law," or Torah. However, with no other clues to confirm a Judean/Jewish connection, it could refer to voluntary associations (see below), who had νομοί ("laws") to govern behaviour. Regardless of the nature of the regulations they espoused and thought they had the right to teach, the author says they "reject conscience" and blaspheme (1:19–20), and they "forbid marriage and demand abstinence from foods" (4:3). There appears to be a connection between these teachings and problems with younger widows (5:14) with profoundly negative perceptions of their behaviour (5:15; see chapters 7 and 8). Paul says that he rejected two of these opponents, specifying Hymenaeus and Alexander, having "handed [them] over to Satan" (1:20; see also 5:15). The opponents are "conceited, understanding nothing, and [have] a morbid craving for controversy and for disputes about words," considering duty and devotion a way to profit (NRSV; 6:4–5), making wealth more important than the true faith (6:10).[5] Paul advises Timothy himself to behave differently from the opponents (4:7, 12–16; 6:11–14, 20) and to convey the proper instructions to the (fictive) community so that they will avoid the improper behaviour encouraged by the opposing teachers (1:3, 11; 3:15; 4:6; 6:17–18).

The *content* of the opposing teachings offers a hazy picture compared to the *impact* of those teachings on the behaviour of the community (see also Fatum 2005, 186, 198–201). The author seems deeply troubled by a lack of harmony; the narrative suggests that the opposing teachers were upsetting the order of the community (1:3; 4:1–4; 5:15). Even though the opponents and their followers evidently had been, or were still, part of the community (Pietersen 2004, 28–34), in the fictional narrative of the letters, the author specifies that opponents have turned away from the best interests of the group (1:6, 19; 4:1–3; 6:3–5, 10; also 6:21). The author encourages his audience (through Paul's exhortation to Timothy) to maintain social distance from them (6:11, 20), and to correct behaviours that caused division (e.g., 2:8).[6]

These three aspects of the fictive layer of this letter – the rhetoric of an older man advising a younger man, proper behaviour in the "household of God," and the activity of the opponents – are meant to inform and direct the real audience of the late first century. The fiction was meant to reflect their own experience (from the point of view of the author). Just as Paul's stated purpose is to exhort Timothy "to direct certain people not to teach other things" (1:3) and to show him "how one ought to behave in the household of God" (3:15), so the author is addressing the effects of real opponents whose teachings and behaviour are causing members to display problematic conduct. In other words, the author is using Paul's authority and reputation within the community (1:1) to address a new and difficult situation, namely, the one created by the opposing teachers.⁷ The author encourages ideal (conventional) moral behaviour in contrast to the opposing teachings in hopes that it would enhance outsiders' opinions of their community (see 3:7, 5:15), particularly the perception of their integrity, morality, and/or honour (see also Zamfir 2013, 37–8, 60–137).

Opposing Teachers and Reputation

The (real) opposing teachers have been the subject of much debate in early Christian scholarship, even given what little information we have about the opponents' point of view (Towner 2006, 41–7). Typically, the identity and characteristics of the opponents are not specified for 1 Timothy alone but derived from all three letters to Timothy and Titus. Admittedly, in all three letters, deviant teaching is a problem, and there are some striking similarities in the descriptions of the opponents. For example, they are associated with teaching (1 Tim. 1:7, 6:3; Titus 1:11; cf. 2 Tim. 3:7) but reject or are bereft of "truth" (ἀλήθεια; 1 Tim. 6:5; 2 Tim. 2:18; Titus 1:14) and talk foolishly (ματαιλόγος, Titus 1:10; ματαιλόγια, 1 Tim. 1:6). They are labelled as disobedient, conceited, and generally seen as immoral (1 Tim. 6:4; 2 Tim. 3:1–5; Titus 1:16), perhaps out for dishonest gain (1 Tim. 6:5; Titus 1:10).⁸ However, in this study, I am concerned about the situation of 1 Timothy specifically, being cautious about deriving information about 1 Timothy directly from 2 Timothy and Titus, as if they were all one text (see discussion in chapter 1).

The identity of the "real" opponents in 1 Timothy is not readily comparable to other early Christian groups. Pauline communities had rival factions from the beginning (e.g., Gal. 1:6–7; 2 Cor. 11:3–5), but the opposing teachings of 1 Timothy reflect a later time period, some decades later, in fact, when the community faced intense crises that seem to have involved rival interpretations of Paul's message (MacDonald 1983; Zamfir 2013, 174–5). Comparisons with Gnosticism (Houlden 1976, 30–1) or a "Gnosticizing form of Jewish Christianity" (Kelly 1963, 12; also Hanson 1966, 16–17, 23; Young 1994b, 10–11) have been successfully refuted (Dibelius and Conzelmann 1972, 65–7; Marshall 1999, 50; Towner 2006, 43;

Zamfir 2013, 165–78). Arguments for the ascetic character of the opponents are more convincing (opponents identified with Judaism, largely based on Titus 1:10, less so); however, mixing all three letters obscures the situation of each letter in this regard. Studies of the specific social aspects of the letters born of a real power struggle are more persuasive (e.g., Verner 1983, MacDonald 1988; Pietersen 2004, 4, 139).[9]

In 1 Timothy, it is clear that the opponents are accused of promoting a form of asceticism, for "they forbid marriage and demand abstinence from [certain] foods" (4:3, NRSV; Zamfir 2013, 174–5). Both aspects of asceticism connect to the historical Paul. Paul's undisputed letters indicate he had encountered opponents who forbade eating certain foods (Rom. 14:2, 1 Cor. 8:1–13, 10:23–31; also Col. 2:16). In 1 Cor. 7, Paul encourages the members of the community to remain as they are, whether married or unmarried, specifying that those who are unmarried and widows should not marry or remarry if they can keep their passions under control (7:8–9). Dennis R. MacDonald argues that the opponents of 1 Timothy encouraged sexual asceticism on the basis of oral legends that were eventually written down in the *Acts of Paul and Thecla*.[10] In the story, Thecla, who is a young virgin, hears an ascetic Paul preach about the virtues of celibacy and abandons her fiancé and mother to become his follower. If the *Acts of Paul and Thecla* reflects one trajectory of how Paul's teaching was interpreted, especially his teaching not to marry or remarry (1 Cor. 7:25–38), then the letters to Timothy and Titus represent another trajectory that requires marriage for women and for leaders (1983, 45, 99).

Margaret Y. MacDonald makes clear that the direction for young widows to remarry because of public scrutiny (1 Tim. 5:11–15) points to the author's desire to limit the number of unmarried women and to curtail women's behaviour that could be viewed by outsiders as shameful (like teaching, 1 Tim. 2:11–15; 1988, 179; 1996, 160–5).[11] This seems to me to be likely. Several times the author alludes to the superiority of marriage and household duties in direct contrast to celibacy; namely, women should marry, manage a household, bear and raise children (2:15; 5:9–10, 14), and (male) overseers and *diakonoi* must be married with children (3:2, 4, 12).[12]

These allusions suggest that teachings involving celibacy posed what the author of 1 Timothy saw as a threat to familial structure in the community. Philip H. Towner finds parallels to sexual asceticism in the "spiritual enthusiasm" and misunderstood resurrection in 1 Corinthians, where the Corinthians questioned the validity of marriage and valued celibacy over family duty (2006, 45, 48–50; see also Marshall 1999, 47; Dibelius and Conzelmann 1972, 66).[13] Paul's reasoning for affirming the possibility of celibacy (while not condoning it for everyone) in 1 Corinthians was linked to a belief that "the present form of the world is passing away" (7:31; also 1 Thess. 4:13–17; Lane 1965; Marshall 1999, 535). The author of 1 Timothy works against this apocalyptic notion of Jesus's imminent return. He characterizes the faith as a lifelong struggle ("fight the good fight of the faith; take hold of the eternal life, to which you were called when you made the good confession in the presence of many witnesses," 1 Tim. 6:12, NRSV; also 1:18), admonishing his readers to "keep the commandment without spot or blame until the manifestation [ἐπιφανεία] of our Lord Jesus Christ, which he will bring about in the right time" (6:14–15; NRSV), literally "which he will display in his own fixed times" (ἣν καιροῖς ἰδίοις δείξει; see also 2:6). The delayed parousia was an issue in some early Christian communities, as evidenced by 2 Pet. 3:3-4: "in the last days scoffers will come, scoffing and indulging their own lusts and saying, 'Where is the promise of his coming? For ever since our ancestors died [literally: our fathers fell asleep], all things continue as they were from the beginning of creation!'" (3:3-4, NRSV). Likewise, in late first-century Corinth, some apparently with "doubt in their soul" said things like, "We have heard these things from the time of our parents, and look! We have grown old, and none of these things has happened to us" (AF 2003, 1:79, 1 Clem. 23.3). If the opponents' ascetic teachings in 1 Timothy pointed to a notion of an imminent parousia, hearkening back to Paul's reasoning in 1 Cor. 7:31, the author of 1 Timothy thought otherwise. Whatever the case, their teachings were a problem in the view of the author, and the real situation of the letter presupposes two conflicting ideologies, and perhaps two views of the historical Paul – one ascetic and the other focused on the traditional social roles of the household.

This points to another, perhaps less obvious issue: why did these divergent trajectories develop at this time? The model of generational stability and social change (and the life course approach that informs it) suggests that particular historical circumstances precipitate social change. I contend that this letter was written at a time of profound social change and intergenerational conflict when the very identity of the community was unstable, a time during which age structure could be more easily challenged because of, among other things, a loss of living memory, and thus a time when intergenerational relationships were in flux.

CHALLENGES TO AGE HIERARCHY IN THE ANCIENT MEDITERRANEAN

Intergenerational conflict as a theme in classical literature has an "exhaustive collection of literary references" (Parkin 1997, 139). Similar to the modern Mediterranean ethnographies examined for the model, there were two main types of conflict: private, familial conflict (usually associated with life course changes like marriage or the introduction of step-parents; Dixon 1999, 166–7),[14] and public, political conflict, where the younger generation publicly came into conflict with their elders in a time of crisis (Parkin 1997, 140; Plescia 1976, 143). Historians point to two major instances of intergenerational conflict documented in the political histories of Greece and Rome: the heyday of democratic Athens (fifth century BCE), and the end of the Roman Republic and beginning of the Empire (first century BCE to first century CE). Both demonstrate times of social upheaval correlated with challenges to age hierarchy. Both also help to illustrate aspects of the model of generational stability and social change: over time, the generational cycle tended to have a moderating effect, and age hierarchy was generally reaffirmed and associated with the resolution of the conflict.

The first record of significant public intergenerational conflict in the ancient Mediterranean was in the city-state of Athens when democracy (among free men) dominated political life (508–322 BCE). A number of surviving literary texts reflect conflict between the younger and older generations, a "polarized two-generational pattern" of νεωτέροι (younger men) and πρεσβύτεροι (older men; Reinhold 1970, 356).[15] Reinhold attributes the uprising of youth, and its generational consciousness, to the failure of the older generation to protect Athens in the Peloponnesian War (1970, 356). In Athens, the implementation of democracy among male citizens of all (adult) ages, along with the Socratic teaching of reason above obedience, gave young people impetus to assert their ideas in the public realm (353–4).

Intergenerational tension in ancient Greece was a popular theme in comedy and tragedy, as well as a topic for philosophers. For example, Aristophanes's comedy *Clouds* (written in 423 BCE) highlights differences between a traditional father and a spendthrift, young adult son. Things get worse when the son comes home with new ideas he learned from Socrates – a reflection of common sentiments about Socrates, the so-called corruptor of youth (see Xenophon *Memorabilia* 1.2). One scene recounts intergenerational conflict that escapes the private sphere: the son refuses the father's request to sing during dinner, a traditional element of the feast. He also refuses a compromise to recite from Aeschylus, but rudely puts forth a piece from Euripides about incest (*Clouds* 1353–76). The son's education had radically changed his values and thinking (Reckford 1976, 99) so that the ensuing argument ends in the son beating the father (*Clouds* 1321–34) – a reversal of the parent-child roles (Reckford 1976, 92–3) and an allusion to parricide (108–9), but ending in comedic laughter, "the sign of life" (109). Kenneth J. Reckord argues Aristophanes used humour to highlight the difficulties of social change (104–5), bringing healing and hope to his audience (117). The play also affirms age hierarchy.

Roman society could be described as being comparatively intergenerationally integrated, replicating a sense of duty and reverence for elders in each generation. The *mos maiorum* (ancestral models of virtuous behaviour), the discipline and virtues taught to and expected of the young, and the power of the *paterfamilias* in the household, all promoted deference to the elderly (Reinhold 1970, 363). Even so, in popular Roman literature, two main themes in intergenerational conflict were present: the elderly wanting the young to behave in a more moral way, and a son rebelling against his conservative father (usually in comedy; Parkin 1997, 140).

A major intergenerational conflict occurred during the tumultuous time at the end of the Roman Republic and beginning of the Roman Empire. Emiel Eyben suggests that the young men had won the Punic War (218–201 BCE) for Rome, but the older men were threatened by them, and actively sought to restrict their power (1993, 7).[16] They passed laws to limit young men's financial responsibility, to prevent men under twenty-five from entering the army, and to restrict access to public office (24–8).[17] There was an explosion of wealth and building in Rome after their conquests. The residents of Rome experienced great extravagance, which especially affected youth, elite and non-elite alike (Polybius, *Histories* 31.25.2–8).[18] When its resources were exhausted, Rome suffered an economic crisis around

138 BCE, resulting in unemployment, debt, and food shortages. A constitutional crisis arose in 134 BCE when Tiberius Gracchus garnered support from the *populares* (a non-elite political body that previously had no de facto power) for a bill to relieve unemployment in the city. In addition, a cultural revolution resulted from the political and philosophical influence of Greek teachers among the progressive elite – especially among young men – because of their openness to Hellenistic ideas (Plescia 1976, 156–9). In a conflict similar to the one in Athens, when the economic crisis was not adequately addressed by the older generation, young men publicly acted against the older generation (Falkner and de Luce 1992, 27).

In the late Republic, young men were important players in the game of political power and were actively recruited by older men. Cicero, Julius Caesar, and others vied for support from young men, including non-elite youth, who likely had hopes of social advancement (Eyben 1993, 56–65). A patrician named Catiline, who advocated for the poor and dispossessed to bolster his dying political career (Badian 2003, 1393), was characterized by Sallust as a man who capitalized on the gullibility, inexperience, passion, and foolishness of young men to join him in a life of vice and crime (63 BCE; *Catiline* 12–14; see also Harlow and Laurence 2002, 70–1).

For elite youth, the usual future reward of political and military power normally promoted harmony between the generations (Reinhold 1970, 363; see also Foner 1984, 130–2). The *cursus honorum* was a progression of public offices, where one's status, authority, and political position increased with age. Power and control were always in the hands of the older generation (Harlow and Laurence 2002, 121, 198; Saller 1994, 131). Few elite men attained public office before the age of thirty. Anyone under thirty was considered too "rash" for public office and restricting ages for each position meant that those competing for office were of roughly equal age (Harlow and Laurence 2002, 106–10).

Octavian, later known as Caesar Augustus, acquired political power at a strikingly young age, forcing his way into the position of consul at a younger age than anyone before him (Eyben 1993, 66–7) and skipping the age requirements of the *cursus honorum* (outlined in an inscription of Augustus's autobiography, *Res Gestae* 1). Octavian "succeeded *in spite of* his youthful age" (Eyben 1993, 69).[19] He was most certainly an exception, yet his story demonstrates the dynamics of both social change and generational stability.

Octavian was named Julius Caesar's successor at the age of nineteen, gaining power in the face of opposition from the older generation. He "was to place a challenge on the entire age structure of the Republic and, more importantly, challenge the very basis for such age restrictions themselves" (Harlow and Laurence 2002, 111). Cicero, who was an older man in his sixties when Julius Caesar was assassinated, publicly supported the young Octavian but had private reservations about his competence (Cicero, *Atticus* 16.8.1). According to Appian, Cicero recommended to the Senate that Octavian be made consul, but with the provision that they "choose as his colleague an older man of good sense to be a firm guide for his youthfulness" (2020, 155, 3.82).

Cicero and Octavian exemplify the tension between older and younger men in Rome: one who climbed the *cursus honorum* through traditional age ranking (Cicero)[20] and one who thwarted traditional age status (Octavian). Cicero wrote *On Old Age* at the age of sixty-two, the same year as Julius Caesar's assassination and his own sidelining in politics, thus "appealing for the honour and position he considered his experience entitled him to" (Harlow and Laurence 2002, 24). Cicero also expresses some anxiety about younger men's power: "For old age is honoured only on condition that it defends itself, maintains its rights, is subservient to no one, and to the last breath rules over its own domain" (1923, 47, 11 [Falconer's numbering, 38]; see also Harlow and Laurence 2002, 111–12, 123).

As part of politically motivated social change, Augustus dropped the ages for office holders,[21] in part to have political peers who were younger than he was, but also to encourage young men from senatorial families to participate in public office. He also lowered ages for entering the military. Demographics played a part in lowering ages, since from the first century CE, the population declined due to low fertility (Osiek and Balch 1997, 64–5; Angel 1972, 100–1).[22] Yet, even with the drop of ages, the conservative element of the generational cycle was evident. Augustus promoted traditional Roman values and *pietas*, especially when it came to family roles (Harlow and Laurence 2002, 119; Hoklotubbe 2017, 13–54). He instituted the *Lex Papia Poppaea*, a law which required widowed and divorced men and women to remarry in order to receive inheritances, and encouraged women to have children, offering them freedom from tutelage if they had three (four for a freedwoman). In addition, he advanced a familial metaphor for the empire, characterizing himself as the Father of Rome. It became a citizen's duty to submit to the Emperor as a son submitted to his father (Rawson 2003, 38). In a time of social turmoil, Augustus encouraged the traditional definition of hierarchical relationships in conjunction with "forces of cohesion," namely, the metaphor of the household and family (Garnsey and Saller 1987, 107).

Older men maintaining precedence over young men in the public sphere is the situation reflected in the model of generational stability and social change (and in modern traditional Mediterranean settings). Meyer Reinhold argues that in the ancient Near East social norms were maintained by myth, ritual, the economic dependence of the young, and socialization of the young to be obedient and respectful toward elders. He also suggests that "insecurity and fear of change served to maintain basic generational harmony as being mutually advantageous to both younger and older generations" (1970, 347–8). These sentiments reflect my basic hypothesis that when intergenerational relationships were in flux, the conservative nature of the generational cycle in Mediterranean cultures kept cultural norms relatively stable. However, social and cultural change is inevitable, and challenges to the system of age structure are more frequent and constant than Reinhold's statement suggests.

AGE IN THE MILITARY AND VOLUNTARY ASSOCIATIONS

To illustrate the nature of intergenerational relationships among men beyond the household and in the public realm in less tumultuous times and more commonplace spaces, we look briefly at the military and voluntary associations. Here again, we can detect some challenges to age hierarchy, but ultimately an affirmation of age structure.

In the military, enrolment, roles, and "retirement" were determined by age (Harlow and Laurence 2002, 146). Recruits could be any age but tended to be young adult males.[23] Duties differed according to age: the young fought, and the older soldiers ideally moved up in rank (Hope 2007, 119). According to Polybius (second century BCE), in the Roman Republic younger soldiers were sent to the front lines in battle (6.20–22; Harlow and Laurence 2002, 75), and military formation was arranged according to age and social class:

> When they come to the rendezvous, they choose the youngest and poorest to form the *velites*; the next to them are made *hastati*; those in the prime of life *principes*; and the oldest of all *triarii*, these being the names among the Romans of the four classes in each legion distinct in age and equipment. They divide them so that the senior men known as *triarii* number six hundred, the *principes* twelve hundred, the *hastati* twelve hundred, the rest, consisting of the youngest, being *velites*. If the legion consists of more than four thousand men, they divide accordingly, except as regards the *triarii*, the number of whom is always the same. (Polybius 2011, 353, 6.21.7–9)

Leaders were chosen from each age group, with the exception of the youngest men (6.24). The *velites* had less elaborate equipment and dress than the others (6.22–3). The camp was formed with the *triarii* (oldest men) in a central (protected?) position among the legions (6.29).[24]

In the Roman army in general, older men assessed the young men's performance and planned strategy (Harlow and Laurence 2002, 75). Men were no longer expected to fight after age sixty (2002, 76). Young soldiers were thought to need discipline and role models (Hope 2007, 118).[25] An experienced soldier was still considered in his prime at the age of forty or forty-five, and soldiers might continue military service into their fifties and beyond.

Age conflict occurred in the military, though probably most insubordination was dealt with through physical discipline (like flogging). According to Livy (first century BCE), the twenty-five-year-old Scipio[26] stepped forward to be the supreme commander of the army when no one else would; the elders did not trust him because he was προπέτεια (rash) – a trait of youth (26.18.11; 26.19.9). Scipio continued to climb the ranks before the usual age to do so and continued to be challenged by older men.[27]

The models of Scipio and Octavian, along with the earlier Alexander the Great, illustrate that the military was a "legitimate" sphere in which a capable young man could establish himself in leadership, but young men who succeeded were the exception. This sphere may have been less threatening than the political or family realm because military rank could more easily override age distinctions, even if such ambition did not go unchallenged.

It is notable that the author of 1 Timothy employs a military analogy to exhort Timothy to "serve as a soldier [in] the good military campaign in these things [στρατεύῃ ἐν αὐταῖς τὴν καλὴν στρατείαν]" (1:18).[28] Indeed, like young men in the Roman army, Timothy is portrayed as on the "front lines" of the fight against the opponents, having been called by prophecy (1:18) and the affirmation of the council of elders (4:14). As an older man in the fictive tale, Paul is directing the younger Timothy to act appropriately (e.g., "placate an older man," 5:1), but also encouraging him to take responsibility, teach, and be an example to others in legitimate ways, directing the community toward duty and devotion (εὐσέβεια). The military analogy might moderate the age differential and demonstrate the way a "good soldier of Christ" (to borrow from 2 Tim. 2:3–4) could legitimately rise into positions of honour or responsibility even if he were young – namely, by proper behaviour and teaching.

Another important venue for intergenerational relationships in the public realm in Roman times were voluntary associations (Latin: *collegia*). From an emic perspective (an insider's point of view), the author of 1 Timothy conceived of the community in familial terms, as a "household of God" (3:15), but from an etic perspective (an outsider's point of view), voluntary associations provide the closest analogy to Christ groups (Tertullian, *Apology* 39; Stegemann and Stegemann 1999, 273–4; Wilson 1996, 1).[29] Like many voluntary associations, they had religious and social functions, offered a sense of belonging, provided social and financial support for those who did not have the security of kin (especially in the city, and including providing a proper burial), and allowed the potential for honour, prestige, and authority by replicating the political structure of the polis (city). Members joined voluntarily, and membership entailed reciprocal obligations (in fact, similar to the expectations within a household; Ascough 1998, 74–8). Voluntary associations could function as fictive kin or "fictive polities," especially when the state or kin had failed to fulfill a person's needs (Walker-Ramisch 1996, 132, 134; Stegemann and Stegemann 1999, 286).[30] Even if a member's family did not formally belong to the association, the association might provide support to them in a crisis (*IG* II² 1275). On the other hand, holding meetings in households suggests that for some members, associations might be an extension or "expression" of family life instead of an alternative to it (Wilson 1996, 14; Kloppenborg 1996a, 23).

Membership of voluntary associations was commonly drawn from non-elite or lower classes (i.e., the urban poor, slaves, freedmen), ranging from poor to relatively wealthy and influential. The associations had a formal organization and "organizational hierarchy" (Wilson 1996, 10). They often had patrons, who may or may not have been involved in the group (10–11). The non-elite had very little chance to gain status by serving in civic government because of their social position,[31] but voluntary associations provided public avenues for the non-elite to pursue honour and prestige, and thus to gain status (MacMullen 1974, 77). The associations themselves had little political influence and little interest in political affairs, except perhaps at a local level.[32] However, political ambition could be pursued within the *collegia* since positions and titles were similar to municipal organizations. Non-elite persons could "participate in a *cursus honorum* to which he or she could never aspire outside of the association" (Kloppenborg 1996a, 18; see also 23, 26). The voluntary association was a "polis writ small" (Kloppenborg 1996a, 26); they were "miniature cities" (MacMullen 1974, 76), "miniature republics" (Meeks 1983, 31). Whether or not the "power" was real in a political sense, titles and rank were important for the sake of honour.

Voluntary associations were often intergenerational in nature. Similar to elite politics, younger men were encouraged to join and participate in associations to keep them viable for subsequent generations.[33] At least some voluntary associations encouraged intergenerational involvement. The Rule of the *Iobakchoi* (164/65 CE, *IG* II² 1368; Kloppenborg and Ascough 2011, 241–57), an inscription detailing rules of an association dedicated to Dionysius, demonstrates that the association encouraged multigenerational membership. Those whose fathers were members receive a discounted membership fee (lines 37–41, Kloppenborg and Ascough 2011, 242–3, 246, 251), and a young boy (παῖς) could be a member if he had paid the fees and his father offered a libation (lines 55–58, Kloppenborg and Ascough 2011, 243, 246–7, 252). Some associations had *tutores* (guardians) from their own membership rather than outsiders serve the children of their fellow members (*Digest* 27.1.17.3), which also encouraged intergenerational membership.

In the organizational structure of voluntary associations, as senior members grew older, junior members inevitably took over more responsibilities. It was evident in the public political struggles of the Roman elite that juniors could resent the power of their elders. Younger men may have joined associations in hopes of gaining prestige before their rightful time came according to the norms of age status.[34] Older men may have been threatened by younger men's potential or used young men to help them with their own ambitions. Unfortunately, we have little evidence for intergenerational conflict in voluntary associations. Evidence of conflict among rival families within associations is common. It is possible that some of the warnings in The Rule of the *Iobakchoi* (IG II² 1368) address intergenerational conflict because actions such as speaking out of turn and sitting in someone else's seat (lines 73–4) are explicitly signs of disrespect when a young man does such things to his elder in Mediterranean settings (see chapter 2). We can imagine that when non-elite young men challenged age structure, voluntary associations would be a setting in which they might see possibilities for gaining power, honour, or office before they reached the "proper" life stage for such a position.

Among the elite and non-elite alike, seniority and age dictated hierarchical relationships in the public realm, but authority based on age could be challenged by politically active younger men. The tumult of war and concomitant questions around the effectiveness of age hierarchy could open the possibility for younger men to question their elders. However, the generational cycle remained steady, and such challenges did not eliminate the basic form of age structure.

THE CRISIS IN 1 TIMOTHY: LOSS OF LIVING MEMORY

Returning to 1 Timothy, the rhetoric of the older Paul and younger Timothy and the number of references to age and age structure could suggest that the author was simply using the authoritative voice of Paul as a strategy to combat the opponents. However, the intensity of the author's rhetoric around age points toward challenges of age hierarchy amid a time of crisis. The nature of that crisis is not clearly stated. However, if indeed the letter was written at the end of the first century, a strong possibility is the dwindling presence of the original members of the group. On the basis of demographic trends (see chapter 1), we can suppose that very few members of the original community would still be alive in the last two decades of the first century.[35] Frances M. Young suggests, "It seems entirely plausible that the 'senior citizen' [elder] carried what we might call the community memory and was therefore commissioned to teach the tradition" (1994a, 146). By the end of the first century, those who had been part of the original community were either very old or had died, so that the founding generation of the community – along with its living memory – was quickly disappearing. Losing the remaining members who had a tangible connection to the community's beginnings meant that the living memory they carried would be lost. In a predominantly oral culture, this would constitute a profound change and shift – perhaps even crisis – in their group identity.

In fact, such a crisis of identity may have precipitated the creation and/or need to copy a number of the written texts that are now important primary sources for early Christian scholarship (some of which also became part of the canon). One likely reason that the canonical gospels and their sources were widely distributed in written form was the need for consistent records about Jesus and the movement's inception, especially when eyewitnesses grew scarce. Eusebius documents that a desire to have Peter's oral recitation of Jesus's teachings recorded in writing led to the beginnings of the Gospel of Mark (*Ecclesiastical History* 2.15; see also Bauckham 2006, 155–82).[36] The author of Luke characterizes the events of Jesus's life as "handed on to us by those who from the beginning were eyewitnesses and servants of the word" (1:2, NRSV).[37]

Other texts promoted the memory of certain influential people connected to the foundations of the Jesus movement, such as Peter and Paul. The author of 2 Peter wrote in Peter's name (1:1) as a way of affirming Peter's authority over against opposing teachers (2:1). The letter is framed as a "testament," or a statement of Peter's wishes made before his death: "I think it right, as long as I am in this body, to refresh your memory, since I know that my death will come soon, as indeed our Lord Jesus Christ has made clear to me. And I will make every effort so that after my departure you may be able at any time to recall these things" (1:13–15; NRSV). The author of 2 Peter affirms the authority of – and implicitly the need to preserve – Paul's letters, stating, "So also our beloved brother Paul wrote to you according to the wisdom given him, speaking of this as he does in all his letters" (3:15–16, NRSV). Likewise, Polycarp praises Paul, affirming that his letters carry authority for his own generation at the beginning of the second century (*Phil.* 3.1–2).

For modern scholars, and indeed for Christian scholars through the centuries, written texts are the crucial evidence for the early Christ followers. However, writing in the early second century, Papias suggests that for first-century Christ groups, the oral testimony as living memory of their founders was superior to written texts.[38]

> I also will not hesitate to draw up for you, along with these expositions, an orderly account of all the things I carefully learned and have carefully recalled from the elders [παρὰ τῶν πρεσβυτέρων]; for I have certified their truth ... But whenever someone arrived who had been a companion of one of the elders [τῶν πρεσβυτέρων], I would carefully inquire after their words, what Andrew or Peter had said [εἶπεν], or what Philip or what Thomas had said, or James or John or Matthew or any of the other disciples of the Lord, and what things Aristion and the elder John, disciples of the Lord, were saying [λέγουσιν]. For I did not suppose that what came out of books would benefit me so much as that which came from a living and abiding voice." (AF 2003, 2:98–9, frag. 3.3–4, Eusebius, *Ecclesiastical History* 3.39)[39]

It is clear that Papias valued oral testimony – "a living and abiding voice" – from people who were with Jesus himself or had heard from his disciples.[40]

Papias's insistence on living witnesses when he himself is providing a *written* account is ironic (and even more ironic that his account only survived in fragments in others' writings). His written account attempted to capture the "truth" they passed on to him, but for him it was clearly an inferior way to learn about the historical teachings and events associated with Jesus. Papias recognized that few witnesses who knew Jesus's disciples were still alive. Those with a "living voice" were most likely to be older persons, and when they were gone, that living link to Jesus would be gone as well. Papias captures the intensity of what this living link meant for his age cohort.[41] In a similar vein, Irenaeus recounts how, as a child, he heard Polycarp's speeches that recall conversations with John and eyewitnesses who had seen Jesus, remembering what he had heard about Jesus's miracles and teaching (Eusebius, *Ecclesiastical History* 5.20.6; see also Munck 1959, 229). If Polycarp was born around 70 CE, as Ehrman suggests (AF 2003, 1:362), he would have been a young man when any disciples of Jesus who survived beyond 60

CE were old.⁴² Papias and Irenaeus valued the living connection of Jesus's disciples, suggesting an analogous desire to retain connections to the founders of the Christ assemblies (like Paul), in Asia Minor and elsewhere.

It is plausible, then, that the rhetoric found in 1 Timothy is meant to address an identity crisis precipitated by the deaths of the original community members, coupled with (or even manifesting in) the threat of opposing teachings and public suspicion in this time of change. The crisis triggered various teachings, including a defensive reaction to some of those teachings in the form of this letter, which defined lines of authority meant to reinforce traditional age hierarchy through the "story" of Paul and Timothy. The author invoked the names of Paul and Timothy specifically to endorse what he considered proper teachings and behaviour in the face of this crisis because Paul and Timothy represented authoritative continuity with the past that could speak to his present situation, namely, continuity with the founding movement, and most importantly, with founding members. The letter itself was meant to substitute for Paul's presence and authority, leveraging his role as an older man.

The rhetorical strategy affirms the post-Pauline heteronymity of the letter (see chapter 1). We know from Paul's undisputed letters that factions rallied behind certain teachers and/or founders involved in the community (1 Cor. 1:12; 3:4–9; *1 Clem.* 47.14) and Paul had to argue for his place among the apostles (Gal. 1:11–2:10). In contrast, the author of 1 Timothy has Paul argue for his own authority and calling without any reference to others (1:1, 12–16, 20; 2:7). The statement that Paul was "appointed a herald and an apostle (I am telling the truth, I am not lying), a teacher of the Gentiles in faith and truth" (1 Tim. 2:7, NRSV) functions as a validation and reminder of his foundational role in the community. This letter replaces the voices of those who had passed away but who had actually known Paul (and Timothy).

Paul is portrayed as a mentor and example (1:12–16),⁴³ but also an ambassador and apostle (κῆρυξ καὶ ἀπόστολος). That is, in the fiction of the letter, he sees himself as a man with a special calling from God, to be God's messenger and hand down his wisdom, defined as a deposit (παραθήκη) to be guarded (6:20), to his trustworthy protégé. Timothy would in turn become an example for the rest of the community (4:12). Paul is a sort of testator,⁴⁴ bequeathing to Timothy (and thus to the real audience through the fictional Timothy) an inheritance of "truth" (2:4, 7; 4:3).⁴⁵

In the Roman world, inheritance was important, and not just for the elite (see *Shepherd* of Hermas, Visions 20.3.12). Given the demographic realities, life was precarious and longevity was not certain. People sought to ensure their property would be passed on to those for whom they intended it through wills (Saller 1994, 155–60; P. Mich 322). In the fictive story of 1 Timothy, the inheritance in question was not property, but "truth" and "healthy teaching" from God (1:11). The inheritance being passed on from the fictive Paul, the founding apostle, to the fictive Timothy, a trustworthy heir, was also shared by the real audience in their reading of the letter. Their share of the inheritance solidified an identity that had continuity with the past, but relevance for their present problems and perspective. That inheritance was the healthy teaching (ἡ ὑγιαινούση διδακαλία, 1:10, 4:6, 6:3) that God entrusted (πιστεύω) to Paul (1:11), and that Paul now entrusts to Timothy in the letter.[46] The author of 1 Timothy may have intended for "Paul" to convey the value of age in a way that resembles something Augustus reportedly said as an older man, illustrating the strength of the conservative tradition when a person grows older. Addressing young men who were behaving badly, Augustus declared, "Listen, young men, to an old man to whom old men listened when he was young" (Plutarch 1936, 85, 10:784D).

The rhetoric of a personal letter to a well-known companion of Paul was a powerful medium to put forward the author's agenda in the midst of this identity crisis. We know from Paul's undisputed letters that he considered the historical Timothy to be like a son who adhered to and promulgated Paul's teaching. He praised Timothy's worth, "how like a son with a father he has served with me in the work of the gospel" (Phil. 2:22, NRSV), calling him "my beloved and faithful child in the Lord" (1 Cor. 4:17, NRSV). He sent Timothy to Corinth as his protégé to remind them of his teachings (1 Cor. 4:17; cf. 1 Thess. 3:2), stating that Timothy was "doing the work of the Lord" just like Paul (1 Cor. 16:10, NRSV).[47] In 1 Timothy, not only is the younger Timothy adopted by Paul (1:2), called by God (6:12), and approved by the council of elders (4:14), but the example of a young man par excellence (4:12). Timothy is depicted as dutifully submitting to the authority of elders, reflecting proper order and behaviour. The centrality of the father-son relationship in the household (see chapter 2; figure 3.1) lends further social weight to this rhetoric and format.

Figure 3.1 | Grave stele with the busts of a father and son (mid-second century CE) in which Xanthios honours his father Xanthos. Digital image courtesy of Getty's Open Content Program.

The documented times of crisis outlined above in which young men publicly challenged their elders in Greek and Roman times may also help illustrate why the author of 1 Timothy couched his letter in the rhetoric of an ideal intergenerational relationship between Paul and Timothy. If indeed it was a time of crisis, when the oldest living voices of the community were disappearing and its social identity in flux, the rhetoric of the letter, framed as an older man advising a younger man to guide and lead the community, suggests that challenges to age structure might have been at the heart of the situation, with younger men vying for power, perhaps by aligning themselves with the opposing teachings (see chapter 9). Timothy is portrayed as a younger man who has power to lead, but his leadership does not arise out of his own ambition: he is loyal to Paul (1:2), called by God (6:12) through prophecies (1:18, 4:14), displayed in his exemplary behaviour (4:12) and confirmed by his submission to the elders (4:14).

In the face of social change (and crisis), the household metaphor with its inherent age structure provided continuity for the movement just as generations provide continuity for biological families.[48] And yet the rhetoric of the letter suggests advocating proper behaviour that reflects ideal virtues and honourable behaviour in the *public* realm. The author of 1 Timothy chose to write his piece as a letter from an older Paul to a younger, idealized Timothy to present an ideal model of a young man in a publicly visible intergenerational relationship with Paul. His service to Paul and model behaviour portray the "correct" way to behave, but also contrast with those who challenged age hierarchy in the midst of social crisis. These challenges are explored in the following chapters.

A RHETORICAL IDEAL FOR A REAL AUDIENCE

In the midst of crisis, the author of 1 Timothy frames his letter in such a way that it is aligned with a conservative view, especially associated with the traditional hierarchies found in the household. For the real audience, this is the voice of Paul addressing Timothy's situation with strong echoes for their own late first-century concerns. Within the letter, the fictive Paul is clear about why he is writing this letter to Timothy, and it involves not just Timothy's conduct, but the conduct of all who are in the community. This is plainly stated as the purpose of the letter, which is to give direction for "how one ought to behave in the household of God [πῶς δεῖ ἐν οἴκῳ θεοῦ ἀναστρέφεσθαι]" (3:15), and it is directed at the real audience who is to "overhear" the instructions.

Used figuratively, the passive form of the verb ἀναστρέφω means to "act, behave, conduct oneself, or live in the sense of the practice of certain principles ... always with the kind of behaviour more exactly described" (BDAG 2000, 72; see also *1 Clem.* 21:8). The author of 1 Timothy outlines "the kind[s] of behaviour" he deems appropriate throughout the letter: submission to political hierarchies (2:1–2), submission to gender hierarchies (2:11–12, 5:14), submission to hierarchies based on social rank (6:1–2), and submission to age hierarchies and performance of concomitant responsibilities (5:1–2, 4, 8, 17, 20). He recommends quiet, non-argumentative, and harmonious behaviour (2:2, 8; 3:3, 8; 5:19), though he is willing to argue with those who promote opposing teachings. He urges respectable behaviour for men (3:2–5) and modest behaviour for women (2:9–10), which includes good household management (3:4–5, 12; 5:9–10, 14), good works (2:10; 5:10, 24; 6:18), and generosity (5:16; 6:19). There are also behaviours of which the author disapproves. He disapproves of any disregard for gender hierarchies (2:12) and hierarchies based on social rank (6:2). He condemns the mistreatment of elders and widows (5:1, 4, 8), as well as false accusations (5:19), idleness (5:13), drunkenness, slander, haughtiness, and greed (3:6, 8, 11; 6:9, 17). He rejects arguing over words, especially when someone is ignorant of their meaning (1:6–7; 6:5, 20).

Many of the appropriate behaviours have direct connections with what was expected in an ancient household (see chapters 2, 4, and 5; Zamfir 2013, 60–159). Although household relationships entail cooperation and (ideally) concord, the analogy of the community as the "household of God" (3:15) also implies hierarchy, with distinct roles of superiority and subordination between men and women, slaves and masters, and older and younger members (Elliott 1981, 172–200; Zamfir 2013, 218–36).[49] The "household of God" was an effective metaphor for a community with members of different ages.[50] The real audience is invited to follow Timothy's example and Paul's instruction to promote "proper" households as well as proper household behaviour.

There are some distinct grammatical clues about the real audience in this letter. The first is the use of first-person indicative. Many uses of the first-person indicative are about Paul's identity (e.g., "I myself was entrusted [with the gospel]," 1:11; "I was shown mercy," 1:16) or directives to Timothy (e.g., "I encouraged you to stay in Ephesus," 1:3; "I command you before God," 6:13). However, there are three instances of the first-person indicative in which the author directly requests something of the community using the authoritative voice of Paul: "I urge [that] entreaties, prayers, petitions and thanksgivings be made on behalf of all humanity" (2:1); "I want men to pray [and women to adorn themselves]" (2:8); and "I want young women to marry" (5:14).[51] These directives appear to be for an implied audience, with hopes the "real" audience will see themselves in the implication.

The second-person imperative is used frequently by the author in the form of Paul exhorting Timothy toward various actions,[52] imposing his "will" on the younger Timothy (Wallace 1996, 485; see also Brooks and Winbery 1979, 127). This involves defining examples of proper behaviour (e.g., "reject profane myths and old wives' tales," 4:7 [NRSV]; "cultivate these things," 4:15; "do not jab at an older man," 5:1) and insisting on actions that would benefit the community (e.g., "command and teach these things," 4:11; also 5:7, 6:17) or benefit particular members (e.g., "do not accept an accusation against an elder," 5:19). Again, the implied audience is clearly in view as those who need to check their behaviour and listen to "these things [ταῦτα]" (3:14; 4:6, 11, 15; 5:7, 21; 6:2b, 11) which is suggestive for the real audience.

In addition, the author's use of the third-person imperative may allow us to peel back the narrative layer even further to glimpse the real audience.[53] The third-person imperative is usually translated to convey a sense of offering consent or permission, since English has no direct equivalent (i.e., "let" the person "do" something), but the force of a command or entreaty is often intended (Wallace 1996, 486; Brooks and Winbery 1979, 129). For example, the translation "*let* a woman *learn* [μανθανέτω] in full submission" (2:11) suggests that Paul is telling Timothy to consent to a woman learning in submission, but the sense in the Greek is more like "a woman should learn in full submission."[54] With a third-person imperative the emphasis changes from the direct recipient (ostensibly Timothy) to others, namely, the "real" audience of the letter (Signor 1999, 22). In the phrase "let no one look down on [καταφρονείτω] you because of your youth" (4:12), Paul is commanding Timothy not to allow anyone to scorn him, but the action (in this case a prohibition) should come from a third party, namely, people in the community who refrain from looking down on him. Thus, the focus is not on Timothy's resistance but on the community's behaviour toward Timothy. By directing a third party through the rhetoric of directives to "Timothy," the author addresses the implied audience and (by extension) his directives for the real audience. In some occurrences, Timothy is not involved at all; someone else is being asked to do the action (Signor 1999, 22n117; 28n150). For example, in 1 Tim. 5:17, the phrase "let the elders who shepherd well be worthy [ἀξιούσθωσαν] of double honour" (5:17) ostensibly directs Timothy's *community* to treat elders properly, suggesting that elders are not receiving their due from those who should be honouring them (see chapter 9). By using this construction, the author is illuminating issues that are part of the experience of the "real" audience and places where the audience could, and was encouraged to, insert itself into the fictive story.

Given the keen concern with the teachings of the opponents, the age-related rhetorical strategy in 1 Timothy must have been employed, at least in part, to interrupt their influence. The author of 1 Timothy was concerned that the opponents' teachings were encouraging dishonourable conduct that was visible beyond the private realm (1 Tim. 3:4, 12; MacDonald 1996, 165–78). How a man managed his household was a private matter. However, the results of his management (or mismanagement) would be evident in a public way (e.g., if his children were acting dishonourably in public places), and thus visible to outsiders. Such conduct included women teaching and exercising authority over men (2:11–12), adult children not caring for their parents (5:4; see chapter 5), young widows running about in public (5:13; see chapter 7), and younger men accusing and not submitting to older men (5:19–20; see chapter 9). In the rhetoric of the letter, the author urges that this conduct required a conservative approach, a return to traditional Roman-type virtues reflective of ideal behaviour found in an ideal household. He wanted community members to conform to social norms, while retaining a distinct identity as Christ-followers (Donelson 1986, 171–81; Elliott 1981). The author's apologetic stance is also suggested in his instructions to pray for the state rulers (2:1–2), which would demonstrate the community's loyalty to the emperor and to civil order, even if they did not participate in the cult of the emperor (this evidently caused problems later; e.g., *Martyrdom of Polycarp* 9.3). As the model suggests, the generational cycle tends to have a moderating effect, and age hierarchy is generally reaffirmed. This is the effect the author wanted to achieve in writing this letter.

CONCLUSION

Ostensibly written by Paul to Timothy, 1 Timothy is a message for the author's real late first-century CE audience. Subtle clues help us discern the real situation of the community, identified as the "household of God" (3:15). Employing the rhetoric of an older man addressing a younger man, the author reflects ideal intergenerational cooperation in the public sphere. Using models of age and intergenerational relationships, I posit that at the end of the first century, as tangible ties to the founders of the communities were disappearing, different teachings were causing rifts amidst the instability, and the reputation of the community was at stake. Evidence from Greek and Roman histories, as well as intergenerational patterns in the military and in voluntary associations, suggests that intergenerational conflict (among men) was a ubiquitous reality in the ancient Mediterranean, resolved either privately or, when it arose publicly, through public reinforcement of age hierarchy. In the situation that precipitated the writing of 1 Timothy, I suggest that intergenerational conflict was intensified because of the loss of living memory as founders were dying. This caused a crisis of identity and created an opportunity for challenges to age status norms. With the community's identity in question, 1 Timothy represents polarized opinions about how the community should proceed during this time of crisis and change. The opponents are represented as holding an ascetic view, advocating against usual and familiar social roles. The author of 1 Timothy promoted a conservative strategy that strongly encouraged submission to age hierarchies, contributing to continuity in communal identity that would be replicated as the members of the community of Christ followers grew up and grew old.

As we now turn to the specifics of some of these conflicts and their age dynamics in 1 Tim. 5, we see directives that are framed using the metaphor of the household (3:15). The model of generational stability and social change (chapter 2) suggests that the family or household is the most common forum for conflict and cooperation in intergenerational relationships in the Mediterranean, and the author of 1 Timothy hoped the metaphor would pull the community through this time of crisis by reinforcing the conservative element of age structure. Among other things, the young should placate older people (5:1), display duty and devotion in caring for their parents (5:4, 8), and not disrespect their elders (5:19–20). The underlying message is about maintaining an honourable reputation through proper behaviour befitting a younger person. An honourable reputation was essential for someone aspiring to have a role with responsibility within the group (3:7). The author hoped that the community's reputation with outsiders would improve, they would have fewer tensions internally, and they would be able to live "a quiet and peaceable life" (2:2).

4

Ideal Behaviour in the "Household of God" (1 Tim. 5:1–2)

The author of 1 Timothy begins his section on age-related issues (5:1–25) with an idealization of the traditional age structure (5:1–2) that hints at the problems he is addressing. Using familial terminology as an analogy for intergenerational relationships, he sets the stage for the following two sections, which deal with widows (5:3–16) and elders (5:17–25), addressing behaviour that is evidently far from ideal.

The directives in 5:1–2 address a young man's behaviour[1] toward four sets of people: an older man, younger men (ostensibly Timothy's peers), older women, and younger women – all presumably adults, categorized according to age and gender, and all relationships associated with the household.

Πρεσβυτέρῳ μὴ ἐπιπλήξῃς ἀλλὰ παρακάλει ὡς πατέρα,
νεωτέρους ὡς ἀδελφούς,
πρεσβυτέρας ὡς μητέρας,
νεωτέρας ὡς ἀδελφὰς ἐν πάσῃ ἁγνείᾳ.

Do not jab an older man but make peace with him as a father,
younger men as brothers,
older women as mothers,
younger women as sisters, in all purity. (1 Tim. 5:1–2)

Earlier in the letter, Timothy is portrayed as an exemplary young man who has modelled this ideal behaviour by submitting to his elders (4:14), and throughout the letter Paul expects Timothy will follow his directives (e.g., 1:3, 18–19; 4:6–16; 6:11–12). In 5:1–2, Paul exhorts him to continue in his ideal behaviour as a model for others, making the age-related aspect of this section of the letter explicit.

"OLDER" AND "YOUNGER" AS AGE CATEGORIES

The Greek terms for older and younger are often used as nouns but are actually comparative adjectives. Thus, πρεσβύτερος (meaning "older") is used as a substantive noun, meaning an "older man," in this case one who is from a generation older than the one represented by Timothy, who is "youthful" (νεότης, 4:12). The term πρεσβύτερος, like the typical English translation "elder," can refer to age or leadership (see chapter 9), but it is clear in 5:1–2 that πρεσβύτερος (older man) and πρεσβύτεραι (older women) are age designations.

The labels "older" and "younger" do not have a basis in strict chronological ages. They are fluid categories. This binary age distinction of older (πρεσβύτερος) and younger (νεώτερος) was typical in ancient Mediterranean designations of age (Barclay 2007, 227–32).[2] In the ancient Mediterranean life course, physical and social attributes related to life stages were more important to a person's relative age than chronological age labels (e.g., when a person became a grandparent, or stepped down from public duties). This fluidity, and potential confusion, over the definition of young and old is illustrated in one legal expert's opinion about age designations: "Titius provided in his codicil as follows: 'To Publius Maevius I wish to be given all the young men in my service.' Question: By what upper and lower limit of age are young men to be defined? Marcellus replied that it was for the person taking *cognition* of the matter to decide whom the testator wished to indicate by the words stated. For in the case of wills, one surely must not stoop to definitions, since most people speak carelessly and do not employ the right names and words. But one could hold that a young man is one who has passed adolescence and has not yet begun to be counted among the older men" (Justinian 1998, 3:42–93, *Digest* 32.69). Marcellus does not mention chronological ages, but stages of the life course, and clearly designations of "old and young" depended on context.

In the ancient Mediterranean, how the young and old interacted with one another largely resulted from life course expectations and experiences. Mary Harlow and Ray Laurence note that "in practice, qualities of the young or the old might have been emphasised for the benefit of the participants" (2002, 150). In 1 Tim. 5, the author employs these fluid designations for old and young to denote proper behaviour.

A METAPHORICAL HOUSEHOLD AND FICTIVE KIN

In 1 Tim. 5:1–2, the author categorizes older and younger men and women using household terminology of parents and siblings. Culturally, each group would have been treated differently according to gender and age. These four groups reflected the composition of the Roman household, the basic social unit of the Roman Empire (also Titus 2:3–7; Verner 1983, 1–13, 171–3; see chapters 2 and 11).

David C. Verner finds reminiscence in 1 Tim. 5 of the household codes, or *Haustafeln* (1983, 83–111).[3] The *Haustafeln* were seen as the traditional way of understanding the household in Greek and Roman times, articulated, for example, by Aristotle, found in Stoic duty lists, and used by the Neopythagoreans and Hellenistic Judeans in the first century CE.[4] The household codes were used to motivate certain behaviour on the basis of household groupings and roles, namely, husband and wife, parent and child, master and slave. The early Christian interpretation of the codes prescribed reciprocal behaviour between superior and subordinate parties. Wives are to be subject to their husbands, and husbands are told to love their wives and not be harsh. Children should obey their parents, and fathers should not provoke or discourage their children. Slaves are to obey their masters, and masters are to treat their slaves justly (Col. 3:18–4:1; see also Eph. 5:1–6:1, 1 Pet. 3:1–7). Instead of the usual husband-wife, parent-child, and slave-master relationships, the text of 1 Tim. 5 adapts this basic structure to emphasize relationships between different age groups.[5] Verner suggests that 1 Timothy (and Titus) involves a complex application of the *Haustafeln*, where the roles of women are especially limited, slavery is not questioned, and age is highlighted, so that the author can promote a good reputation and control opposing teachers (1983, 13–24, 83–111; also Lührmann 1981).[6]

Like the *Haustafeln*, the directives in 1 Tim. 5:1–2 are ideals based upon real relationships. Traditionally, biologically related households functioned as kin, but in urban environments, other groups, such as voluntary associations, might also function *like* kin (see also chapter 3; Barclay 1997, 72–3; Hareven 2001, 152).[7] At the time of the historical Paul, individual adherence to a new group may have challenged family stability, since honour and concord in the family were intertwined with religious identity and practice (Sanders 1997, 162). Karl Olav Sanders suggests we avoid an "over-idyllic picture" of fictive kin (156), since it was probably patriarchal from the beginning. When Paul asks Philemon to rethink the status of the slave Onesimus, inequality is very much evident: Philemon is still Paul's benefactor, and Paul does not challenge Philemon's status as master (156–62). However, by the late first century, whole families belonged to the community and may have made up the bulk of the membership (1 Tim. 3:4, 12; 5:4, 8, 14). Thus, it is little surprise that the author promotes behaviour that reflects conventional family life, including recognizing "elders" as authority figures who promote stability (1 Tim. 5:17; cf. Titus 1:5; Barclay 1997, 77–8).

Fictive kin is often an element of social support in modern Mediterranean networks, providing an analogy with the late first century. For example, Peter Benedict found that nuclear family households in a Turkish town tend to use neighbouring households, which may or may not be related, to function like extended kin in rural areas. They cooperate and provide mutual support, for example, in preparing winter foods, and fulfilled "social obligations such as assistance in times of birth, marriage and death" (1976, 226). Networks of men are found in common occupations, coffee-house groups, voluntary associations, and neighbours, and networks of women (connecting through passages between courtyards) are based on daily contact with neighbours, visiting, or prayer groups (227; see also Kongar 1976, 205–7, 213–15).[8]

Similar forms of cooperation may be reflected in the urban setting in which early Christ groups were successful, operating as fictive kin. The familial similes in 1 Tim. 5:1–2 suggest that intergenerational relationships replicated tangible kinship-like functions that undergirded the call for ideal behaviour.

THE ROMAN IDEAL

Turning to the Roman ideal of age-related behaviour, we see clear reflections of the model of age status and generational stability (chapter 2). In the ancient Mediterranean family, honour prescribed appropriate and ideal age-related behaviours for members

Figure 4.1 Grave naiskos of Sime, a woman honoured by her husband and grown children (about 320 BCE).
Digital image courtesy of Getty's Open Content Program.

of a household, at least in public. The Stoic philosopher Epictetus (55–135 CE), a freedman, described the duties of a son as follows: "To treat everything that is his own as belonging to his father, to be obedient to him in all things, never to speak ill of him to anyone else, nor to say or do anything that will harm him, to give way to him in everything and yield him precedence, helping him as far as is within his power" (1925, 271, 2.10.7; Eyben 1993, 206). Plutarch lists honouring parents and respecting elders as important elements of proper conduct: "that one ought to reverence the gods, to honour one's parents, to respect one's elders, to be obedient to the laws, to yield to those in authority, to love one's friends, to be chaste with women, to be affectionate with children, and not to be overbearing with slaves" (1927, 35, *Education of Children* 10, [Stephanus's numbering] *Moralia* 1:7E).

The ideal behaviour of youth toward elders was deference, not only to one's parents (figure 4.1) but to anyone who was older. Philo determined the proof of one's filial piety by the courtesy one would show to a person who shared the seniority of the person's parents. In other words, if someone respected an aged man or woman, this reflected his remembrance of his father and mother (*Special Laws* 2.237).[9] Philo gives us a clear sense of hierarchical ordering of age, both in the family and in other social settings, taking into account how one was to behave according to one's position in the age hierarchy. "And a father and mother deserve honour [τιμή], not only on this account, but for many other reasons. For in the judgement of those who take account of virtue, seniors [πρεσβύτεροι] are placed above juniors [νεωτέρων], teachers above pupils, benefactors above beneficiaries, rulers above subjects, and masters above servants. Now parents [γονεῖς] are assigned a place in the higher of these two orders, for they are seniors and instructors and benefactors and rulers and masters: sons and daughters are placed in the lower order, for they are juniors and learners and recipients of benefits and subjects and servants" (1937, 446–9, *Special Laws* 2.226-27). Similarly, Dionysius of Halicarnassus, writing in Asia Minor during the reign of Augustus, stated that the "proper" order of offering opinions within the senate was to begin with the oldest, then allow a turn for those progressively younger (*Roman Antiquities* 11.6.3, 6). "I ask you to come forward and deliver your opinions – first the oldest members, as is customary and fitting for you, next those of a middle age, and last the youngest" (1950, 25, 11.6.6).

Cicero also explains how the old and young should interact in different ways according to their age: "Since, too, the duties that properly belong to different times of life are not the same, but some belong to the young (*iuvenum*), others to those more advanced in years (*seniorum*), a word must be said on this distinction also" (1913, 125, 1.34.122). Cicero then outlines the expected behaviour of the young:

> It is, then, the duty of a young man (*adulescentis*) to show deference to his elders and to attach himself to the best and most approved of them, so as to receive the benefit of their counsel and influence. For the inexperience of youth requires the practical wisdom of age to strengthen and direct it. And this time of life is above all to be protected against sensuality and trained to toil and endurance of both mind and body, so as to be strong for active duty in military and civil service. And even when they wish to relax their minds and give themselves up to enjoyment they should beware of excesses and bear in mind the rules of modesty. And this will be easier, if the young are not unwilling to have their elders join them even in their pleasures. (125, 1.34.122)[10]

Cicero suggests the young need to be reminded to practise modesty (*verecundiae*, which can also mean reverence or shame). In modern Mediterranean cultures (chapter 2), we saw that conflict between old and young is quite common in private, but rarely happens in public because such behaviour would threaten family honour. We also saw that modesty is an attribute of the young in the context of their elders (Abu-Lughod 1986, 113). Cicero affirms a similar pattern of intergenerational relationships: in public, the young should practise modest behaviour; seniority was usually derived from age, and with seniority came the right of precedence, including correcting and monitoring public behaviour of the young.

Roman writers refer to a golden age in which the young revered their elders (which might sound familiar to a twenty-first century Western audience!). Juvenal describes a past time in which a youth would rise before his elders; even a wealthier (and thus higher status) young person would rise before a less wealthy older person (*Satire* 13.53–59). Ovid also recalls the traditional reverence for the old and their wisdom. The young would not dare to speak shamefully in the presence of their elders (*Fasti* 5.57–70). Valerius Maximus recounts an ideal past in which elite young men would treat older men like fathers. A young man would escort an older man to the senate, waiting outside the door to serve him and accompany him back home. This became training for future public service. At dinner parties, young men would be careful to arrive after older men so their elders could be seated first, and allowed their elders to get up and leave before they did. They rarely spoke in the presence of their elders, and if they did, it was with modesty (2000, 2.1.9). These writers lament the lack of reverence or respect among the youth of their own day.

Though respect for parents and elders was a common motif in Roman literature (explored further in chapter 5), these laments suggest that a consistent and uniform expression of ideals does not necessarily mean such ideals were accepted and performed in an ideal way (see also Yarbrough 1993, 53). Repeated presentations of ideals could just as easily point to a general lack of respect and perceived need to exhort people to respect their elders.[11] Indeed, writers commonly lament the rebellious nature of youth (explored in chapter 9). It is unlikely there was a "golden age." Most likely, there were just ideals that continued to be lamented by each successive cohort of older men.

Still, respect for elders remained a strong cultural value. In his treatise on old age, Plutarch promotes respect for old age:

τό δ'ἀπὸ τοῦ χρόνου πρωτεῖον, ὃ καλεῖται κυρίως πρεσβεῖον, ἀζηλοτύπητόν ἐστι καὶ παραχωρούμενον· οὐδεμιᾷ γὰρ οὕτω τιμῇ συμβέβηκε τὸν τιμῶντα μᾶλλον ἢ τὸν τιμώμενον κοσμεῖν, ὡς τῇ τῶν γερόντων.

The primacy which comes from time, for which there is the special word *presbeion* or "the prerogative due to seniority in age," arouses no jealousy and is freely conceded; for of no honour is it so true that it adorns the giver more than the receiver as of that which is paid to old age. (1936, 100–1, *Moralia* 10:787D)

In other words, when someone gives honour to an older person as an act of deference on the basis of age, that younger person acts honourably; he acquires honour by giving honour where it is due.[12] The younger person (ideally) does not compete for this kind of honour, for (hopefully) he will receive it himself as he grows older.

It is noteworthy, however, that, as in the modern Mediterranean (e.g., Campbell 1994, 286; see chapter 2), respect was not guaranteed.[13] Whether or not an older person received respect depended at least in part on whether he (or she) had wealth or status and/ or maintained an honourable character in the perception of others (Harlow and Laurence 2002, 117). Karen Cokayne points out:

> Respect ... had to be earned by conforming to what society believed was the correct behaviour in old age. Industriousness and diligence (*industria*) brought that respect, which in turn led to self-confidence and a way of coping with physical burdens of old age. It was not necessarily old age itself that earned reverence, but the actions of individuals stimulated by the drive for affiliation and (self-)esteem. Nor did old age itself invite contempt; rather, those who failed to live up to society's expectations of them were marginalised – which in turn encouraged many to remain physically and mentally active as long as they were able. (2007, 219–20)

To illustrate, Plutarch argues that old men should continue to be active in politics, to keep themselves in vigorous health (1936, *Moralia* 10:792D–E), and to be models and teachers for the young (10:790E–F, 10:795A–F). An old man who was inactive, ill, and unable to function could be a target of ridicule.

To summarize, the Roman ideal of age-related behaviour prescribed respect for elders. Deference from younger people was associated with good order, duty, modesty, and honourable behaviour. Respect for one's elders was expected and lamented as lacking at times. Given this context, it is most likely that among early Christ followers, age always had some precedence because it was such an ingrained cultural value. John M.G. Barclay points out that Timothy is distinguished as an exception to the rule of age hierarchy (2007, 238–9). He is young, but clearly considered experienced enough to take a leadership role in Paul's stead. Yet, his position is tenuous, for Paul must argue that he is suitable for the responsibility (4:12), despite his being sanctioned by the council of elders (πρεσβυτέριον; 4:14). Barclay highlights another exception from the early second century found in Ignatius's *Letter to the Magnesians*. Damas is a young overseer, but wise, and the "holy elders [οὓς ἁγίους πρεσβυτέρους]" (my translation) yield to his decisions. Ignatius's admonishment for the church in Magnesia to respect him (AF 2003, 1:242, 3.1) indicates that not all community members did. As Barclay argues, in both cases, the authors must take pains to convince their audiences that these exceptional young men were worthy of respect *despite* their youthful age (2007, 238–9).¹⁴ By and large, people who grew up and grew old within the early Christian movement (such as those who were faithful "from youth to old age," AF 2003, 1:149, *1 Clem.* 63.3) and retained a good reputation probably gained precedence through their seniority of age. At any rate, this was the expected ideal.

IDEAL RELATIONSHIPS IN 1 TIMOTHY 5:1–2

This ancient Mediterranean context of proper behaviour between old and young frames 1 Tim. 5:1–2. The comparison of the older man to a "father" implies the precedence that comes with seniority of age. Paul admonishes Timothy as a young man not to ἐπιπλήσσω (jab or strike at) an older man but παρακαλέω (conciliate, mollify, placate, or make peace with) him as a father. The contrast between a public display of disrespect and an ideal familial model of concord implies that some younger people in the Christian community were not treating their elders appropriately.

The meaning of ἐπιπλήσσω ranges from "rebuke" (verbal jab) to "strike at" (physical jab) and occurs only here in early Christian literature. Other instances of this word in the Greek literature reveal a sense of having social power over someone, or, as someone might say colloquially, of "putting someone in their place."¹⁵ In the public realm in the ancient Mediterranean, true insults, including physical violence, were measured with honour because they denoted "domination and subjection" (Saller 1994, 142). Public humiliation was a brutal affront to a person's honour.¹⁶ In Acts 16:22–39, Paul and Silas were stripped and beaten in Philippi; the following day they demanded the magistrates lead them out of prison as a matter of honour (Acts 16:37–39; see also Aulus Gellius, *Attic Nights* 10.3.17). Richard P. Saller notes that proper conduct toward freeborn members of the household was similar to proper conduct in the public sphere, namely, using words rather than beating, with the goal of instilling a sense of shame and honourable behaviour (1994, 143–4). In 1 Timothy, the author's exhortation for Timothy not to "jab" an older man alludes to the need for proper behaviour between adults in the public realm, particularly of younger men to older men. In the ancient Mediterranean, a son would rarely have rightful social power over his father (except perhaps if he was senile) and striking one's father was a reprehensible action (as it is in the modern Mediterranean; see chapter 2).¹⁷ In ancient literature it might be an allusion to parricide (1 Tim. 1:9; Aristophanes *Clouds*; see chapter 3). In the Hebrew Bible, anyone who struck or cursed a parent was subject to the death penalty (Exod. 21:15, 17; Lev. 20:9; Deut. 21:18–21, 27:16), and it was shameful to display disrespectful behaviour toward parents (Prov. 19:26, 20:20, 28:24).

The opposite action, the ideal that Timothy should display, is represented by the verb παρακαλέω. One might expect the author to reflect the *Haustafeln* with a word like *obey* (Col. 3:20, Eph. 6:1, 1 Tim. 3:4), but this is not the case. This verb παρακαλέω is used elsewhere in 1 Timothy to mean "exhort" or "encourage" (2:1, 6:2), but these glosses seem awkward here because they suggest overtly offering advice. In modern Mediterranean cultures, as noted in chapter 2, when younger people offer advice to their elders, it may be heard but it is not usually openly heeded, since the older person has the right to make decisions. In addition, παρακαλέω in 2:1 (urging prayers) and 6:2 (teach and urge these things) are followed by an accusative object, whereas there is no content for the exhortation in 5:1.

The context suggests the opposite of speaking harshly or "striking" a father; thus, the NRSV translation of "speak" is not intense enough. Since the verb is borrowed for the younger men, older women, younger women (all accusative), the meaning must apply, at least somewhat, to them as well. The word can have the sense of "treat someone in an inviting or congenial manner, someth[ing] like our 'be open to the other, have an open door': invite in, conciliate, be friendly to or speak in a friendly manner" (BDAG 2000, 765). This sense of the verb is found in other intergenerational exchanges. In Luke 15:28 (the parable of the lost son), the father tries to conciliate with ("plead," NRSV; παρακάλει αὐτόν) the older son, who was angry that his father treated his wayward younger brother so well.¹⁸ Paul also uses the term with an intergenerational analogy: "As you know, we dealt with each one of you like a father with his children, *urging* and encouraging you [παρακαλοῦντες ὑμᾶς καὶ παραμυθούμενοι] and pleading that you live a life worthy of God" (1 Thess. 2:12, NRSV). A translation that captures a sense of conciliation would be more apt here than the NRSV's gloss of "urging." A sense of conciliation or apology is also found in Acts 16:39. As mentioned above, the city magistrates had ordered Paul and Silas to be flogged. The next day, after hearing that Paul and Silas were Roman citizens, they apologized to them (παρεκάλεσαν αὐτοὺς), with a sense of making peace with them. Paul insisted that they not let them go in secret because they had been dishonoured in public (16:37–38; see also 2 Macc. 13:23). The apology was meant to restore honour. In each of these cases, the verb παρακαλέω is followed by an accusative of person, as in 1 Tim. 5:1–2. We find one more parallel in Paul's use of the word that does not have an accusative of person, but does have a sense of making peace: "when slandered, we make peace [or seek goodwill; δυσφημούμενοι παρακαλοῦμεν]," (1 Cor. 4:13, my translation).[19]

Thus, in 1 Tim. 5:1 a sense of conciliate, mollify, placate, or make peace (with the intent of seeking goodwill and concord) contributes to the author's theme of promoting concord. It emphasizes how Timothy was to treat an older man but clearly suggests how he should behave toward the other three groups in 5:1–2 as well. For younger men, if the admonition not to participate in the sins of others (5:22) refers to Timothy's peers – that is other younger men – then the directive to "make peace" with them is also appropriate. Peer relationships could have been fraught with potential honour challenges. Sibling relationships were hierarchical in nature: older brothers had precedence over younger brothers. Still, brothers ideally strived for concord (Aasgaard 2004, 100–1; Plutarch, *On Brotherly Love, Moralia* 6:484D). The appropriate treatment of older women is reflected in the directive to "honour real widows" (5:3) and more subtly in the verses that follow (5:9–10, 16). Finally, his behaviour toward younger women is highlighted with the phrase "in all purity [or chastity; ἐν πάσῃ ἁγνείᾳ]," implying that Timothy should protect a young woman's reputation as if it was his sister's (and thus his family's) reputation.[20] As with other directives in 1 Timothy, the behaviour toward all these groups is idealized, but hints at some of the problems the author is tackling.

CONCLUSION

In the rhetoric of 1 Timothy, Timothy is exhorted to be conciliatory with four groups of people, distinguished by age and gender, whom he should treat as if they were family: father, mothers, brothers, and sisters. The categories of "older" and "younger" were fluid but were clearly based on seniority and age. Through the fictive instructions of Paul to Timothy, the author invites the audience to behave in the "household of God" in the same way that they were expected to behave (ideally) in the literal Roman household. However, these relationships would relate to more than just a metaphor, since early Christ followers probably functioned like fictive kin: members who were not biologically related acted as kin to one another in their urban environment – a phenomenon also found in voluntary associations at the time. Ideal intergenerational relationships involved the young deferring to their elders and acting with modesty so as not to shame their community. As in the modern Mediterranean, respect was not automatic; honour was due to an older person if she or he had cultivated virtue over her or his lifetime. A young man was not to rebuke an older man but make peace with him (and with others as well). Thus, the author was reflecting both an ideal behaviour expected in the community and a reality of how the community was expected to function publicly in its urban environment. As we will see, for the author of 1 Timothy, proper behaviour would function to allay suspicions, appear honourable to outsiders, and promote concord in the face of divisive teachings.

What we see in 1 Tim 5:1–2 is the framing of a section on age-related behaviour (5:1–25) that begins with Paul instructing Timothy to strive for an ideal: have proper respect for others in the community as if they were members of the household, according to age and gender. As an ideal young man who displays honourable and proper behaviour (4:12–16), Timothy is meant to uphold an ideal and to stand in contrast to some in the actual community who were not behaving ideally. Since the group was under suspicion from outsiders, the author advocated honourable behaviour as a way to demonstrate their moral uprightness, thereby mitigating the problems caused by the different teachings (1:3, 6:3). The directives that follow (5:3–22) suggest that some activity in the community was violating normal cultural practice, namely, not caring for parents (chapter 5), older women not taking responsibility for younger women (chapters 7, 8) and young men falsely accusing their elders (chapter 9).

5

Categorizing Widows: Definitions and Responsibilities

The author of 1 Timothy promotes a traditional view of age structure that is modelled after the household, reflecting the ideal pattern of age structure in the Roman world and the expectation of acting as fictive kin. The real audience is implicitly invited to take up this directive and expectation for themselves by observing proper age hierarchies. There is no grammatical transition between 5:2 and 5:3, but the theme of age categories and age hierarchy continues from 5:1–2 as the author now turns to a discussion about widows. This rather lengthy section of the letter (5:3–16) continues with directions related to age-related expectations.[1]

This section on widows is one of most enigmatic in the Pauline corpus.[2] Using a culturally sensitive understanding of age structure, demography, and life course in the ancient Mediterranean world, I employ a critically informed imagination to try to make sense of the problems and proposed solutions around widows, starting in this chapter and continuing in the next three.

WIDOWS IN THE ANCIENT MEDITERRANEAN

The term χήρα means widow ("a woman left without a husband") but could also apply to a divorcée ("a woman living without a husband") (Stählin 1979, 440).[3] In both cases, such a woman was sexually experienced but no longer in a sanctioned sexual relationship. Though one term covers both situations, it was socially more respectable to remarry after widowhood than after divorce (Humbert 1972, 68, 73).[4] Early Christian texts reflect this point. In Mark, Jesus condemns remarriage after divorce (10:12), as does

Paul: "A wife is bound as long as her husband lives" (1 Cor. 7:39, NRSV; also Rom. 7:2). While Paul discourages remarriage for a widow, he does not condemn it: "But if the husband dies, she is free to marry anyone she wishes, only in the Lord. But in my judgment she is more blessed if she remains as she is" (1 Cor. 7:39–40, NRSV; Stählin 1979, 457). The association of the shame of adultery with divorce may have contributed to a negative attitude toward remarriage after divorce.[5]

In early Christian literature, χήρα normally refers to an adult woman who is no longer married, usually as a distinct group of women, separate from the category of "wife" (γυνή).[6] The ὄντως χήρα ("real widow") in 1 Timothy is described as "alone" (5:5), which probably means she has no kin (neither husband nor children, in this case), but it is possible she is a divorcée. The χῆραι over sixty were to have had one husband (1 Tim. 5:9), which suggests they were women whose husbands had died. If the difference between death and divorce mattered for the author of 1 Timothy, he does not mention this explicitly, though he does distinguish widows in other ways (see below). He was more concerned about the behaviour of and toward these women than about how they became χῆραι.

With the five- to ten-year age difference between husbands and wives upon first marriage (see chapter 1), a Mediterranean woman generally could expect to become a widow. In fact, "the social world of adult women could be crowded with widows" (Cokayne 2007, 200).[7] On the basis of demographic and papyrological evidence, Jens-Uwe Krause concludes that perhaps 10 to 15 per cent of women up to the age of thirty were widowed (or divorced),[8] but between the ages of thirty and fifty, about 40 per cent of women were widows. Overall, he suggests that 30 per cent of adult women were widows (1994, 73). While these estimates may be high (McGinn 1999, 631),[9] they do suggest that after the age of about thirty, a married woman could expect her chances of becoming a widow to rise.

For the Romans, a respectable adult woman was usually married (McGinn 1999, 631). Marriage marked her transition from childhood to adulthood, and most non-elite young women likely married in the late teens or early twenties (Shaw 1987, 44; Harlow and Laurence 2002, 81, 94).[10] Both men and women were expected to remarry if they were still in their childbearing years (Treggiari 1991, 500–1).[11] Younger widows generally strove to remarry (Krause 1995, 110) and were encouraged to do so in part because their sexuality was connected to familial reputation (McGinn 1999, 632). Augustus's promotion of traditional family values in his marriage laws also reflected remarriage as a cultural expectation.[12] A woman's identity and function in the family was largely associated with childbearing within marriage, having been raised from the time she was a girl to be a wife and mother. Some elite women may have chosen not to remarry while still in their childbearing years (Humbert 1972, 77), but whether non-elite women did or even could make such a choice is not certain (Parkin 1992, 196n196). A non-elite widow might inherit from her dead husband or from her father,[13] but she might also be left in poverty (Treggiari 1991, 500–1).

A widow would not typically remarry if she was past the age of childbearing (Treggiari 1991, 499). Augustus ruled that a woman named Septicia was too old to be remarried to an "old man [*senex*]" because she was "no longer capable of bearing children," and "the marriage had not been for the purpose of procreating children" (Valerius Maximus 7.7.4, 2000, 174–5). Her inheritance, which was put into question by her marriage, was awarded to her sons rather than becoming a dowry to her new husband. Valerius Maximus, who records the incident, is in full agreement with Augustus's decision: "If Equity herself had taken cognizance of this matter, could she have given a juster or weightier decision? You spurn those to whom you gave birth, sterile you marry, you confound testamentary order by your malevolence, and you are not ashamed to assign your whole estate to the man beneath whose body, already laid out for burial, you spread your withered senility. So thus conducting yourself, even down in the underworld you were blasted by a celestial thunderbolt" (7.7.4, Valerius Maximus 2000, 177).

Widowhood in the modern Mediterranean may offer some further insights. Older women typically do not remarry (Chapman 1971, 110). Their identity and status can vary. On the one hand, the death of her husband might mean a poignant loss of identity and authority for a widow. Whereas a new bride may feel like an outsider in her new marital family, a woman's married identity becomes primary. One seventy-eight-year-old Greek widow describes her keen sense of loss following her husband's death: "You see I wear black. But it isn't only the clothes I wear which are black. My man is dead. In the house of your mother, father, sisters, brothers, you are a guest [*mousafiri*]; you are an outsider [*xeni*]. You live with them but you are an outsider. But with your man you are a *nikokyra* [female householder]. When you are a *nikokyra* no one says you didn't do this right, or come and eat this food which was made for you. I don't have my own household. I don't have anything anymore" (Salamone and Stanton 1986, 118n4). In a Turkish village, a woman should have a man to arrange business, to protect and to advise her. If her husband is dead, a widow's grown son may take this role (Stirling 1965, 196–7). However, an older widow without a son is especially likely to be alone, either tolerated by her husband's kin or dependent on charity or neighbours who have no familial obligation to her (1965, 115, 174).[14] These examples of modern Mediterranean widows suggest we consider various scenarios and identities for the women and widows in the ancient Mediterranean.

It was probably evident that ancient Mediterranean women typically had their last children in their early forties as their fertility slowed before the onset of menopause (Parkin 1992, 123; 192n137; Frier 1994, 320–1). At that time, a woman's identity became more associated with her motherhood role as she directed and/or was supported by her adolescent or adult children.

Whether or not a widow could or did remarry, her respectability and reputation were most important. Younger widows (especially under thirty-five, perhaps) were encouraged to remarry because they were still able and willing to have children. While a widow who remained unmarried and gained a good reputation for this choice may have been celebrated in some circumstances (e.g., as a *univira*, see chapter 6), remarriage was the norm (Treggiari 1991, 235).

Remarriage meant women would appear respectable and conform to social norms, but many widows probably also wanted to remarry to secure their financial situation (Krause 1995, 109). Remarriage may have been the most secure financial choice for a widow (109).[15] In Parkin's estimation, "In classical Roman society ... a childless widow would have been in a singularly unenviable position when she grew old, with no form of state support, and so she would have had every reason to remarry while the opportunity was available. It would appear that most women at this time, of the elite class at any rate, did remarry and remain potentially productive throughout their childbearing years" (1992, 133). But beyond their child-bearing years, women's financial security depended largely on whether they had children, especially sons, or wealth of their own (see below).

CATEGORIES OF WIDOWS IN 1 TIMOTHY 5:3–16

This range of circumstances in which a first-century widow may find herself provides context for the widows of 1 Tim. 5:3–16. There are four categories of widows in this text. (1) The "real widows" (τὰς ὄντως χήρας, 5:3, 16; ἡ ὄντως χήρα 5:5)[16] are introduced in 5:3 as a group of women Timothy should honour. In 5:5 "real widows" are defined as having been left alone (μεμονωμένη),[17] and in 5:16 they are specified as the group Paul wants the assembly (ἡ ἐκκλησία) to support. (2) There is a widow with family, namely, one who has children and/or grandchildren (5:4, also 5:8). The family members are exhorted to care for such a widow because she is the responsibility of her family members.[18] (3) There is an exemplary old widow (5:9–10). This widow is "not less than sixty," has been married only once, and is well-known for her "noble deeds." This widow is often equated with the real widows, although they are not specified as such in the text. I do not equate the two categories. (4) There are "younger" widows (5:11–15), whose behaviour is problematic, and, in the view of the author, in dire need of correction. The four groups of widows represent a range of ages and stages of life.[19]

The author overtly presents what he considers two main problems related to widows in 1 Tim. 5:3–16, one financial and the other behavioural. Before I explore these perceived problems, it is worth considering whether these are actual problems, whether they are part of the fiction of the letter, or whether there is a mix of real and fictional elements. In other words, since the author constructed other elements of the letter, he might have constructed these problems for rhetorical reasons. Although the rhetoric is fairly consistent with the author's fictional portrayal of Paul's words to Timothy, the detailed, lengthy, and rather perplexing descriptions and emphatic directives suggest that at least some of the problems are more real than constructed. If the rhetoric served only to regulate the general behaviour of women in the author's day, many of whom may have been widows, this section might have been much more straightforward. Instead, the section involves a complex array of social relationships and categories of women, implying an underlying problematic situation involving widows in the real community.

Although the author does not abandon his fictional narrative in 1 Tim. 5:3–16 (second-person imperatives occur in 5:3, 7, 11; the first-person indicative occurs in 5:14), the shift in grammar (third-person imperatives in 5:4, 9, 16; third-person indicative and subjunctive woven through most of the text) also suggests that he had in mind a specific situation that the real audience was experiencing rather than a general set of instructions.[20] The author's perception of and proposed solutions to the underlying situations are idiosyncratic, to be sure, reflecting his own conservative stance and perspective. Nevertheless, however obscure the details of the real situation behind his descriptions and suggestions might be, this section reflects situations the author himself was facing in his community, using Paul's voice and authority to propose solutions.

The first problem appears to be that the church was "burdened" with its support for widows (5:16). Paul's solution was twofold: have widows' families care for them as an expression of proper behaviour toward parents (5:4, 8), and have any believing woman who "has widows" support them (5:16). This would leave support for the "real widows" (5:16) who were alone (5:5) and without any other support. The author intimates that some adult children (and grandchildren, 5:4) along with the believing woman (5:16), were responsible to support widows associated with them but were derelict in their duties. The first problem, then, is the behaviour of members of the community who are shirking their responsibility to support widows.[21]

The second problem is connected to the first but represents a more obvious threat to the community: some women were behaving dishonourably (5:6, 13, 15), which was affecting the community's reputation with outsiders (5:14) and compromising the honour of the group (MacDonald 1996, 157–60; see also Zamfir 2013, 97–127, especially 106–8). The author suggests that younger widows, who were both compromising the community's honour and burdening the community, should marry and take up the marital responsibilities normally expected of a woman (5:14). They would then be cared for by their husbands (solving the first problem), and kept busy with childbearing, childrearing, and domestic duties (solving the second problem). These elements of Paul's directives are fairly clear, but as we consider the real audience, a number of the other details are more difficult to explain. These will unfold in the next few chapters. In the remainder of this chapter, I discuss real widows (5:3, 5, 16) and then widows with family (5:4, 8) and the cultural context of how children are to treat their parents (filial duty).

Real Widows

As in 5:1, Paul begins the section on widows (5:3–16) using an imperative to express what Timothy should do: "honour widows who are real widows [χήρας τίμα τὰς ὄντως χήρας]" (5:3). The verb τιμάω means to honour or revere, often directed toward someone of higher status (like gods or elders).[22] Aristotle's sentiments would probably be applicable to the Roman era as well: "Honour (τιμή) is also due to parents, as it is to the gods, though not indiscriminate honour: one does not owe to one's father the same honour as to one's mother, nor yet the honour due to a great philosopher or general, but one owes to one's father the honour appropriate to a father, and to one's mother that appropriate to her" (*Nicomachean Ethics* 9.2.8–9 [1165a, Bekker's numbering], 1926, 526–7). The context of 5:3 suggests that Timothy, as a young man, is to honour a real widow as he would a mother because she is his elder (5:2). It is worth noting that honour can also sometimes mean having esteem for someone in a lower position (e.g., a father honouring a son; Homer, *Odyssey* 14.203; Hesiod, *Theogony* 532;), which reflected the position of widows with no financial support.[23] The term has a clear sense of the worth or value of the one who (or that which) is honoured (BDAG 2000, 1005; LSJ 1940, 1793–4; see also Malherbe 2008 on 1 Tim. 5:17). Since this section in 1 Timothy begins and ends with the real widows (5:3, 16), it is likely that "honouring" the real widow meant, at least in part, providing aid in the form of communal and financial support (5:16). The imperative here hints at an irony: widows were often not seen as honourable because of their liminal position of being women who were neither virgins nor married.

As noted earlier, no state care or public charities for the elderly were available (until later Christian times), nor was the public care of the elderly as such a great concern for the ancient Romans; it was a private affair (Parkin 2003, 216–19, 225). Poverty in old age in the ancient world would be devastating: "If ... poverty happened to befall a man (ἀνήρ) when he had become old, he would himself pray to be free totally from life: this is because of his deprivation in all respects, not having anyone to guide him, nor a source of support, not having adequate clothing, and lacking shelter and food. There are times when he does not have anyone to draw even some water for him" (Juncus; Stobaeus 50.2.85; translated by Parkin 2003, 225). Seneca reveals why a widow might be anxious: "I shall have no one to protect me and no one to keep me from being despised" (*De Consolatione ad Marciam* 19.2, Seneca 1932, 65). Someone who was utterly poor in old age might become a sex worker (considered a base and ridiculed position, especially for an old woman; Cokayne 2003, 139) or a beggar (Parkin 2003, 224–5), but relief might only come with death: "someone who is older and has already given up all hope because of his bodily weakness and poverty looks forward to nothing except the last day of his life" (*Shepherd* of Hermas, Visions 20.2, AF 2:223, 225).

Older men may have found care through a younger wife.[24] Older women, however, tended not to remarry (see chapter 6). A poor widow could find support from her family (her natal family if she were young enough, or her own children if she were older), or a patron (Cokayne 2003, 139). Failing the presence of children and spouse, there might be kin or neighbours willing to help an older person. But, in Roman society in general, if an old person had no children, she or he "was dependent primarily on the initiative they themselves showed and the authority they possessed" (Parkin 2003, 217). She might be able to support herself by offering special skills, such as midwifery, healing arts, weaving, wool working, occasional harvesting, or becoming a wet-nurse if she was young enough (Bremmer 1987, 196–7, 200; Cokayne 2003, 139). Older women could sell products in public since they had more freedom of movement in the public realm than younger women did (Bremmer 1987, 197). But, in the end, an old widow with no children to care for her may have a difficult time supplying her basic needs.[25] This is certainly the strongest image of "the widow" in the ancient world; some widows were poor, but not all, of course. The widow eventually became a symbol of "dependence on God" (Van der Toorn 1995, 20).

The "real widows" in 1 Timothy are described as alone (5:5), too old to remarry and thus set in contrast with the younger widows whom the author thinks need to remarry (5:14). If Timothy was to make peace with older women as mothers (5:2), then the rhetoric in 5:3 suggests he would be expected to model what it meant to honour them as children would honour parents – that is, with care (5:16). In the end, honouring real widows appears to mean that the assembly (ἡ ἐκκλησία) will assist them, supporting them or caring for their needs because no one else is available to care for them (5:5, 16; Verner 1983, 163). And this was not purely charity, for the real widow reciprocated with her prayers (5:5).

Widows with Family and Filial Duty

The intervening verse (5:4), between the directive to honour real widows and the description of real widows, focuses on the needs of the second category of widows: widows who do have family.

εἰ δέ τις χήρα τέκνα ἢ ἔκγονα ἔχει,
μανθανέτωσαν πρῶτον τὸν ἴδιον οἶκον εὐσεβεῖν
  καὶ ἀμοιβὰς ἀποδιδόναι τοῖς προγόνοις·
τοῦτο γάρ ἐστιν ἀπόδεκτον ἐνώπιον τοῦ θεοῦ.

But if some widow has children or grandchildren (descendants), *they should learn* first to perform their duty and devotion to their own household
  and to reciprocate support to their parents (ancestors),
for this is pleasing before God. (1 Tim. 5:4)

The subject of the sentence in 5:4 shifts from the singular widow ("some widow" [τις χήρα]") to the plural ("let *them* learn [μανθανέτωσαν]"). The author's focus moves away from his fictive narrative at this point (indicated by using second-person imperative in 5:3) to discuss people in the implied audience (and thus with an intent to address his real community) through the use of the third-person imperative. The widow in 5:4 is a passive figure; if she has children or grandchildren (descendants), *they* are responsible for her (rather than the community, 5:16). The author emphasizes that children and grandchildren were obligated to support the older widows who were their own kin.

The widow in 5:4 had to be old enough to have adult children and/or grandchildren that were capable of providing for her, and was probably a "permanent" widow, meaning she would not remarry (Bremmer 1995, 31; see chapter 6). If a non-elite woman became a mother sometime around age twenty (Saller 1994, 37; see note 10) and continued to have babies until her late thirties (Frier 1994, 324) or early forties, she would be in her mid-thirties to late fifties when her children reached an age of some adult responsibility (between the ages of fourteen and eighteen). If her daughters also married around twenty years of age, then she may be between forty and sixty years old when she became a grandmother. While a woman could potentially be a maternal grandmother in her late thirties, she was less likely to become a paternal grandmother until fifty or so (if a first-born son married and had a child at about thirty). Her grandchildren would not be able to provide for her until she was in her mid-fifties, at the youngest (assuming her daughter's children might take such a responsibility), but more likely mid-sixties. Therefore, with waning childbearing capability and the age at which a woman would have grown children and/or grandchildren, we would expect these widows with family would be, at minimum, around forty years old.

The children and grandchildren are to "learn" to "perform their duty and devotion [εὐσεβεῖν]" and "reciprocate support [ἀμοιβὰς ἀποδιδόναι]" to their parents (τοῖς προγόνοις). The term πρόγονοι means "forebearers," and can refer to parents, grandparents, or ancestors. The use of πρόγονοι instead of other possible terms (like "mother and grandmother"; 2 Tim. 1:5) reflects a larger cultural ideal of respect for one's forebearers, as well as respect for the past and for tradition, and perhaps for the Roman value of *mos maiorum* (the way of the ancestors).

The verb μανθάνω (to learn) may reflect the influence of the opposing teachers. It is also used in 5:13 (the younger widows "learn to be idle," [ἀργαὶ μανθάνουσιν]) and in 2:11 ("in silence, a woman should learn with all submissiveness" [γυνὴ ἐν ἡσυχίᾳ μανθανέτω ἐν πάσῃ ὑποταγῇ]). In all three contexts, the author highlights problematic behaviour and desires proper behaviour. The author implies that the opposing teachings influence the hearers toward improper behaviour, namely, leading them to neglect their mothers and grandmothers. The irony is that proper behaviour toward their older family members should not need to be learned, for such neglect was considered highly improper behaviour in the ancient Mediterranean context. Indeed, neglecting their own made them worse than unbelievers (5:8).

Even though the specific situation entails widows who are in need of support, the author's exhortation has a basis in a cultural expectation of one's duty to parents and grandparents, and the two verbs clearly convey this. The verb εὐσεβέω reflects the concept of living in a dutiful and right way, including duty to parents, and reflecting the idea of proper behaviour elsewhere of 1 Timothy. The verb ἀποδίδωμι means to "recompense" or "make a return," and carries a sense of obligation, duty, and reciprocity (BDAG 2000, 110). The addition of the noun ἀμοιβὰς, which also carries the meaning of a "recompense" or "return" (BDAG 2000, 54), emphasizes the reciprocal nature of caring for aging parents. It is worth examining the literary and cultural context associated with each of these verbs.

Εὐσεβέω: PERFORMING DUTY AND DEVOTION

The verb εὐσεβέω is a cognate of the noun εὐσέβεια, roughly the Greek equivalent of the Latin *pietas*.[26] It broadly refers to the idea of fulfilling one's obligations, especially the duty one has toward God (or the gods, if one was a polytheist), to country, to parents, to children, and to kin.[27] Mary Rose D'Angelo posits that "the version of εὐσέβεια [the letters to Timothy and Titus] proposed ... reflects the imperial virtue of *pietas*, a combination of devotion to the deity with the proper respect for one's superiors and responsibility toward one's dependents, especially as familial duty" (2003, 158).[28] Such piety especially entailed proper respect for those who controlled one's life (Malina and Neyrey 1996, 45). It was a political as well as social obligation that required careful negotiation within society and within the community (Hoklotubbe 2017, 56, 79). In other words, one of the difficulties with translation is that, in its ancient context, the concept combined religious devotion (to God or the gods) with duty to the traditional structures of family and society (moral or ethical dimension) – two ideas that were separated after the Enlightenment. Therefore, I have chosen to translate the noun εὐσέβεια as "duty and devotion" and the verb εὐσεβέω "to perform duty and devotion" in order to cover both aspects. It also had an emotional aspect. In the so-called *Laudatio Turiae* inscription, the woman's filial piety (*pietas*) was demonstrated in avenging her parents' murders (1.4–9, in Wistrand 1976).

For the author of 1 Timothy, εὐσέβεια is a pivotal value. It is a virtue to pursue, along with righteousness, faith, love, endurance, and gentleness (6:11). Proper behaviour in the "household of God" is associated with the mystery of εὐσέβεια (3:15–16), which the author defines in a formulaic christological statement: "[Christ] was revealed in flesh, vindicated in spirit, seen by angels, proclaimed among the Gentiles, believed in throughout the world, taken up in glory" (NRSV). In this sense, εὐσέβεια has a basis in how the author and his readers understand the nature of Christ – the focus of their religious devotion.

The manifestation of εὐσέβεια was in one's posture or way of being. It was to be found in prayer for the state rulers (2:2), in women's modest behaviour and appearance (2:11), as well as in filial duty of adult children (5:4). A cognate of εὐσέβεια is used for women who should dress modestly and with good works (2:10). The teaching that "is in accordance with εὐσέβεια" is set in contrast to the opposing teachers who disagree with "healthy teaching" (6:3). The opposing teachers are associated with vices, including "thinking that εὐσέβεια is a way to procure (financial) gain [πορισμὸν]" (6:5). The author states that while εὐσέβεια does provide "great gain [πορισμὸς μέγας]" when it is combined with contentment (6:6), desiring to be rich (πλουτεῖν) is a trap that ends in destruction (6:9).[29] For the author of 1 Timothy, εὐσέβεια is the opposite of seeking financial gain, which is attached to vices such as excess and self-indulgence – the vices evident especially among certain women in the group (2:9, 5:6; see chapter 8). The author of 1 Timothy touts the usefulness of training in εὐσέβεια instead of listening to old wives' tales (4:7–8), presumably associated with the opponents. He suggests that the law (which the opponents seek to teach) is for those who are lawless, rebellious, sinful, and ἀσεβέσιν (1:9) – the antithesis of εὐσέβεια – without a sense of piety, duty, and devotion.

The idea of duty and devotion was associated with affection and appreciation, which ideally motivated children to provide support to their parents as they aged. Hierocles states, "For what gain is so great to a child as piety and gratitude to his parents?" (*On Duties* 4.25.53; translation in Malherbe 1986, 91). The notion of εὐσέβεια (*pietas*) included "reciprocal affectionate duty" (Saller 1994, 227).[30] In a first-century letter from a soldier to his mother, the emotional connection between mother and son is evident: "If the gods wish it, whenever I find an opportune time to do it, I am coming to you with letters ... Everybody who comes will testify to you how I am trying to come every day. If you want to see me a little, I want it a lot, and I pray to the gods every day that they soon give me an easy passage for coming" (*P.Mich.* III 203; translation in Rowlandson 1998, 93–4). Similarly, in a series of letters to his mother (in the late second century), a man named Sempronius becomes increasingly anxious to hear from his mother, wanting to know about her well-being. He addresses her as "mother and lady," and consistently mentions he prays for her good health (*P.Mich.* XV 751–52; translation in Rowlandson 1998, 144–5). In a letter to his brother, Maximus, he lauds her; "For we ought to honour as divine the lady who gave us birth, especially since she is so very good" (*Sel.Pap.* I 121.27–28;

translation in Rowlandson 1998, 144n2; figure 4.1). A similar bond between mother and son, as well as grandmother and grandson, may be implied in 2 Tim. 1:5 where Timothy's "sincere faith" mirrors the faith of his grandmother Lois and mother Eunice.[31] Mothers might be the more common parents to receive such affection, partly because mothers often outlived fathers.[32]

An act of εὐσέβεια generated out of intense affection is recorded by Valerius Maximus. A woman was imprisoned for a capital crime. The jailor had pity on her and allowed her daughter to visit, but made sure she gave the old woman no food as he intended to starve her to death. After several days he wondered why she was not dying. He looked into the cell and saw the daughter nourishing her mother from her own breasts. When the jailor told the authorities, the sentence was dropped on account of the daughter's extreme act of *pietas*. Valerius Maximus concludes: "This might be thought to be against Nature, if to love parents were not Nature's first law" (*Memorable Doings and Sayings* 5.4.7; translation in Parkin and Pomeroy 2007, 126–7). Pliny the Elder also recounts this story, noting that a temple dedicated to *Pietas* was built on the site where this act of *pietas* occurred (*Natural History* 7.121).[33]

The author of 1 Timothy uses the term εὐσεβεῖν (5:4) to highlight the importance of one's duty and devotion to parents as part of overall εὐσέβεια (duty and devotion) that reflects foundational moral expectations. In 2:3, prayer leads to "a quiet and peaceable life in godliness [εὐσέβεια] and dignity" (NRSV) which "is good and pleasing before God our Saviour." Almost the same phrase describes the reason for performing duty and devotion (εὐσεβεῖν) in 5:4: "for this is pleasing before God." The repetition of key words and ideas in 5:4 suggests that filial duty is also proper behaviour for peaceable living – and the kind of life that would reflect a good reputation.[34] In short, "proper behaviour" of community members, as manifested in prayers for state leaders and duty toward parents, both as expressions of εὐσέβεια, would project honourable behaviour in the perception of outsiders.

Filial Duty as Reciprocity

The second verb phrase in 5:4, "reciprocate support [ἀμοιβὰς ἀποδιδόναι]," suggests a repayment that would never match the debt that children owe their parents for bearing and rearing them. For Cicero, the "services [of parents] have laid us under the heaviest obligation" (*On Duties* 1.17.58 [58, Miller's numbering], Cicero 1913, 61). The second-century Stoic philosopher Hierocles states, "our gratitude to [parents] is perpetual and unyielding eagerness to repay their beneficence, since, even if we were to do a great deal for them, that would still be far too inadequate" (*On Duties* 4.25.53; translated by Malherbe 1986, 91). He goes so far as to say that children's actions are not even their own, but really an extension of their parents' actions. Parents are "the images of the gods" as well as "benefactors, kinsmen, creditors, lords and the finest of friends" (*On Duties* 4.25.53; translated by Malherbe 1986, 91; also Aristotle, *The Nicomachean Ethics* 8.12.5). Similarly, Philo states that the "duty of honouring parents ... stands on the border-line between the human and the divine," suggesting that parents are like God in that they have produced children, and children are obligated to honour them (*On the Special Laws* 2.225 [section 38], 1937, 447).[35] Harlow and Laurence summarize: "Old age had never brought guaranteed respect or right to position, but the Roman virtue of *pietas* enshrined the idea of respect for one's parents and an obligation to look after them in their old age in return for the care they had shown already" (2002, 119).

Hierocles notes that children secured not only their parents' care, but also their grandparents' care in old age: "We should consider that in children we not only beget for ourselves helpers, persons who will take care of us in our old age, and who will share with us in every fortune and circumstance; we beget them not only on our own behalf, but in many ways also for our parents. For the procreation of children pleases them since, if we should suffer some calamity before they die we would leave them someone to take care of them in their old age" (24.14; translation in Malherbe 1986, 103). Hierocles suggests that when the ancient sources discuss care for parents, they probably imply grandparents as well. In practice, as noted above, demographic realities suggest adult children would more often be required to support their mothers and grandmothers than their fathers and grandfathers.

Filial duty was particularly important in frail old age, when an elderly parent was in their last stage of life.[36] Hierocles equates physical care of parents in old age with the care they gave to their children when they were infants: plenty of food suitable for old age, bed, sleep, healing salves, baths, clothing, and anticipation of their needs (*On Duties* 4.25.53). Hierocles also explains that children should pay close attention to their parents' emotional and social needs (their "soul"). He says children should spend time with their parents, especially as they near the end of their lives, "performing seemingly servile duties such as washing their feet, making their beds and standing ready to wait on them" (*On Duties* 4.25.53; translation in Malherbe 1986, 92–3; see also Sir. 3:12–16).

In the ancient Mediterranean, it was a social expectation, a cultural obligation, and common moral teaching that adult children would care for and support their elderly parents.[37] Most people relied on their adult children to care for them as they aged, especially among the non-elite (Parkin 2003, 221). In his *Controversies*, Seneca the Elder indicates that filial support could mean to give food to a parent in a time of need.[38] In the family of Psyphis and Tetosiris (*P.Mich.* V 322),[39] their adult children received their inheritance but were asked in return to provide their elderly parents with wheat, oil, and cash for expenses and clothing on a monthly basis, to take care of any private or public debts their parents incurred, and to provide an appropriate funeral when they died.

Adult children in the ancient Mediterranean expected to care for their parents just as they would expect care from their children when they aged. Children's obligation of repayment to their parents was a binding cultural value. This was, of course, part of the generational cycle. As the model of generational stability suggests, in a society where honour was a pivotal value, such attentiveness toward one's aged parent would also be recognized as honourable behaviour. The directive in 1 Tim. 5:4 suggests some members of that community were neglectful of their parents and grandparents – dishonourable behaviour indeed.

"One's Own, Especially the Household" (5:8)

To reiterate the gravity of the situation, a few verses later, the author makes a second statement about those who were not properly supporting family members:

εἰ δέ τις τῶν ἰδίων καὶ μάλιστα οἰκείων οὐ προνοεῖ,
τὴν πίστιν ἤρνηται
καὶ ἔστιν ἀπίστου χείρων.

> And if someone does not provide for his or her own,
>   and especially members of a household,

he or she has denied the faith
and is worse than an unbeliever. (1 Tim. 5:8)

The author of 1 Timothy expected members of the "household of God" to behave properly in the community (3:15) but also, as suggested in 5:8, in their familial roles in their own households (e.g., 3:4, 12, 5:14; see chapter 4). The verb προνοέω has a sense of caring, not so much out of obligatory reciprocity, but out of deliberate, thoughtful attention or provision, with a connotation of careful planning ahead of time (BDAG 2000, 872), similar to Hierocles's ideal of foreseeing and fulfilling a parent's requests (*On Duties* 4.25.53, translated in Malherbe 1986, 92; see above).

Those who care for the elderly members of their household are pleasing to God (5:4), but to neglect members of the household is to deny the faith (τὴν πίστιν ἤρνηται, 5:8). This implies that one who has faith, or is faithful, should behave in ways that are morally superior to those who do not. Perhaps they should be especially morally superior to the opposing teachers, who have evidently turned away from "the faith" (e.g., 1:19, 6:21). Neglecting the elderly made the person worse than someone with no faith or faithfulness (ἔστιν ἀπίστου χείρων, 5:8). This repetition emphasized how serious the neglect was but also how such behaviour was part of "the faith" (see chapter 8).

The author specifies that one should "especially [μάλιστα]" provide for "members of a household" (5:8). The meaning of μάλιστα is a matter of some debate (also found in 5:17; see chapter 9). It can mean either "especially" (which delimits a select group within "one's own," namely, the members of one's household) or "in other words" (thus equating "one's own" with "members of the household"). Employing the second meaning, R. Alistair Campbell suggests that 5:8 does not refer to one's literal household but to fellow believers in the metaphorical "household of God" (1995, 157–60). While I am unconvinced by Campbell's argument,[40] his study does highlight that it is not clear whether the widowed mothers and grandmothers were themselves Christ followers.[41] Carolyn Osiek and David Balch suggest that individuals involved in the community may have had family members who needed care and were not Christ followers (1997, 166–7). Either way, the author is clearly distinguishing between the filial responsibility of family members (5:4) and the responsibility of the assembly (ἡ ἐκκλησία, 5:16). The phrase μάλιστα οἰκείων ("especially of a household"), serves to emphasize the importance of responsibility to close kin associated with the household.[42] And it may be deliberately ambiguous.

Social Sanction

Filial duty would have been especially important for widows whose children survived into adulthood, especially with no Roman laws to enforce filial duty[43] and little or no financial leverage like that available to a *paterfamilias*.[44] In addition to the cultural and social expectation of εὐσέβεια (Parkin 2003, 215–16), a widow's children may have been motivated by affection (as discussed above). However, there was another way to ensure care for aging parents: social sanction (Foner 1984, 149–53).

In a society where one's honour is paramount, social sanctions are powerful. As we have seen, looking after parents was considered a moral duty, as well as part of honourable behaviour that maintained family prestige and reputation. Family wealth was an important part of status and honour maintenance (Saller 1994, 155), but even among the relatively poor, an honourable son would treat his father (and mother) with respect, particularly in public. Not caring for elderly parents would compromise one's honour (see Brandes 1995, 14). Susan Treggiari notes, "How a person behaves with his nearest and dearest spills over into the public sphere, where he is observed by outsiders" (2005, 10–11).

In *P. Mich*. V 322 (mentioned above), aging parents legally ensured their care by outlining the provisions they expected from their children.[45] Expectations for provision as outlined in a legal document would likely be public knowledge, such that if the children did not fulfill their duties, they would be subject to social sanction.[46] They would bring dishonour to their family if their peers perceived that they were acting immorally toward their aging parents. Of course, older parents who were not receiving proper care from their families could also complain – a strategy to ensure care through the mechanism of social sanction (Foner 1984, 112; Brandes 1995, 20). Voicing a concern would reinforce the cultural norm and could also compromise honour – both of an individual and of the family – which people would take pains to avoid.

Osiek and Balch argue that because the ancient texts suggest the elderly were constantly concerned about having children care for them and provide a proper burial, there must have been significant neglect of elderly parents (1997, 165–6). Demographic realities reflect some credible concern, for some parents did outlive their children. And some children did neglect their parents.[47] However, this evidence does not suggest significant overall neglect. Parents might have voiced their concerns about old age so frequently not because their children were negligent, but because parents wanted to be sure they would not be, or wanted to ensure more than minimum efforts. Seneca commended Marcia on the filial devotion she displayed toward her aging father, contrasting the lowered standard of filial duty in his day, "in an age when the supremely filial was simply not to be unfilial!" (*De Consolatione ad Marciam* 1.2, Seneca 1932, 5). Seneca does not lament the *neglect* of parents, which would have been quite concerning, but the minimal efforts of children toward their parents. Rather than think of the treatment of parents as either dutiful or neglectful, a continuum of more or less pious behaviour would better reflect reality.

What we might call "religious sanction" was also a factor: "Parents were often equated with gods, so that disrespect, violence, or neglect of obligations to them was equated with impiety" (Reinhold 1970, 352; also Carter 2001, 46–50; Philo *Special Laws* 2.224–25). On a social level, religious sanction functions as social sanction. Accusing a person of impiety or irreverence might shame them into proper behaviour (e.g., Cicero, *Atticus* 9.9).[48] This takes us back to the model of generational stability and social change (chapter 2): conflict within the family is normal, especially in contexts of social change, but conflict that shows up publicly is subject to social sanction and lowers a family's perceived honour.

This appears to be at issue for the community addressed by the author of 1 Timothy. In the list of qualities for overseer and *diakonoi*, the author requires leaders to manage their own households well and have submissive children who treat their parents with respect (3:4, 12). If a man's children were not respectful and did not order themselves properly under the authority of their father, they would bring shame on their family, which in turn would have brought shame on the Christ group. In other words, the honour of an individual household that belonged to the Christ group would also reflect the honour of the community as a whole. Likewise, if adult children did not adequately care for their widowed mothers and grandmothers, this would be perceived as dishonourable behaviour, reflecting on both "families."

Unlike the paranaesis in 1 Tim. 5:1–2 that encouraged ideal behaviour, in 5:4 and 5:8 the author suggests that community members needed to live up to *conventional* behaviour in providing for their own relatives, lest their behaviour be worse than that of unbelievers (5:8). Calling into question one's commitment to "the faith," a form of religious sanction, is an important tactic of the author of 1 Timothy. He emphasizes duty and obligation toward one's parents to avoid social sanction from outsiders. The author's language is meant to shame certain community members into proper behaviour, namely, at least in part, taking care of widowed mothers and grandmothers.

Given that the reputation of the community was at stake, the author of 1 Timothy motivates his audience toward filial piety primarily by reinforcing cultural obligations of reciprocity (5:4), as well as religious and social sanction (5:8), most fervently by appealing to members' sense of εὐσέβεια, that is, their duty and devotion.

CONCLUSION

The author of 1 Timothy wishes to address two problems associated with widows: some widows have become a burden for the community (5:16), and certain behaviours were compromising the community's reputation (5:15). It seems fairly clear from the outset that the church should assist the "real widows" (5:16), but not be burdened with other widows who had other choices, namely, the widows with family to care for them (5:4, 8), and the younger widows who can and should remarry (5:14). In 1 Timothy, the author appeals to his listeners' sense of εὐσέβεια (duty and devotion) as the basis for proper behaviour, behaviour that would ensure the community was perceived by the outside world as honourable. Caring for parents was a primary part of εὐσέβεια, for Mediterranean cultures place a high priority on revering and supporting parents, especially as they age.

The directives in 1 Tim. 5:4 and 5:8 are intended for adult children, emphasizing the importance of fulfilling this duty as an act of reciprocity and obligation, and as part of proper behaviour. The phrasing suggests that the problem was more than a financial burden for the community; neglecting proper behaviour by avoiding filial duty was compromising the honour of the group. The author implies that some adult children were not fulfilling this obligation, which would have appeared as dishonourable, opening them to social sanction and ridicule.

The deference due to one's elders (5:1) was an ideal the author wanted his audience to strive for. However, given the specificity of the instruction ("reciprocate support to their parents," 5:4), as well as shaming language ("he or she has denied the faith and is worse than an unbeliever," 5:8), the author indicates that some people were failing to perform *normal* duties; they were behaving in culturally inappropriate ways that endangered the reputation of the community.

6

Why Sixty?

While the author was appalled at the behaviour of certain people who did not adequately care for their aging mothers and grandmothers, he was delighted by a group of elderly widows whom he presents as models of virtue. We turn from widows with family (5:4) to another category of widow: the exemplary widows of 5:9–10. Since they are not labelled as such, these widows are not "real" widows, as specified in 5:3, 5, and 16. Rather, they are a special class of widows who stand out for their ideal attributes and life-time of virtuous activities. These widows are described as "having become not less than sixty years old [μὴ ἔλαττον ἐτῶν ἑξήκοντα γεγονυῖα]" (5:9). Why sixty?

There are surprisingly few references to chronological ages in the early Christian literature (see chapter 11), and no other early references of which I am aware that distinguish a particular age group in this way.[1] Furthermore, specifying the age of sixty for women in the ancient Mediterranean world is rather odd because a woman's social age was normally determined by life stages rather than chronological age. Though commentators have attempted to account for this age in various ways related to financial aid, the power of leadership, marriage, and/or sexuality, none has adequately addressed the specificity of the age of sixty.

OLD WOMEN, REPUTATION, AND THE SIXTY+ WIDOW

In the Roman Empire, an older woman's experience of life depended on many factors, but familial roles and social status were among the most influential. A married woman would continue to function under her husband's authority, though as she aged her influence increased, especially if she had grown children. She would be influential in their lives, including helping to procure marriages (see chapter 7). Becoming a grandmother did not necessarily mark her as "old" (especially if she was in her late thirties or early forties; Harlow 2007, 208), but it did "age" her since she entered a new stage of the life course (2007, 202).

Information about older women in Roman society comes mostly from men, whose attitudes toward older women varied widely. Since early Christian texts were written by men, the stereotypes reflected in ancient texts are themselves quite relevant. Recognizing that these are *perceptions* of older women is crucial, lest we equate perception with reality. For the Roman male writer, the biological or chronological age of a woman was not as relevant as social age, that is, "attitudes and behaviour expected of an individual at any given stage" (Cokayne 2007, 197). For instance, male Roman writers tended to refer to women in relation to men, especially in their roles as daughters, sisters, wives, mothers, mothers-in-law, and grandmothers.

Older women were often loathed, sometimes ignored, and occasionally highly respected by male writers. Cokayne argues that there were two opposite stereotypes of older women: "a woman was either a respectable wife and mother, or she was disreputable" (2003, 134). These stereotypes were often connected to appearance and life circumstances (Parkin 2003, 15–26). In Greek and Roman literature, men tended to comment on women's physical aging as visually unattractive (Cokayne 2003, 220). They were stereotypically "disgusting, haggard, stinking, toothless, and sex-crazed" (Parkin 2003, 86; see also Bremmer 1987, 203–4, Horace, *Epode* 8; Martial *Epigrams* 3.93), or excessive gossips and alcoholics (Harlow and Laurence 2002, 129–30; Cokayne 2003, 148–9; Bremmer 1987, 201–2; see also Titus 2:3).[2] Cokayne emphasizes that such negative stereotypes were based on an old woman's apparent lack of self-control (2003, 145) in light of the expectation that women were to be chaste and respectable their whole lives (135).

On the other hand, a few old women were portrayed in the ancient literature as the epitome of female self-control – the ideal Roman matron. For example, Pliny the Younger praised a woman named Ummidia Quadratilla, who died at seventy-nine years of age. She raised her grandson to be a good citizen, and prudently bequeathed her wealth to family members, despite the many admirers who undoubtedly hoped for a share (*Letters* 7.24). She is elsewhere attested as a generous patron in her local town (CIL 10.5183; Harlow and Laurence 2002, 129). Pliny also describes a deceased thirteen-year-old girl as having "all the wisdom of age [*anilis prudentia*; literally, "wisdom of an old woman"] and sedateness [*gravitas*] of a matron though joined with youthful sweetness and virgin modesty" (*Letters* 5.16.2; Parkin 2003, 245). The application of this stereotype to a young woman demonstrates its influence as a public image.

Similar stereotypes are present in the modern Mediterranean, but there are some nuances to consider. A woman's reputation in old age is a reflection of her reputation throughout her life course. In her younger years, a woman's sexuality threatens family honour and must be protected.[3] Men are usually considered the protectors, but women also have an active role in protecting their sexuality, and thus the honour of the group.[4] When a woman reaches menopause and is beyond her childbearing years, she is no longer considered sexual, has more freedom, exercises more power, and submits to fewer people (Abu-Lughod 1986, 163). According to J.K. Campbell, among his Sarakatsan informants (who were probably mostly men), a woman is cunning (*poniros*), an attribute which is a constant threat to men's honour, but (ideally) she can redeem the family honour through her sexuality by bearing sons who will protect the honour of community (1964, 277). He states that an old Sarakatsan woman, "past the period of sexual activity"[5] whose son is reputable, has "almost overcome the moral disabilities of her sex" (1964, 277–8) – almost, but not quite. In fact, women continue to pose a potential threat to the honour of their family throughout their lives, but how they pose a threat changes over the life course.

A modern traditional Mediterranean woman's lifelong reputation is an important factor in her role in family honour. Her reputation is inherited by her children, for, as we have seen, an individual's honour is shared with all family members (Pitt-Rivers 1977, 29, 78; chapter 2). It can affect whether her daughters can secure an honourable marriage, for example. An older woman can help preserve the reputation of female members of her family, both in upholding her own reputation and helping to protect theirs against potential gossip of other women. As with all other family members, old women can threaten or strengthen family honour. Or, more accurately, the *perceived* virtue or malice of old women, based on a lifetime of honourable or disreputable behaviour, can affect her own and her family's honour. Julian Pitt-Rivers notes that since honour is based on reputation, "it is gossip rather than the truth which is relevant" (1977, 39; see also Kartzow 2009).

Stereotypes of old women as either an old hag or ideal matron, of course, are not reflections of real women's lives, but male perceptions of women, which is the case in 1 Timothy. Specifically, the widow in 1 Tim. 5:9–10 reflects the positive stereotype of the ideal old woman. The author uses this characterization when he describes the sixty+ widow:

Χήρα καταλεγέσθω,
   μὴ ἔλαττον ἐτῶν ἑξήκοντα γεγονυῖα,
   ἑνὸς ἀνδρὸς γυνή,
   ἐν ἔργοις καλοῖς μαρτυρουμένη,
εἰ ἐτεκνοτρόφησεν,
εἰ ἐξενοδόχησεν,
εἰ ἁγίων πόδας ἔνιψεν,
εἰ θλιβομένοις ἐπήρκεσεν,
εἰ παντὶ ἔργῳ ἀγαθῷ ἐπηκολούθησεν.

A widow should be put on a list
   having become not less than sixty years old,
   the wife of one husband,
   being well attested in noble works
if she has raised children,
if she has shown hospitality,
if she has washed the feet of the saints,
if she has assisted those who are afflicted,
if she has pursued every good work. (1 Tim. 5:9–10)

The author's use of a third-person imperative ("let her be put on a list"; καταλεγέσθω) likely reveals a glimpse of the real situation behind the letter, or at least how the author perceives the situation.[6] The phrase "a widow should be put on a list" is conditional; she must fulfill the qualifications outlined. The first implicit qualification is her age, "having become [γεγονυῖα]" an age that is "not less than sixty years [μὴ ἔλαττον ἐτῶν ἑξήκοντα]"; that is, she should have attained this age (the sense of the perfect participle is an achievement). The author also notes her marital status ("wife of one husband") and describes her current reputation, "being well attested in noble works." The verb μαρτυρέω means to bear witness or testify, but since it is in the passive voice, it suggests *others* speak well of her and can attest to her noble works (BDAG 2000, 618). These three present attributes are followed by five explicit conditional statements describing her *past* activities that have led to her current reputation (discussed in more detail below). In fact, we see a *lifelong* reputation reflected in the description of what the sixty+ widow has accomplished over her life course. Her enduring reputation of virtuous behaviour is at least part of the reason the author highlights this widow of advanced age. However, it does not explain the specificity of "not less than sixty years old."

CHRONOLOGICAL AGE AND PROBLEMATIC ASSUMPTIONS

As discussed in chapter 4, the identification of age is usually contextual, employing the terms "old(er)" and "young(er)" (e.g., Luke 1:7, 18; Philem. 9; 1 Pet. 5:5; see Barclay 2007, 227–32). Indeed, the author of 1 Timothy chose comparative age designations (older/younger) to set up the section related to age groups (1 Tim. 5:1–2), and to identify certain "younger" widows (5:11, 14; cf. Titus 2:2–8). On the other hand, even when chronological ages are specified in early Christian texts, they often correspond to life stage rather than chronological age. For example, Jesus was "about thirty" according to Luke (3:23) when he began his teaching and healing. Thirty was the age of maturity and sound judgment for a man.[7] Jesus raised a girl from the dead who was twelve years old (Mark 5:42), the legal minimum age for marriage (Harlow 2007, 197). In a social sense, her death would have meant a loss of connection to another family through marriage. In both cases, the chronological ages are specified likely because they correlate with a stage of life. They both also refer to specific individuals rather than a group, which is implied in 1 Tim. 5:9. Thus, the specification of "not less than sixty" 1 Tim. 5:9 is an anomaly.

While some commentators merely mention the phrase in 5:9 without elaboration (e.g., Collins 2002, 139),[8] others pass over the reference entirely (Dibelius and Conzelman 1972, 75; Houlden 1976, 93). Discussion of the age of sixty usually revolves around one of several explanations: (1) setting a minimum age requirement that restricted the number of widows who qualified for aid or that restricted women's power; (2) specifying an age at which women were less likely to remarry or have sexual passion; or (3) setting the threshold of old age. Each of these explanations is problematic.

Restricting Financial Aid

One of the most common arguments about the directive to enlist sixty+ widows is pragmatic: it limited the community's liability for supporting widows (e.g., Knight 1992, 230; Marshall 1999, 593; Young 1994b, 117; Johnson 2001, 264, 274; Towner 2006, 346; Barclay 2020, 276). Supporters of this hypothesis suggest that the qualifications listed in 1 Tim. 5:9–10 reduce the number of widows receiving aid from the church, so that the church is not overly burdened (5:16). The community would be financially responsible only for a small number of widows, and for a short time, since life expectancy at sixty was short (Johnson 2001, 264, 274; see below). George W. Knight, III (1992, 230) and Towner (2006, 346) suggest that these widows could no longer support themselves because of their advanced age. Age restrictions were accompanied by other restrictions; widows who receive aid must also have been married only once (5:9) and possess proven domestic virtue (5:10; Johnson 2001, 264, 274). Some suggest the support is remuneration for ministry (e.g., Hanson 1966, 57).

The idea of restricting aid rests on two major assumptions, both problematic. The first assumption is that the word "enlist" (καταλέγω) refers to a list that *restricts* the number of widows. The meaning and use of the word does not explicitly correspond to a received action (like receiving charity). This is not to say that such a context is impossible, but it is not a strong possibility, especially given other contexts in which we find this term (discussed below). The word "enlist" is typically set in opposition to the phrase introducing younger widows in 5:11, usually translated "but deny the younger widows," with a sense of (or explicit wording for) not putting younger widows on a list (5:11). This translation and interpretation I dispute in chapter 7. There is no grammatical reason to connect the sixty+ widow (5:9) and the younger widows (5:11) in this way.

The second problematic assumption is that the sixty+ widow in 5:9–10 is the same as the "real" widow (specified in 5:3, 5, 16) who is explicitly meant to receive aid (5:16). For example, Bruce W.

Winter states, "The 'real' Christian widow had an age qualification and was known for her faithfulness in marriage. She distinguished herself in her service as a Christian ... She had no immediate family or relatives to support her financially. This was how the 'real' Christian widows were defined in the Pauline community in Ephesus (1 Timothy 5:4, 9, 10, 16)" (2003, 123). Towner recognizes that "the reference to widow is here generic, χήρα (without the art[icle])" but posits that "the argument developed to this point in the passage makes it clear that the 'real widow'... is meant" (2006, 345n70). This is circular reasoning. In order to make his argument clear, he must begin with an assumption that the sixty+ widow is equated with the "real" widow.⁹

The "real widows" and "sixty+ widows" are not the same group of widows. The text does not explicitly equate the two, and the author emphasizes different characteristics for the two groups. The real widows were needy and devoted to prayer (5:5); the "enrolled" widows were distinguished by their age and exemplary past behaviour (5:9–10; Kidd 1990, 104).

The author is careful to specify "real" widow(s) three times in the text. In the first instance, Paul exhorts Timothy to "honour widows who are real widows," (χήρας τίμα τὰς ὄντως χήρας, 5:3; see chapter 5). In the second instance, the author indicates that the "the real widow" (ἡ ὄντως χήρα) was solitary and left alone (μονόω, 5:5). In the third instance, Paul uses the third-person imperative to direct the assembly (ἡ ἐκκλησία) to provide aid (ἐπαρκέω) to "the real widows" (ταῖς ὄντως χήραις, 5:16). He does not use this phrasing in 5:9. The author explicitly contrasts the "real widows" with two other types of widows: widows who have children and/or grandchildren (5:4), and the widows that a believing woman "has" ("if some believing woman has widows [εἴ τις πιστὴ ἔχει χήρας]," 5:16).

Not all commentators equate the real widows and sixty+ widows. C. Spicq considers 5:9 the beginning of a new section introducing an "order of widows" that is not equated with real widows (1947, 532; see also Verner 1983, 165).¹⁰ However, Bassler rightly posits that the textual unit must be 5:3–16 because the author begins and ends with the "real" widows (5:3 and 5:16) (2003, 136). Reggie M. Kidd proposes that the real widows and "enrolled" widows are two different groups, and that the latter represent "an office being opened up precisely to patronesses of the church in consideration of their beneficence to the church ... verses 9–15 indicate the official recognition the widowed woman of means is to be afforded for her service" (1999, 105). Unfortunately, Kidd ignores the content of 5:11–15 regarding the troublesome younger widows. More importantly, however, he does not address the question of what motivated the author of this letter to write this extended section on widows.

A significant problem with the equating of the "real" widow with the sixty+ widow is that if the text in 5:9 serves to limit the numbers of those who receive charity, no widows under the age of sixty would be eligible. A destitute widow could be any age (Bassler 1996, 97).[11] Young widows typically remarried in Roman society (see chapter 7), but, as discussed in chapter 5, an older widow was at risk of utter poverty, especially if she had no children (Cokayne 2003, 152; 1 Tim. 5:5). It is unlikely that the community would reject the destitute widows who could no longer remarry, but who were not yet sixty, solely on the basis of age. Given that average life expectancy at sixty years of age was fairly short (Parkin 2003, 50, 280), the majority of widows who were alone and needed support were probably *under* sixty.[12] There is no solid evidence in the text to demonstrate that aid was restricted to women who would have taken over forty years to prove their domestic virtue in order to be worthy of receiving aid. In the fourth century, the *Apostolic Constitutions* (in part an interpretation and application of parts of 1 Timothy), clearly state that the church should provide aid to all who were in need, especially the poor, the sick, and those with many children (3.1.4).[13] In a small community in the late first century, it is unlikely the author is attempting to restrict aid to the poor on the basis of age.

Another significant problem with equating real widows and sixty+ widows is that if the younger widows remarried (as they were being encouraged to do in 5:14) and were subsequently widowed a second time, they would *never* qualify for support because an enlisted widow was to be "the wife of one husband" (5:9; Kidd 1990, 104). Again, this seems unlikely. The author would hardly advocate for the community turning her away if she was in need; indeed, he admonishes whose who have wealth to be generous in giving to others (6:18). It is possible to take this phrase to mean marital fidelity rather than literally the wife of one husband for her entire lifetime, but one wonders why clearer phrasing was not used if this were the case.

The point of 5:9–10 is not to define who should receive aid. The sixty+ widows are not equated with the "real" widows, and there is no evidence to suggest charity is at issue. In fact, the sixty+ widows appear to have had some wealth since they are described as having provided hospitality and care for others.

Restricting Power (an "Order of Widows")

A second major argument for "why sixty" suggests that it is an age limit that restricts the number of widows to be "enrolled" in some kind of ministry, often arguing for an "order of widows." Restricting the number of widows would mean women had restricted power in the leadership of the community. This argument suggests that widows in 5:9 were "enrolled" as a "special class" of widows (Dibelius and Conzelmann 1972, 75), especially a kind of ecclesiastical office, which was (or developed into) the later "order of widows" (*ordo viduarum*; Spicq 1947, 532; Thurston 1989, 44–53; MacDonald 1988, 185).[14] In this interpretation, the author listed the sixty+ widows separately because of the special nature of the group (Thurston 1989, 44)[15] and in order to put limits on which particular women could be part of the order (53).[16] Specifically, it excluded the widows who were younger (5:11) and who had married more than once (5:9). In this interpretation, the real widows who need assistance (5:5, 16) cannot be equated with the official "order" of widows.[17]

Although an "order of widows" is evident in later literature,[18] it is difficult to justify such a role in this text. First, if the author were setting up qualifications for an ongoing "order of widows," his directives to younger widows would be at odds with his long-term goal. If the younger widows remarried, as they were encouraged to do in 5:14, they would never qualify to become part of the "order," since they must be the wife of one husband (5:9), an observation recognized by some scholars (e.g., Bassler 1984, 33–4), but not adequately accounted for (e.g., Guthrie 1990, 114).

Moreover, though the list of qualifications and attributes bears some resemblance to the lists found in 1 Tim. 3:1–13 for overseer, *diakonoi*,[19] and female *diakonoi* (or wives of *diakonoi*),[20] the lists are not convincingly parallel. There are very few qualifications and characteristics that actually overlap, as a close comparison demonstrates (table 6.1).

All three categories refer to having one wife/husband (3:2, 12; 5:9). This could mean married only once, but in a culture of frequent death and divorce among (younger) adults, this could disqualify many

Table 6.1 | A comparison of overseer, *diakonos*, and sixty+ widow

Someone who aspires to be an overseer	*Diakonos*	Sixty+ widow
the husband of one wife (μιᾶς γυναικὸς ἄνδρα, 3:2)	the husband of one wife (μιᾶς γυναικὸς ἄνδρες, 3:12)	the wife of one husband (ἑνὸς ἀνδρὸς γυνή, 5:9)
wants a noble work (καλοῦ ἔργου ἐπιθυμεῖ, 3:1)		is attested (by others) in noble works (ἐν ἔργοις καλοῖς μαρτυρουμένη, 5:10)
hospitable (φιλόξενον, 3:2)		has shown hospitality (ἐξενοδόχησεν, 5:10)
shepherd (manage) his household well, and keep his children submissive with all respect (τοῦ ἰδίου οἴκου καλῶς προϊστάμενον, τέκνα ἔχοντα ἐν ὑποταγῇ, μετὰ πάσης σεμνότητος, 3:4)	shepherd (manage) their children and their households well (τέκνων καλῶς προϊστάμενοι καὶ τῶν ἰδίων οἴκων, 3:12)	has raised children (ἐτεκνοτρόφησεν, 5:10)

otherwise apt people. If it is taken to be a reference to marital fidelity (Collins 2002, 139–40), it might fit well with the overall argument of advocating for proper behaviour in all aspects of moral life, though, as noted above, it is oddly specific.[21] Perhaps most importantly, because of cultural perceptions of gender, a woman without a husband was seen quite differently from a man without a wife.

The man who aspires to be an overseer wants a "noble work" (a reference to his potential future appointment; 3:1) whereas the sixty+ widow's "noble works" refer to her current reputation that rests on past good works (5:10; also 2:10). The overseer candidate and sixty+ widow are both associated with hospitality, but the author uses different terms (3:2; 5:10).[22]

Why Sixty? 123

All three are assumed to have children. As fathers, the overseer and *diakonoi* are required to exercise authority over their children in the present (3:2, 4, 12), whereas the sixty+ widow raised children in the past (5:10). The parallels do demonstrate the author's concern for proper familial behaviour, but do not suggest that the author is outlining a present office for the sixty+ widows.

In addition, the grammatical structure suggests different purposes for the lists. The list of attributes (adjectives and attributive participles) for overseer and *diakonoi* follows the phrase in 3:2, "must be [δεῖ ... εἶναι]" (3:8 borrows the phrase in 3:2 to make sense of the sentence). The purpose of this list is to outline current qualities found in those who will be (future) reliable, faithful, and active leaders in the community. The widow's list follows the passive third-person imperative (καταλεγέσθω): let her *be put on the list* (if she qualifies). The widow's current qualities are listed as attributive participles (5:9), but her deeds are listed in the aorist indicative – a past tense. The purpose of this list is to select particular women based on their age, marital status, reputation, and *past* female accomplishments (Fee 1988, 125; see also Johnson 2001, 264, 274; Barclay 2020, 277). While the author of 1 Timothy specifies the aspiration of someone to be overseer (ἐπισκοπῆς ὀρέγεται; 3:1) and the action of serving as *diakonoi* (διακονέω; 3:10, 13), neither aspiration nor action on the part of the widows is implied in the directive to "enlist" them (5:9).

Finally, the context of the overseer and *diakonoi* constitutes a new section of the text (following the phrase πιστὸς ὁ λόγος, 3:1), designated for listing qualifications of these leaders. In contrast, the widow's description is listed amid directives to various groups in the community who are acting improperly.[23]

In sum, arguing that the widow in 5:9–10 holds an "office" parallel to that of the overseer and *diakonoi* in 3:1–8 on the basis of the qualification lists is unfounded.

There are two final reasons that it is unlikely that sixty+ widows represented an "order of widows." The first is that those who posit an "order" or "circle" of widows assume the list in 5:9–10 to be prescriptive of a distinctly renewable role in the community.[24] They suppose the list outlines which current and future women are qualified to belong. Although these verses are used this way later in the church (e.g., Tertullian, *On the Veiling of Virgins* 9.2), one cannot assume they were meant to be used this way originally. The authority of the "office" itself is not clear in 1 Timothy (even in 3:1–13).

This is in contrast with Ignatius's description of the overseer and *diakonoi*, for example, which betrays signs of the beginning of institutionalization such that the role itself, rather than the person in the position, held authority (*Mag.* 6.1).

Finally, women of this age (and older) would be, on average, too old to *begin* a set of ongoing duties (Guthrie 1990, 114). Disqualifying widows who were under sixty from a position of power would certainly curtail the power of women (Krause 2004, 100), especially if women over sixty were often frail. C.K. Barrett considers most sixty+ widows "too infirm" to actively serve the church (1963, 75). Conflating real widows and sixty+ widows, I. Howard Marshall suggests that they were not able to care for their own needs any longer (1999, 593). Bonnie Bowman Thurston tentatively posits they were less mobile, so less prone to gadding about (1989, 47). However, since she argues for an order of widows, Thurston notes their "duties" may include visitation. She acknowledges the weakness of such reasoning (47).

Indeed, in the second-century story of the *Acts of John*, the old women of Ephesus were gathered together to receive care (section 30). Of those who were over sixty, only four were healthy; the others were sick and debilitated. John attributes their poor health to the devil and seeks to heal them so they can be useful. It is curious that John is surprised at the number of ill women who are over the age of sixty, for illness and physical weakness could hardly have been uncommon for aging women in the ancient world. The author of the *Acts of John* may have known the specific reference to sixty in 1 Tim. 5:9, which was also associated with Ephesus, and assumed women over sixty had an important role to play in the community.

On the other hand, older women did possess power. Mediterranean women, modern and ancient, tend to gain more power as they progress through the life course. After menopause or becoming a grandmother, a woman was freer to function outside her household, perhaps employed as a mourner, midwife, or messenger (Bremmer 1987,197–8). She usually earned respect from her children, especially if she had inherited some wealth. Parkin interprets this freedom not so much as a privilege but as a sign of her lack of status, that is, her unimportance in society (2003, 246, 259). His description of old women in the Roman world is rather negative, focusing on their lack of "usefulness" in their post-reproductive stage of life. But if old women were wholly without power, there would probably not be such strong emotions and stereotypes portrayed in the public domain, such as in comedy and art – or indeed in this letter (1 Tim. 4:7; also Titus 2:3).

Timothy is told, "Have nothing to do with [παραιτοῦ] profane myths and old wives' tales [τοὺς βεβήλους καὶ γραώδεις μύθους].[25] Train yourself in [εὐσέβεια], for while physical training is of some value, [εὐσέβεια] is valuable in every way, holding promise for both the present life and the life to come" (4:7–8, NRSV; see also chapter 5). The contrast of the women who tell stories in 4:7 (who may not necessarily be *old* women; Zamfir 2013, 181) with the exemplary old widows of 1 Tim. 5:9–10 parallels ambivalence toward older women in the ancient Roman sources explored above. As in the modern Mediterranean (Campbell 1964, 290; Chapman 1971, 44; Brown 1982, 145), older women in particular in the ancient Mediterranean were associated with magic and witchcraft (Propertius, *Elegies* 4.5.9–20; Bremmer 1987, 204–6). "On the one hand, this is an obvious case of stigmatising due to the marginal position of old women, but on the other hand, old women of all times have made use of magic to strengthen their feeble position within society" (205–6). This sort of power or threat might be behind the negative connotation of "old wives' tales" in 1 Tim. 4:7 (see also MacDonald 1983, 4). If this portrayal of older women and their potential power over others (younger people, especially) represents a negative stereotype, then 1 Tim. 5:9–10 offers a description of the *positive* stereotype of older women – the epitome of domestic duty and self-control.

Men may have been threatened by the power of older women, some of whom were at the height of such power, especially with their influence over their grown children.[26] Indeed, if the only women granted power were those who had reached the advanced age of sixty, this would most certainly restrict the power of middle-aged women under sixty. However, 1 Tim. 5:9–10 does not explicitly restrict women's power; rather, it highlights certain women as ideal matrons.

As with the hypothesis that the age of sixty was meant to restrict women from receiving aid (above), it is not clear that "enlisting" widows means to *restrict* the number of widows in 5:9–10 who were gaining power. It is clear, however, that the author was concerned about women's behaviour. Whereas some old women in ancient Mediterranean society were despised, these old widows would have been revered. Beyond the fact of its later development, there is no compelling evidence to suggest that the author of 1 Timothy intends to establish an "order of widows" as an active office, nor an organized group starting a ministry at age sixty.[27]

PAST ACTIVITIES FOR A PRESENT SITUATION

I have argued that the author is not asking the widows in 5:9–10 to be put on a list to restrict them (either for aid or for leadership). However, he is highlighting this widow as a model of virtue demonstrated by her good deeds. Her life experience over the various stages demonstrated consistent virtue that remained for her into old age. She is an example of an ideal πρεσβύτερα (older woman, 1 Tim. 5:2; cf. πρεσβύτιδος, Titus 2:3), highlighted to exemplify the traits she has cultivated over a lifetime that other women – namely, middle-aged women – should be striving for and modelling to the younger women (chapter 8). In 1 Tim. 5:9, the author was not considering *future* widows over sixty years old, but thinking about *present* widows in his community, or at least a present ideal. In 5:9–10 the widow's *current* qualities resting on *past* deeds reveal that she is meant to be seen as exemplary. I now examine these past deeds in some detail.

Wife of One Husband

According to 1 Tim. 5:9, a sixty+ widow must also be "a one husband woman" (ἑνὸς ἀνδρὸς γυνή). For Romans, a woman ideally married only once in her lifetime.[28] Lifelong marriage to one husband was considered morally superior to multiple marriages, even though remarriage after being widowed was "strongly encouraged by kin, society and state" if she was still of childbearing age (Harlow and Laurence 2002, 95; see chapter 7). Being married to only one man reflected ideal chastity, but it was also considered good fortune, for many husbands died before their wives at relatively young ages. If a woman was married to only one man in her lifetime, this usually meant that either he outlived her or she was an older woman when he died (and therefore unlikely to remarry if she was no longer able to bear children). She was considered fortunate because of the longevity of her husband (Treggiari 1991, 235).

A woman married only once was known in Latin literature as a *univira* – a term associated with public image. The label *univira* (once married) occurred in inscriptions, often erected by a woman's children (Humbert 1972, 68–70; Treggiari 1991, 499). Humbert suggests the rarity of the *univira* rather than the frequency may have given this title its status (1972, 75; also Parkin 1992, 132). The most important attribute of a *univira* was her marital faithfulness (*la fidélité conjugale*).[29] Moreover, the objective of the epitaph was to promote a positive public image (Humbert 1972, 68). In other words, a widow's reputation, cultivated over many years of chastity after her husband's death, was the object of praise.

Univira came to be associated with virtuous widows in early Christianity, but Marjorie Lightman and William Zeisel argue that this was an adaptation of the original term. For the Romans, the virtue of a *univira* was related to consistently being under male authority in her life, first her father's and then her husband's authority (1977, 20). In late antiquity, the Christian church provided a kind of "surrogate for male authority" that allowed widows to appear virtuous and chaste (28–30). But Romans did not normally associate widowhood with virtue or esteem; they considered it a regrettable and unlucky circumstance (26).

A *univira* had certain ritual rights because of her chastity and good fortune, such as a role of *pronuba* in which she joined a bride to her new husband. A *pronuba* had to be married only once with a living husband, presumably to confer the same kind of fortune on the bride (Isidore, *Etymologies* 9.7.8; Treggiari 1991, 233). Also, only a *univira* could sacrifice to the goddess Pudicita ("Chastity"; Livy *History of Rome* 10.23).

Lightman and Zeisel posit that in the late Republic divorce was more common than it was in the early Republic (for evidence, see *Laudatio Turiae* 1.27 in Wistrand 1976). *Univira* took on a new meaning of a woman who was exceptional in her female virtue and fortune in contrast to a *matrona* who might be married several times over her lifetime (Lightman and Zeisel 1977, 24–5). Funerary inscriptions from this time demonstrate that the term was used by the non-elite as well as the elite, especially men who wished to increase their social status and display respect for traditional virtues (*mos maiorum*; 26). Their wives, whom they describe as *univira*, were often actually quite young (Treggiari 1991, 235).[30]

A young widow may have felt some tension between the status given to *univira* versus the social and legal expectations to remarry (Harlow 2007, 206n72). One marriage meant one sexual relationship, and this kind of loyalty signified other virtues as well. In an idealization of the days of old, Valerius Maximus describes women married once in laudable terms: "Women who had been content with a single marriage used to be honoured with a crown of chastity. For they thought that the mind of a married woman was particularly loyal and uncorrupted if it knew not how to leave the bed on which she had surrendered her virginity, believing that trial of many marriages was as it were the sign of a legalized incontinence" (2000, 131, 2.1.3). Plutarch portrays Cornelia, the mother of Tiberius and Caius Gracchus, as an exemplary widow who was devoted to her sons (Harlow and Laurence 2002, 68, 89). After her husband died, leaving her with twelve children, she refused to marry again even when Ptolemy the king requested her hand. Although only three children survived to adulthood (one daughter and two sons), her sons became famous for their public activity in Rome. Plutarch attributes their exemplary virtue to their mother's conscientious care (*The Life of Tiberius Gracchus* 1.3–5).[31] Cornelia was from an elite family, and revered by the people for her role as a mother. They erected a statue in her honour, as mother of the Gracci (*The Life of Caius Gracchus* 4; Pliny *Natural History* 34.31). After her sons were killed, Plutarch recounts that she retained her virtuous behaviour because of her strength of character, recalling their great deeds without grief. He describes her entertaining and interacting with noble men, with hospitality and honour (*The Life of Caius Gracchus* 19.1–3). Notably, Plutarch focuses on her reputation rather than her sexuality or marital status.

This evidence suggests that widows did not have social prestige because of their widowed state (indeed, they were anomalous since they were without male protection), but an older widow might have authority and honour for other reasons, namely, family connections, wealth and/or age, especially when she wielded authority over younger women (Krause 1995, 113–15; Treggiari 1991, 498). Thus, there are a number of possible connotations of the sixty+ widow being "a one husband woman" (5:9), but it is most likely that it points to the ideal of her faithfulness to her husband and the public honour this would elicit.

Noble Works

A sixty+ widow "is attested in noble works [ἐν ἔργοις καλοῖς μαρτυρουμένη]" (5:10). This phrase implies that on the basis of having witnessed her past activities, others can verify her honourable reputation in the present. Plutarch uses the phrase ἔργα καλά (good works) to denote the carefully cultivated fruit of a virtuous man who should remain in office in his old age (1936, 94, *Moralia* 10:786D).

The first of her past deeds is that she should have raised children (ἐτεκνοτρόφησεν).[32] Motherhood was the most important role a woman could have; devotion to her children was a moral ideal (Zamfir 2013, 259, 270; see also 257–78; van Bremen 1993, 234). Certainly, a woman may have become a widow after her children became adults,[33] but it was relatively common for a widow to keep and raise her underage children, even if they legally belonged to their father's family (Treggiari 1991, 467–8). She may also have had grandchildren whom she helped to raise. Along with childbearing, childrearing was an important female task. Plutarch's description of Cornelia demonstrates that a mother's exemplary virtue was instrumental in her children's virtue (*The Life of Tiberius Gracchus* 1.4–5).

The sixty+ widow should have provided hospitality (ἐξενοδόχησεν). This may have been in her own home (if she inherited or was granted the right of habitation of a house; e.g., Justinian 1998, 7.8.2.1, 7.8.4–9), or could apply to helping with tasks related to hospitality in households that belonged to kin or other community members. Food preparation would be an important part of hospitality. This is women's work (see, for example Danforth 1982; Kenyon 1991). Similarly, she was to have assisted those in distress (θλιβομένοις ἐπήρκεσεν). This might mean tending the sick, injured, or grieving. This sort of task was also connected to women's work, especially tied to networks of women who would band together for such purposes. In female networks in modern Mediterranean societies, where many women come together to make proper preparations, older women have positions of authority, usually women in their forties and fifties, past caring for young children and with more freedom and resources to organize rites of passage and assist with various life crises (Sacks 1992; 1–6; also evident in Titus 2:3–5; LaFosse 2017a). The word for "assist" (ἐπαρκέω) has a sense of being "strong enough" to be of assistance (LSJ 1940, 610). The term is repeated twice in 5:16, admonishing the believing woman to *assist* the widows she has, and the community to *assist* the real widows (see chapter 8).

In addition, the sixty+ widow was to have washed the feet of saints (ἁγίων πόδας ἔνιψεν). This is a unique and enigmatic phrase. It is found in a fourth-century inscription honouring a female *diakonos* with phrases found in 1 Tim. 5:10 (Eisen 2000, 164–7). Ute

Eisen notes that washing feet was a way to honour guests and an act of love. Rather than menial work, it may have been an honourable task, perhaps hearkening back to the woman who washed Jesus's feet in Luke 7:36–50 (2000, 166).[34] The word ἅγιος means holy, sacred, or set apart, but here used as a plural noun (ἅγιοι) means "holy ones" but often rendered "saints." The term is not found anywhere else in the letters to Timothy and Titus, but occurs frequently in Paul's undisputed letters, where it refers to all believers (e.g., Rom. 1:7, Phil. 1:1, 2 Cor. 13:12, Philem. 5, 7).[35]

Finally, this widow had been devoted to every good work (παντὶ ἔργῳ ἀγαθῷ ἐπηκολούθησεν). The author makes a subtle distinction between the virtuous noble deeds (ἔργοις καλοῖς) of an established older woman that others have witnessed, and the everyday good works performed willingly over a lifetime of service. Perhaps the emissaries sent to Corinth from Rome in *1 Clement* provide an apt parallel to the sixty+ widow: they were "faithful and temperate men [ἄνδρας πιστοὺς καὶ σώφρονας] who have lived blamelessly among us from youth to old age [γήρους]" (AF 2003, 1:148–9, 63.3). In both cases, their lifelong commitment and virtue were seen as essential characteristics to help in problematic situations.

In a culture where an old woman was perceived in the public eye as either ideal and virtuous or a haggard old crone lacking self-control, the sixty+ widows exemplified all that the author hoped for in women's behaviour. On the other hand, to call too much attention to these women would not be prudent (Osiek and MacDonald 2006, 3). They exemplified virtue and pointed to the truth in a way befitting a woman in cultural context – not in words (2:12, 5:13), but in deeds, past and enduring, to which others could bear witness (5:10). That they did not command too much public attention – except, or course, for their respectability – was, ironically, the point of highlighting them as models of virtue.[36]

REMARRIAGE AND SEXUAL PASSION

The exemplary nature of the sixty+ widow is clear. However, we still have no clarity on the specificity of sixty. Suggestions for this age distinction include two other possibilities: these widows were unlikely to remarry (Easton 1947, 153; Knight 1992, 223; Bassler 1996, 97; Johnson 2001, 264)[37] or at this age they were less likely have sexual passion (Kelly 1963, 115; Thurston 1989, 47).

Why Sixty?

The argument that the author specified the age of sixty because these widows were unlikely to remarry holds very little merit. *Any* widows who were *beyond childbearing age* were not likely to remarry (Cokayne 2003, 121–5). Though concord and mutual benefit were valued in marriage (e.g., 1 Cor. 7:2–5), marriage was generally seen as a union formed primarily for procreation. This is illustrated by a second-century story of a contentious marriage. In defence of his marriage to Pudentilla, a wealthy widow with grown children, Apuleius denied that he used sorcery to gain her affections and that he was a legacy hunter, trying to rob her sons of their inheritance. Apuleius's opponents held that Pudentilla was sixty, but Apuleius proved she was just over forty (*Defense* 3.67, 4.89). She was deemed an unlikely candidate to remarry, in part because remarriage might compromise her children's inheritance. Apuleius was adamant that her surviving son's inheritance would not be jeopardized by his marriage to their middle-aged mother.

Men understood the implications of menopause, of course.[38] The Augustan laws made fifty the upper age limit of remarriage for widows or divorcées, which was likely based on the observation that by this age women were no longer fertile (Cokayne 2003, 122; Parkin 2003, 194–8). A woman's decline in fertility is associated with the process of menopause, although a woman's fertility declines before her menstrual cycle ceases. The ancient sources differ as to when they suggest a woman reached menopause. Pliny the Elder observed that "a woman does not bear children after the age of fifty, and with the majority menstruation ceases at forty" (*Natural History* 7.14.61). A few ancient (male) authors stated that some women menstruate up to their sixtieth year (e.g., Soranus *Gynaecology* 1.20, first or second century CE), but it is unlikely that the author of 1 Timothy was aware of and referring to obscure medical tradition subscribing sixty as the upper limit of women's menstruating years. As Soranus pointed out, menopause varied from woman to woman. Nevertheless, the age of fifty seems to have been when the ancient male authors typically thought a woman reached menopause.[39]

Thus, a significant problem with the "unlikely to remarry" theory is the gap between the age when men thought menopause normally occurred (around fifty), and the chronological age of sixty. Marshall notes the "gap" between supporting widows sixty and older and the younger widows of childbearing age, but disregards its implications by stating, "these instructions are probably more in the nature of ideals than precise regulations" (1999, 593). Yet the author *is* very precise about the age of "not less than sixty"; Marshall's comment does not address the deliberate specificity of the phrase.

Harlow points out that menopause itself is not visible or public, so it is a poor marker for determining women's age (2007, 199–200).[40] Bremmer argues that "the Greeks" (presumably men) "saw women primarily as producers of heirs and objects of love or lust. Menopause and (approaching) old age therefore constituted a fundamental change in the man-woman relationship in antiquity" (1987, 191).[41] However, male authors did not normally use menopause as a measure of old age.

Other indicators of age are visible and thus more obvious markers, such as physical appearance (hence the negative stereotype of old women) and familial roles (hence potential positive stereotypes). The changes in women's roles as their sons become adults and they have grandchildren are particularly important (Harlow 2007, 199–200). Appearing to act in ways appropriate to one's life stage is an important cultural value. In modern Greek culture, mothers may continue to be fertile after their children are adults but are embarrassed to be pregnant at that stage of their lives, when they are close to being grandmothers. Also, an adolescent son would be embarrassed if his mother was pregnant because this reveals her sexuality (Beyene 1989, 114). Menopause and becoming a mother-in-law and grandmother may occur at around the same time for many women, but their stage of life rather than their biological cycle is socially visible (see Brown 1992, 18). Though they were no longer valued for their fecundity, older women did have influence in their families (see de Luce 1993a, 42).

The other suggestion for why the author of 1 Timothy specified the age of sixty is less chance of sexual passion. This argument especially contrasts the behaviour of younger widows in 5:11–13 (Kelly 1963, 115; Thurston 1989, 47). The merit to this idea is that in the ancient Mediterranean, a woman's behaviour was directly correlated with male honour and was strongly associated with her chastity, specifically with her reputation for chastity (MacDonald 1996, 253). An adult woman was "normally" in a monogamous sexual relationship within marriage. Both widowhood and old age were therefore liminal states for women. Since widows were both sexually experienced (unlike virgins) and no longer had male "control" over their sexuality, they were anomalous, and automatically considered suspicious (Buitelaar 1995,

8). An old woman, in the male perspective, was beyond childbearing years and should no longer be in a sexual relationship (see the example of Pudentilla above). Negative stereotypes and marginalization of old women were tied to the abhorrence Romans had for old women who were still sexually active. In their view, female sexuality was tied to reproduction (Cokayne 2003, 135).[42] The sex-crazed old woman was a common character in comedy (Aristophanes, *Assemblywomen* 877–1111; see chapter 7). In the ancient male mind, an ideal old widow was not sexually active.[43]

To suggest that the age of the sixty in 1 Tim. 5:9 had to do with menopause or sexual passion helps us to consider context but still does not explain the specificity of sixty. While it is probably true that women over sixty were unlikely to remarry, and they may have been perceived as having less sexual passion, this was just as true of women over fifty. Again, the gap of a full decade should hardly be ignored.[44] Therefore, suggesting that widows would not remarry or be sexual after sixty is not an adequate explanation for the specificity of sixty.

THRESHOLD OF OLD AGE

Still other scholars have pointed to sixty as the threshold of old age in antiquity (Spicq 1947, 532–3; Barrett 1963, 75; Thurston 1989, 47; Kelly 1993, 115; Bassler 1996, 97; Marshall 1999, 593). Roman textual sources were not consistent about sixty as the commencement of old age. "Old age" could start as early as forty-six (Cicero, *On Old Age* 17.60) or as late as sixty-nine.[45] Parkin argues that it is convenient for *scholars* to consider the age of sixty as the start of old age,[46] but sixty was not an age at which someone was suddenly old (2003, 16).

That said, some ancient sources did specify the chronological age of sixty as the threshold of old age, but often for rhetorical effect. "Age terms as labels might be used as a means of imposing authority, of showing respect, or of causing calculated affront" (Parkin 2003, 23). For example, Apuleius's detractors said that Pudentilla should not remarry because of her advanced age of sixty (*Defense* 3.67, 4.89), even though, as noted above, Apuleius demonstrates that she was just over forty by producing public documents recording her birth and the number of consuls since she was born (4.89). The detractors chose the age of sixty as a polemical strategy to argue that Pudentilla should not have remarried.

In his comments on the sixty+ widows of 1 Tim. 5:9, Spicq states that sixty was the typical age of retirement (1969, 532), but this is true only for elite men.[47] For men, the age of sixty was associated with entering a time when adult male responsibilities diminished. An elite man could retire from military and public office at the age of sixty, although sources differ on the exact age (see Parkin 2003, 290–1). Roman senators were no longer required to attend the senate after the age of sixty (Seneca, *De Brevitate Vitae* 3.5). The age was evidently lowered from sixty-five (Seneca *Controversiae* 1.8.4), but the evidence is unclear as to when or why (Parkin 2003, 126–7). From a study of papyrological evidence from Roman Egypt, Parkin argues that men were exempt from the poll tax at the age of sixty (raised to sixty-two in the second half of the first century; 2003, 157–62), and from public services (152–3), although Parkin notes that exemption from the latter was usually based on a combination of age and infirmity (153–4). Release from civic duties may be why a man was no longer required to remarry after the age of sixty if he was widowed or divorced, according to Augustan marriage laws (198–9).[48] In the Mishnah, a man who is sixty is an elder (*m. Aboth* 5.21). The Damascus Document (among the Dead Sea Scrolls) specifies that a man over sixty is no longer eligible to be "Judge of the Congregation" (10.7). In sum, within the male life course, the age of sixty as old age was generally correlated with the cessation of active public life and civic duties (Harlow 2007, 197).

Sixty is also portrayed as a time when full personhood was diminished, as in the case of senicide (killing an elderly person) in Roman comedy. In Lucian's *Downward Journey* those over sixty who had died are described as old and wrinkled like raisins (5–6). Lucian's Peregrinus strangled his old father who was sixty (*Passing of Peregrinus* 10), and Gryllus is told to die and become ashes at age sixty (Herondas, Stobaeus 50.2.56). There are more serious references to senicide. According to Diodorus Siculus, in a pejorative description of a group of apparently cave-dwelling people, an old man who could no longer tend flocks (or who was disabled) killed himself, or was killed, so that no one among them was over the age of sixty (3.33.6). The phrase "sixty year olds over the bridge" probably related to military voting, but some ancient writers did use the phrase to allude to senicide in the far Roman past (e.g., Ovid *Fasti* 5.623–24; see discussion in Parkin 2003, 264–72).[49]

These references are hardly applicable to women. The ancient Romans perceived men's and women's life stages differently, as demonstrated by the Augustan marriage laws, for instance, where men were required to remarry between the ages of twenty-five and sixty, and women between twenty and fifty. Admittedly, references to women who were sixty do demonstrate that sixty is considered an advanced age. For example, a young boy says of his great aunt that she is "extremely old [γῆρας μακρόν]: apparently she's lived more than sixty years" (P. Sakaon 40.12–13; translated in Parkin 2003, 20).

Sixty is an age at which a woman might engage in particular public activities. In Plato's *Laws*, he specifies that priests *and priestesses* in his ideal city should be "not less than sixty years old [ἔτη ... μὴ ἔλαττον ἑξήκοντα]" (1926, 420–1, 6.759D; Spicq 1947, 532).[50] The age specified for men and women is the same.[51] Notably, the high reputation of the households the candidates represent is also of great importance (6.759C). It suggests that sixty was old, but not too old to hold a sacred religious position; in fact, it was a stipulation for this position.[52] However, the priests and priestesses would hold the sacred office for only one year. Though the phrasing mirrors that of 1 Tim. 5:9, there is no time limit or specific function listed for the sixty+ widow of 1 Timothy. Plato's priestesses are mentioned in the context of public religious roles in a male context. By comparison, the context of 1 Tim. 5:9 does not indicate a public activity although it does allude to a widow's *reputation* in public. The sixty+ widow is also mentioned in the context of other women, not men.

Funerary Rites

A possibility that has not (to my knowledge) been suggested elsewhere is associating sixty+ widows with funerary rites. According to funeral regulations in ancient Greece, Solon specified that women who were sixty and older were the only women, besides close female kin, allowed in the room where the deceased was laid:

> The deceased shall be laid out in the house in any way one chooses, and they shall carry out the deceased on the day after that on which they lay him out, before the sun rises. And the men shall walk in front, when they carry him out, and the women behind. And no woman less than sixty years of age shall

be permitted to enter the chamber of the deceased [γυναῖκα δὲ μὴ ἐξεῖναι εἰσιέναι εἰς τὰ τοῦ ἀποθανόντος], or to follow the deceased when he is carried to the tomb, except those who are within the degree of children of cousins; nor shall any women be permitted to enter the chamber of the deceased when the body is carried out, except those who are within the degree of children of cousins. (Demosthenes 1939, 102–3, "Against Macartatus," *Private Orations* 43.62)

Old women in the modern Mediterranean are often associated with laments and tending graves, especially in Greece (Danforth 1982).[53] One explanation for why old women, especially old widows, fulfill this role is that they are on the "threshold" between life and death, both as old women and as women whose husbands have died. In many cultures, old women provide important ritual functions because their liminal status affords them a mediating role in rites of passage, like funerals (Buitelaar 1995, 10). Solon does not provide direct insight as to why sixty was the age specified for women's involvement in burial, though it appears to relate to the public nature of their involvement (since they are outsiders to the family).

Interestingly, there are no obvious allusions to laments and grave tending in the list of past deeds for the sixty+ widows in 1 Tim. 5:9–10. I have several suggestions for why, but all are purely speculative. Since laments contain elements of protest to the status quo (Abu-Lughod 1990, 46–7), the author might have considered them improper. Rituals for the dead were probably enmeshed with polytheist elements, which may have been problematic for the early Christ groups. This may have been especially true of women's laments. On the other hand, another possibility is that "washing the feet of the saints" (1 Tim. 5:10) could allude to a death ritual.[54]

SIXTY AS PUBLICLY HONOURABLE

Of the many references to the age of sixty in the ancient literature, a select few may help us to understand why the author of 1 Timothy specified this age. It is probably true that the author uses sixty at least in part because it was considered the threshold of old age, an age at which a woman is prone to illness and physical weakness (*Acts of John* 30), and an age at which a woman should not remarry (e.g., Apuleius's detractors regarding Pudentilla). The phrasing of "not less than sixty" is probably used with the rhetorical effect of labelling such a woman as old, perhaps because of its association in popular thought with old age in men. However, it is years of honorable reputation cultivated over a long life that was of utmost importance to the author of 1 Timothy, especially in a time when reaching this age was not something the majority would achieve. Sixty was also used to refer to roles for some women in the public sphere and public ritual, as with Plato's priestesses and old women attending funerals. The age of sixty in 1 Tim. 5:9 appears to have a similar public element with regard to a widow's exemplary reputation. She exhibited all the admirable female virtues expected of women for an honourable "household." The emphasis is on her behaviour rather than on teaching (2:12), stories (4:7), or gossip (5:13). Thus, she is presented as an older woman, "not less than sixty," having been married only once and having others around her testify to her lifetime of "noble works," having cultivated a notable, respectable, and honourable set of present attributes over many years. Her lifetime of experience points to her trustworthiness as a model of feminine virtue and activity.

The Meaning of καταλέγω

Another exegetical question still remains: why was an old widow of virtuous character being "put on a list" (καταλεγέσθω, 5:9; Johnson 2001, 264)? As we have seen, the standard suggestions are to receive financial support, or to affirm qualifications for an office, namely, the "order of widows," usually with a sense of restricting numbers of widows on the list. However, as I have been arguing, rather than restricting numbers of widows, the author is highlighting exemplary widows who were chosen on the basis of their character and reputation. A closer look at the meaning of καταλέγω (enlist) suggests that that author's motive is around honour.

The verb καταλέγω in the active voice means "to pick out, choose," with connotations of telling (lengthy and orderly) stories of "kings or ancestors" (LSJ 1940, 897). In the passive voice, as it is in 5:9, καταλέγω means "to be enlisted, enrolled" (Towner 2006, 345n71) or possibly "be recounted" (LSJ 1940, 897).[55] The word is not used elsewhere in the New Testament. That the author of 1 Timothy wants particular widows chosen and highlighted is certain, but the contextual meaning of καταλέγω needs some clarification.

In first-century literature, καταλέγω commonly refers to conscripting young men to fight in an army (e.g., Plutarch *Antonius* 5.4, *Sertorius* 4.2, *Pompey* 59.1-2, *Galba* 18.2, *Cicero* 12.3). Commentators often adopt this meaning when they translate the word "enlist" in 1 Tim. 5:9 (e.g., Collins 2002, 139; Houlden 1976, 93; Dibelius and Conzelmann 1972, 75). For soldiers, enlistment was an act of obedience. "But when Pompey began *to levy* [καταλέγειν] recruits, some refused to obey the summons, and a few came together reluctantly and without zest, but the greater part cried out for a settlement of the controversy" (Plutarch 1917, 270-1, *Pompey* 59.2). The enrolment of men for the army, which entails obedience to military hierarchy, provides an awkward analogy for virtuous old widows!

Philo uses the word καταλέγω to denote virtuous character, reflecting a similar context to that found in 1 Timothy: "But the ruler of the whole nation, infusing into the ears of his people doctrines of piety, and charming the souls of his subjects with them, *selected* [καταλέγει] and picked out a thousand men of each tribe, choosing them with regard to their excellence" (1939, 188-9, *On the Virtues*, 42). Plutarch also employs the word for selecting specific people because of their proven character: "And in his *selection* [καταλέγων] of the men in authority that were to accompany him on his expedition he included also Lucius, the brother of Vitellius, without either increasing or diminishing his honours" (1926, 286-7, *Otho* 5.1). In this example, the selected men were already in responsible positions, chosen for a special task. Similarly, "[a particular] incident strengthened the party of Brutus and Cassius; and when they were *taking count* [καταλέγοντες] of the friends whom they could trust for their enterprise, they raised a question about Antony" (1920, 166-7, *Antony* 13.1). In this example Plutarch intimates the selected friends were considered trustworthy to accomplish their goals. The author of 1 Timothy may use καταλέγω with a similar nuance, telling Timothy to *enlist* specific elderly widows because of their virtuous character.

However, the examples from Philo and Plutarch use the active voice and are involved with men in the public sphere. A more fruitful source of word usage, including use of the passive voice, can be found among inscriptions for voluntary associations. In an inscription from Pergamon, the passive form of καταλέγω is clearly used to enroll a member, since the stipulation about fees is based on whether or not a man's father has been enrolled for a certain amount of time: "But if the son should enter [the association] at the same time as his father, or before five years has elapsed from the father's enrolment [καταλελέχθαι, literally: having been enrolled], he shall enter and pay the same entrance fee as if his father had not been a member" (*AM* 32.1907.293, 18; translation by Kloppenborg and Ascough 2011, 251).[56]

The following inscription suggests a similar list of members among the Areopageioi in Attica, specifying who was eligible (lines 76–81):

ἐάν τινες ἐξ Ἀρεοπαγειτῶν ἐν τοῖς [Πανέλ]-
λησιν ὄντες τήμερον καταλημφθῶσιν τὴν τριγονίαν παρασχεῖν μὴ
δυνάμενοι, οὐ διὰ τοῦτο ἀπ[εω]-
σθήσονται τοῦ συνεδρίου· πρὸς δὲ τὸ μέλλον οὐδεὶς ἄλλος ἐξ
Ἀρεοπαγειτῶν τοῖς Πανέλλησιν ἐνγρα[φή]-
σεται ἢ ὅσοι πρὸς τὰς χειροτονίας ἀφικνεῖσθαι δύνανται τὴν τριγονίαν
ἔχοντες. τὸ προς τὴν βου[λὴν]
τῶν Πεντακοσίων φέρον [ἄ]ποχρώντως ἔχει ταύτηι τετάχθαι ὥστε
αὐτοὺς τοὺς **καταλεγομένους** ε[ὐ γε]-
γονέναι.

If some of the Areopageioi who are today among the Panhellenes are found to be unable to demonstrate three generations [from slavery], they are not to be for this reason ousted from the council; but in the future, no one else from the Areopageioi is to be registered [ἐνγρα(φή)σεται] in the Panhellenes except whoever is able to enter the elections having three generations [from slavery]. As to what concerns the council of the Five Hundred, it is sufficient that it has been arranged that those on each occasion enrolled [τοὺς καταλεγομένους; i.e., those who had been **enrolled**] be themselves of good birth. (*SEG* 29:127.ii.76–81; Attica, 174–75 CE).[57]

Marcus Aurelius commissioned this inscription to address the problem of freedmen gaining the vote in the Athenian assembly. A person became a member of the Aeropageioi if he had been an archon (or in a similar role), or if he received an honorific membership based on the performance of a liturgy or benefaction. The inscription suggests a new policy whereby a person was required to show that he was three generations away from slavery (see line 70, not translated here). In this inscription, enrolment required a set of particular qualifications and meant that one obtained a seat on the council of the assembly – a position of honour.

In an inscription from Attica, a woman named Timothea is described as "enrolled" in her duties of carrying a holy basket in sacred rites for the Great Dionysia in Athens. The main focus of this section of the inscription is on her father, who is appointed for certain tasks, but he is identified by his daughter's position rather than his own. The woman is presumably fairly young because her father is young enough to be taking on active duties.

[Ξένων] Ἀσκληπιάδου Φυλάσιος εἶπεν· ἐπειδὴ ὁ [ἄ]ρχων Ζώπυρος [ἀπο]φαίνει τὸν πατέρα τῆς **καταλεγείσης** κανηφόρου Ζώπυρο[ν] [πέ]μψαι τὴν θυγατέρα τὴν ἑαυτοῦ Τιμο[θέα]ν οἴσουσαν τὸ ἱερὸν κανοῦν τῶι θεῶι κατὰ τὰ πάτρια, προσαγαγεῖν δὲ αὐτὸν καὶ θῦμα ὡς ἠδύνατο κάλλιστον, ἐπιμεμελῆσθαι δὲ καὶ τῶν λοιπῶν τῶν καθηκόντων ἑαυτῶι εἰς τὴν πομπὴν καλῶς καὶ φιλοτίμως

Zenon son of Asklepiades, a man of Phylē, made the following motion: Whereas Zopyros the archon appointed Zopyros the father of the canephore [basket carrier] who **had been enrolled**, to send his own daughter Timothea, who will carry the sacred basket for the gods, in accordance with ancestral custom, and that he would bring a sacrifice that was as beautiful as possible, and would also honourably and zealously take responsibility of all the other things that were appropriate for the procession, at his own expense. (*IG* II² 896; see also *IG* XII, 8 666)

Here, καταλέγω suggests the woman has an official and special duty to perform. The basket carrier was central to the rituals of the Great Dionysia. The fact that the father's identity is established by his daughter's enrolled status suggests that the *honour* of being a basket carrier is more important than the duty itself.[58]

Finally, an Egyptian inscription (238 BCE) specifies enrolment restrictions in a new tribe (φυλή) of priests serving Ptolemy Adelphos. Those who already had been priests were not to transfer to the new tribe.

εἰς δὲ [τὴν φυλὴν]
ταύτην **καταλεχθῆναι** τοὺς ἀπὸ τοῦ πρώτου ἔτους γεγενημένους ἱερεῖς καὶ τοὺς
προσκαταταγησομένος ἕως μηνὸς Μεσορὴ τοῦ ἐν τῶι ἐνάτωι ἔτει καὶ το[ὺς τούτων]
ἐκγόνους εἰς τὸν ἀεὶ χρόνον, τοὺς δὲ προυπάρχοντας ἱερεῖς ἕως τοῦ

πρώτου ἔτους
εἶναι ὡσαύτως ἐν ταῖς αὐταῖς φυλαῖς ἐν αἷς πρότερον ἦσαν, ὁμοίως δὲ
καὶ τ[οὺς ἐκγόνους]
αὐτων ἀπὸ τοῦ νῦν καταχωρίζεσθαι εἰς τὰς αὐτὰς φυλὰς ἐν αἷς οἱ
πατέρας <ε>ἰσίν·

[For good fortune, it is decreed that] those who have become priests from the first year [of the reign of Ptolemy Adelphos] shall **be enrolled** in this tribe, and those assigned until the month of Mesorē of the ninth year and their children for eternity, and those who had been priests up to the first year, likewise, shall be in the same tribes in which they were formerly, and likewise also their offspring shall be registered from now on in the same tribes as their fathers. (Delta I 989,1.20–23)

Those enrolled in the new tribe were priests serving from the time of Ptolemy Adelphos. As an extension of their continuing roles, their children would automatically be registered in the same new tribe.

In each of these occurrences of καταλέγω, a person was enlisted because of specified qualifications. Enlistment may have entailed explicit duties (such as those of the basket carrier), but the honour of being "enlisted" was more important than any duties associated with enrolment/enlistment. Interestingly, each of these instances of καταλέγω is also associated with intergenerational relationships, such that enrolment, or enlistment, was related to the rights and responsibilities of family members in different generations – one person's honour or right is automatically connected to his or her parent's or offspring's honour or right.[59]

This use of καταλέγω harmonizes well with the language used to describe the sixty+ widow explored above: she has specific qualifications; she is being honoured for her lifetime of virtue more than for a particular function; and this section of 1 Timothy features the importance of intergenerational relationships in 5:1–2 (see chapter 4) and in 5:4, 8 (see chapters 5 and 7).

Enlistment can suggest a literal "list" of people. In fact, lists are common in inscriptions for voluntary associations. They were used to demonstrate publicly who was a member of the association, sometimes including men and women together. For example, in a third-century inscription from Athens, a list of fifty-eight names lists thirty-seven men and twenty-one women (the women are listed without any male associations). The inscription declares that these members intend to honour their benefactor publicly "on account of his excellence and the piety he has shown to the Goddess [ἀρετῆς ἕνεκεν καὶ εὐσεβείας τῆς εἰς τὴν θεόν]" (*IG* II² 1297, lines 16–17, Kloppenborg and Ascough 2011, 133–4). Such honour is meant to challenge and encourage others to act as generous benefactors as well (lines 6–7, 133–4). By including their names in the public declaration of honour, the members are held accountable for following through on honouring their benefactor (they are liable to pay a fine if they do not; lines 17–18, 133–4). There is some sense that the members share in the honour of such a generous patron; the list implicitly honours their membership in the group as well.

In a related inscription of the same association, the names of some members are explicitly listed in order to be honoured publicly for their proper administration of matters related to the gods, if they have paid their dues. The inscription lists six men and five women (probably one more woman's name appeared originally; *IG* II² 1298).⁶⁰ Similarly, on a third-century inscription in Salamis, a list of members is displayed in order to honour them:

τούσδε ἐστεφάνωσεν τὸ κοινὸν τῶν θιασωτῶν ἀρετῆς ἕνεκα καὶ δικαιοσύνης τῆς εἰς τὸ κοινὸν τῶν θιασωτῶν·

On account of their excellence and honesty that they have shown to the association of *thiasōtai*, the association of *thiasōtai* (voted) crowns for (the following): [a list follows] (*IG* II² 2347, lines 5–6, Kloppenborg and Ascough 2011, 74).

John S. Kloppenborg and Richard S. Ascough point out that members of the Dionysos association listed in *IG* II² 1325 (also *IG* II² 1326) possessed some wealth and rank (2011, 167). This is most obvious in the description of the founder's benefactions (*IG* II² 1325, lines 22–29), but others on the list can be identified as honoured individuals from other inscriptions (Kloppenborg and Ascough 2011, 165, 167). Thus, the list seems to serve to honour their rank and generosity. All these examples point to the listing of names on inscriptions for honorary purposes (see also examples in van Bremen 1996, 97–108, 231–6).

While καταλέγω might refer to a literal list in 1 Timothy,⁶¹ the author might also be using it metaphorically to indicate the kind of public honour a woman would receive if her name was included on a public list. Either way, the result would be the same: public recognition of the sixty+ widow's contribution to the group's honour through her exemplary reputation.

Such a public honour for a woman is found in IG II² 1328B. A woman named Metrodora is honoured publicly for her past work as a priestess and an attendant to other priestesses in the *orgeōnes* of the Mother of the Gods.

> In the year that Sonikos was archon, in the month of Mounichion, at the regular assembly, the *orgeōnes* approved the motion that Kleippos of Aixoneus proposed: Whereas Metrodora, having been deemed worthy by the priestess Archedikē (who became priestess during the archonship of Hippakos) to serve as an attendant and to co-administer with her for a year, devoted herself (to this role) and co-administered the matters pertaining to the goddess honorably [καλῶς],[62] appropriately [εὐσχημόνως], and piously [εὐσεβῶς][63] and fulfilled her obligations both to the priestesses and to the *orgeōnes* without reproach [ἀνέγκλητον];[64] and (whereas) accordingly, when Simalē became priestess in the year that Sonikos was archon, and when she requested that the *orgeōnes* agree to appoint [κατασταθῆναι] for her Metrodora as an attendant; and after (the *orgeōnes*) agreed with her, she co-administered the priesthood honorably and appropriately and in a pious manner – what pertained to the goddess, to the priestesses, and to the *orgeōnes* – on account of which the priestesses also are eager to appoint her as attendant to the goddess for life. Therefore in order that they might be seen to be taking the best care of the goddess and that they might act honorably and piously in relation to the matters of the goddess; for good fortune it has been resolved by the *orgeōnes*, on the one hand to act in all matters that pertain to the decree that was proposed by Simon of Poros, and on the other, that the *orgeōnes* appoint Metrodora as an attendant to the goddess for life and that she serve indefinitely those who happen to be priestesses, and that she meet their needs honorably and appropriately; and that they take care that all things pertaining to the goddess occur piously, just as her mother, Euaxis, continued to do these things. And let the secretary inscribe this decree on the stele of the *orgeōnes*.
> (Kloppenborg and Ascough 2011, 169–71)

In the first part of the inscription (not reproduced here), written eight years earlier, the association declared that a woman could not hold the position of priestess or attendant for more than a year.[65] Metrodora's appointment to the position for life indicates she "must have distinguished herself in some extraordinary way to merit this honor" (Kloppenborg and Ascough 2011, 174). Metrodora was given this position for "good fortune [ἀγαθεῖ τύχει]" (line 37, 2011, 170–1) and to ensure the best and most pious care for the goddess and matters related to the goddess (lines 35–7). Her role appears to be one of guiding and mentoring priestesses who are newly appointed each year so that they function in their duties with proper piety (lines 40–2). The tangible activities associated with pious behaviour are not specified, but piety (εὐσεβῶς) toward the goddess is a crucial element of Metrodora's past activity and responsibility in teaching new priestesses. The public nature of the inscription also suggests that the whole group benefited by honouring her in this way.

The inscription also mentions Euaxis, the mother of Metrodora, who apparently had similar responsibilities (line 43). The intergenerational aspect of this inscription suggests that her mother's honourable behaviour was an important element in appointing Metrodora. Her mother's pious behaviour reflects on hers, and she continues in her mother's footsteps.[66]

There are no direct indications of Metrodora's age when she is appointed as attendant to the goddess for life. If she is a mentor, the cultural norm of age hierarchy would suggest she is older than the newer priestesses. It is difficult to imagine that an appointment for life would be made unless Metrodora had established her reputation over a good part of her lifetime.

The honour bestowed upon Metrodora resembles and is suggestive for understanding the enlisted widow in 1 Tim. 5:9. Exemplary pious behaviour is of utmost importance. Metrodora is appointed because of her past pious service to the goddess as well as her apparent ability to mentor new priestesses in similar pious service. Similarly, for the sixty+ widow, the list of her past activities demonstrates the kind of behaviour that sets an example, specifically for other women. This might be the kind of behaviour the author has in mind when he equates "proper behaviour" in the household of God with εὐσέβεια (3:14–16), especially since it contrasts starkly with the female behaviour he condemns in 2:9–15. In both cases, previous pious activity is rewarded publicly by encouraging a role and position that would last for life. This is made clear for Metrodora. In the case of the sixty+ widow, who could not expect to live much longer, her honour would presumably last for the rest of her life. Metrodora would not be performing the activities of the priestesses herself; she would be teaching such activities to new priestesses. This suggests mentoring or walking alongside (perhaps in a maternal role) rather than front-line activity. The sixty+ widow may be a role model or mentor for other women (see chapters 7 and 8). In addition, the sense of intergenerational continuity for Metrodora, a kind of mothering of a new generation, is suggestive for the context of 1 Tim. 5:9 since the author frames this section with a definition of how intergenerational relationships within the community should function – like relationships in a household context (5:1–2). If older women were like mothers (5:1), this would include modelling proper behaviour for the younger members of the group, as a mother does for a daughter.

The inscription is a public declaration of Metrodora's reputation and honourable behaviour. But the honour was not hers alone; it reflected the reputation of her whole community (see also van Bremen 1993, 236; 1996, 108). The idea of "enlisting" exemplary widows in 1 Tim. 5:9 reflects a similar sense of awarding public honour to those who behave properly and piously – those who embodied the ideals of a virtuous women over her lifetime.[67] By implication, withholding public honours or shaming for problematic behaviour (e.g., 5:4, 8, 20; chapter 5) is a complementary strategy for the author of 1 Timothy.[68]

THE RHETORICAL VALUE OF SIXTY FOR THE SIXTY+ WIDOW

Given the heteronymous nature of 1 Timothy, we cannot peel back the layers to find out if the author had in mind actual widows who fulfilled the description in 5:9, or if he was constructing an ideal old widow as a model for others. We can see women grouped into specific types: those who should not teach (2:11); female *diakonoi* or wives of *diakonoi* (3:11); real widows (5:3, 5, 16), younger widows (5:11) – but no women are named.[69] These categories of women work to his advantage: on the one hand, he can portray his main character's (Paul's) authoritative recommendations in a way that was general enough to appear to apply to a community several decades earlier. This rhetoric is reminiscent of Paul's directives in 1 Cor. 7 for how women and men should approach marriage and remarriage, but the author of 1 Timothy writes with a stronger authoritative tone.[70] On the other hand, he was able to address what he perceived as pressing issues for the real audience through his fictional story. While the author of 1 Timothy may have specific women in mind when he addresses issues related to women (especially 2:9–15, 3:11, 5:3–16), he does not use his fiction to address them directly.

The evidence suggests leaning toward the sixty+ widow as a rhetorical ideal, an exemplary older woman who is given the honour of being put on a list for public recognition of her life-long virtue.[71] This image of an exemplary woman may also have provided a way to remind younger generations of the inheritance they received from their forebearers, the founders of their Christian community. Portrayed as being in her last stage of life, the special distinction and recognition of the sixty+ widow was not nearly as important for her as an individual as it was for the community.[72]

CONCLUSION

First Timothy 5:9–10 was not intended to be prescriptive, nor was it a solution for a long-term future of Christian communities. It was not a way to limit the number of widows needing assistance. Neither was it a definition of an "order of widows" or a way to limit women's power. It is true that the phrase "not less than sixty" can point to old age, the unlikely event of remarriage, and lowered sexual threat (versus younger women of childbearing age). Yet, the author could have expressed most of these sentiments by simply conveying that they were old (γέρας) or beyond marriageable age, beyond childbearing years, or post-menopausal. Yet he used the specific phrase "not less than sixty."

Sixty was considered by some ancient authors to be the threshold of old age. Though this age mostly applied to men and public life, for this woman, the specificity of sixty suggests that the author wished to highlight her exemplary lifetime of virtuous behaviour and honour her good deeds in a public way. His rhetoric suggests that her virtue would be evident as a matter of public reputation, reflecting "how one ought to live in the household of God" (3:15). If women embodied the honour of the group, the sixty+ widows were the epitome of this embodiment. Singling out this group was not a way to set up future leadership, but rather dealt with a particular present situation in the community. The sixty+ widow is highlighted as an ideal example of proper behaviour, a woman who cultivated "good works" throughout her lifetime to which others could bear witness. The need for such an exemplary model is disclosed in the next segment of the letter, revealing *why* the author highlighted the sixty+ widows as models of female virtue in attempting to solve the problems the community faced. We turn to those problems next.

7

Younger Widows and Age Hierarchy among Women

As we have seen, proper behaviour was a guiding principle for the author of 1 Timothy. He advocates for proper behaviour toward the older generation and one's own generation (5:1–2; chapter 4) and proper behaviour of children toward their widowed mothers and grandmothers (5:4; chapter 5). The virtuous reputation of the sixty+ widows was established by a lifetime of exemplary behaviour (5:9–10; chapter 6).

We now turn to the younger widows (5:11–15), who were of particular concern because their improper behaviour was directly connected to the reputation of the community.[1] In the history of the Christian tradition, this particular section on younger widows has received great attention, not least because it presents a perplexing set of issues.[2] It is clear that the younger widows are causing problems that include immodest behaviour and worse, for "some have turned away after Satan" (5:15). The fictive Paul puts forward this solution: these young women are to adopt proper roles in the context of the "household of God" (3:15): marry, bear children, and manage their own households (5:14). This solution seems fairly clear, except for two looming questions. First, despite the threat posed by the situation, Paul curiously does not exhort Timothy to reprimand these women directly – he "wants" (βούλομαι) a solution (5:14). Second, even though the solution is to have the young women marry, apparently they already *want* to marry – and this is presented as a dire problem (5:12)!

These enigmatic elements are explored over the next two chapters. By applying insights from ancient Mediterranean age structure and focusing on women's ages and stages of life in cultural context, implicit categories of women come to the fore. We have already considered the four categories of widows in 1 Tim. 5:3–16 (real widows, widows with family, exemplary widows, and younger widows; see page 97). But I suggest that there is another group of women that is critical to solving the problem of the younger widows: middle-aged women. These women were powerful in the community, and some were caught up in the "other teachings" the author opposed. The solution to the problem of the younger widows involves the actions of these women. We have a glimpse of them in 5:6, but they are explicitly revealed at the climax of this section, with the label of "believing woman" (5:16). The whole section on widows culminates in the directive Paul gives as a third-person imperative: this "believing woman" should aid the widows she "has," namely the younger widows (5:11–15) because it is her duty to do so. The behaviour of younger widows is clearly a problem, but in the context of age hierarchy among women, the author does not see them as entirely at fault. The responsibility lies with the "believing woman."

The argument for middle-aged women as the implicit target of the author's frustration is explored more fully in chapter 8. In this chapter, we examine the grammar of 5:11–15, the cultural reasons behind younger widows "wanting" to marry, and the cultural context of age hierarchy among women. These elements strongly suggest that in 5:11, the sense of the verb (παραιτέομαι) needs to be revisited. Normally, the verb is translated to denote a command to "deny" (παραιτοῦ) the younger widows (especially to keep them from being on a list, borrowing the idea from 5:9). However, a more culturally sensitive translation, given the situation and rhetoric of the letter, points to Paul asking Timothy to "intercede for" (παραιτοῦ) the younger widows by approaching the middle-aged women on their behalf.

CONTRASTING WIDOWS

In the whole letter of 1 Timothy, we encounter the younger widows only in 5:11–15. However, the problems surrounding them are discussed at some length, with more direct attention given to them than any of the other women in this letter. The argument flows together, but can be divided into two sections:

νεωτέρας δὲ χήρας παραιτοῦ·
ταν γὰρ καταστρηνιάσωσιν τοῦ Χριστοῦ,

γαμεῖν θέλουσιν
  ἔχουσαι κρίμα ὅτι τὴν πρώτην πίστιν ἠθέτησαν
ἅμα δὲ καὶ
  ἀργαὶ μανθάνουσιν
    περιερχόμεναι τὰς οἰκίας,
  οὐ μόνον δὲ ἀργαὶ
  ἀλλὰ καὶ φλύαροι καὶ περίεργοι,
    ἀλοῦσαι τὰ μὴ δέοντα.

But **intercede for** the younger widows;
for when they behave immodestly moving away from Christ,
  they want to marry,
    resulting in having judgment because they "rejected
    their first faith,"³
but also at the same time,
  they are learning to be idle
    going around households,
  and (they are) not only idle
  but also foolish and meddlesome,
    saying things that are not necessary.
      (1 Tim. 5:11–13)

βούλομαι οὖν νεωτέρας
  γαμεῖν, τεκνογονεῖν, οἰκοδεσποτεῖν, μηδεμίαν ἀφορμὴν
  διδόναι τῷ ἀντικειμένῳ λοιδορίας χάριν
ἤδη γάρ τινες ἐξετράπησαν ὀπίσω τοῦ Σατανᾶ.

Therefore, I desire young women
  to marry, to bear children, to manage a household,
  to give to the adversary not even one chance for
  condemnation,
for already some have turned away after Satan. (1 Tim. 5:14–15)

These verses are notoriously difficult to unravel. The basic traditional view is that the younger widows are to be *denied* (παραιτοῦ) the privilege of being put on the list for aid or ministry because of their behaviour, their age, and/or because the church is financially overburdened (see chapter 6). More specifically, most interpretations of this text contrast the widows over sixty in 5:9 with the younger widows in 5:11 (e.g., Marshall 1999, 598; Spicq 1947, 170–1). The phrase νεωτέρας δὲ χήρας παραιτοῦ (5:11) is usually translated in direct opposition to 5:9, borrowing the idea of "enlist" from 5:9 to make sense of the wording: "but refuse to put younger widows on the list" (NRSV; so also BDAG 2000, 764). In other words, the νεωτέρας χήρας, the "younger widows" in 5:11, are compared to the widows in 5:9 who are explicitly at least sixty years old (e.g., Marshall 1999, 598; Van Neste 2004, 59). This translation (and interpretation) implies that the age of sixty is the boundary line for who can be on the list and who cannot, either for receiving aid, which equates the real widows (5:3, 5, 16) with the sixty+ widows (5:9–10), or for enrolment in an "office" or position of leadership (usually understood to be the so-called "order of widows").

As discussed in chapter 6, serious problems arise from these standard interpretations comparing the sixty+ widows (5:9) and younger widows (5:11) since, if we follow the logic of these conventional interpretations, a woman must be married only once in order to be on the list (5:9), but younger widows who are supposed to remarry (5:14) could never qualify for enrolment in their old age, thus cutting them off from either aid (in the first scenario) or an apparent ministry opportunity (in the second scenario). Also, if the only two categories of age in the author's mind are over and under sixty, this poorly reflects the range of ages and life stages of widows who are likely to be part of the community (see Krause 1994 ,73). However, the comparative noun νεωτέρας (younger) cannot simply refer to widows under sixty (5:9) because these "younger" widows were clearly a specific group of women still able to bear children, as is evident in 5:14.[4] There is a significant gap between the average age of menopause (somewhere closer to fifty years of age; see chapter 6), and the age of sixty that cannot be accounted for if νεωτέρας means "under sixty." Thus, νεωτέρας should be understood as a description of the (perceived) rebellious widows who are young enough to remarry and have children (5:11–15), not a designation meaning "under sixty."

In fact, the grammatical structure does not lend support to the conventional interpretations. Both verbs are imperatives, but 5:9 is a third-person imperative ("let a widow be enlisted"; χήρα καταλεγέσθω), whereas 5:11 is a second-person imperative, ostensibly directed at Timothy: παραιτοῦ the younger widows. In addition, χήρα in 5:9 is singular, whereas χήρας in 5:11 is plural (see figure 7.1).

The term νεωτέρας (younger women) is a comparative adjective used as a substantival (noun) in 5:1 and 5:14 without an object of

5:9	χήρα	καταλεγέσθω
5:11	δὲ	
	χήρας	παραιτοῦ
	νεωτέρας	

5:9	a widow	let her be put on a list
5:11	but	
	widows	deny [them]
	younger	

Figure 7.1 | The typical contrast between 60+ widows (5:9) and younger widows (5:11)

comparison, but the δέ ("and" or "but") in 5:11 strongly suggests νεωτέρας (younger) may in fact have an antecedent of comparison. The best possibility for a grammatical parallel to 5:11 is found in 5:3: χήρας ... τὰς ὄντως χήρας, the widows who are "real" widows. This phrase offers both an antecedent to the comparative (younger) and clearly parallel verb and noun forms. The noun "widows" (χήρας) is a plural direct object matching the plural direct object in 5:11 (νεωτέρας). The verb is a second-person singular imperative (τίμα, "honour"), matching the second-person singular imperative in 5:11 (παραιτοῦ, "intercede for"). Thus, in the fiction of the letter, the grammatical structures suggests that Paul tells Timothy to honour (τίμα) real widows and intercede for (παραιτοῦ) the younger widows (see figure 7.2). These actions are directed toward the two most vulnerable groups of women in the community.

As discussed in chapter 5, the "real widow" is defined as a widow who is alone (μεμονωμένη); that is, she has no husband, no parents, and no offspring to care for her. The real widow hopes only in God and prays constantly (5:5). As argued in chapter 6, the sixty+ widow of 5:9 is not the same as the "real widow," so the attributes of 5:9–10 do not apply to the real widow. The real widow is defined in contrast to the widow who has adult children (5:4; chapter 5). The real widows probably belong to a similar age group and life stage as the widows with children; otherwise, they would be expected to remarry

5:3	χήρας	τίμα
	τὰς ὄντως χήρας	
5:11	δὲ	
	χήρας	παραιτοῦ
	νεωτέρας	

5:3	widows	honour
	[who are]	
	the real widows	
5:11	and	
	widows	intercede for
	[who are]	
	younger	

Figure 7.2 | A contrast between real widows (5:3) and younger widows (5:11)

(5:14). Paul tells Timothy to "honour" (τίμα) the real widows, who are without family, denoting respect and filial duty (chapter 5).

This contrast between real widows and younger widows might seem to justify the typical translation of παραιτοῦ, which would mean *deny* the younger widows the honour given to the real widows. In other words, if the real widows are to be honoured with material support, the young widows were to be denied such support (Johnson 2001, 206; Marshall 1999, 582). If honour denoted an attitude of responsibility and respect toward those like one's mother (5:1, 4), it would be obvious that a younger widow, who was not yet at the life stage in which she had adult children (5:11, 14), was not worthy of this kind of honour. Admittedly, Paul may be seeking to limit an existing activity, namely, assistance (5:16; Bassler 2003, 136). The text may suggest that the community (ἡ ἐκκλησία) was burdened with supporting widows (5:16; see chapter 8), though we cannot rule out the possibility that the burden is rhetorical in nature, woven into the fiction of the letter to provide a greater sense of urgency. Still, Paul directs anyone with a widowed mother or grandmother to support them (5:4), and a believing woman who "has" widows to support them (5:16), leaving the community to aid real widows only (5:16). And, indeed, the section begins and ends with real widows (also Van Neste 2004, 56). However, we can say that the most pressing problem does not appear to be with supplies but with the behaviour of the younger widows (again, whom he discusses in more detail than any of the other groups of women or widows; 5:11–15), and the community's reputation.

PERCEPTIONS OF BEHAVIOUR AND REPUTATION

The author describes, in some detail, the young widows' involvement in what he deems shameful behaviour that is causing problems for the community's reputation (Kartzow 2009, 160). Their behaviour apparently could or did give the "adversary" (ὁ ἀντικείμενος)[5] an opportunity to bring condemnation or discredit (λοιδορίας) upon them (5:14). The author emphasizes the problematic *perception* of their actions, which would affect the reputation of their families and of the community (MacDonald 1996, 149–65, esp. 157–9; see also Delaney 1987, 44). The emphasis on community reputation throughout the letter suggests that the author himself had such perceptions about a troublesome group of young widows in his real community. Unfortunately, there is no way to ascertain the *actual* behaviour of the young widows (either in the author's real community or in the author's narrative of Paul's directives). Given the intensity of this part of the letter, the behaviour described here likely had some connection with real behaviour, but the most potent aspect of the behaviour was the *perception* of the younger widows. And for the author, this was a critical issue for the real audience.

Winter is convinced that the young widows were in fact engaged in sexually immoral behaviour. "It is not a case of one-off sexual indiscretion but rather a promiscuous lifestyle that is under discussion" (2003, 133). He cites the portrayal of young widows by elite Roman men as evidence that widows really were promiscuous. For example, Petronius (*The Ship of Lichas*, 110–111, first century CE) recounts a story about a young especially chaste widow who sat in her dead husband's tomb for five days refusing to eat because of her grief. On the fifth evening a soldier posted near the grave persuaded her to eat, and they became lovers that very evening. The story was meant to illustrate the "sexual fickleness" (Winter 2003,

130) of even the most chaste woman. Winter argues that women in 1 Timothy were following the patterns of the elite women in the first century CE labelled "new" women, who imitated the culturally tolerated sexual exploits of young men (129–31). However, Winter does not adequately account for men's cultural need to protect the honour of their family by protecting women's chastity. Promulgating a stereotype of women as easily seduced, especially the anomalous figure of the widow, provides a strong cultural reminder that honour is at stake if he fails to protect his female kin. Again, we cannot know whether the author of 1 Timothy actually observed this kind of behaviour among the young widows (or imagined that Paul did), but it is more likely, given his anxiety about reputation, that he is reflecting the perception of their behaviour rather than actual behaviour (see Huizenga 2013, 301n41).

MacDonald convincingly argues that early Christian women could be accused of sexual promiscuity simply because their ambiguous role straddled the private and public realms (1996, 67–73). She derives her insights by applying Juliette du Boulay's anthropological study of women in a modern, traditional Greek context (see MacDonald 1996, 240–3.). Du Boulay observed that a woman's activity may be *perceived* as sexually immoral even if she has been chaste. Her observation of the Mediterranean concept of women's shame (modesty) in Greek village life is worth reviewing at length:

> There are two factors in village society which bring it about
> that a woman's reputation, essentially located in her sense of
> shame, extends into fields of activity which are not concerned
> with sexual relations. One is the practical fact that absence from
> the home or irregularities in customary activities which can-
> not be minutely and indisputably accounted for in society, will
> almost inevitably be taken as evidence of surreptitious liaisons.
> The other is the fact that since, according to the conception of
> feminine nature, a woman's shame is the seat of her virtue, lack
> of virtue in aspects of life completely unrelated to sexuality may,
> if occasion arises, be referred back to a woman's basic moral
> nature. Thus evidence of infidelity is direct proof of a wom-
> an's worthlessness in all other fields, and, conversely, careless
> behaviour about the house and neglect of household duties
> are referred back to the basis of a woman's honour and cause
> aspersions to be cast on her chastity. It is because of this that to

be thought to be "good" (*kalē*) in the sense in which this word is used to denote "chaste," a woman must not only be literally chaste, but must be loyal, hard-working, obedient to her husband, and diligent in household duties such as cooking, washing, and cleaning. A woman's place, in fact, is in the home, and any prolonged absence from it except for matters directly related to the welfare of the family is disliked by the husband and adversely noted by the community. (1974, 130-1)

The description of the young widows in 1 Tim. 5:11-15 reflects these very values. They are said to be καταστρηνιάσωσιν, which has a rough base meaning of "behaving immodestly" (5:12), with a connotation of sexual behaviour that is out of place (see below). They "have judgment" (5:12), assumedly from those who are perceiving their behaviour as problematic, while rejecting their "first faith" (see discussion in chapter 8). They are described as idle or unproductive (ἀργαί), the opposite of a hard-working, loyal wife. They publicly display foolish and gossipy talk (Kartzow 2009).[6] Their activity outside the household (5:13) appears as an unaccountable "absence from the home" (in du Boulay's words) and thus immodest. Moreover, the author explicitly "desires" (βούλομαι) to fix the situation with the types of domestic activities that, according to du Boulay, demonstrate modest behaviour for women: being married and managing a household (5:14). Younger widows were in a particularly precarious situation, especially in their childbearing years, because without a male protector, they would always be under some scrutiny for their behaviour (Buitelaar 1995, 10). Notably, the description of the behaviour of younger widows in 5:13 culminates not with a condemnation of sexual impropriety but with the young widows' public image; they should be married, raising children, and managing a household "to give to the opponent no occasion for condemnation" (5:14).

The problems are also connected to the opposing teachers. The author says the young widows "learn" (μανθάνουσιν) to be idle as they go around to different households. The verb μανθάνω is also used in two other contexts of improper behaviour in 1 Timothy. In 5:4, the author uses the third-person imperative admonishing children and grandchildren who are shirking their responsibilities for supporting their widowed mothers and grandmothers. In 2:11, he states that a woman should learn (μανθανέτω; third-person imperative) in quietness and all submission (2:11). In all three cases, women are directed to learn what the author deems proper behaviour. The author is implying that the women are "learning" the wrong things, or from the wrong teachers; in all three cases, their lack of learning the right things is placing them in compromising circumstances that affect the reputation of the community.

Problematic Behaviour (5:11–13)

The introduction of the younger widows begins with highlighting their problems: they "behave immodestly moving away from Christ [καταστρηνιάσωσιν τοῦ Χριστοῦ]," which makes them "want to marry [γαμεῖν θέλουσιν]" (5:12). As a *hapax legomenon*, the exact meaning of the verb καταστρηνιάω is difficult to determine. BDAG translates the phrase "when they feel sensual impulses that alienate them from Christ," on the basis of καταστρηνιάω being defined as "to be governed by strong physical desire" (2000, 528). Winter rightly argues that "there is no basis for this rendering of the verb in terms of feelings rather than actions" (2003, 132–3), since the related verb στρηνιάω refers to behaviour that LSJ describes as "run riot" or "wax wanton" (1940, 1654). In Revelation, στρηνιάω is used to describe the immoral activity of the "whore of Babylon" and the kings who join her (18:7, 9; Spicq 1947, 171). Marshall suggests καταστρηνιάω means "their sexual impulses form a temptation that leads them away from devotion to Christ," and in so doing they turn to follow Satan (1 Tim. 5:15; 1999, 599).[7] Indeed, the young women are perceived as "dangerous and unpredictable beings," sexually motivated and vulnerable to opposing teachers (Verner 1983, 165–6; also MacDonald 1996, 160–1). The term καταστρηνιάω introduces the young widows as behaving in a problematic, sexualized manner, but given the cultural context explored above, it need not be *actual* sexual activity. The perception of immodesty was enough to put their behaviour into question and to threaten the community's reputation.[8]

Furthermore, the use of the genitive τοῦ Χριστοῦ (Christ) after the verb καταστρηνιάω (where κατά has a sense of "against") probably gives the phrase a sense of motion away from Christ as a result of this perceived immoral behaviour.[9] Elsewhere in 1 Timothy, "Christ" is always found in the phrase "Christ Jesus" (1:1, 2, 12, 14, 15, 16; 2:5; 3:12; 4:6; 5:21). Perhaps the use of "Christ" on its own in 5:11 signifies a focus on the *community* of Christ and not as much on the person or devotional focus of Christ (Jesus). Thus, the sense is that the younger widows behave shamelessly, which results in moving away from all that Christ represents. This is in line with Spicq's argument that the author's use of καταστρηνιάω in 1 Tim. 5:12 emphasizes his indignation toward immoral activity that is self-focused, turning away from their obligation to Christ and his service, and against the community's best interests (1974, 171). However, we are still working within the *perception* of women's behaviour and how that perception affected the community.

The reason Paul wants Timothy to do something with the younger widows is this: "for when [ὅταν γὰρ] they behave immodestly moving away from Christ, they want to marry [γαμεῖν θέλουσιν]" (5:12). This is a particularly enigmatic sentence. In the male perspective, marriage preserved the family structure and family honour. It also perpetuated the generational cycle. Clearly, men desired women to marry. Ancient male authors also thought women wanted to be married. Philo describes the women in the Judean monastic communities near Alexandria as "aged virgins, who have kept their chastity not under compulsion, like some of the Greek priestesses, but of their own free will in their ardent yearning for wisdom. Eager to have her for their life mate they have spurned the pleasures of the body and desire no mortal offspring" (*On the Contemplative Life* 68–9; translation in Kraemer 1988, 27). Philo alludes to the sexual desire of Greek priestesses who are compelled to remain virgins. He also suggests that women normally expected and desired marriage and children by emphasizing that elderly Judean virgins *exchanged* a sexual relationship and children for wisdom. This evidence suggests the author of 1 Timothy is not projecting a stereotype of young women desperate to marry,[10] but rather a scenario in which younger widows wanted another marriage as an expected part in a woman's life course (see chapter 5).

There were a number of reasons why a young widow herself would want to remarry (see chapter 5), including wanting to secure her material well-being. Krause argues that the "emancipatory" element of female asceticism is overestimated, and posits that the material need of most women, especially among the non-elite, would motivate them to remarry (1995, 109–10). A widow might have received an inheritance or legacy from her husband (van Bremen 1996, 256–61),[11] but her standard of living might also have dropped significantly after his death (Treggiari 1991, 500–2). A poor young woman would want to remarry to secure her material future; a woman from a family with some property or wealth would want to remarry to qualify for inheritances, as specified by the Augustan marriage laws (Harlow and Laurence 2003, 88–9).

A second marriage would reinstitute a "normal" status for a widowed woman. In the Pythagorean letter *Theano to Nikostrate*, the author states, "widowhood is not bearable for young women" (in Huizenga 2013, 72, 326). In patriarchal cultures generally, widows whose husbands died (or women whose husbands divorced them) are the victims of circumstance, yet they are often viewed with suspicion (Buitelaar 1995, 7–10), perhaps associated with the "power, awe or dread" of the dead or dangerous because they have outlived their husbands (10, 15; see also MacDonald 1996, 49–126).[12] At the very least, widowhood is an ambiguous category,[13] not just because of no husband, but also because of no household (Philo, *The Special Laws* 3.69–75), made worse if a woman did not have children (Catullus, *Poems* 61.199–223).[14] Krause suggests that the desire to be mothers far outweighed the risks of pregnancy and childbirth (1995, 109–10).

Marriage was an important identity marker in a woman's life and the usual key to her increasing influence as she progressed through the life course. A woman's role as wife and mother evolved as she aged, and her age afforded her greater power and freedom, especially if she had children who grew to adulthood. Young women could foresee their own rise to power within the domestic sphere on the basis of the examples of their mothers, mothers-in-law, grandmothers, and other female kin and neighbours. Among the elite, women who survived their husbands often promoted their sons (e.g., Cornelia, the mother of the Gracchi; see chapter 6). The situation would have been similar among the non-elite. A young widow, especially if she had no children or young children (who may or may not survive to adulthood) was in a vulnerable position with very little social power. Her normal avenue for gaining power over the life course would be to re-establish herself as a wife and matron of a household.

In short, though sexual desire (implied in 1 Tim. 5:12) is a possible reason why younger widows would want to marry, there were other compelling reasons: it alleviated material need or secured financial well-being; it would allow them to escape the suspicion associated with their widowed status, and it would permit them to pursue the life course that typically afforded women power as they aged. Because of her anomalous status, any unusual behaviour on the part of a young widow would prompt an accusation of sexual misconduct even if a social faux pas had nothing to do with sexual activity. All of their behaviour reflected on the honour of the family and the men who were bound to protect them. Marriage was the best way to protect women's chastity. Marriage was also a cultural and social expectation.

In 1 Tim. 5:11–13 the desire to remarry seems to be a problem that goes hand in hand with what is perceived as "immodest behaviour" (5:11), namely, idleness, meandering from house to house, and spewing unnecessary words (5:13). Roman urban women were not confined to the household or private sphere, but in the public realm, women were typically "socially invisible" (Osiek and Balch 1997, 54; Osiek and MacDonald 2006, 3, Zamfir 2013, 128–37) – or at least they were supposed to be (see du Boulay's observations above). The accusation of going around to different households (5:13) would compromise a woman's modesty, for this would be "visible" activity. The concept of "idleness" does not suggest the young women ceased all activity but that they "fill[ed] their time with the wrong kind of work," the kind of work of which the author disapproved (Kartzow 2009, 147). If women's idleness was equated with immorality, then moral conduct involved women being always engaged in tasks, keeping themselves busy with chores or duties or (in the ancient world), at the very least, with weaving (Winter 2003, 133–4). Kartzow suggests that the author uses the rhetoric of gossip to contrast the ideal woman who concerns herself with domestic duties (2009, 157–8). Gossip may even be associated with magic (149–51; Pietersen 2007). But the major point here is that young widows' behaviour is perceived as being sexually immodest because it was visible and not filled with what the author of 1 Timothy thought were proper activities for women.

Not a Command, but a Desire? (5:14)

After describing the young widows' problematic behaviour, the author offers a solution. He "wants" or "desires" (βούλομαι) young women to marry, bear and raise children, and run a household (5:14) – that is, to assume the domestic responsibilities of a wife and mother. The author does not specify young widows here, but young women (νεωτέρας), perhaps because all young women were expected to be married (though he seems to have the young *widows* primarily in mind). It is noteworthy that he does not emphasize marriage alone, but also having children and managing a household. As we have seen, these were typical expectations for young women in the ancient Mediterranean.

Paul's statement that he desires (βούλομαι) young women to marry (5:14) creates a strange paradox because, as we have seen, these women are characterized as wanting to marry! And this wish to marry is presented as problematic, namely, as the unfortunate outcome of the young widows' immodest behaviour (5:12). It is curious that two similar verbs of desire (θέλω and βούλομαι) are used with the infinitive γαμεῖν (to marry), but with such different connotations. The younger widows "want [θέλουσιν] to marry" (5:12); that is, they have the desire or willingness to marry, perhaps with a sense of purpose (BDAG 2000, 448). However, there is a lack of agency or resolve when compared to βούλομαι, which implies determination, order, and a plan to bring about that which one desires (BDAG 2000, 182). When Paul "desires [βούλομαι] young women to marry" (5:14), he means that he has a strategy for this desire to be acted upon, a commitment to see it happen.

Even so, given how serious the situation is, the author's choice of language is surprising. The use of the term βούλομαι in the first-person indicative has a less forceful tone than other directives in the letter.[15] By comparison, in 1:20 and 2:12, the author's much more authoritative language in the first-person indicative denotes Paul's action related to problematic teachings and behaviour. In 1:20 Paul says he has turned over (παρέδωκα) two men to Satan. In 2:12 his forceful directive is for women in the public setting: "I do not permit [οὐκ ἐπιτρέπω] a woman [or wife] to teach or have authority over a man." Yet in 5:14 – even in such a threatening situation – the author does not use this kind of commanding language for the young widows.

The word βούλομαι is also used in 2:8 where he also makes a request of community members: he desires (βούλομαι) men to pray without division and women to adorn themselves modestly.[16] Marshall suggests both instances refer to "a strong directive" (1999, 604), but the only substantiation for this claim is the context of the author's urgency. Dibelius and Conzelmann state that the strength of the verb βούλομαι comes from its use elsewhere in "legislative regulations" (1972, 75). Neither explains why the author of 1 Timothy uses much more directive language elsewhere (including second- and third-person imperatives) but refrains from using more forceful language in 5:14 (and in 2:8, for that matter).[17]

Neither does Paul instruct Timothy to correct the young women directly, a notable contrast with his instructions elsewhere in the letter.[18] If the author thought that Paul or Timothy (in the fiction of the letter) could have direct authority over the young women, he would have used that authority. But as a man, Timothy was not in a position to direct younger women; that is, the appropriate course of action was not in the purview of a man.[19] Rather, these were women's affairs. A consideration of cultural context and age hierarchy among women indicates that Paul's "plan" (implied with the use of βούλομαι) involved middle-aged women who were responsible for the younger widows.

Older and Younger Women in Titus 2:3–5

In Titus 2:3–5 we glimpse the dynamics of female age structure – especially the responsibility of older women to younger women. Similar to 1 Tim. 5:14, "Paul" offers directives for young women to embrace a domestic role, but the directives are focused on the responsibility of older women who were to teach and discipline younger women (τὰς νέας; 2:4–5).

In Titus 2:1, "Paul" addresses Titus directly:[20] "But you – you speak the things that are suitable [πρέπει] for healthy teaching" (my translation)[21] in contrast to the opposing teachers (Titus 1:10–16). The content of "suitable things" highlights what is especially suitable to particular age and gender categories found in the household – the same categories we find in 1 Tim. 5:1–2: old men (2:2), old (and young) women (2:3–5),[22] and younger men (2:6),[22] with Titus as an example of a younger man (2:7–8).[23] While old men, old women, and younger men are addressed directly, young women are not;[24] they appear to be the responsibility of the old women.[25]

> Likewise, old women [πρεσβύτιδας] are to be suitably reverent [ἱεροπρεπεῖς] in demeanor, not slanderers or slaves to much wine, teachers of what is good [καλοδιδασκάλους], so that they might discipline the young women [ἵνα σωφρονίζωσιν τὰς νέας] to be lovers of their husbands [φιλάνδρους εἶναι], lovers of children [φιλοτέκνους], self-controlled [σώφρονας], pure [ἁγνὰς], good

household managers [οἰκουργοὺς ἀγαθάς], submitting to their own husbands in order that the word of God might not be blasphemed. (Titus 2:3–5, my translation)

Old women (πρεσβύτιδας) are exhorted to be "suitably reverent in demeanor" (note the repetition of the cognate πρέπει from 2:1) and to thwart the stereotypes of gossiping and drinking to excess often associated with old women (see chapter 6). They are to teach what is good or noble (or be good teachers; καλοδιδασκάλους),[26] namely, teaching young women. Their teaching would result in (ἵνα) providing sensible guidance or discipline (σωφρονίζωσιν) to young women to be faithful in their domestic roles. The word σωφρονίζω means "to instruct in prudence or behavior that is becoming and shows good judgment" (BDAG 2000, 986), with strong connotations of self-control and moderation (Malherbe 2006, 48–65). Abraham J. Malherbe points out that it is the "primary virtue of women in antiquity" (2006, 59).

Older women's teaching should manifest in what becomes a fairly long list of characteristics for the young women. Not only would they be married, but they would be women who loved their husbands (φιλάνδρους) and loved their children (φιλοτέκνους). Interestingly, the term for self-control and moderation (σώφρονας) is repeated with a close cognate (another cognate is used for young men as well; σωφρονεῖν, Titus 2:6). They are to be pure (ἁγνάς), which is related to the way Timothy was to treat younger women in 1 Tim. 5:2. The last two characteristics are associated with their specific domestic roles: being "good household managers [οἰκουργοὺς ἀγαθάς]" – which is similar to the action in 1 Tim. 5:14 (οἰκοδεσποτεῖν) – and "submitting to their own husbands [ὑποτασσομένας τοῖς ἰδίοις ἀνδράσιν]" (2:5). The purpose for teaching this long list of characteristics is so that "the word of God might not be blasphemed" – a comment related to the reputation of the community of the faithful. A similar sentiment completes the list of Paul's desire for the younger women in 1 Timothy – to marry, bear children, manage households, give the adversary no occasion for condemnation (5:14).

Titus 2:3–5 provides a clear sense of the relationship between older and younger women in a community similar to one found in 1 Timothy. By virtue of their experience and freedom from the domestic responsibilities of younger women, older women would be in a

Figure 7.3 | Cameo set in a modern ring (100–1 BCE) featuring a woman and a young girl, perhaps taking part in a religious procession. Digital image courtesy of Getty's Open Content Program.

position to support and mentor younger women. The characteristics and actions of the younger women are pivotal for the group's reputation (Huizenga 2013, 288), but older women are explicitly responsible for the younger women: the rhetoric places the young women fully under the jurisdiction of the older women; they are not to be addressed directly by Titus. This question of jurisdiction suggests that Paul uses the word "desire" (βούλομαι) to address the younger widows in 1 Tim. 5:14 instead of a using command because it was not Timothy's place to deal with them. The author wanted the traditional female hierarchy to make things right because it was *their* responsibility to do so.

WOMEN IN TRADITIONAL MEDITERRANEAN CULTURES

As a means of considering what such relationships among women might look like in an ancient Mediterranean setting and to suggest a comparable setting for the women in 1 Timothy and Titus, I turn to ethnographic data related to age hierarchy among women and women's worlds.

Some anthropologists have observed that the women's realm in modern traditional Mediterranean cultures is largely separate from the men's realm. For example, Stirling notes that in Turkey, "men and women live in different social worlds. Only within the household do the two worlds touch closely, and even here the separateness of the sexes in the society at large affects individual relations between them" (1965, 112; see also 98, 101). Chapman also comments with regard to rural Sicilians, "On the whole the fields of activity of men and women are complementary and only rarely overlap" (1971, 33). This guarantees women a certain amount of independence "to manage their own affairs without interference" from men (Stirling 1965, 118; Campbell 1964, 151).[27] Likewise, Fernea describes the women's world in rural Iraq in the 1960s as separate from men. A woman spent time either at home with her husband, or with other women, in their homes or participating in religious celebrations and activities. In order to visit friends' homes across town, they would navigate back alleys to avoid public places where men gathered (1965, 151).

Women network with one another in order to share certain domestic duties and socialize on a daily basis, provide support to one another in times of crisis, and prepare for rites of passage (Kennedy 1986, 130). In Edremit, Turkey, the "world of women" is a "private world of the houses and courtyards," according to Fallers and Fallers (1976, 246), where women cooperate to fulfill their responsibilities. For a boy's rite of passage (circumcision at age six), his mother and "a squad of neighbours and kinswomen prepared food in the courtyard kitchen for [two hundred] guests" (256). A woman learns specific social behaviour: "to make oneself a welcome member of women's society ... all learn ways of contributing to the social gatherings of women," which is often in the context of work for poorer women, or formal visiting for wealthier women (252). In this Iraqi village, kin and neighbours worked side by side (the women wondered why Fernea never did her laundry with them at the river). They supported one another emotionally (in the illness of a child, or in the grief of a loved one's death), socially (storytelling and visiting is important; also Abu-Lughod 1993), and ritually (for example, preparing for and participating in marriage ceremonies; Fernea 1965). In the Turkish village, women within the household are in constant daily contact, sharing tasks and child-minding, as well as gossip (Stirling 1965, 174).

On the other hand, from her observations of a Greek village, Juliet du Boulay argues that the strength of family loyalty overrides female solidarity, observing no female "subculture" in rural Greece. Family ties are primary. A mother aligns herself with her son in opposition to her daughter-in-law, who threatens the mother's position of affection with her son and her role as mistress of the house (1986, 147). Women also tend to judge other women who are prone to argue or gossip (148). According to du Boulay, "the family, or the house, is the villager's sole unequivocal refuge, accommodating different generations and sexes impartially and demanding and receiving the total loyalty of each" (146). If women and men operated separately, she argues, this would be a betrayal of the family (146; also Campbell 1964, 275; Dimen 1986).

While du Boulay's observations in part point out cultural differences between specific communities, they also identify some important considerations for women's networks among ancient Mediterranean women. Loyalty to one's family places limitations on "female solidarity," if we take this to mean women defending other women against men. Family loyalty is a strong feature of Mediterranean cultures (see chapter 4). Since a woman often lacks the life-long continuity of kin relationships that men have in patriarchal families (Stirling 1965, 107; see also Brown 1992, 25),[28] her loyalty is primarily to her own marital family as mistress of her own home and informal guardian of her children's inheritance (Campbell 1964, 71). Dimen observes that Greek women "begin as daughters, attain adulthood only as daughters-in-law, get no satisfaction until they are mothers of sons, and become powerful only when they are mothers-in-law. Thus, their lives communicate the inevitability and personal necessity of social connection. The most important connection is to family" (1986, 64).

However, loyalty to one's family need not preclude the reality and functions of women's networks. In the Greek village of Vasilika, Friedl observed that "women have their own conversational groups of working neighbors which men do not join" (1962, 90; see also Benedict 1976, 237). In Milocca (Sicily), kin and marriage relationships take precedence over friendship (Chapman 1971, 124), but during the day, women's main contacts are their immediate female neighbours, who help each other, especially in heavier household tasks. Or they may sit in doorways knitting, spinning, or cleaning wheat. Families reunite in the evening (21).[29] In a Cretan village, women form friendships with other women even though visiting in other neighbourhoods is not socially acceptable (Dimen 1986, 130). While neighbours might provide emotional support to one another, they recognize that to maintain family honour, their loyalty to family must take precedence (Kennedy 1986, 130).

A woman's stage of life influences her involvement in women's networks. While she is involved in childbearing and childrearing, there is less time for activity outside domestic duties, especially limiting younger women's relationships beyond the family (Kennedy 1986, 130). Dimen observes that friendships usually start either before or after childbearing and early childrearing because women have little extra time for visiting while caring for young children (1986, 130). She observes that women are lonely in their isolated work, but "they look forward to their old age when they will be permitted to socialize, to share gossip in the afternoon with friends while daughters or daughters-in-law interrupt their lone labors only to serve them coffee" (61–2; also Cool and McCabe 1983, 66–7).[30]

It follows that a woman's primary (or sole) way to gain power is through the changes that occur as she progresses through the life course in the context of her family.[31] Foner finds that cross-culturally, older women typically experience more freedom as they age, participating in the public sphere, influencing community decisions by informally advising husbands and sons, and sometimes controlling resources (1984, 67–91). Older women are considered to make up the active senior generation, and as such receive deference from younger women (deference these elder women once gave their senior female kin). They have the right to claim authority over younger female kin regarding labour and decision-making (such as who among the younger generation will marry, and to whom; Brown 1992, 18–21; Friedl 1962, 90).

In modern traditional Mediterranean societies, whether a woman achieves these privileged roles depends on marital status, reputation, and having adult sons. Following her childbearing years, and perhaps while still raising some younger children (Cool and McCabe 1983, 64), a woman typically becomes a mother-in-law.[32] An older woman exerts her authority as the senior member of the domestic unit (Campbell 1964, 76–8; Whitaker 1976, 200).[33] Older women have more control over family decisions. Older women's life experience gives them authority over younger women. Older women also have greater flexibility, and often more wealth, to offer support for younger women (Danforth 1982).

Older women are responsible for the behaviour of younger women. They offer advice and problem-solving skills to younger women (Chapman 1971, 32). Older women also have power over younger women's reputations because their opinions and judgment are credible in the community (Cool and McCabe 1983, 65–6). In this way, older women may be the most ardent preservers of younger women's subordination (Foner 1984, 90–1). Foner notes that "old women in many societies have a strong interest in keeping young women in their place" (1984, 68), which may manifest in gentle guidance or authoritative directives. Such older women might best be termed "middle-aged women," meaning women who are at the stage of their life course when their children have become adults, but they are not yet frail or dependent (Sacks 1992, 2; Brown 1992, 18).

In sum, though family remains the focus of loyalty, this does not preclude the presence of women's networks in Mediterranean cultures. Women share in certain domestic tasks and support one another in preparations for rites of passage or in crises. Women's networks include kin and neighbours. Patrilocal marriage patterns mean that women may have fewer connections to their natal kin through the life course, but their relationships with their children might be especially important since a woman gains status when she moves through the life course. As her children become adults, she has the potential to achieve the height of her status, including domestic authority, public visibility, increased mobility, and mentoring roles.

ANCIENT MEDITERRANEAN WOMEN'S NETWORKS AND AGE HIERARCHY

The patterns found in these modern Mediterranean ethnographies are suggestive for investigating ancient women's identity, networks, and age hierarchy, especially since ancient Roman sources, written mostly by elite men, limit our view of women's lives, often revealing little more than perceptions and ideals in the framework of familial roles (Harlow 2007, 208).[34] Labels for women in 1 Timothy, namely, γυνή (which can mean woman or wife; 2:9–15) and χήρα (widow, a woman who is no longer a wife; 5:3–16), suggest that family loyalty and identity were of primary importance, at least in the description of women (e.g., Anna is identified by her marital status in Luke 2:36–37, but we know nothing of Simeon's age or marital status; 2:25–35; LaGrand 1988).[35]

Urban, non-elite women would have needed other women to help fulfill their social obligations in a manner similar to modern Mediterranean women (e.g., food preparation for rites of passage, support in times of crisis). Treggiari comments on informal female networks in the Roman world: "Although we hear little of women entertaining, there could normally be no objection to visits from women friends and relations. Young married women visited and received their mother, their husband's kinswomen and their own, older matrons and widows, their own contemporaries, and unmarried girls. It was, of course, a courtesy for younger or socially inferior women to call on their elders and superiors and for friends to call on the sick or pregnant and women in childbed" (1991, 421). This kind of socializing may be especially true of elite women (Dixon 1988, 211), but is suggestive for female networks among the non-elite.

Osiek and MacDonald argue that a women's realm existed in the early Christian world. They describe it as "a world of women about which the texts remain silent – a world of sisterhood, conversation, and exchange among women on issues of hospitality, childcare, service and allegiance to Christ under the authority of a (sometimes) pagan *paterfamilias* as a wife, daughter, or slave, a world where distinctions among various categories of women possibly broke down" (2006, 19). We glimpse networks of women in Christ groups such as Tabitha's devotion to good works among the widows in Acts 9:39, as well as in Titus 2:3–5 (as outlined above). The wealthy young martyr Perpetua, and her slave and fellow-martyr Felicitas share a bond of camaraderie in the *Martyrdom of Perpetua*. In the *Acts of Paul and Thecla*, the crowd of women in the arena is highlighted by the narrator (32). They cry for justice for the young woman; they shout as the lioness lies at Thecla's feet in the arena; they mourn when the protective lioness is killed; and they throw herbs and flowers into the arena to put the beasts to sleep (33–5). Thus, their collective voices and action affect Thecla's victory. Afterward, within Tryphaena's household, many of the female servants convert (39). These unnamed women may represent a female network of support, found both within and outside of the household.

Early Christian women may well have relied on female networks in an urban setting but found special connection to the women in their Christ group network. Christ communities valued instruction from one generation of women to another (Osiek and MacDonald 2006, 91). It was these women they would visit and call upon for help in domestic crises and women's preparation for rites of passage. In addition, older women might also have fictive "mothering" roles, such as nurse, foster-mother, and other "surrogates" (Osiek and MacDonald 2006, 76; Dixon 1988, 141–61). Whether women's age hierarchy (e.g., Titus 2:3–5) includes relationships that are based on household ideals, or on real household (or extended kin) relationships largely depends on post-marital residence (Brown 1992, 24–6). By the end of the first century, it was unlikely that "the household relationships have been replaced by relationships in the Christian community" (Verner 1983, 171). Rather, these roles were likely filled by a mix of non-kin and "extended households" (Quinn 1990, 134; also 130), including a woman's own mother and mother-in-law. Urban households in the Roman East were likely neolocal, but fairly near the wife's family, though patrilineal customs persisted. In this scenario, mothers would have more influence over young wives than their mothers-in-law would if they were in a patrilocal setting (see LaFosse 2017a).[36]

There are clues from the ancient evidence about the nature of the age hierarchy among women. In ancient Greek society, women's seclusion restricted female friendships, but old women were freer to move around, no longer impeded by the "pollution of childbirth" (Bremmer 1987, 197–8) and able to visit, and influence, younger women as door keepers and midwives (195), likely with some involvement in their marriages as well (199–200).[37] Older women had roles in marriage rites of younger women, as expressed by the

Roman poet Catullus (first century BCE): "You honest matrons, well wedded to ancient husbands, set the damsel in her place [i.e., array the maiden in her marriage bed]" (1913, 81, 61.179–81; on the *univira* see chapter 5). The Vestal Virgins had a strict age hierarchy involving mentoring, according to Plutarch.[38] In the *Acts of Paul and Thecla*, Thecla (a virgin) is involved in two relationships with older women. She rebels against her mother's rightful authority by refusing to marry (8), but later returns to her mother, perhaps to convert her or to support her as was her filial duty, or both (43). Later, Queen Tryphaena, who is an older woman and mother figure, aids, protects, and provides for Thecla as a daughter in place of her own deceased daughter (27–32, 39).

The Pythagorean letters were ostensibly from older to young women, offering advice and instruction that reflects a cultural norm of older women teaching younger women (Osiek and MacDonald 2006, 91). In Annette Burland Huizenga's study of these letters in comparison to the letters to Timothy and Titus, she observes that "the dominant gender ideology decrees that older women ought to act as teachers for young women, to supply the appropriate amounts of reminding and censure" (2013, 294). Kartzow highlights the ideal of older women teaching family values to younger women and the disapproval of older women who influence poor behaviour (gossip, idleness) in younger women reflected in the letters to Timothy and Titus. Younger women were vulnerable to such influences (2009, 149).

The older women who would be in the position of power within the hierarchy of women were mothers, mothers-in-law, and grandmothers. They were no longer childbearing, and not very old or frail; they were "middle-aged" women (Saller 1994, 50), probably in their forties and fifties, mothers of adult children. They were women who were at the most powerful stage of their lives (Sacks 1992, 1–6; also see above). At this stage of life, these older women were also more likely to have wealth at their disposal.[39] And in the context of the cultural norms of the ancient Mediterranean, they would have been expected to guide and have authority over younger women in a way that reflected modesty, thus maintaining family honour. For the author of 1 Timothy, this looked like proper order in the "household of God" (3:15), and a middle-aged woman with influence over and responsibility for younger women – this was the "believing woman" (1 Tim. 5:16).[40]

Meaning of παραιτοῦ

Given the nature of age hierarchy among women, we now turn back to 1 Timothy, considering the presence of middle-aged women responsible for the younger widows. In this scenario, the translation of παραιτοῦ is pivotal (5:11). It denotes what Paul was commanding Timothy to do with regard to the younger widows. The word παραιτέομαι has two main connotations: "to decline, refuse, avoid, reject" or "to make a request, ask for ... ask for someth[ing] in [sic] behalf of another, intercede for τινά someone" (BDAG 2000, 764). Admittedly, this word means "deny" in 1 Tim. 4:7: "refuse [παραιτοῦ] (to hear)" the myths that are profane and associated with old women. The word is used similarly in 2 Timothy: Timothy is told to refuse to hear stupid and senseless controversies (2 Tim. 2:23). In Titus 3:9, a comparable sentiment is expressed about controversies, but with the verb περιΐστημι (go around so as to avoid). Directly following this admonition, the author of Titus uses παραιτοῦ to denote avoiding or rejecting, or perhaps even driving out, a divisive person after one or two warnings. Though the grammatical structure in this last instance is similar to that of 1 Tim. 5:11 (παραιτοῦ with an accusative of person), the meaning cannot be the same. Even though some of the young widows in 1 Tim. 5 displayed problematic behaviour, and some had already "turned away after Satan" (5:15), they themselves are "learning" wrong behaviour (5:13); they do not appear to be the kind of instigators that are mentioned in Titus 3:9. And even the divisive person in Titus 3:9 had one or two warnings before being rejected.

Therefore, the translation of "deny, reject, or avoid" does not fit the context of 5:11. In fact, if the young widows were to be avoided or rejected, the author would have little reason to spend time describing the problem with their behaviour and how such behaviour should be corrected within the community.

I propose that Paul is directing Timothy "to intercede for" the younger widows (LSJ 1940, 1811, III). Similar translations of παραιτέομαι demonstrate a need for someone to speak on behalf of a person(s) who needs help. In a story told by Herodotus, King Darius had imprisoned a woman's brother, husband, and sons. The woman rationalized why she would choose her brother when forced to choose only one (she could have another husband and children, but not another brother). Darius decided to release her brother ("the one for whom she had interceded [τοῦτόν τε τὸν παραιτέετο]") and her oldest son (both accusative; Herodotus 1921, 146–7, 3.119). The second-century BCE Roman historian Polybius records that an embassy was sent to Ptolemy to intercede [παραιτεῖσθαι] for a man who was being held prisoner by Ptolemy (2010, 462–3, *Histories* 4.51.1). Similarly, in Mark 15:6, Pilate vows to release a prisoner for the Judeans: "and at [the] feast he used to release to them one prisoner for whom they interceded [ὃν παρῃτοῦντο]" (my translation). In all three examples, the persons in need of intercession are prisoners, but not necessarily criminals. In all three, they are powerless to effect their own release; others spoke on their behalf. Similarly, I suggest that Paul directs Timothy to *intercede for*, that is, speak on behalf of, the younger widows, for they were (perceived as) powerless to act on their own behalf. Thus, Paul introduces the problems associated with the young widows by telling Timothy to find help for them. Though it is not made explicit in this verse, the cultural context suggests he would find the solution among the middle-aged women who were responsible for younger women in the group.

INTERLUDE: FEMINIST CRITIQUE

Feminist interpreters of 1 Timothy tend to focus on the patriarchal oppression of women and the author's squelching of women's leadership roles in 1 Timothy (e.g., Thurston 2003, 172). For example, on the letters to Timothy and Titus, Linda M. Maloney states, "These letters are both frustrating and depressing to the Christian woman who reads them: their tone (especially as regards women and their roles) is negative to the point of ferocity, and it is this negative and oppressive quality that has dominated interpretation and authoritative application of these texts in the succeeding two millennia ... there can be no doubt that the author of these letters had an agenda, and that agenda did not include fostering the advancement of women, whatever their class or rank, nor of slaves, male or female. The point of view is androcentric and patriarchal almost to the point of absurdity" (1994, 361). Some women are highlighted for their roles (362), but the hierarchical overtones of the author are hard to miss.

The feminist critique has been enormously helpful in prompting scholars to illuminate women's lives in the ancient world, to draw attention to how interpretations of these texts have been harmful for people throughout Christian history, including their role in justifying slavery and colonization, and to consider alternate interpretations. The pioneering work of Elizabeth Schüssler Fiorenza (1983) is a great example. The angst that comes with the presuppositions of Western, twentieth- or twenty-first-century lenses is justifiable from this perspective.

My goal as a historian is to examine 1 Timothy within its own setting using insights from anthropology to uncover the cultural dynamics and occasion behind the text as well as the expression of cultural values that emerges from the text. In this, I follow other women working on the social history of women (e.g., Osiek and MacDonald 2006, Cohick 2009). The language of "freedom," "equality," or "equity," important values that have developed over centuries of Western thought, were simply not values espoused in ancient Roman society and were highly unlikely to have been on the minds of first-century Mediterranean women (Kloppenborg 1996b). They had their own way of thinking about how their world worked. Developing insights about the social and cultural milieu of the ancient Roman world contributes to an ongoing conversation around how we understand the texts from a historical perspective. For example, in Bassler's recent reassessment of 1 Tim. 5:3–16, she notes that Gal. 3:28 is not about equality, as she assessed earlier (1984, 23, 29), as much as it is about sexual differentiation based on the masculine as the norm (2003, 125–6). I always read the text through my own lenses and training, but I hope the ongoing conversation with others (academic and non-academic) is generative.

The examination of women's worlds and age hierarchy among women, then, is meant not to criticize or condone that world, but to examine it, looking for the real experiences of women, however difficult the task may be and however much we are beholden to the historical sources we have. But historical work also matters in our own time and place, at least in part because it illuminates aspects of our present realities that may not otherwise be noticeable and can open conversations we might not otherwise have.

CONCLUSION

The younger widows of 1 Tim. 5:11–15 have long been an enigma. By considering the roles of women's networks and age hierarchy among women in modern and ancient Mediterranean cultures, I suggest that the real problem is the middle-aged women – women in the stage of life in which they have their greatest social power – who are not stepping up to their responsibilities in the way the author sees fit. No longer responsible for young children, and with younger female kin (daughters, daughters-in-law, nieces) to take on the bulk of domestic chores, middle-aged women had more time and freedom to pursue other interests, but also had responsibility for the younger women. In the view of the author, they were not fulfilling their responsibilities. The result was that younger widows appeared as scandalous to outsiders, eroding the community's reputation.

In Mediterranean cultures, older women control, guide, and teach younger women apart from men. It would be culturally inappropriate for Paul to have Timothy direct young women himself since the responsibility for correcting younger widows' behaviour rested with older women. Thus, Paul asks Timothy to intercede for the younger widows (5:11), ultimately in order to correct their behaviour (which involved marriage), but the intercession would actually be about correcting the behaviour of the *middle-aged women*. If younger widows *wanted* to remarry (5:12), perhaps they found themselves not *able* to remarry. This is where the middle-aged woman also had a particular role to play as a "believing woman" (5:16).

8

A Believing Woman

The author of 1 Timothy perceives the behaviour of the younger widows as causing problems for the community's reputation (5:14). In the last chapter, I argued that despite the serious threat that this perceived behaviour posed, rather than admonishing or punishing them, the fictive Paul tells Timothy to intercede for (παραιτοῦ) them (5:11). This changes how one understands the author's perception of the younger widows. Instead of seeing them as perpetrators of the problem, I suggest that the author sees them as vulnerable victims in need of assistance. In cultural context, older women were responsible for the teaching and behaviour of younger women (Titus 2:3–5). They were to protect, aid, and guide the younger widows.

One might wonder where we see these middle-aged women in 1 Timothy. Though their age is not made explicit, Paul's appeal to a "believing woman who has widows" (5:16) is the most obvious and direct moment at which the author addresses the middle-aged women in the community. He likely also points to their selfish ways in 5:6 and implicitly directs their gaze to their ideal role model in 5:9–10. Identifying the "believing woman" as the middle-aged woman behind the problematic younger widows is especially fitting if these older women were being influenced by those who taught other things (1:3, 6:3), such as forbidding marriage (4:3), because the middle-aged women would have been responsible for arranging the marriages of younger women. In fact, the presence of the middle-aged women at the climax of the section on widows helps to explain the rather odd conundrum of the author condemning younger widows who want to marry (γαμεῖν θέλουσιν, 5:11), yet desiring younger women to marry (βούλομαι οὖν νεωτέρας γαμεῖν;

5:14). His desire for them to marry, bear children, and run households puts them in their "proper" female roles as a way to mitigate the problems their behaviour has caused for the reputation of the group. In addition, elsewhere in the letter, the author is concerned with the proper behaviour of women who seem to have some level of influence (2:9–15, 4:7, 5:6). This level of influence suggests that, according to the ancient Mediterranean life course, they were most likely middle-aged women. If such women were influenced by or even promoting the "other teachings," then the author was invested in bringing them back to what he understood to be "sound teaching" (1:10, 6:3). Because of their significant influence in the community, he would prefer them to be allies, which he demonstrates by labelling them "believing" and/or "faithful" (πιστή).

ASSISTING THE VULNERABLE

The last sentence of the section on widows should be taken as a solution to all the problems involving widows (5:3–15), but especially the problems involving the younger widows (5:11–15). Since the author has taken such pains to describe the situation of the younger widows (5:11–15), the exhortation in 5:16 is meant to finally resolve these issues:

εἴ τις πιστὴ ἔχει χήρας,
   ἐπαρκείτω αὐταῖς
καὶ μὴ βαρείσθω ἡ ἐκκλησία,
   ἵνα ταῖς ὄντως χήραις ἐπαρκέσῃ.

If any believing (faithful) woman has widows,
   she should aid them
and the assembly should not be burdened,
   in order that it might aid the real widows. (1 Tim. 5:16)

There are clearly two situations in parallel here, both of which involve aid (ἐπαρκέω). A "believing woman" should help widows connected to her, and the community (ἐκκλησία) should help "real widows" (5:3, 5). The mention of "real widows" brings the whole section on widows (5:3–16) full circle: the exhortation for Timothy to honour real widows (5:3) is completed with a third-person imperative directing the assembly, through Timothy, to aid them.[1] This verse also serves as the climax of the entire section (5:3–16), with an emphasis on the act of helping others who are vulnerable (the final word is ἐπαρκέω).

The "believing woman" has a pivotal role. Her actions affect the assembly as a whole since neglecting her responsibility to aid the widows in her care became a burden for the community. Interestingly, the sixty+ widow is described as having aided (ἐπαρκέω) those who were in distress (θλιβομένοις ἐπήρκεσεν; 5:10) as part of her exemplary past deeds.[2] As an ideal older woman, she has helped those who were vulnerable, as the believing woman should. As Barclay argues, "women are the linchpin" of a system "bound together in gift-exchange, in a network of households like that imagined in 5.9–10" because women "manage the everyday practices of the household through which ... 'good works' are resourced and exchanged" (2020, 278; see also 284–5).

The widows who are connected to the believing woman in 5:16 are not explicitly identified, but the verb ἔχω suggests a "close relationship," like that of relatives (BDAG 2000, 420).[3] It must refer to widows addressed earlier in this text. The believing woman's widows cannot be the real widows[4] because in 5:16, the real widows are clearly contrasted with the believing woman's widows. The repetition of the verb ἐπαρκέω indicates that one set of widows (those belonging to the believing woman) should be assisted by the believing woman, and the other set of widows (explicitly described as the "real widows") should be assisted by the assembly. If the believing woman is not doing her duty in this respect, the assembly is assumedly "burdened" (βαρέω) with both sets of widows. Neither can the believing woman's widows be the widows with family.[5] The author is not returning to older widows after an extended description of how problematic the younger widows are. The believing woman's widows also cannot be the sixty+ widows (who are not real widows) because they are highlighted for their exemplary virtue, not need (see chapters 5 and 6). Thus, the most logical conclusion is that the widows associated with the believing woman (5:16) are the *younger* widows (5:11–15) and that 5:16 is the author's solution to the problem. More specifically, the believing woman represents a group of women in the real audience of the letter who are to aid those for whom they are responsible – the younger widows – as part of recovering the honourable reputation of the community. The issue of problematic behaviour threatening the community's reputation was probably the most pressing issue in the author's own occasion for writing the letter (as opposed to the fictional narrative layer of the letter; chapter 3), and the use of the third-person imperative to address the believing woman points to this issue.

The two specific uses of the third-person imperative for women in 1 Timothy have notable connections to proper behaviour amid descriptions of alarmingly improper behaviour (in the author's perspective). The phrase "let a woman learn [μανθανέτω] in full submission" (2:11) is embedded in the context of Paul's directives for women's dress and modesty, and his declaration that he does not allow a woman to teach or have authority over a man (2:9–15).[6] The phrase "let the believing woman who has widows take care of [ἐπαρκείτω] them" (5:16) directly follows the section on the poor behaviour of young widows, some of whom have even apparently turned away after Satan (5:15).[7]

Thus, the culmination of the section on widows (5:3–16) rests on the actions of the believing woman, who is to assist the younger widows in her care (5:16). Her responsibilities are that of an influential, middle-aged woman in the community.

THE BATTLE FOR FAITH AND FAITHFULNESS (AND JUDGMENT)

The designation of the middle-aged woman as a "believing woman" (πιστή)[8] in 5:16 deserves closer examination, especially because this section also contains three other instances in which cognates of the term are used. In 5:8, the one who neglects family responsibility denies the faith (πίστις) and is worse than an unbeliever (ἄπιστος), and in 5:12, the younger widows are accused of setting aside their "first faith" (πρώτη πίστις).

Within early Christian literature and within the New Testament, the terms πίστις (noun) and πιστός (adjective) have a range of meanings. The noun form (πίστις) can mean putting confidence or trust *in* someone who is reliable (faith); trustworthiness *of* someone who is reliable (faithfulness); or the *essence* of what one has faith in, especially a set of teachings ("the faith"; BDAG 2000, 818–20). Similar to the first two meanings for πίστις, the adjective represents either "being worthy of belief or trust" or "being trusting" (BDAG 2000, 820–1).

The terms πίστις and πιστός are used in several senses in 1 Timothy.[9] God judged Paul as faithful (πιστόν) and appointed him to serve

God (1:12), as an example for those who trust (πιστεύειν) in Christ Jesus (1:16) and as "a teacher of the Gentiles in faith [ἐν πίστει] and truth" (2:7). Timothy is to have faith (πίστιν) and a good conscience (1:19), being a good model for the faithful (τῶν πιστῶν) in speech, behaviour, love, faith (ἐν πίστει), and purity (4:12), and rejecting improper things so he can pursue righteousness, devotion (εὐσέβεια), faith (πίστις), love, endurance, and gentleness (6:11). *Diakonoi* are to hold "the mystery of the faith [μυστήριον τῆς πίστεως]" (3:9); women who are *diakonoi* (or wives of *diakonoi*; see chapter 6, note 20) should be faithful (πιστὰς) in all things (3:11). Those who serve well "have great confidence in faith/trust [ἐν πίστει] in Christ Jesus" (3:13). God is the saviour of all people, especially those who are faithful (πιστῶν, 4:10).[10]

On the other hand, the opposing teachers "promote speculations rather than the divine training that is known by faith [ἐν πίστει]" (1:4, NRSV). They forbid marriage and eating certain foods, but the author states that those who believe (τοῖς πιστοῖς) and know the truth should gratefully receive these things (4:3). There are those whose faith (τὴν πίστιν) has been shipwrecked (1:19). Some who are eager to be rich have strayed away from the faith (ἀπὸ τῆς πίστεως; 6:10), and some who profess knowledge that is false have "missed the mark with regard to the faith [τὴν πίστιν]" (6:21).

One's status as someone who has faith affords them certain obligations. If someone does not take care of their own, they "have denied the faith [τὴν πίστιν ἤρνηται]" and are "worse than an unbeliever [ἔστιν ἀπίστου χείρων]" – someone with no faith (5:8). A believing woman (πιστή) who has widows should assist them (5:16), and slaves with believing (πιστούς) masters should be especially obedient because their service benefits believers (πιστοί; 6:2).

This brief survey of πίστις / πιστός suggests that in 1 Timothy, one's actions should demonstrate their trustworthiness in relationships and their faithfulness or trust in the teachings. It is also apparent that πίστις denotes boundaries about who is "in" the group and who is not. Even if God "is the saviour of all humanity" (4:10), God is especially the saviour of those who are faithful (μάλιστα πιστῶν; 4:10).

I suggest that opposing teachers were using this term for their own purposes (4:1, 6:21; see below), in which case the author of 1 Timothy was attempting to reclaim it as the rightful legacy of Paul and his way of understanding the truth (2:4, 4:3). Timothy himself is put forth as an example of faithfulness in contrast to the opposing teachers; his faithfulness can be admired and emulated by the author's hearers (4:1–16).

The word πιστή in 5:16 is an adjective functioning as a noun (substantive), and thus can be translated "faithful woman" (able to be trusted) or "believing woman" (one who trusts someone else). The word could refer to her faithfulness in serving God (as Paul had, 1:12) or her trust in Christ (as Paul did, 1:16). In the context of 5:16, it likely meant both. Thus, the woman is called a "believing/faithful woman" (πιστή, 5:16) to highlight her membership in the group and to point to her responsibilities. If the opposing teachers were using this semantic domain to promote their views, the author is claiming it for his own as a way to define those who were (and were not) *faithful* in the "household of God" (3:15) and *trusting* in Christ. In the case of middle-aged women, he is perhaps using it to shame them into behaviour he sees fitting for someone who professes to be devoted to God (2:10). Thus, when the author identifies τις πιστή ("any believing woman") in 5:16, he is appealing to real women in the community who are influenced by the "different teachings" but whom he hopes to sway back to his way of thinking, exhorting them to be truly faithful, as he understands it.[11]

Countering the rhetoric of the opposing teachers may also be in view in 5:12: "for when [the younger widows] behave immodestly moving away from Christ, they want to marry resulting in having judgment because they 'rejected their first faith' [πρώτην πίστιν ἠθέτησαν]."[12] Typical interpretations of this phrasing suggest that their sexual desire drives them to want to marry, which turns them against Christ, who is their "first faith." Though such an interpretation does reflect views of female sexuality in the first century, it assumes a determinedly individualist (modern Western) viewpoint with regard to "faith." It is important to recall that women embodied the honour of their group through their modest behaviours. Widows were seen as anomalous since they were neither virgins nor wives and more prone to appear immodest. Younger widows were especially perceived as being out of place in society and were much more likely to be accused of sexual immodesty (see chapter 7). In addition, the fact that they wanted to marry (5:12) was a normal desire because the typical life course for a woman unfolded through marriage (chapter 7).

Another possibility for the meaning of "first faith" is that they were turning against a specific commitment to prayer (Johnson 2001,

266), but this assumes that all widows were expected to pray, not just "real" ones (5:5). Bassler argues they deny their faith by rejecting a vow of celibacy (2003, 131). That celibacy "could provide women a basis for increased autonomy and power" (126), especially freedom from "hierarchical dominance" of a father or husband, the dangers of childbirth, and the rigours of childrearing (139; also 129–30). While there is strong evidence for some celibate women in the early Christian communities (especially in the second century and later),[13] vows of celibacy were largely a later development that we cannot assume for the early stage of the Christian community represented by 1 Timothy. Bassler admits that celibacy was "not a real option for most women in this world" (127), especially in the long term. The Vestal Virgins remained celibate for thirty years (and beyond, if they chose not marry after this; Plutarch, *Life of Numa Pompilius* 10), but Treggiari notes, "lifelong celibate women are otherwise practically unexampled, although nothing can be proved for the lower class" (1991, 83).[14] Thus, it is difficult to confirm that the "first faith" was a vow of celibacy that the younger widows intended to keep.

Winter posits that a young widow's desire to remarry was a wish "to abandon her faith in order to secure a husband who would not marry her if she remained a Christian" (2003, 137).[15] Similarly, Collins argues that the young widows' loss of their "first faith" refers to the loss of faith a young widow would experience if she married a polytheistic (outsider) husband (2002, 141). If women were expected to participate in their husband's religious practices,[16] and a young woman's first marriage involved loyalty to her husband and to Christ, then later marrying a polytheist could mean giving up her "first faith" and her community. By the end of the first century, we can imagine that a woman who was widowed while still in her childbearing years probably either grew up in the Christian community or became part of the community when she married a man who was already part of it. Some caution is needed here, however, for some women with polytheistic husbands did belong to Pauline and post-Pauline communities (1 Cor. 7:6–8; 1 Pet. 3:1).

On the other hand, the issue might be about *remarrying*. In the beginning of the third century, Tertullian desires his wife not to remarry at all, but he is especially against her marrying someone outside of the faith community (*To His Wife* 2.1.4).[17] Since Romans tended to consider the early Christ groups a superstitious movement,[18] a polytheist husband may be loath to accept a new wife who belonged to the movement. Religious unity of the married couple (or sectarian endogamy, or both) may have prompted Paul in his directive to the Corinthians to marry "in the Lord" (1 Cor. 7:39).

However, this picture of a young woman rejecting her personal faith continues to promote a rather individualistic view of faith in a primarily collectivist community that was concerned for their reputation. Instead, I propose that the rhetoric of the phrase "the first faith" has to do with the opposing teachers that the author is convinced are behind the issues in his community. The exact phrase "the first faith" occurs nowhere else in the letter, but the phrase "the faith" (ἡ πίστις) occurs in contexts that suggest the author may be turning his opponents' rhetoric to his own advantage (as suggested above), emphasizing what the author understands to be Paul's correct teaching and condemning the opponents' teachings. "The faith" is known by those who know the truth (4:3). "The faith" is in Christ Jesus (3:13); it is in accord with a clear conscience (3:9) and healthy teaching (4:6), and it involves a "good fight" (6:12). In 4:1 Paul states that in later times some will renounce "the faith," and concludes the letter with lamenting that some have missed the mark regarding "the faith" (6:21).[19] The deliberate use of this phrase in the letter, especially with regard to the opposing teachers in 4:1 and 6:12, suggests that the author is using their terminology in a battle of rhetoric. He reverses their usage in an attempt to demonstrate to his hearers that even if the opponents tout what they call "the faith," it is actually what Paul has entrusted to Timothy in this letter (6:20) that will direct them in the ways of the truth, as manifested in the assembly (ἐκκλησία) of God (3:15) and keep them in "the [true] faith" (6:21).

The result of the young widows' desire to marry is judgment, but *who* is judging them is not clear. It could be that the community is judging them for their wanton behaviour or that God is judging them for giving up their faith in Christ (another individualistic-centred conclusion). However, if the opposing teachers were using πίστις / πιστός for their own purposes, the phrase "first faith" may have related to rhetoric *used by the opposing teachers* to encourage young widows to remain unmarried, since they are said to forbid marriage (4:3).[20]

I suggest that the *opponents* accused the younger women of not following "the faith" (as they understood it) because these women wanted to marry again. And the opponents judged them for this desire. In my translation, I place the "first faith" phrasing in quotation marks to denote a saying that the author is quoting from his opponents when they accuse the younger widows of rejecting their teaching. Though the opponents would see their teaching as the right way to understand the faith, obviously the author of 1 Timothy disagrees. Thus, the younger widows "want to marry, resulting in having judgment [from the opposing teachers] because they [the younger widows] 'rejected their first faith' [or so the opposing teachers say]" (5:12). This would help explain why the author appears to condemn their wish to marry (5:12), but then states he wants them to marry and take on traditional roles (5:14) – he is speaking against the opposing teachers' view and their judgment of the younger widows.

Furthermore, if the believing woman who was to care for the younger widows was influenced by this teaching, perhaps these young women were incurring judgment *from the middle-aged women* themselves who were actually discouraging them from marrying on the basis of the opposing teachers' instruction not to marry (4:3). Indeed, the author condemns anyone who does not provide for their own with "faith" rhetoric, saying they (including the middle-aged women, perhaps) are denying "the [true] faith" and are worse that someone outside the community of the faithful (5:8).

In sum, an examination of πίστις / πιστός in 1 Timothy suggests that the author turned the rhetoric of the opponents against them to counter their teachings. Their version of "the faith" included forbidding marriage (4:3), so that young widows wanting to remarry would incur the judgment of the opponents (5:12). The author attempts to reclaim the phrase "the faith" (4:1, 6:21), including quoting their phrase ("first faith") in 5:12. He wants to demonstrate that the opponents were wrong when they advocated against remarriage for younger widows and when they judged these women for wanting to remarry (5:12). If the middle-aged women were influenced by this opposing teaching, they also were judging the younger widows for not wanting to follow the agenda of the opposing teaching. In other words, the younger widows' wish to remarry and not keep a vow of celibacy resulted in the opponents' judgment – a judgment that the author rejects, for he desires that they do marry for the good of the reputation of the community (5:14).

MATCHMAKING AND DOWRIES

As discussed in chapter 7, the author's solution for the problematic younger widows is that they should marry, bear children, and run a household, which he does not dictate or command, but "desires" (βούλομαι). If 5:16 finalizes the solution to the problem outlined in 5:11–13, then the author was relying on the believing woman to enact this solution. The nature of the believing woman's assistance to the younger widows must, therefore, relate to marriage.

The believing woman was to come to the aid (ἐπαρκέω) of the younger widows, and this included tangible support from her resources.[21] If the believing woman followed through with this duty, then the assembly would be free to aid the real widows without burden. But if she neglected this duty, the assembly would be burdened (βαρείσθω), that is, weighed down, oppressed, and treated unjustly (BDAG 2000, 166). While it is possible that the author has a financial burden in mind, the troubled reputation of the community may be foremost. The actions of the believing woman would help to alleviate this burden if she aided the younger widows. Indeed, the cultural context suggests that one of the roles of older women in the ancient Mediterranean was to be involved in the arrangement of marriages and dowries for younger women.

In the ancient Mediterranean world, marriage was not a romantic union but rather a family-driven and socially sanctioned duty arranged by family members, with an aim to produce legitimate children. According to the *Lex Julia*, "people who wrongfully prevent children in their power from marrying, or who refuse to provide a dowry for them ... can be forced by proconsuls and provincial governors to arrange marriages and provide dowries for them. Those who do not try to arrange marriages are held to prevent them" (Justinian 1985, 202, 2:23.2.19). Family members continued to have an obligation to get involved in marital relationships when need be. According to Bradley, marriages inevitably included "intervention, management, and manipulation, the natural corollaries, in fact, of marriage by arrangement" (1991, 191).

In modern, traditional Mediterranean cultures, older women, by virtue of their experience and freedom from certain domestic responsibilities, are in a position to support and mentor younger women, which includes a lead role in marriage arrangements.[22] In the ancient Mediterranean, while fathers (if they were alive) had the final say about marriage, a mother had some responsibility in choosing marriage partners for her children (Dixon 1992, 50). Treggiari emphasizes that a young man's mother, especially a widow, would actively seek a wife for her son.[23] This involved "being approached by other *matronae*" who obviously represented young women in that context. Treggiari also notes that "where possible, women should deal with women and men with men" (1991, 134–5; see also Noy 1990, 395n105). Livy recounts the story of a mother's indignation at her husband arranging a marriage for their daughter without her consent:

> The betrothal agreement was thus duly made at this public ceremony, and when Scipio went home he told his wife, Aemilia, that he had arranged the engagement of their younger daughter. Aemilia, just like a woman, was angry that he had not consulted her at all about a daughter who belonged to them both and added that the girl's mother should not have been left out of the decision even if it were to Tiberius Gracchus that he was betrothing her. Scipio was reportedly delighted with the correspondence of their opinions and replied that this was the very one to whom she was engaged. (2018, 195, 38.57.6–8)

Virgil recounts the story of Queen Amata who, feeling that her mother's rights over her daughter's marriage had been disregarded, wept over her daughter's marriage to Turnus, the Trojan, who was to take her daughter away (Virgil, *Aeneid* 7.402).[24] In the *Acts of Paul and Thecla*, no father is mentioned, so Thecla's mother was likely a widow who secured a highly desirable marriage for her daughter. Thecla's mother probably felt her own welfare was secured with such a marriage to the well-positioned Thamyris (43). When Thamyris and Thecla's mother realize Thecla has abandoned them for Paul's message, they weep, along with the servants, for their lost future wife, daughter, and mistress (10).

A letter from Jerome (late fourth century CE) to a middle-aged woman illustrates mother-daughter dynamics between a widowed mother and her "virgin" daughter within the later Christian community. The young woman appears to be in a questionable relationship with a man (Jerome, *Letter* 117.3). Jerome recommends that living with her mother will protect the young woman's chastity. He indicates that the daughter had not wanted to live with her mother because her mother was behaving in a "worldly" manner, but Jerome emphasizes the mother-daughter bond: she carried her in her womb, raised her with affection, washed her clothes, sat with her when she was ill, bore the challenges of pregnancy to bring her life, reared her to become a woman, and taught her to love Christ (4). He exhorts the mother to focus on helping her daughter (11; Kraemer 1988, 170–7). Jerome implies that the mother is responsible for her daughter's chastity and/or marriage.

Aunts, married elder sisters, and matrons who were family friends might help a young virtuous virgin be noticed by other women in hopes of a good offer of marriage; women's networks provided ways to find out about potential brides (Treggiari 1991, 135, 138). Treggiari describes Cicero's negotiations for his daughter's third marriage that involved a number of women who presented their candidates. Cicero's wife was heavily involved in the process (1991, 127–31). Cicero recounts a story of a woman whose sister's daughter wanted to marry. The young woman and her aunt went to receive an omen, which Cicero notes was an ancient custom. After waiting a long time, the young woman asked to sit in her aunt's chair; the aunt replied that her niece could take her place. This action was the omen, for the young woman married the aunt's husband after the aunt unexpectedly died (Cicero, *On Divination* 1.104).

Older women were also sometimes employed as professional matchmakers in the Eastern empire (Arjava 1996, 30; Noy 1990, 385).[25] This is not likely to be the case here in 1 Timothy, as the middle-aged women are more likely benefactors, but it does point to the possibility of such a role for older women. Marriage arrangements involved a material component, namely, the dowry (Treggiari 1991, 323–64). Dowries were usually provided by a woman's family or a patron. The dowry represented wealth from a bride's natal family and could give her a kind of authority and security in marriage. In the propertied classes, a widow would have received back her dowry, and perhaps a legacy, usufruct, or inheritance from her deceased husband (usually the inheritance that would be passed on to his [their] children, who would continue the family lineage) if she was married *sine manu* in Roman times (Treggiari 1991, 324–64). This meant that she continued to be a member of her natal family, under her father's *potestas* (power) rather than her husband's, as long as her father was alive. In other words, a woman belonged to her father's *familia* but to her husband's *domus*. In the first century CE, women were typically married *sine manu* (Bradley 1991, 4, 9–10; Saller 1994, 74–83; Parkin and Pomeroy 2007, 72).

If a young widow's family could not provide a dowry, an older woman in the community might have come to her aid as a patron.[26] Patronage between women of different status was common. Even modestly wealthy women were patrons of freedwomen (and freedmen; see Osiek and MacDonald 2006, 202–3, 214–19). In a second- or third-century epitaph, a woman named Epiphania is praised for providing financial aid to other women, motivated by εὐσέβεια (duty and devotion; see chapter 5): "And to friends abandoned as woman to women I provided much, with a view of piety [φίλες τε λειπομένες ὡς γυνὴ γυνῆξι πολλὰ παρέσχον, εἰς εὐσεβίην ἀφορῶσα]" (SEG 24 1081; Horsley 1981, 2.55–56; see also Zamfir 2013, 112n72). Treggiari notes that wealthy women were known to make charitable donations to young women for dowries (it was less acceptable for men to do so; 1991, 344). For example, Livia, the wife of Augustus, helped to pay dowries of many young women, for which an arch was built in her honour (Dio Cassius, *History of Rome* 58.2.3). In the so-called *Laudatio Turiae* (CIL 6.1527), a husband praises his wife for helping her female kin by taking them in and providing dowries. He states, "For you brought up your female relations who deserved such kindness in your own houses with us. You also prepared marriage-portions for them so that they could obtain marriages worthy of your family" (Wistrand 1976, 23, 1.44–49).[27] Since young women receiving the gift would not necessarily be direct descendants of the donor, such action offers another piece of evidence for the importance of female networks (see also Barclay 2020, 283). It also points to the rhetoric of the household metaphor in 1 Timothy (3:15) and call for faithful community members to take care of their own (5:8) within the community.[28]

Marriage was a complicated affair, and remarriage even more so, since a woman often retained ties with the family of her first marriage, especially if she had children.[29] If over a quarter of all adult women were widows (Krause 1994, 73), we cannot expect that all young widows *could* remarry.[30] They often had a large dowry as compensation for their lack of virginity. They might be more assertive than virgins, and the fact that they already had one husband die was suspicious – a potential sign of women's power that a man might want to avoid (Apuleius, *Defense* 92:6–11; Harlow 2007, 202; see also Buitelaar 1995, 10, 15). Parents were typically involved in the choice of a second marriage. In the *Laudatio Murdiae* (CIL 6.10230), Murdia had become a widow with one son. She remarried a second time and had subsequent children. The inscription states, "she upheld the marriages to worthy husbands that had been provided by her parents," suggesting that her parents were integral in her finding a second husband as well as the first (Lindsay 2004, 93). On the other hand, previously married women had "greater freedom" to "take some initiative in finding new husbands" (Treggiari 1991, 135).[31]

The believing woman in 1 Tim. 5:16, as a member of the "household of God," would have been expected to aid widows with her resources, including dowries when needed. The present aspect of the verb implies an ongoing commitment from the believing woman, which would include arranging a marriage and supporting the marriage in the long term. Whereas the community's aid to the real widows is expressed with the aorist aspect (ἐπαρκέσῃ), giving it a general sense of assistance for the real widows, the present aspect (ἐπαρκείτω) gives the verb a sense of continuous, possibly "timeless," action (Signor 1999, 64) toward the younger widows.

The author of 1 Timothy required *women* to marry because he pushed for traditional household roles for women, children, and slaves in order to gain more positive outside opinions of the community (Bassler 2003, 133). But the author also required *men* to marry and take up traditional male roles related to the household. This was a stipulation for men who wanted to be considered for positions of responsibility in the community, namely, overseer and *diakonoi* (3:1–10, 12; see chapter 6, also Krause 1995, 109). If the opponents promoted abstaining from marriage (4:3), their teaching probably affected both women's and men's decisions about remarriage. Bassler argues that the opposing teachers who reportedly forbade marriage (4:3) had special success among women (also 2 Tim. 3:6–7), since the author of 1 Timothy is so adamant about women being married (1 Tim. 2:15, 5:14; also Titus 2:4–5; Bassler 2003, 132). While Bassler is probably referring primarily to younger women, it is more likely the older women who were influenced. Perhaps mothers were encouraging their sons not to marry (or remarry if widowed) either.[32] For a man, marriage included the potential connections that such a marriage would secure to increase his status.[33] The lack of a father-in-law might change the prospects for a young man's status.[34] The opposing teachers may have suggested other ways the younger men could gain status (see chapter 9) without relying on older women to get them married.

If young men were choosing not to marry (and widowers were choosing not to remarry), then there may have been a dearth of believing men for young women to marry. This would especially be the case for young widows, who were already at a disadvantage for marriage prospects. If a young widow had no father, perhaps suggested by her unrestrained behaviour in 5:13,[35] she may be a less desirable mate. And so she may have gone looking for a husband herself,[36] perhaps outside the group. This may be one reason she is accused of being out of place, going around households being foolish and saying things she should not say (5:13; Collins 2002, 141).

The wording and cultural context of 1 Tim. 5:16 support an interpretation of the believing woman as an older woman who was responsible for helping younger widows to secure suitable marriage partners and providing dowries. If the middle-aged women were part of the problem, the author of 1 Timothy was convinced they were also part of the solution.

MODELLING PROPER BEHAVIOUR

In addition to their responsibility for finding suitable marriage partners for the younger widows, the author's choice of words leveraged the full self-identity of the middle-aged women as "believing/faithful women" (5:16). If they were truly women of faith, as they probably professed to be, they would also fulfill their true obligations in modelling and providing guidance in virtuous behaviour expected of a believing woman.[37] As we saw in chapter 7, older women, according to Titus 2:3–5, are to provide instruction to younger women, but they are also expected to be models of modest, reputable behaviour themselves, to be "suitably reverent in demeanor, not slanderers or slaves to much wine" (Titus 2:3). In a similar way, the women who are highlighted in 1 Timothy for their behaviour were probably older women responsible for embodying virtue themselves, but also for modelling behaviour to their juniors.

In fact, we glimpse the middle-aged woman earlier in 1 Tim. 5:3–16, namely, in the brief and enigmatic phrase in 5:6: "but the woman who lives luxuriously is dead while she is living [ἡ δὲ σπαταλῶσα ζῶσα τέθνηκεν]." Although this verse occurs in the context of widows, the participle only indicates female gender, not a particular category of woman. The description of this woman is reminiscent of the one in 2:9–10: women who were more worried about their appearance than about their modesty. In fact, the woman in 5:6 looks very much like the women in 2:9 because of her decadent behaviour, "indulg[ing] [her]self beyond the bounds of propriety" (σπαταλάω, BDAG 2000, 936). In neither instance is the woman portrayed as modelling the kind of behaviour that was proper for virtuous women. If a woman was "living luxuriously," she was not being responsible for her own behaviour, and neither was she being responsible for the behaviour of those in her care. She was selfish and ungenerous, spending time, money, and effort on herself rather than on others.[38] In 5:6, the author hints at what her lack of responsible action leads to: it is tantamount to death, for in death, the person is no longer able to act.

Earlier in the letter (2:9–10) the author paints a picture of a woman who is using her wealth for herself rather than for others in the community. This kind of selfishness may also be implied in the word used for the younger widows who "behave immodestly moving away from Christ" (5:11; see discussion in chapter 7) – behaviour that could understood as a manifestation of the poor *modelling* of their female elders.

There are noteworthy parallels between the women in 2:9–15 and the sixty+ widows. In chapter 6, I argued that the sixty+ widows were set up as an ideal to which the middle-aged women of the community were to aspire. The similar phrasing in 2:9–15 and 5:9–10 reflects a picture of the ideal behaviour of a virtuous woman as an expression of her devotion to God.

In 2:9–15, the author conveys concerns for women's behaviour when the community was gathered together. He wanted women to dress and act "with modesty [shame] and moderation [μετὰ αἰδοῦς καὶ σωφροσύνης]" and adorn themselves not with ornate hairstyles and jewels (2:9) but with that which was "suitable" (πρέπει), "through her good works [δι' ἔργων ἀγαθῶν]," 2:10). The word αἰδώς (shame or modesty) is found only here in the New Testament (except for a variant in Heb. 12:28). It is clearly part of honour language, with a sense of "a respect for convention" (BDAG 2000, 5). Paired with σωφροσύνη, it is a call for women to behave with modesty and self-control, which is the foundation of female virtue in the ancient Mediterranean world (Malherbe 2006, 59). They should be adorned (κοσμέω) with that which is suitable (πρέπει)[39] "for women professing duty and devotion to God [γυναιξὶν ἐπαγγελλομέναις θεοσέβειαν]" (2:10). A cognate of εὐσέβεια, θεοσέβεια has a sense of honouring traditional religious and social structure, which is a fundamental value for the author (see chapter 5). A woman's virtue and demeanor would manifest "through good works" (δι' ἔργων ἀγαθῶν, 2:10). Of course, all women were expected to act modestly, but interestingly, this phrase is paralleled only one time in 1 Timothy: for the *past* deeds of the sixty+ widows in 5:10 ("every good work [παντὶ ἔργῳ ἀγαθῷ]").[40] If the author has a middle-aged woman in mind in 2:10 when he declares that her duty and devotion should be expressed "through good works," then he upholds as her model the exemplary sixty+ widow who has already, in her virtuous past, influenced others through "every good work."

We find a hint of female age hierarchy and duties in 1 Tim. 2:15. This is a notoriously difficult verse, especially the author's use of σώζω (save). My interest here, however, is on what it may reveal about roles of women related to age. After refusing to have women teach or have authority over a man (or husband), the author references the deception and disobedience of Eve (2:12–14). Then he states in 2:15, "But she will be saved through having children, if they remain in faith and love and purity with self-control [σωθήσεται δὲ διὰ τῆς τεκνογονίας, ἐὰν μείνωσιν ἐν πίστει καὶ ἀγάπῃ καὶ ἁγιασμῷ μετὰ σωφροσύνης]." Whatever the author might mean by "being saved," he switches subjects mid-sentence from the woman (singular) to her children (plural). The switch is similar to the change in subjects in 5:4: if any widow (singular) has children or grandchildren, they (plural, i.e., the children and grandchildren) should learn first their duty to their own household (chapter 5).[41] Thus, a woman (referring back to the woman not permitted to teach in 2:12) will be "saved" through having children (διὰ τῆς τεκνογονίας).[42] Interestingly, a similar word related to bringing up children (τεκνοτροφέω) is used for the past deeds of the sixty+ widows in 5:10, one of the activities that makes her an ideal model of female virtue.

The subject shift in 2:15 then focuses on the children, who will ideally "remain in faith and love and purity with self-control [ἐὰν μείνωσιν ἐν πίστει καὶ ἀγάπῃ καὶ ἁγιασμῷ μετὰ σωφροσύνης]." The implication is that the woman would teach (and model) these virtues which would manifest in her children. As we have seen, faith (πίστις) is a multifaceted concept and important in this letter, in part as an identity marker of faithfulness and commitment to one's responsibilities within the group (5:16; see discussion above). The virtue of

Figure 8.1 | Statue of a Roman woman (third century CE), namely, a middle-aged *matrona*. Digital image courtesy of Getty's Open Content Program.

moderation, σωφροσύνη, is listed as an attribute the woman herself should have (2:9), so that she is to both model and teach it. Similar to Titus 2:5–6, both young women and younger men were to have self-control and moderation (variations of σωφροσύνη), which is consistent with encouraging proper behaviour of younger people, who embody the shame of the community (chapter 2).[43]

The language used in 1 Tim. 2:9–15 suggests that the women the author has in mind are powerful women with significant influence. He endeavours to end their public teaching (2:12) and admonishes them to return to traditional roles in their own behaviour (2:9–10) and in their "proper" sphere of influence, namely, their children (2:15). Women with this kind of influence would most likely to be middle-aged women with adult children whose behaviour mattered for the reputation of the community.

The author closes the letter with a condemnation of focusing on one's own pleasures rather than the needs of the community (see 1 Tim. 6:9–10).[44] The contrast between the woman who lives luxuriously (5:6) and the real widow (5:5) demonstrates this: a real widow has nothing to give others except her prayers. Even in her devastating circumstances, her focus on God and constant prayers are more life-giving than the selfish ways of the luxurious woman who has so much more to give but refuses to do so. In her selfishness, such a woman is dead even as she lives (5:6). She is socially dead,[45] at the very least, because she is not acting as part of the community with a focus on caring for others. Someone who is dead is no longer part of the reciprocal relationships that make up a community (or household).[46]

Directly following the phrase about the self-indulgent woman, the rhetoric of Paul to Timothy returns with this instruction: "and command these things, so that they might be blameless [καὶ ταῦτα παράγγελλε, ἵνα ἀνεπίλημπτοι ὦσιν]" (5:7). The antecedents for ταῦτα (these things) and the plural subject for "they" (ὦσιν) are both unclear. "These things" could refer to any of the directives in this section that are directly or indirectly aimed at the community, for all of these directives relate in some way to the reputation of the community.[47] "They" could refer back to the family members who are shirking their responsibility (5:4; Marshall 1999, 589), but it could also refer to any or all of the members of the community implied in the directives in this section. The next verse (5:8) emphasizes neglect, identifying "someone who does not provide for their own (with forethought), especially their household" (5:8), suggesting those whom the author wants to "be blameless" are the neglectful kin of 5:4 and the luxurious woman of 5:6.

It is striking that such a person denies the faith and is worse than an unbeliever (5:8), since this clearly contrasts with the author's label of "believing woman" in 5:16. Thus, the author seems to have in mind the same woman in 5:16 that he has in 5:6 – painting her as selfish, uncaring, and "luxurious" in 5:6 in order to call her out of those ways and toward her proper duties, hoping that the label "believing woman" in 5:16 appeals to her sense of duty and devotion toward the real faith rather than that of the opponents – or to her sense of shame, that is, to her sensitivity to the importance of the honour of the group and her role in preserving it.

The line of thought would therefore follow this logic: real widows are alone and spend their time praying (5:5), which contrasts with the middle-aged woman who is selfish in her behaviour (5:6). By following "these things" (5:7) specified in 5:8–16, these women would become blameless, which they currently are not. In fact, shirking responsibility is the point of the following verse, which states that "if someone does not care for one's own," that person "denies the faith" and is "worse than an unbeliever" (5:8) – a statement of social sanction (chapter 5).

Understanding the believing woman to be a middle-aged woman who has not been fulfilling her responsibilities toward younger women also makes sense of the parallel grammatical structure in 5:4, 8, 16 (see also Van Neste 2004, 57–8):

5:4   εἰ δέ τις χήρα τέκνα ἢ ἔκγονα ἔχει
5:8   εἰ δέ τις τῶν ἰδίων καὶ μάλιστα οἰκείων οὐ προνοεῖ
5:16 εἴ   τις πιστὴ ἔχει χήρας

In 5:4, the author states, "**and if some** widow has children or grandchildren" they should be caring for the widow with family. In 5:8, he states "**and if some** person does not take care of one's own especially those of one's own household," they are denying the faith. It is sufficiently ambiguous so that it may indirectly link the problem of adult children avoiding their filial duty with the problem of middle-aged women avoiding their responsibility for the younger women, whose behaviour was out of control. And in 5:16, he states, "**if some** believing woman has widows," she needs to assist them – the ultimate solution to the problem of the younger widows.[48]

CONCLUSION

If the middle-aged woman is in view in 5:6, we can follow the whole line of reasoning in 5:3–16 this way: Timothy should honour real widows (5:3), contrasted with the widows whose family members should care for them (5:4), because real widows are alone (with no one to care for them), yet they are devoted to prayer (5:5). In contrast, the middle-aged woman is self-indulgent, and even though it appears she is better off than the lonely widow, she is more dead than alive (5:6). Timothy is to "command" the following things (as well as what was already said about family members of widows) so that those who need to be admonished are "above reproach [ἀνεπίληπτος]" (also 3:2, 6:14); this is paramount, since the community's reputation is at issue (5:7). If someone is not taking up their responsibility to take care of their own (their own children, or mothers and grandmothers, or others for whom they have responsibility), they are worse than those with no faith or faithfulness (5:8).

The description of the sixty+ widow, then, logically follows this harsh statement about neglect because she provides the exemplary model (chapter 6) to which the middle-aged women should aspire. Several of the same words are used in the list of the sixty+ widow's past deeds that are used for the middle-aged women: having children (2:15, 5:10), doing "good works" (2:10, 5:10), and aiding (ἐπαρκέω) those who are vulnerable (5:10, 16). In addition, her hospitality demonstrates she is not focused on herself, unlike the self-indulgence implied in the behaviour of women in 2:9 and 5:6. The sixty+ widow is the ideal that the middle-aged woman should emulate.

After highlighting the exemplary sixty+ widows, Timothy is told to intervene for the most vulnerable people in the scenario, the younger widows, whose poor behaviour is perceived in such a way that it is manifesting into a significant problem: the "adversary" (outsider) is condemning their behaviour (5:14), and some young widows have "already turned away after Satan" (5:15). This is the result of the older women neglecting their duties. The author finishes with a statement directed at the believing woman – a *middle-aged woman* – and her responsibility for younger women – the widows she "has" (ἔχω; 5:16). The solution is that she should aid (ἐπαρκείτω) those widows in her care (5:16), in a manner reminiscent of the aid sixty+ widows have offered to the afflicted (5:10). If the believing woman fulfilled her responsibility of getting the younger widows married, the assembly would no longer be burdened (βαρείσθω) with a troubled reputation and would be able to simply help the real widows. In the cultural context of the time, the believing woman's aid involved matchmaking, providing dowries, and modelling proper behaviour.

The need for Timothy to intercede suggests that the young widows are confused and in need of guidance and intervention (5:11). As was typical of young women (or so the author would have thought), they wanted to remarry. But their middle-aged mentors did not want to help them find new marriage partners, for they were influenced by the instruction of the opposing teachers (4:3) and encouraging them instead to remain unmarried. When the young widows appeared to behave immodestly by trying to find their own husbands, perhaps outside the community, they were moving away from Christ, and thus away from the community (5:12), threatening the reputation of the community because of the perception of their behaviour (5:14). Nor were the middle-aged women encouraging the unmarried *men* to pursue matrimony (hence the stipulations of marriage for men pursuing leadership roles; 3:2, 12). Since the middle-aged women condemned marriage, they may have followed the opponents in "judging" the young women for wanting it, saying that they had abandoned their "first faith" – a phrase, I argue, that was used by the opponents (5:12). In the view of the author of 1 Timothy, true faith for women (5:16) was found in cultivating behaviour appropriate for women in the "household of God" (3:15), as exemplified by the sixty+ widows (5:9–10), especially demonstrated in "good works" (2:10, 5:10). For younger widows, this meant the author wished them to marry, have children, and run a household of their own (5:14). For the author of 1 Timothy, proper behaviour and order was the antithesis of the opposing teachers and their influence, and using Paul's voice, his exhortations, meant to be heeded by the middle-aged women, would overcome the influence of the opponents and help restore the reputation of the community.

There were, however, other problems of reputation, for the younger men were also behaving improperly, in ways that contrasted sharply with the exemplary young man, Timothy.

9

Elders

In 1 Tim. 5:1–16, the author weaves together the fictive directives from Paul to Timothy with instructions to his real audience, often providing indications of their actual situation. He introduces cultural expectations of age hierarchy, including respect for the older generation (5:1–2), filial piety (5:4), and proper behaviour of middle-aged women toward younger women (5:11–16) modelled by exemplary old widows (5:9–10). The next section, 1 Tim. 5:17–25, represents a continuity of directives related to age, but a shift in topic from women to men, beginning with the πρεσβύτεροι, or men who were "elders."

Though in later times the term πρεσβύτερος is associated with an "office" (static rank or position), in the late first and early second centuries, it carried a strong sense of age and seniority associated with the pervasive and fluid cultural value of honour. Though elders are at the centre of this situation, I suggest that it is actually younger men who are causing problems by not acting honourably toward their elders according to the conventions of age-related roles. The author's response emphasizes his conservative view of age structure: the young should properly respect the old lest they compromise the reputation of the community. Using the voice of Paul, the author's rhetoric reflects his anxiety about younger men's potential power in his own time of social crisis.

ELDERS IN 1 TIMOTHY

The word πρεσβύτερος is aptly translated as "elder." That is, it can be a reference to age (literally, the word is a comparative adjective functioning as a noun, meaning "older man") or it can denote a role and title of authority and/or leadership. The distinction between the two meanings is not clear. In 1 Tim. 5:1, the word clearly refers to age, namely, an older man as compared with Timothy (a younger man) and other younger men (νεώτεροι, 5:2; see chapter 4). Elsewhere in literature associated with Christ groups it conveys a role rather than age, though attainment of some age in order to have the role cannot be ruled out. The word is used for Judean elders in the gospels (e.g., Mark 11:27, Luke 20:1, Matt. 21:23), and elders of the church (e.g., Acts 15:22; 20:17; Titus 1:5–6; Ignatius, *Eph.* 2.2, 4.1; *Mag.* 2, 6.1, 7.1; *Trall.* 3.1, 12.2; *Smyr.* 8.1; Rev 4:4).

The meaning of πρεσβύτερος in early Christian communities is part of a long-standing discussion about the development of leadership roles within the movement. The term certainly developed in the Christian church to become the title for a distinct "office," but when this development occurred and how this title relates to other "offices" has been much debated.[1] The scholarly literature on the function of elders in early Christ groups and Christian communities often attempts to work out how it relates to the role and function of overseer (ἐπίσκοπος).[2] The debate centers on two major questions: the origins of the designation, and the function or role of the πρεσβύτεροι in early Christianity. The second question focuses on reconciling the use of the term in 1 Tim. 5:17, where it stands alone, with the use of the term in Titus 1:5–9 (and, to a lesser extent, Acts 20), where it is often interpreted as equated with the ἐπίσκοπος (overseer).[3] Various attempts to solve the problem presented by Titus 1:5–9 include the development of the monarchical episcopate (Campbell 1994), the merging of two different systems of leadership (von Campenhausen 1969), and an evolution of official roles as the community required more structure (Burtchaell 1992). The identity and function of elders and the overseer is difficult to determine on the basis of texts that clearly are not concerned with the distinction, nor were they meant to endorse a particular church structure (Young 1994b, 108; Verner 1983, 150).

In studies of leadership roles in the early church, elders have traditionally been grouped together with overseers and *diakonoi* as a tripartite leadership structure.[4] Even though it has often been characterized as such (e.g., von Campenhausen 1969), the tripartite grouping is *not* obvious in 1 Timothy. Viewing the roles of overseers, *diakonoi*, and elders together in this letter is anachronistic at best and does not reflect the progression of the letter (Malherbe

2008; Hutson 2013, 82). In 1 Tim. 3, Paul presents the characteristics and qualifications for someone who aspires to be overseer (3:1–7) and qualifications for *diakonoi* (3:8–10, 12–13) and their wives or female *diakonoi* (3:11; the context does not make it clear which is in view; see chapter 6, note 20). The section that discusses elders (1 Tim. 5:17–25) occurs significantly later in the rhetorical argument of the letter. The "elders" in 1 Tim. 5 are not presented as a third "office." Seeing them as such skews the actual intent of this section, which focuses on matters of age. Furthermore, the characteristics listed in 1 Tim. 3 for overseer and *diakonoi* do not mirror the directives regarding elders in 1 Tim. 5:17–19; the sections have differing contexts and differing purposes (Stewart 2014, 148). The author simply does not conceive of the three together.

In line with my challenge to the perceived unity of the letters to Timothy and Titus (chapter 1), we cannot assume that the meaning of "elder" in 1 Tim. 5:17 is exactly the same as the one in Titus 1:5 (so also Stewart 2014, 148–9). Moreover, we cannot *begin* with an assumption that the term "elders" represented roles that were already developed "offices," even if certain responsibilities in the community might be associated with them (149). It is also worth considering that the meaning and use of πρεσβύτεροι did not remain continuous during these times of social change, and that other connotations or functions might have nuanced the use of the term in various contexts. A review of the secondary literature on the topic of elders, particularly as it relates to 1 Tim. 5, may be instructive.

The majority view has little to do with age because it posits that elders in 1 Timothy represent an office derived from leadership in the Judean/Jewish synagogue. For example, Burtchaell (1992) articulates the designation of "elders" as a functional office adapted by Christians from the normative Judean organization, eventually altering roles and terminology to distinguish themselves from their Judean roots. In this view, in the early church, power was in the hands of the charismatic leaders, namely, prophets and apostles, while the officers (especially elders) presided in the background. When the church's unity was challenged, the officers became more powerful and important in maintaining order.

The assumption of an "office" for 1 Tim. 5:17 is problematic, for there is compelling direct evidence of an age designation, namely, the use in 5:1 for age. In keeping with the theme of intergenerational relations and age in 1 Tim. 5, it follows that the introduction of πρεσβύτεροι in 5:17 has the connotation of age rather than a title (or office). If it did not connote age, this would signify a radical change in subject matter (Malherbe 2008, 282).

Though it is a minority opinion, a few scholars have asserted that age was central to the term πρεσβύτερος (in 1 Timothy and Titus). For example, Joachim Jeremias states that elder "nicht Amts-, sondern Altersbezeichnung ist [is not a designation of office but a designation of age]" (1949, 32). A.E. Harvey suggests that elders were imbued with authority because they could offer counsel to local communities on the basis of their age, senior status, and likely social status (heads of prominent families) in the community. Elders were not "appointed," but certain men (perhaps the first converts and most senior members) were chosen for special responsibilities, namely, the responsibility of bishop or "overseeing" (1974, 325; Titus 1:5–7; Acts 16:23; *1 Clem.* 44; see also *1 Clem.* 47:6, 55:1). Frances M. Young argues that elders were not an office parallel to overseer and *diakonoi*, but "were originally a council of senior Christians recognized as the bearers of the apostolic tradition" (1994b, 148).[5]

R. Alastair Campbell focuses on "elders" as a reference to both seniority and old age (1994, 2). Campbell's starting point is drawn from the work of Rudolph Sohm (1892), who posited that elder was not originally an office; rather, elders were a group of men honoured for their senior status and proven character in the community. For Campbell, the term "elders" denoted honour and respect, applying to senior men of noble or influential households in both Judean and Greco-Roman communities. He understands elders as those in roles of "seniority" in the early church, paralleling the basic structure of the household (see also Verner 1983 and Maier 1991). Like Harvey, Campbell argues that holders of official positions, such as overseer, were drawn from this group.[6] Campbell has much to say about age that is valuable, although his argument for a monarchical episcopate relies too heavily on Ignatius with little corroborating evidence. Similar to Campbell, Johnson posits a single overseer "who functions as part of a 'board of elders'" on the basis of 1 Tim. 4:14, hinging on 1 Tim. 5:17 where elders "govern" as a "basic job" with other duties "depending on gifts and needs" (1996, 218).

The most convincing treatment of these issues to date is in Alistair C. Stewart's recent volume *The Original Bishops* (2014). He argues that the collective πρεσβύτεροι within individual congregations were not derived from the Judean/Jewish synagogue (for which he finds almost no evidence; 132–8), but from Hellenistic voluntary associations, especially in Asia Minor. In these associations, πρεσβύτεροι hold positions of honour because of their age, social rank, and wealth as patrons and men of influence (121–43).[7] Regarding the role of πρεσβύτεροι in Titus 1:5–9 and 1 Tim. 5:17, Stewart argues that the use of the term is qualified in both instances and used in two different ways. In Titus, a letter that assumes an audience of multiple churches, the phrase κατὰ πόλιν πρεσβυτέρους ("elders of the city"; Titus 1:5) refers to leaders from each congregation (likely overseers in their individual churches) who would come together to form a kind of federation, a structure that Stewart demonstrates is evident in Rome and elsewhere (38–44). However, in 1 Tim. 5:17, the elders refer to an entirely different group within a single congregation (led by an overseer). The phrase οἱ καλῶς προεστῶτες πρεσβύτεροι ("elders who shepherd well")[8] refers to older men who are honoured patrons in the congregation, similar to those who functioned in associations (147–65).

Stewart's careful research clearly conveys πρεσβύτεροι as a term of honour due to older age rather than a term for an office. This points to a recent trend in scholarship toward an understanding of age as central to the use of this term. Malherbe (2008) clearly moves in this direction, focusing on old age in 1 Tim. 5:17–19 and arguing for a connection between Greco-Roman moral tradition and 1 Timothy. This culturally sensitive analysis suggests that attitudes toward old age and intergenerational conflict in Roman culture form the most appropriate background of this text, specifically highlighting honour and financial support for elderly men and women.

THE ELDERS IN 1 TIM. 5:17–18

Given my focus on age structure, I begin with the assumption that instructions related to elders in 5:17–23 logically deal with *age-related issues* involving elders because they are set within the *framework* of age-related issues (1 Tim. 5:1–2). Having addressed problems among the older and younger women in 5:3–16, the author now turns to the men.[9] The anacoluthon in 5:17 suggests a subtle change of thought, but clearly the themes of age and improper behaviour continue from 5:1–16:

Οἱ καλῶς προεστῶτες πρεσβύτεροι
διπλῆς τιμῆς ἀξιούσθωσαν,
   μάλιστα οἱ κοπιῶντες ἐν λόγῳ καὶ διδασκαλίᾳ.

The elders who shepherd well
should be considered worthy of double honour,
   namely, those who toil in word and teaching. (1 Tim. 5:17)

Here, the author presents yet another third-person imperative ("let them be considered worthy [ἀξιούσθωσαν]"), indirectly addressing the real audience about an issue in the author's own time (see chapter 3). The identity, function, and importance of the elders for the rest of the section (5:18–25) justifies a rather lengthy explanation of the details of this verse.

G. Bornkhamm argues that πρεσβύτερος has a "positive element of venerability" as compared to the more negative sense of other words for age (e.g., γέρων, παλαιός; 1964, 652). However, in his treatise *Whether an Old Man Should Engage in Public Affairs*, Plutarch makes little distinction; "Cato, for example, used to say that we ought not voluntarily to add to the many evils of its own which belong to old age [τῷ γήρᾳ] the disgrace that comes from baseness. And of the many forms of baseness none disgraces an aged man [ἄνδρα πρεσβύτην] more than idleness, cowardice, and slackness, when he retires from public offices to the domesticity befitting women or to the country where he oversees [ἐφορῶντα] the harvesters and the women who work as gleaners" (1936, 80–1, *Moralia* 10:784A). The author of 1 Timothy only uses the term πρεσβύτεροι to describe older men and elders (1 Tim. 5:1, 17, 19). Given their current level of activity, we need not posit men who were very old (dysfunctional); rather, they were the active senior members of the community, in fact, probably around the same age as middle-aged women (chapters 7 and 8).

Clearly, the elders who "shepherd well [οἱ καλῶς προεστῶτες]" (5:17) have important functions in the community that provide stability and authoritative roles as part of their honourable behavior in the household of God. The term προΐστημι has two possible meanings: one of leadership and authority, and the other of showing concern, with the notion of acting to provide care (BDAG 2000, 870). However, one meaning did not necessarily supersede the other, as illustrated by an inscription honouring Artemis in second-century

Ephesus. It declares that the edict was publicized "while Titus Aelius Marcianus Priscus, son of Aelius Priscus, a man very well thought of and worthy of all honour [τειμῆς] and acceptance, was leader [προεστῶτος] of the festival and president of the athletic games" (Horsley 1987, lines A.16–21; 4.19). As the leader of the festival, Priscus had authority over its proceedings, but such a position required the care of a benefactor as well. In this way, both senses of the verb are implied: "the inscription ... reflects the ease with which Graeco-Roman urban dwellers accepted the compatibility of the two notions of benevolent actions and structured authority" (Horsley 1987, 82; see also Marshall 1999, 611). Glosses for the phrase in 1 Tim. 5:17 such as "lead" or "manage" tend to favour the nuance of "ruling"; I have chosen the gloss "shepherd" because it contains the aspect of leadership as well as caring that would befit a patron (see a similar argument in Stewart 2014, 138).

The dual function of the word προΐστημι is also reflected in 1 Tim. 3:4–5 in the list of qualifications for overseer. Someone who aspires to this position must "shepherd his own household well [τοῦ ἰδίου οἴκου καλῶς προϊστάμενον]," having "submissive children with all respectfulness" (3:4). The author goes on to clarify, repeating the action: "if someone does not know how to shepherd his own household [εἰ δέ τις τοῦ ἰδίου οἴκου προστῆναι οὐκ οἶδεν]" (3:4), how can he care for [ἐπιμελήσεται] the church of God?" (3:5). The verb προΐστημι has a sense of authority and care that is inherent in the role of *paterfamilias*, or male head of the household (Marshall 1999, 481). While it normally takes the genitive, this is not supplied in 5:17. However, the community is almost certainly in mind.[10]

The elders who "shepherd" do it "well" (καλῶς) – a word that carries a notion of noble and honourable behaviour.[11] The phrase οἱ καλῶς προεστῶτες (1 Tim. 5:17) also describes the man aspiring to be overseer (as noted above) in 3:4 (καλῶς προϊστάμενον) and the *diakonoi* in 3:12 (καλῶς προϊστάμενοι), who were all expected to shepherd their own households, including their children.[12] This suggests that the overseer and *diakonos* should reflect the same noble and caring shepherding skills that the older men already displayed (5:17). The phrase καλῶς προεστῶτες ("shepherding well") is commonly used to describe the character of ἐπιμελήται (supervisor/benefactor) in association inscriptions: they serve honourably (with an additional phrase not found in 1 Timothy: "with ambition"; *IG* II² 1256, *IG* II² 1262, *IG* II² 1277, *SEG* 2:9; see also Plutarch, *Moralia* 10:783C).[13]

In 1 Tim. 5:17, προΐστημι is coupled with κοπιῶντας (growing weary).[14] A similar pairing is found in 1 Thess. 5:12 (Malherbe 2008, 283): "we ask of you, brothers and sisters, to respect those who toil [κοπιῶντας] among you, and shepherd [προϊσταμένους] you in the Lord and correct you" (my translation). In both instances (1 Thess. 5:12; 1 Tim. 5:17), the author uses the image of "growing weary" to describe the great effort put into the work of leaders who care for and work on behalf of the community. The goal is to get the community to recognize the necessity of respecting and honouring these leaders.

Interestingly, the word κοπιάω (grow weary) is used elsewhere in what appears to be a popular negative stereotype of old men, which is quite different from the use in 5:17. Plutarch states, "It is not right to say, or to accept when said by others, that the only time when we [older men] do not grow weary [κοπιῶμεν] is when we are [profiting by] making money [ὡς κερδαίνοντες μόνον οὐ]" (1936, 80–1, *Moralia* 10:783F). The author of 1 Timothy condemns the love of money (ἡ φιλαργυρία) as a root of all kinds of evil (6:10),[15] and the opposing teachers appear to have this very vice, "imagining duty and devotion to be a means of [monetary] gain [νομιζόντων πορισμὸν εἶναι τὴν εὐσέβειαν]" (6:5). The word πορισμός can mean to earn a living, but 6:9–10 makes it clear that this word has a negative connotation related to obtaining material wealth for its own sake (LSJ 1940, 1450).[16] This is in line with the meaning of Plutarch's κερδαίνω (1936, 80–1, *Moralia* 10:783F), which means to gain profit or advantage (LSJ 1940, 942).

Perhaps the author of 1 Timothy has this stereotype in mind when he describes the elders, using the word in 5:17 in an ironic sense. That is, there may be some in the community who stereotype these older men as growing weary in their efforts to take advantage of others, perhaps especially because of their age. If so, the author may use this language to point out they are in fact growing weary in their honourable activity for the good of the community. The author implies they are not motivated by selfish gain, as inferred from Plutarch's saying about older men, and as indicated in the description of the opposing teachers (6:9–10). Instead, they grow weary from living up to their responsibilities (also 4:10), namely, "shepherding well [καλῶς προεστῶτες]" in their active duties "in word and teaching [ἐν λόγῳ καὶ διδασκαλίᾳ]." They speak and teach in the right way, in contrast to the opposing teachers who fight over words (λογομαχίας,

6:4; cf. 1:6, 2:8) and teach other things (ἑτεροδιδασκαλεῖ, 6:3; cf. 1:3). They are elders deserving of honour.

The word μάλιστα in 5:17 has been hotly debated (in this verse as well as in 5:4; see chapter 5). The word can mean "especially," highlighting a subgroup within a group in contrast with "false or idle" elders (e.g., Kim 2004, 367), or it can mean "namely," further defining the attributes of a group (e.g., Marshall 1999, 612). For the author of 1 Timothy, healthy teaching is performed by those who are able to manage or care for the church. An overseer, for instance, should be an apt teacher and a good manager of his household (3:2, 4; also Titus 1:9). The two functions are apparently not exclusive of one another. Since the author is explaining roles that have not yet been universally defined, it is noteworthy that he marks teaching as a more important function than financial or cultic duties, especially in light of comparable terminology used in the association inscriptions (as discussed in this section). Thus, the word μάλιστα does not denote a different set of people or highlight a subgroup of elders (implied with the translation "especially"). Rather, the translation "namely" more accurately demonstrates that the speaking ("word") and teaching functions help "define" the elders who shepherd well (Campbell 1994, 200–1, following Skeat 1979).

The elders who perform their duties "should be worthy of double honour [διπλῆς τιμῆς ἀξιούσθωσαν]." "Double honour" probably did not refer to monetary payment per se, but it may have been an honorarium (Malherbe 2008, 285), or more probably double portions of food at the communal meal (Schöllgen 1989; Marshall 1999, 615; Stewart 2014, 150).[17] Several ancient parallels corroborate this interpretation. In one association inscription, a member who becomes *quinquennalis* (chief officer of the society, a post held for five years) is freed from certain obligations and should receive a double portion of what was distributed (*CIL* 14.2112, second century). Plutarch notes various rewards for public service including festivals, food, and other material rewards (*Moralia* 10:787B). Handouts in the Roman city (of cash or food) were distributed by rank, and favoured the elite, not the poor. This was because "honor qualified, [but] rarely need" (MacMullen 1974, 118). This was also the case with the *gerousia*, associations for mature men. It was not so much a person's need or age, but their social status that qualified an older person for a kind of pension (e.g., *P.Oxy.* 3099–3102; El-Abbadi 1964, 167).[18] In the ancient Mediterranean, the wealthy simply got more rewards (Malherbe 1983, 99).[19]

By middle age, men were at the height of their power as *paterfamilias* in the household, as a father of adult children, and in the eyes of their peers. It was culturally expected that elders exhibited maturity, self-control, and wisdom and had authority over younger people (Plutarch *Moralia* 10:790E–F). Ptolemy's idealized description of old age suggests older men would labour less but fulfill a function as advisors (*Tetrabiblos* 4.10). Men of lower status would likely have worked until they were physically unable. As they grew older, men retained a certain amount of authority even as their activity declined if they were still reasonably independent, especially those who had roles of a *paterfamilias* and patron. But not all older men would have the same level of respect or authority, which is reflected in the statement of qualification of who deserved more honour in 1 Tim. 5:17 ("namely, those who toil in word and teaching").[20]

"Honour" is an important theme in 1 Tim. 5, included at the beginning of each major section (5:3, 5:17), but the two instances are quite different from one another in substance: Timothy is told to "honour" the real widow (5:3), and the elders are to be seen as "worthy of double honour" (5:17). The author may have a vague comparison of the elders and the real widows in mind here (Kim 2004, 366–7), though it is a rather weak semantic parallel. The two instances of "honour" are not the same grammatically (verb versus noun) or contextually. Real widows are depicted as women devoted to prayer (5:5) but in need of care (5:16), whereas elders are to be respected because of their positions of responsibility, assumedly because they provided care to others (through benefaction). The sense of honour for these two sets of people was also different culturally because honour was not demonstrated the same way for mothers and fathers (Aristotle, *Nicomachean Ethics* 9.2.8–9; see chapter 4). "Double honour" for elders (5:17) was meant to be similar to honour given to a father (5:1), including a material manifestation of that honour (as described above), which was part of a public display of deference.

Finally, in 5:18, the author quotes two sources to support this contention that elders are worthy of double honour. They are not directly quoted from the Hebrew Bible but derived from tradition

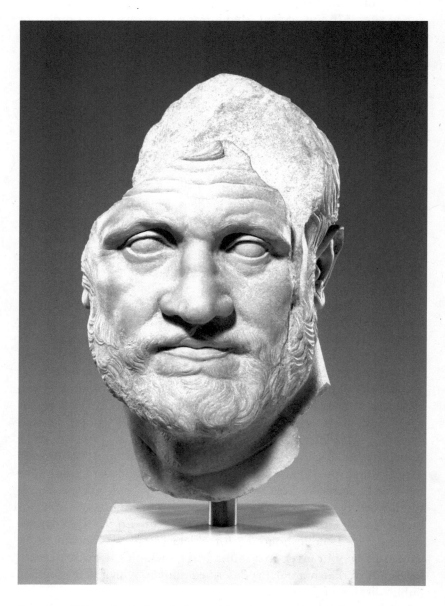

Figure 9.1 | Portrait of a bearded man (about 150 BCE), namely, an older man from Asia Minor. Digital image courtesy of Getty's Open Content Program.

familiar to Christ followers (Malherbe 2008, 287; also 1 Cor. 9:8). The appeal to tradition suggests that the author needs to convince his audience of the importance of honouring elders, especially for their efforts in correct teaching (versus the opposing teachings).

In short, the elders in 5:17–18 are deserving of honour because of their age and active and noble responsibilities in the community, caring for, teaching, and guiding in honourable and proper ways. The elders clearly have roles of responsibility, likely including patronage, but the author's point is to emphasize how elders are to be treated as older men (i.e., with "double honour"; reflecting 5:1). The roles of older men demonstrate they are deserving of honour rather than mistreatment. These are issues, as we will see, that are related to age structure.

The Honour of Age

The position of elders as presented in 1 Tim. 5:17 reflects a "traditional mode of authority" more than a "bureaucratic institution" (Elliott 2003, 6). Stewart comments, "The failure to recognize the language of patronage and honor in the phrase *kalōs proestōtes presbuteroi* [elders who shepherd well], and thus to see this as the language of office, is a fuller failure in the interpretation of the Pastoral Epistles" (2014, 164). As the model of generational stability and social change (chapter 2) suggests, honour is a crucial element of age structure in the ancient Mediterranean. Within the community, not all older men would have been patrons and able to exercise authority, for this also depended on one's social position and status. The designation of πρεσβύτεροι in 5:17 reflects a traditional age-related role of senior members of the community of social standing – men who had gained honour as they matured and cultivated their reputation (probably primarily through benefaction and its related authority; see Zamfir 2013, 44–59).

As the modern Mediterranean settings and model of the generational cycle (chapter 2) suggest, older people generally deserve honour because of their age, and those who are weaker or younger are expected to be modest and submissive. These relationships depend on reciprocity. The senior person is obligated to protect and provide for his dependants; the dependants respect the elder, demonstrated by modest behaviour in his presence. However, age does not guarantee a person's right to authority or honour (precedence) – one must be morally worthy. With age a person tends to hone his self-control (an important aspect of honour) and is increasingly responsible for others. Also, as he ages, those who once had authority over him pass away, and he gains respect from his juniors (Abu-Lughod 1986, 92).

In 1 Tim. 5:17–22, the author uses the age designation πρεσβύτεροι because he appeals to the privilege that rightfully belongs to older men who are morally worthy of respect when they fulfill their role honourably (καλῶς; 5:17; see above). In other words, by using this term, the author appeals to culturally appropriate behaviour according to age structure: these older men have responsibilities to protect and support the younger members of the community, and they deserve respect and deference from younger members (see also 1 Pet. 5:5). Cicero states that "the crowning glory of old age is influence (*auctoritas*)" (1923, 72–3, *On Old Age* 17.61), meaning that an older person's "views were accepted without too many questions" (Cokayne 2007, 210).

Plutarch states that older men were to be models for younger men, especially in the public forum: "old men [γέροντα] should engage in affairs of the State for the education and instruction of the young [νέοι] ... the statesmen, not only by speech or making suggestions from outside, but by action in administering the affairs of the community, directs the young man, whose character is moulded and formed by the old man's actions and words alike [ἔργοις ἅμα καὶ λόγοις]" (1936, 116–17, *Moralia* 10:790E–F). Although Plutarch focuses on politics among the elite, the roles of old and young men were likely similar among the non-elite. Modelling may not be the focus in 1 Tim. 5:17, but someone who deserves honour, in this case "double honour," achieves this status only through modelling in actions (shepherding and teaching) and spoken word (ἐν λόγῳ). The expectation of modelling honourable behaviour has parallels with the expectations of middle-aged women (chapter 8), though clearly they were gendered accordingly.

Any lack of respect and deference would threaten the reputation (honour) of the older men because, to outsiders, it would appear that the older men were not worthy of respect. Paul introduces the elders in 5:17–18 with a sense that those who *should* be giving honour and respect are not doing so.[21] The same sense may be implied in the directives to Timothy to placate an older man rather than jab at him in 5:1. Whereas these directives are part of the story of Paul and Timothy, the urgent tone that builds in 1 Tim. 5 suggests that a real situation compelled the author's fiction. A crisis of identity (chapter 3) formed the context in which "other" teaching (1:3; 6:3) caused problematic behaviour that called the community's reputation into question, namely *younger* men's behaviour.

"Those Who Continue to Commit Wrongs" (5:20)

Malherbe notes that although 5:19 is not connected syntactically to 5:18, the subject – conduct toward elders – has not changed. However, "the tone becomes much sharper," shifting from a third-person imperative (calling for the elders to be honoured) to two directives in second-person imperative. The first imperative calls for Timothy not to accept (μὴ παραδέχου) an unjust accusation against an elder (on the basis of established tradition; 5:19), and the second directs him to rebuke (ἔλεγχε) those who continue to commit wrongs (5:20; Malherbe 2008, 288–9).

κατὰ πρεσβυτέρου κατηγορίαν μὴ παραδέχου,
    ἐκτὸς εἰ μὴ ἐπὶ δύο ἢ τριῶν μαρτύρων.
τοὺς ἁμαρτάνοντας ἐνώπιον πάντων ἔλεγχε,
    ἵνα καὶ οἱ λοιποὶ φόβον ἔχωσιν.

An accusation against an elder – do not acknowledge [it],
    except on the basis of two or three witnesses.
Those who keep committing wrongs – rebuke [them] in front of everyone,

The *incidence* of the accusation was more problematic than the *content* of the accusation. The author reveals nothing explicit about why the elders were accused. He focuses on the fact that these accusations were not made through proper judicial procedure (with two or three witnesses). It follows that accusations were made against elders without merit and that at least some elders were slandered.[22] As we will see, the author is adamant that *these accusations* constitute improper behaviour.

The verb ἁμαρτάνω (the act of wrongdoing) occurs only here in 1 Timothy (as a participle). The usual translation is "those who continue to *sin*." Contested, thick, modern theological understandings of "sin" do not illuminate the sense of the word in 1 Timothy. A definition from the cognate ἁμαρτία, which is also used in the context (5:22, 24), is more helpful: "a departure fr[om] either human or divine standards of uprightness" (BDAG 2000, 50). For the author of 1 Timothy, the concept of ἁμαρτία (wrongdoing) is the opposite of εὐσέβεια (duty and devotion) and δικαιοσύνη (righteousness or right behaviour; 6:11).[23] That is, those who are doing wrong in 5:20 are those who deviate from how "one ought to behave in the household of God" (3:15) including the structural norm of age hierarchy (5:1).

The participle "those who keep committing wrongs [τοὺς ἁμαρτάνοντας]" does not have a clear antecedent. The typical interpretation of 5:19–20 assumes "the wrongdoers" in 5:20 are certain *elders*, contrasted with the "good" elders who preach and teach and deserve "double honour" in 5:17. In this scenario, they were to be rebuked in front of the other elders, taking a clue from the next phrase, that "the rest" were to have fear (Quinn and Wacker 2000, 464; Fee 1988, 130), perhaps to emphasize the "pedagogical value of rebuke" before the rest of the elders (Bassler 1996, 101).[24] But the text is not explicit about who "the rest" are, nor is the rebuke specified as being in front of select others, let alone other elders. In fact, it is clear that the rebuke was to be *in front of everyone* (ἐνώπιον πάντων).

When we consider the proper conduct and attitudes outlined in 1 Timothy, we meet with a rather odd contradiction if we take the wrongdoers to be elders. If Timothy is to *refrain* from jabbing at or chastising an elder (5:1), then being told to *rebuke* (ἔλεγχε) elders, especially in front of others, directly contradicts the first directive of this section: Timothy was to make peace with an elder as he would a father! In 5:20, Paul is clear in his directive that young Timothy is to *rebuke* (ἔλεγχε) the wrongdoers, that is shame or disgrace them in front of everyone for their wrongdoing.[25] In addition to being contradictory to the directives in 5:1, it was culturally inappropriate for an elder to be rebuked (or shamed or questioned), especially in such a public manner. In modern Mediterranean cultures, a junior does not discipline an older person, and submissive behaviour is inappropriate for a superior person.[26] Similarly, Plato states that violence of younger people against older people is shameful, worthy of banishment, and should be subject to punishment by the state (*Laws* 879B–C, 881D, 932A–C).

Given the literary and cultural context, therefore, "those who keep committing wrongs [τοὺς ἁμαρτάνοντας]" are not the elders who have been accused, but rather those *who are doing the accusing*.

Making the accusation is the only "wrongdoing" specified in this context, and according to cultural norms, accusing an elder (especially without the evidence of witnesses) would certainly be understood as wrong.

That the accusers are in view in 5:20 can be justified grammatically as well. The author begins with a singular accusative ("an accusation" done to a singular person "an elder"; 5:19) and ends with a different, but related plural accusative ("the wrongdoers," specifically those who have accused the elders; 5:20). A similar pattern occurs in 2:15 and 5:4 where the nominative subject of the first clause shifts from a singular person (and verb) to a nominative plural verb in the next clause (see chapters 5 and 8). In both cases, the plural actions of the unnamed group can make a significant impact on the singular person for whom the actions matter (the woman who is "saved" in 2:15 impacts the children she is responsible for, and in 5:4 the child or grandchild who has widows should be caring for them). Similarly, in 5:20, the singular person (the elder) is significantly impacted by the actions of the implied group (those doing wrong, that is, those accusing the elders).

Given the rhetoric of the letter in its cultural context, more can be said about the identity of the wrongdoers (accusers). From the perspective of an old man (Malherbe 1994), Paul would not have directed the ideal young man (Timothy) to chastise older men in public. In Greco-Roman thought, however, *younger people* commonly needed to be corrected or disciplined. Thus, Paul is asking Timothy to correct *younger men* who had overstepped their place in the age hierarchy of the "household of God." The only other commentator, to my knowledge, who has considered this possibility is Frances Young. She asserts that the wrongdoers are younger men – individuals who "challenge or refuse to accept teaching of 'seniors,'" that is, those who rightfully carry the traditions and "corporate memory" and apostolic tradition of the community. She rightly points to the age structure of Roman society: "As in any household in antiquity, age bore with it certain status and authority. It was the older people who were guardians of the corporate memory. They were not to be lightly disregarded, still less corrected. Timothy himself was to deal with his elders respectfully" (1994b, 107).[27] As far as I am aware, no subsequent commentator has taken up Young's suggestion (nor argued with it), but cultural context affirms her suggestion.

AGE HIERARCHY AMONG MEN

Across cultures, younger men may demonstrate deference while harbouring resentment toward older men because of the latter's control over roles and resources. Older men may be threatened by younger men's desire to gain autonomy, especially if they are physically or mentally declining. One of the ways such conflict is mitigated is simply through the natural progression of the life course: a man gains power as he progresses through his active adult years (Foner 1984, 31–55).

As we have seen, age hierarchy was evident among men in public life, military and voluntary associations in the ancient Mediterranean, and is suggestive of intergenerational relationships among the nonelite (chapter 4). Plutarch offers insights about relationships between generations in the public realm. Writing as an old man, Plutarch is convinced that the young and old have their respective places in the natural order. Grey hair is a crown created by nature as a symbol of honour (*Moralia* 10:789F). Different stages in the life course dictate roles; that is, "youth is meant to obey and old age to rule" (1936, 111, 10:789D; see also 10:795F). Plutarch recognizes the envy of (φθόνος) and contentiousness toward (φιλονείκας) older men. He advises that older men "should rather extinguish this by power [τῇ δυνάμει] than turn their backs and go away naked and unarmed" (1936, 100–1, 10:787F).[28] Young people are prone to envy (φθόνος) and seeking power (1936, 114, 790C; 142, 10:796A), the greatest evil (μέγιστον κακόν; 98, 10:787C) for public life. Older men have fewer passions and are less prone to envy and discord (10:788E, F). They no longer need to be ambitious because they have had a lifetime of experience, gaining wisdom, learning moderation, and earning respect. Plutarch believes age is the most certain way of being honoured (10:787D).

Plutarch's use of honour-shame language is instructive. His main thesis is that if an old man gives up public life, he is dishonourable; in his (androcentric) language, such a man is a coward, feminine, and domestic – a man lacking in masculinity, as he understands it.[29] Giving up public life makes old age an even more "shameful" time of life than it already is; continuing to be a role model and guide for the young is honourable. He contends that an old man should still seek honour because "the love of honour never grows old [φιλότιμον ἀγήρων]" (1936, 81, 10:783F; see also Thucydides 2.44.4). Plutarch makes an important distinction between the youth's ambition for power and the old man's desire for honour. Desiring honour is not a selfish or self-centred act, but a virtue. Old men desire honour for the good of society, for its stability and continuation.[30] Young men's ambition can upset the balance of society and should be controlled by the older, wiser men. Cicero notes, "the greatest states have been overthrown by the young," who are rash (*temperitas*) "and sustained and restored by the old," who (unlike the young) have prudence (*prudentia*), reason, and good judgment (1923, 28–9, *On Old Age* 6.20).

Young men were thought to be vulnerable to suggestion. As noted in chapter 3, histories of Rome depict young men as deceived into involvement with conspiracies. A strong leader would gain support from gullible young men who were "not yet in control of their bodies or their minds" (Harlow and Laurence 2002, 71). For example, Sallust described Catiline as easily deceiving young men into crime because of their foolishness and proclivity toward excess (*Catiline* 14; Cicero *Catiline* 2.4; Harlow and Laurence 2002, 70–1). Sallust also indicates that the lure of riches caused a decline in young men's virtue. "After riches began to be held in honor and led to the acquisition of glory, positions of authority, and political influence, then virtue began to lose its edge ... they had no scruples and no moderation" (2013, 39, *Catiline* 12.1–2). It is noteworthy that in 1 Timothy, the author names the pursuit of wealth for selfish gain as problematic for the opposing teachings (6:5–10); this suggests that younger men were among those who were influenced by these teachings – or perceived as such.

In the ancient Mediterranean, young men were typically considered rebellious, rash, and impressionable, thought to need direction and supervision (Eyben 1993, 14–21, 28–9, 37; Laes and Strubbe 2014, 43–8). Cicero states, "[nature] has put before the young many slippery paths, on which they can scarcely keep their footing or even enter without falling or stumbling" (1958, 459, *Pro Caelio* 41 [Gardener's numbering], 17). He also suggests that youth is a phase in which to work out rebelliousness in order to become responsible adult men. "I could bring forward the names of many men of the highest rank and distinction who were notorious, some for gross licentiousness in youth, some for utter profligacy, vast debts, extravagances, sensual excesses, but whose failings were afterwards so covered over by numerous virtues, that anyone who wished could excuse them on the plea of youth" (1958, 461, *Pro Caelio* 43 [Gardener's numbering], 18; see also Philostratus, *Lives of the Sophists* 513). He asserted that older men should instruct and train young men (*adulescentis*) for all functions and duties (*On Old Age* 8.29). Seneca notes how zealous young men (neophytes) can attain the highest ideals, if someone teaches them well (*Letters* 108.12, 23, 26–7). But Sallust, less hopeful, recounts his perception of how difficult it was as a young man to work toward virtue:

> I myself as a very young man, like a great many, was initially carried along into politics by my inclination, and there I encountered many setbacks; for instead of modesty, instead of incorruptibility, instead of merit, there flourished shamelessness, bribery and greed. And although my mind, a stranger to evil practices, rejected such conduct, nevertheless amid such rampant vices my youthful weakness was seduced and held captive by the desire for advancement [*ambitione*]; and despite having no sympathy with the evil ways of the rest, nonetheless, the craving for public office [*honoris cupido*] made me the victim of the same ill-repute and jealousy as the rest. (2013, 24–5, *Catiline* 3.3–5)

In retrospect, as an older man, Sallust blames his own poor behaviour as a young man on an innate and immature sense of ambition and passion for public honour.

But as Parkin has pointed out, it was "not just a man's world, it was a young man's world" (2003, 50). Young men had a kind of power that could upset the norms of age hierarchy: physical strength, youthful passion, and ambition. Harlow surmises that the older generation of Roman male elite were threatened by the younger generation, who could push them out of positions of power (2007, 198; Eyben 1993, 27; Reinhold 1970; cf. Plutarch, *Moralia* 10:787F, above).

However, we might question just how rebellious and disobedient young men actually were, since these views were perpetrated by older men.[31] What we see in these Roman sources are ideological notions of young men in a world ruled (largely) by older men, in families, in politics, and in civic society. While some younger men were undoubtedly irrational and erratic, such stereotypes are pervasive in older men's depiction of them. They reflected some level of anxiety among older men about their potentially precarious position in society and helped them to retain power over resources and positions of authority (Cokayne 2007, 210).³² Plutarch notes that old men were hated for squelching opportunities for young men, holding onto their power too tightly. When this happened, old men's "love of precedence and of office is held in no less disrepute than is other old men's love of wealth and pleasure" (1936, 131, *Moralia* 10:793E).

It was in the interest of older men to perpetuate this hierarchical economic and social structure for the sake of stability. But also older men relied on younger men, as students and apprentices, in war, in labour, in political life (and probably in voluntary associations), to affirm their influence and offer their esteem, and to inherit their roles when they were gone.³³

First Timothy is written from the perspective of an older man. Paul is aware that Timothy's youth might undermine his authority (4:12), but also praises Timothy for his exemplary triumph over youthful passions and temptations through his training (4:7) and calling (1:18, 4:14, 6:12). A reading that is sensitive to cultural concepts of age hierarchy among men in the Mediterranean supports a scenario behind 1 Tim. 5:17–22 that involves younger men vying for power, accusing the elders as a way to undermine them. It suggests that the author perceived younger men as seeking gain, resulting in their lack of respect for traditional social roles, including deference to older men. Timothy himself functions in the fiction of the letter as the exact opposite, an exemplary younger man who is a model to others (4:12; chapter 3; see also Pao 2014, 752).

Interestingly, the characteristics of the overseer and *diakonoi* include a component of age that assumes a man who is eligible for the position has matured into a responsible adult: he should be married, a father, and the head of a household (3:4–6, 12; see also Zamfir 2013, 44–5). If younger men were being influenced by the opposing teachers, they may have been refusing to marry (4:3). The stipulations for male leadership ensured men were of a certain age to attain those positions. Though no age is specified, marriage itself denoted an expectation of a certain level of maturity (3:2, 12). For a non-elite man, a first marriage (at age twenty-five or thirty) probably denoted a level of maturity and responsibility beyond the rashness of youth. The fact that men must fulfill this requirement suggests that some men vying for leadership may not yet have been in this stage of life. In addition, they would need to be old enough to have children who obey (3:4, 12) and thus old enough to bring honour (or shame) to the household. An aspiring overseer would need enough experience in the community that others would not see him as a neophyte (3:6) and enough life experience (perhaps as a patron) to have a good reputation with outsiders (3:7). The asceticism of the opponents would threaten this reflection of household structure in the community but also the age structure of the community since without marriage, there would be no future generations.

A consideration of age structure and common rhetoric of older men about younger men points toward the wrongdoers in 1 Tim. 5:19–20 as younger men whom the author believes were behaving badly, accusing and disrespecting their elders. Younger men were upsetting the proper order of the "household of God" (3:16), so that the author is adamant they are in need of correction that deters others from doing the same. The rebuke in 1 Tim. 5:19 appears to be a form of social sanction (see chapter 5) meant to deter others ("the rest [οἱ λοιποί]"), namely, other younger men. The directive for Timothy not to "acknowledge an accusation against an elder" (5:19) would also have helped to discourage unfounded accusations. Timothy himself exemplifies the traits of a *mature* young man, in contrast to the problematic rash young people implied in these verses.

Younger Men in 1 Tim. 5:17–22 and 1 Clement

A similar situation is evident in *1 Clement*, which provides a contemporary context for the set of circumstances in 1 Tim. 5:17–25. Some elders[34] had been deposed by what appears to be a faction of younger people (44.5–6; 47.6; 54.2; 57.1; also 2.3; 3.3; 21.6).[35] In Clement's view, the latter have caused a schism and need to repent of their wrongdoing. Why the schism formed is not clear, but Clement wants to restore proper order (Young 1994a, 106). Though there is modern debate about whether or not the references to age in *1 Clement* are the core issue (e.g., Maier 1991, 87–94; Bowe 1988, 65), age is almost certainly an important element (Horrell 1996, 264n134).[36] L.L. Welborn's (2018) recent monograph contributes a detailed and convincing argument that the conflict does have a basis in age. On two occasions, Clement outlines lists of what proper order means (*AF* 2003, 1:36, 74–7, 1.3 and 21.6–8,; also 1:109, 41.1,): (1) respecting[37] and submitting to their leaders, (2) honouring elders (πρεσβύτεροι), (3) instructing or disciplining young people (νέος) to think moderate and respectful thoughts and to fear God, (4) directing women or wives to be pure, dutiful, respectful, and submissive, and in *1 Clem.* 21.8 (AF 2003, 1:76-7), to train children (τέκνα) in humility, love, and discipline.[38] The elders here are most certainly "older people" (which, as argued above, does not discount some authoritative responsibilities, and these need not be exclusive categories). The letter begins with defining those who are causing trouble as "reckless and headstrong [προπετῆ καὶ αὐδάδη]" (AF 2003, 1:34–5, 1.1) – characteristics that older elite men tended to associate with rebellious young men (Welborn 2018, 21–48).

The situation of *1 Clement* is similar to that of 1 Timothy. Harry O. Maier points out that at this stage of community building some people question why things are the way they are, and others (like Clement) legitimate the order that is already in place. As the first generation of the church passed away, appealing to "order" explained, justified, and made explicit the importance of using tradition to codify memory (1991, 109–21).

The author of *1 Clement* argues that not honouring the elders and the order of the community, which was set up by God, is "exceedingly shameful" (AF 2003, 1:121, 47.6) and wrong behaviour (ἁμαρτία, 1:140, 59.2; compare 1 Tim. 5:20). "Thus you who laid the foundation of the faction should be subject to the [elders] and accept the discipline that leads to repentance, falling prostrate on your heart. Learn to be submissive; lay aside the arrogant and haughty insolence of your tongue. For it is better for you to be considered insignificant but reputable [μικροὺς καὶ ἐλλογίμους] in the flock of Christ than to appear prominent [ὑπεροχή] while sundered from his hope" (1:136–7, 57.1-2). This depiction is very similar to Roman descriptions of rebellious youth who were arrogant and overly ambitious, wanting to gain power before it was their time in the life course to do so (Welborn 2018, 21–48, 68–82).

Furthermore, the perpetrators are said to need discipline (*1 Clem.* 56.2-5, 16; 57.1; AF 2003, 134–7). The primary word for discipline in this context is παιδεύω, but Clement also employs a quotation from Proverbs (1:23–33, Greek Septuagint), which uses ἔλεγχω – the same word used on 1 Tim. 5:20 to rebuke the wrongdoers. For Clement, παιδεύω and ἔλεγχω appear to be approximately synonymous (see also Rev. 3:19), used for disciplining the young so that they will attain righteousness. There are important parallels between

Clement's exhortation to discipline the young, factious men rebelling against their elders in Corinth and Paul's exhortation to Timothy to rebuke the wrongdoers in front of everyone as a form of discipline (1 Tim. 5:20). For Clement, discipline of the young leads to φόβος or fear of God (*1 Clem.* 21.6, AF 2003, 74) – the same phrase used to instill fear for "the rest" who are to witness the rebuke of the accusers in 1 Tim. 5:20, assumedly the fear of God. Philo mentions fear in correlation with respect and affection for parents (*Special Laws* 2.239).

Even though the semantic range for the behaviour of younger men is broader and more explicit in *1 Clement* than in 1 Timothy, the scenario in *1 Clement* demonstrates a parallel and near contemporary situation of younger men dishonouring some older men and disrupting the proper order of the community.

THE SERIOUSNESS OF THE WRONGDOING

In chapter 8, I argue that in 1 Tim. 5:14, Paul's *suggestion* rather than a command in 5:14 ("desiring [βούλομαι] young women to marry, bear children, and manage a household") was an indication that it was the authoritative domain of middle-aged women to direct younger women. By contrast, in 5:20 the author gives a direct and severe order in the form of an imperative: rebuke (ἔλεγχε) the wrongdoers in front of everyone. But this is not just a simple rebuke: this is a matter of utmost importance. The next verse builds the intensity of Timothy's role in solving this problem in the community. In 5:21, Paul uses the first-person indicative with a strong directive to Timothy: "I warn [διαμαρτύρομαι] [you] before God and Christ Jesus and the elect angels, so that you might guard these things." The verb διαμαρτύρομαι emphasizes the "extraordinary importance" of the matter (BDAG 2000, 233), especially by invoking the presence of the divine court. There is only one other time the author uses the first-person indicative with a directive: in 6:13–14 Paul says to Timothy, "I adjure [παραγγέλλω] you to keep the commandment."[39] Here again he calls upon the witness of the divine realm.[40]

Timothy is warned so that he might "guard these things [ταῦτα φυλάξῃς]"; this verb is used only one other time in this letter – when Paul gives his final directive to Timothy (an imperative), to "guard the deposit [τὴν παραθήκην φύλαξον]" with which he has been entrusted (6:20) for the good of the community and its reputation.

"These things" that Timothy is to guard in 5:21 appear to be the directives in 5:19 and 5:20, namely, rejecting unfounded accusations and rebuking those who continue to commit wrongs, but maybe more broadly the social norms of respect for hierarchy, including respect for elders.

The great seriousness of the wrongdoing and the need for correction continue to be elucidated in the next set of phrases. They clearly follow the rhetoric and logic of a *young* Timothy asked to shoulder this responsibility. Paul directs Timothy to proceed "without discrimination, doing nothing on the basis of [your] inclination" (5:21). If we follow the fictional layer of the letter, a young Timothy might be tempted or inclined to favour his peers, but given the gravity of the situation, he must operate without favouritism toward his peers, adhering to the proper code of behaviour in the "household of God" (3:15). This code is reflected in the model of generational stability and social change: younger men rebelling against their elders in a way that was visible to outsiders was unacceptable. The directive to rebuke the younger men would be seen as both constructive and necessary to maintain the structure of honour in the community.

The next sentence portrays two further concerns in the fiction of the letter: appointing leaders and being tempted to join the wrongdoers. Both concerns relate to age structure. Paul commands: "Do not place hands on anyone hastily [χεῖρας ταχέως μηδενὶ ἐπιτίθει]" (5:22). He appears to be concerned that candidates for positions of responsibility in the community should not be affirmed too quickly. It is worth pointing out that this text makes little sense if it were referring to the *appointing* of elders, for they clearly already have responsibilities (5:17–18).[41] In fact, Timothy himself has had a council of elders (πρεσβυτερίος) lay hands on *him* (ἐπιθέσεως τῶν χειρῶν) to bestow a gift (χάρισμα) on him through prophecy (4:14; compare 1:18).[42] The gift is related to his responsibilities in the community. Paul gives Timothy a similar authority to lay hands (5:22), that is, to bestow a role in the community, on others. This directive is reminiscent of the third-person imperative directed at those who would choose suitable men to be *diakonoi* (3:10): let them first be put to the test (δοκιμαζέσθωσαν) and only approved if they are found to be blameless (ἀνέγκλητοι; similar to Titus 1:7–9). Both 3:10 and 5:22 suggest a process of making sure people prove their worth before they are given special responsibilities in the community.[43] Given the descriptions of overseer and *diakonoi* (1 Tim. 3:1–10, 12–13), it may be one or both of these roles that are in mind here, though it is more likely *diakonoi*, who are mentioned in the plural rather than singular (there is only one overseer in 3:1).[44] Part of proving their worth is proper behaviour, including submitting to one's elders and displaying proper behaviour toward elders. Those who continue in wrongdoing by accusing their elders are not abiding by the structure of the age hierarchy, and thus are not appropriate candidates for leadership positions, however ready they may think they are. Indeed, one of the overall concerns in 1 Timothy is to bestow roles of responsibility on those who are worthy and who follow the healthy teaching.[45]

Paul continues in 5:22: "nor join in the wrongdoings that belong to others; keep yourself pure [ἁγνὸν]." The warning hearkens back to the wrongdoers (τοὺς ἁμαρτάνοντας) in 5:20. As a young man himself, the fictive Timothy is directed not to behave like the young men who are wrongdoers, but to continue his proper respect for his elders. The word ἁγνὸν (pure) has echoes of 4:12, in which Paul affirms that despite his youth, Timothy is "to be a model for those who are faithful in word [speech], in conduct, in love, in faith and in purity [ἐν ἁγνείᾳ]" and 5:2, where Timothy is told to act with all purity (ἐν πάσῃ ἁγνείᾳ). The phrase in 5:2 follows his relationship toward younger women, but given the context here, may actually relate to all the relationships listed, including those toward older men and other younger men – relationships that are under scrutiny in 5:17–22.

The very odd phrase in 5:23 clearly follows the fiction of the story as a direction to Timothy: "no longer drink water, but use a little wine because of your stomach and your frequent illnesses." Christopher R. Hutson convincingly argues that this directive has to do with Timothy's purity (5:22) and his age (4:12). Timothy's "behavior with regard to wine contributes to his credibility" as a young man (2013, 83). Drinking wine in moderation was recommended by physicians to balance the body's humours for a young man (83–9), and moderation (including that of drinking wine) was becoming of a teacher and philosopher, especially a young student whose practices would be modelled to others and honed over time (89–91; see Epictetus, *Discourses* 3.13). In the context of Timothy's conduct within the community, this demonstration of purity would model moderation to other younger men.[46]

The last two verses of this section (1 Tim. 5:24–25) also emphasize the seriousness of the situation with a general statement about the visibility of acts of wrongdoing (ἁμαρτίαι) as well as the visibility of noble works (τὰ ἔργα τὰ καλὰ; compare 3:1, 5:10, 6:18). The visible nature of the wrongdoings (5:24–25) strongly suggests that the author was concerned for the community's reputation in the larger society. As we have seen, he demonstrates this concern elsewhere in the letter (2:2, 3:7, 5:14; also 6:1). The rebuke (5:20) was an in-group activity, not meant to be visible to outsiders. As in the model of generational stability and social change (chapter 2), a person can chastise kin for shortcomings in private. However, a person would never allow kin to be accused in public, as illustrated by a proverb among the Sarakatsani: "A relation can speak to his kinsman but he cannot listen to something about him" (Campbell 1965, 112). Thus, the social sanction in 5:20, when Timothy is told to rebuke the wrongdoers in front of the whole community, is meant to be instructive and preventative. Everyone would then be aware of the severity and implications of the wrongdoing.

However, young men defying their elders was a breach of proper behaviour that could be visible beyond the group, prompting potential judgment from outsiders. In the modern Mediterranean, a man is provoked only by extreme insults; the insults themselves are dishonourable for those who hurl them (Campbell 1964, 286). Hurling accusations against the elders (5:19) in public would be seen as particularly shameful if outsiders viewed this. The final statement on the visibility of wrongdoing and noble works (5:24–25) may hint that if outsiders could see what was going on, a harsher social sanction could be enforced. Such an act is probably in view in 1 Tim. 1:20 where the author has Paul say he has handed Hymenaeus and Alexander "over to Satan," an act of ostracism, perhaps with a goal of repentance, but also as a demonstration of maintaining the honour of the group. In the modern Mediterranean, if a kinsman acts very badly, a person will be forced to abandon him, perhaps also condemn him, so that he puts social distance between them. This demonstrates that he supports community values and avoids shaming himself. The potential loss of moral and practical support of kin upholds the norms and values of the community and is an even more powerful form of social sanction (Campbell 1964, 113).

CONCLUSION

In a modern Turkish village, "age is not a criterion for any formal group, but it carries respect and authority" (Stirling 1965, 27). This seems to have been true for the author of 1 Timothy. Age was an important component of social relationships in the ancient Mediterranean, especially honouring elders. The context of 1 Tim. 5:17 suggests that the "elder" was primarily an age designation rather than a role, and almost certainly not yet an office. He describes elders in laudable language: they are fulfilling their honourable duty, especially those who preside, speak, and teach.

The ambiguous term in 1 Tim. 5:19 "those who keep doing wrong" refers to *the accusers* rather than elders. The author has in mind younger men wrongly accusing some of their elders. This action was understood as a grievous wrongdoing. Older men stood to lose respect with such accusations; accusations in the public realm would damage the community's reputation. Younger men demonstrated dishonourable behaviour by accusing their elders and not acting with modesty around them. As an older man, Paul tells Timothy to rebuke (shame) the younger men for their action, and not get swept up in their wayward ways himself. In the view of the author of 1 Timothy, this would encourage honour where it was due, and proper order would be restored. With close parallels to the situation in *1 Clement*, the author reflects urgent anxiety over intergenerational conflict and its problems for the community. Probably an older man himself, the author's anxiety suggests that the rebellion of young men in Paul's fictive letter reflected a similar situation among the members of the real audience, at least as it was perceived by the author in his own time and experience.

10

Intergenerational Conflict in 1 Timothy: The Big Picture

This study illustrates how a culturally informed understanding of age structure illuminates two layers of 1 Timothy: the explicit, rhetorical layer of the fictional directives of an older Paul to a younger Timothy, and an often implicit, real layer of the author's proposed solutions to what he perceives as the problems in his late first-century community. The author hopes to encourage conventional, age-related behaviour in order to maintain (or recover) the community's reputation, both reflecting and promoting generational stability amid social change (chapter 2).

Having worked through the details of 1 Timothy (particularly 1 Tim. 5), I now consider the "big picture" of 1 Timothy, highlighting the problem of intergenerational conflict in the author's community that relates to reputation. In fact, hints of intergenerational conflict are woven through much of the letter, illustrating why the author envisions his community as a "household of God" (3:15) – a community composed of different age groups functioning like a household, with conflict, cooperation, roles, and obligations to one another.

INTERGENERATIONAL CONFLICT IN 1 TIMOTHY 5: A REVIEW OF THE ARGUMENT

In the form of a letter, the author of 1 Timothy creates one side of a dialogue between two well-known characters, Paul and Timothy, who are associated with the founding of the community. The letter represents and embodies Paul's familiar voice of authority for this late first-century audience in Asia Minor. In the rhetoric of the letter, an older Paul directs his younger protégé, Timothy (1:2, 4:12; Malherbe 1994; Huizenga 2013, 322; Welborn 2018, 95), to deal with issues of significant concern around influential teachers (1:3, 6:3) who are steering members of the community away from what he deems the healthy teaching (1:10, 6:3). The author describes and prescribes "proper behaviour" that reflects his own expectations of relationships within the "household of God" (3:15). Even though they are couched in the rhetoric of Paul's directions to Timothy, these directives address the problems within the author's real, late-first-century community. His letter serves to correct certain behaviours that he identifies as being promoted by opposing teachers in a time of social change, namely, a crisis of identity as living witnesses of the founding of the community were passing into memory.

In chapter 3, I suggested that at the time 1 Timothy was written (at the end of the first century CE), its original members were aging and dying, and the community was struggling to define itself in light of losing these connections to their founders. The choice of Paul and Timothy as characters in the letter hearkened back to those familiar and trustworthy names associated with the community's inception. To combat the "other" teachings that arose in this time of change the author of 1 Timothy opted for a socially conservative approach. He advocated traditional values of the household, including values that structured gender and age behaviour in traditional ways, in order to "solve" what he saw as the problems arising from the opposing teachings.

In 1 Tim. 5, the author advocates and condemns behaviours related to specific age groups. Proper and honourable behaviour in the ancient Mediterranean dictated that younger people offered deference to their elders. They were expected to wait their turn to become people of influence in the community as they themselves aged. Proper and honourable behaviour also dictated that older people took up their responsibilities toward their juniors. This reciprocity between older and younger was the cultural norm in the ancient Mediterranean, a norm that has persisted in modern, traditional Mediterranean cultures. The issues addressed in 1 Tim. 5 suggest these norms were being contravened, thus compromising the reputation of the real community.

Framework of Age Structure (1 Tim. 5:1–2)

With these first two verses, the author frames this section as one that has to do with age. Having just outlined specifics of the opponents' teachings that forbid marriage and eating certain foods (4:1–3), followed by a series of exhortations for the young Timothy (4:12) to model and direct others toward proper behaviour (4:11–16), the author turns explicitly to issues of age-related roles in 1 Tim. 5:1–2. In the rhetoric of Paul's directions, he continues his exhortation toward Timothy: he is not to jab at an older man, but he is to make peace with him as if he were his father (5:1). Likewise, older women should be treated like mothers, younger men like brothers, and younger women like sisters, thus emphasizing the typical familial relationships found within the household (5:2). The categories of "older" and "younger" are fluid (Barclay 2007, 227–32), reflecting the way that age structure is characterized in other ancient documents. On the one hand, these were idealized relationships of concord, with younger people deferring to their elders and older people mentoring and supporting younger people. On the other hand, they may well have reflected a common urban experience in the ancient Mediterranean world of fictive kin, filling positions of household relationships due to untimely deaths of biological kin. The relationships provide a direct sketch of how the author conceived of the "household of God" (3:15), hinting at the tensions related to widows and elders that the author is about to address.

Reining in the Wild Widows (1 Tim. 5:3–16)

The section on widows (5:3–16) has been notoriously difficult to interpret. It is critical to begin with the understanding that women had crucial roles to play in the "household of God," for women embodied the honour of the community. Women were typically "socially invisible" (Osiek and MacDonald 2006, 3–4). Women who were "noticed" usually caused significant consternation, since it was shameful behaviour that was generally conspicuous (e.g., 1 Tim. 2:9–12). Nonetheless, on occasion, exemplary women were honoured publicly, often highlighting their admirable reputation (e.g., Phoebe in Rom. 16:1–2; Metradora, see chapter 6).

The author begins with an exhortation to "honour widows who are real widows" (5:3), defining them as widows who are alone (5:5), without husband, children, or others to care for them. "Honour" would dictate that Timothy (in the rhetoric of the letter) would care for real widows, treating them as if they were mothers (5:2). Cultural context would suggest this means providing materially for them. Indeed, the community (ἡ ἐκκλησία) – assumedly revealing the real audience in this phrase – appears to be already caring for their material needs (5:16). By definition, these are older widows, since they are no longer in their childbearing years (unlike the younger widows; 5:14) and thus (apparently) have no reason to be remarried.

Although the care of widows is the focus of 1 Tim. 5:3–16, and this section begins and ends with care for "real widows," the real problem is not with real widows. The specific directive that the community should care for the real widows (5:16) suggests there are issues with resources, though it is more likely that there is a problem with the *distribution* of resources rather than a shortage (implied in 6:17–19).[1]

In fact, the most pressing issues are relational, not financial, and they are associated with two different groups of widows – older widows with families, and younger widows. In both cases, the problems have to do with reputation and expectations for particular stages of the life course. The author proposes that both problems should be solved by those who are tasked, according to social norms, with caring for widows.

The first problem is with a group of widows set in contrast to the real widows: older widows who are *not* alone. They are widows who are beyond their childbearing years (otherwise they would remarry; 5:14) and, unlike the real widows (5:5), they *do* have kin, namely, children and grandchildren (5:4). These widows should receive care from their family members as proper cultural behaviour would dictate (εὐσεβέω), ideally out of loyalty and filial piety. There is a suggestion here of neglect, especially if these children and grandchildren are in mind when the author says anyone who does not care for their own is worse than an unbeliever (5:8). On the other hand, the notion of duty and devotion (εὐσεβέω, εὐσέβεια) – a strong ethos in 1 Timothy (2:2; 3:16; 4:7, 8; 6:3, 5, 6, 11; cf. 1:9) – should dictate the responsibility that children and grandchildren have toward their mothers and grandmothers. Neglecting this tangible manifestation of duty and devotion, if noticed by outsiders, would compromise not just their own reputation, but that of the community as well. Not taking care of one's own was abhorrent behaviour, for in doing so, such a person was worse than someone with no faith (5:8).

The second problem also has to do with care of widows, but it appears to be such a serious issue that it constitutes the focus of this section. A full five verses deal directly with the problem of younger widows, who are still capable of having children (5:14). The flow of the rhetoric suggests that the climactic sixth verse points to the solution to the problem (5:16). This solution, I would suggest, rests with a woman – or more accurately a set of women – who are responsible to make things right: women in their forties or fifties, labelled as the "believing/faithful woman who has widows" (5:16). As middle-aged women, they were at the height of their social power – and responsibility. Clues in 5:6–16 suggest that they were not fulfilling this duty, especially toward the younger widows. The *believing* women with responsibilities for *younger* women were by definition *older* women, the age of mothers of adult children, at the most powerful time of their lives. They were supposed to model proper behaviour and take care of the younger widows by mentoring them and getting them remarried, including helping with the customary dowry.

Such women were benefactors, and thus had some wealth to help provide for their young mentees. By positing that middle-aged women with some wealth are at the root of the problem in 5:3–16, we can make better sense of the text than conventional interpretations have. We catch a glimpse of her (and her wealth) in 5:6 as a woman who lives luxuriously, namely, for herself, rather than fulfilling her responsibilities. Her lack of concern for others is like being dead since she is not contributing to the community, contrasting with the real widow, who has nothing but is still faithful to God and contributes to others with her prayers (5:5). The phrasing for the luxurious woman of 5:6 suggests she is a woman with some wealth and influence, and we also see a glimpse of her earlier in the letter. The author exhorts women to be clothed with good works rather than with adornments that demonstrate wealth (2:9). They are told they should be silent, suggesting they had some influence the author is trying to channel (2:11–12).[2] This is our first glimpse of the women who are supposed to be modelling proper behaviour and using their wealth and influence for the sake of the community, especially helping younger widows. Clearly, the author has not given up on this middle-aged woman because he calls her a "faithful woman" (5:16), though this may also be a way to shame her into her responsibilities (and to reclaim "the faith" from the opposing teachers).

In 5:7, Timothy is exhorted to "command" these things (especially the things that follow) so that these women (and perhaps also those not taking care of their widowed mothers and grandmothers) will be "above reproach [ἀνεπίλημπτος]" (5:7). Like those who need to care for their aging mothers and grandmothers (5:4), she needs to provide for her own, especially those in her household (5:8).[3] To do anything less is a denial of the faith and is worse than someone who is not faithful (5:8). If she is truly "faithful" (5:16), she will step up to her responsibilities.

Typical interpretations of the widow in 5:9–10 as a "real widow" posit a sudden jump back to the topic of 5:5. Instead, it makes more sense of the flow of the text if the author is actually pushing forward, now comparing the middle-aged woman to an ideal widow, who is (in probably a figurative sense) to be honoured by being put on a list, like a list of voluntary association members whose names were chiseled on stone, for all to see and revere. This ideal sixty+ woman has the good fortune of having been married to only one man (*univira*) and having the kind of ideal reputation for good works for which the middle-aged woman should be striving. This sixty+ widow is defined by her past deeds, which demonstrate how she used her wealth and role for others, bringing up children, showing hospitality, washing the feet of the saints, assisting those in trouble, and devoting herself to every noble work (5:10). Her past good works (5:10) include all the duties that middle-aged women of means should aspire to. That is, she is the model that middle-aged female patrons should emulate, responsibly supporting others under their care. Neglect of these duties makes them worse than an unbeliever (5:8) and causes younger widows' behaviour to damage the community's reputation (5:14b).

The author then turns back to his rhetoric between Paul and Timothy with a call for Timothy to take action with respect to the younger widows (5:11). The usual translation of the second-person imperative (παραιτοῦ) suggests Paul is telling Timothy to "deny" the younger widows, assuming from the context that they are to be denied the privilege of being put on the list implied in 5:9. This usual translation contrasts younger widows with sixty+ widows (often interpreted as "real widows," even though this is not the phrase used in 5:9). Thus, most translations suggest Timothy should prevent younger widows either from receiving aid (meant for real widows) or from procuring a leadership position. However, there is little grammatical reason to tie the younger widows to the list in 5:9. Instead, using a lens of age structure, it is more likely that Paul tells Timothy that he needs to *intercede for* (παραιτοῦ) the younger widows because they are the vulnerable group most affected by the middle-aged women's lack of care for others. The clearer contrast in the passage is between the imperatives for Timothy to "honour" real widows (5:3) and "intercede for" younger widows (5:11).

The intercession is necessary because younger widows want to remarry (5:11) and are not readily able to do so without familial aid (or someone acting as kin). Earlier in the letter, the author characterizes the opposing teachers as forbidding marriage (4:3). I posit that the middle-aged women are influenced by this teaching, and thus they do not want to fulfill their duty to find new husbands for young widows. The condemnation the younger widows receive (5:12) is not from outsiders, but from the opponents and the middle-aged women (their female mentors) influenced by them. The opponents and middle-aged women judge the younger widows for their desire to remarry by accusing them of setting aside their "first faith" (5:12). Since the younger widows want to marry – as was expected and anticipated for women of childbearing age – this lack of involvement from their mentors caused what was deemed by the author to be erratic and inappropriate behaviour (5:13). They were not kept busy with the usual tasks of a young married woman but instead were noticed going about others' households on their own (perhaps to find their own husbands). Regardless of why they were "gadding about" (NRSV), their behaviour was at risk of being ridiculed by outsiders and shaming the whole group (5:14). The author goes so far as to say that some have gone astray, following after Satan (5:15). Rather than commanding these women to behave (with rhetorically directive language, like "I permit no woman to teach," 2:9), he uses the softer verb βούλομαι (I want) these younger women married, bearing children, and managing a household. In other words, he wants to see them in their "proper place," behaving in the way they ought, rather than risking the reputation of the community (5:14). However, getting the young women married – matchmaking, dowry, and all – was the responsibility of the "believing woman," whom he turns to directly in 5:16. Like the exemplary sixty+ widow (5:10), she *should* be using her wealth and influence to provide and care for the younger women to whom she was obligated, so that the assembly could provide and care for the real widows, who had no one else to care for them. A "faithful woman" (5:16) should fulfill the responsibilities that were hers as a middle-aged, influential woman.

It is no wonder that the author plays with the idea of "faith/faithfulness" through this section (5:8, 12, 16), and throughout the letter. If one does not care for those for whom one is responsible, it is tantamount to denying the faith (5:8). The opponents are using the language of faith/faithfulness for their own ends, judging the younger widows (5:12) and dictating what they understood to be truly faithful (assumedly indicated in part in 4:3). But the author still holds out hope that the middle-aged women who appear to be influenced by the unhealthy teachings can come back to the healthy teaching and thus truly be "faithful" women – women who fulfill their duties in the "household of God" (3:15) with loyalty and devotion. That is, his phrasing calls them back to step up to their responsibilities to rein in the (perceived) wild younger widows, and thus help the community's reputation.

In short, proper behaviour in the "household of God" (3:15) included caring for one's widowed mothers and grandmothers, as the cultural norm of filial piety dictated (5:4). Widows without family, whose liminal status may have made them targets for outsiders' criticism, were expected to be pious and unseen (5:5). Younger widows should be married again if they were young enough to bear children (5:14). The exemplary sixty+ widow had lived a life that should be a model for older (especially middle-aged) women in the community (5:9–10). Middle-aged women, indicated explicitly in the phrase "a faithful/believing woman" (5:16), were to ensure that their own behaviour and that of younger women was kept in check: modest, unnoticed, and, in the case of younger widows, in another marriage, as proper recognition of honourable behaviour and of their role in the household would dictate.

Elders and Age-Appropriate Behaviour

Having addressed the problems with widows, the author turns rather abruptly to elders (5:17–23). The thread of continuity here is a concern for age-related issues connected to the community's reputation. In 5:17, Paul exhorts Timothy to deem elders worthy of double honour (likely a tangible reward, like a double portion of food). This illustrates one important way that Timothy as a young man is to model being conciliatory toward older men (5:1). Like sixty+

widows (5:9–10) who should be honoured for their ideal behaviour, the elders who have distinguished themselves as worthy of such honour have done so through their service to the community (5:17–18).

In the traditional interpretation of 5:19–23, the elders are at fault and to be rebuked, but the cultural context makes this interpretation untenable. Elders were to be respected, not scolded (5:1) or rebuked in front of others; in fact, such actions toward elders would be considered deeply shameful. A culturally sensitive reading of 5:19–20 suggests that the poor behaviour of *young men* is in view. Timothy is not to "accept as correct an accusation against an elder, except on the basis of two or three witnesses. In front of everyone, rebuke those who keep committing wrongs, in order that the rest also might have fear" (5:19–20). "Those who keep committing wrongs" in 1 Tim. 5:20 are not the elders or a general audience, but rather those who *accuse* the elders (also Young 1994b, 107). The content of the accusation is apparently unimportant; rather, the focus is on the fact that these accusations are underhanded, unlike legitimate complaints that included corroboration by witnesses (5:19). The strong directives in 5:19–22 (along with similar language in *1 Clement*) imply that younger men were rebelling publicly against older men in the community. This may be as a result of influence from the opposing teachings, giving younger men hopes of gaining power in the community before they were mature and not yet identified with traditional constructs of family responsibility (such as getting married, having children, and leading a household of their own). Returning to the rhetoric of the letter, we can say that at least this was how it looked from the perspective of an older man.

Thus, the author confronts a problem of younger men falsely accusing older men in the community, dishonouring their elders, displaying irreverent behaviour, and disrupting the order of the community. Wrongful accusations against an elder was a violation of what constituted proper behaviour – behaviour that could cause problems with the reputation of the group if outsiders were to observe it. Since the deleterious effects of such behaviour affected reputation in a public way, the solution needed to be a deterrent for all of the group to witness. The younger men should be rebuked before the whole community, so that "the rest" of the younger men "might also have fear" (5:20) and thus turn from this deleterious behaviour (5:20).

This action of rebuke is particularly serious because the author warns that God, Christ, and the angels were bearing witness (5:21). While it may be tempting for Timothy, as a younger man himself, to overlook such actions of his peers (5:21), whom he is to treat like brothers (5:2), he is told not to share in their wrongdoings (5:22). He is to remain pure (5:22; also 4:12 and 5:2), which also may be in view with the strange comment about drinking wine for his stomach (5:23; Hutson 2013, 83–91). And given his position of authority as a young man following Paul's authoritative instructions, Timothy is not to lay hands on any younger men for a role of responsibility within the assembly without great care and thought (5:22). Leadership qualifications in the letter (3:1–10, 12) suggest that any man aspiring to leadership should be of a certain age with a demonstrated level of maturity (head of household, husband of one wife, submissive children, not a new convert, etc.).

In short, elders should be honoured, especially those with responsibilities in the assembly. Younger men who disrespect their elders with false accusations should be rebuked in front of the community. Timothy as a young man himself is to act on Paul's authority, condemning this behaviour and not participating in it, and continuing his exemplary behaviour. Perhaps like other older men who wrote about the younger generation around the first century, the author felt the threat of the potential power of younger men in a time of social crisis (chapter 3). By idealizing Timothy, the author is contrasting young men in his real community whom he perceived as disrespectful and insolent, reflecting the similar sentiments about young men in other Roman writings. His rhetoric served to promote his own conservative view of the age structure.

Summary

My interpretation of 1 Tim. 5 suggests that those who taught "other" things (1:3, 6:3) were especially influential among some older (middle-aged) women and some younger men,[4] generating a grave concern for the reputation of the community. The author's opponents forbade marriage (4:3), which would have upset family structures, perhaps by encouraging young women (5:11–15) and men (3:2, 12) not to marry or remarry. In 5:3–16, *the middle-aged women* (glimpsed in 2:9–10 and 5:6 and named the "believing woman" in 5:16) should be guiding and caring for the younger women, whose social visibility (5:13) was a major problem. This would be solved, in the view of the author, by finding them new husbands instead of encouraging asceticism (4:3). In 5:17–23, *younger men* were wrongly accusing their elders (5:19–20), hoping to jump the queue and gain power and influence without waiting until age had proved them worthy. The author asks Timothy to rebuke the younger men for their irreverent behaviour toward their elders (5:20). The opposing teachings also may have encouraged young men to be overly ambitious, desiring positions of power before their age, marital status, and experience granted them such a right. Their behaviour threatened the rightful position of their seniors and seems to be what the author was so adamantly opposing in 1 Tim. 5:17–25. The author is careful to present the elders as morally worthy (5:17–18) and severely reprimands behaviour that displays a lack of respect and proper deference toward them (5:19–25). The haughtiness of their accusers would reflect badly on the reputation of the whole community if outsiders were privy to such disrespectful behaviour.

A subtle comparison ties the two major sections of 1 Tim. 5 together. The author compares the exemplary sixty+ widows (5:9–10) with the middle-aged, "believing" woman (5:16) who is neglecting her duties. Similarly, he compares the exemplary Timothy (e.g., 4:12–16) with wayward younger men (5:19–22).

Since the letter mixes the fictive rhetoric of Paul's directions to Timothy with the real situation of the late first century, it is often difficult to separate the layer of fiction from the layer of the author's community. The author's language in 1 Tim. 5 implies anxiety about adult children and grandchildren not caring for their widowed mothers and grandmothers, about middle-aged women not performing their duties toward younger women, and about young men behaving improperly toward their elders. The urgency of the language used in 1 Tim. 5 suggests that this is a place in the letter where the real audience is invited to apply Timothy's situation to their own. This becomes even clearer in the last verses of the chapter.

WRONGDOING, NOBLE DEEDS, AND REPUTATION (1 TIMOTHY 5:24–6:2A)

The sections on widows and elders are summed up with a general statement about wrongdoing (ἁμαρτίαι) contrasted with noble works (τὰ ἔργα τὰ καλὰ). This statement (5:24–5) serves as a summary of the specifics described in 5:1–23 as well as a further statement about the bearing of community members' behaviour on the reputation of the community as a whole.

> Τινῶν ἀνθρώπων αἱ ἁμαρτίαι πρόδηλοί εἰσιν
>   προάγουσαι εἰς κρίσιν,
>   τισὶν δὲ καὶ ἐπακολουθοῦσιν
> ὡσαύτως καὶ τὰ ἔργα τὰ καλὰ πρόδηλα,
> καὶ τὰ ἄλλως ἔχοντα
>   κρυβῆναι οὐ δύνανται.

> The wrongdoings of some people [not specifying men or women] are known to all,
>   leading the way into judgment,
>   but also following them.
> Likewise, noble works are also known to all,
> and those [honourable works] which might otherwise be hidden are not able [to be hidden]. (1 Tim. 5:24–5)

The phrase "wrongdoings of some people" draws an explicit parallel to those "wrongdoers" who are to be rebuked in 5:20 (for judging their elders) but also carries echoes of the improper behaviour of the children and grandchildren who are neglecting their filial duty to their widowed mothers and grandmothers (5:4), and of the middle-aged women who are neglecting their duties to the younger widows in their care (5:16). Moreover, the author contrasts wrongdoings with noble works (τὰ ἔργα τὰ καλὰ) – the kind of public praise offered in association inscriptions (see chapter 8) and in lifelong virtue of the sixty+ widow, who has had others bear witness of her "noble works [ἐν ἔργοις καλοῖς]" (5:10). The phrase is also found in the list of directives for those who are rich (6:18), who are presumably patrons of the community (male and female).[5] Similarly, an overseer and *diakonoi* should perform their duties nobly (καλῶς; 3:4, 12, 13); the elders already do (5:17).

In other words, just as inappropriate behaviour might incur judgment, honourable works in the form of proper behaviour would present a positive, honourable perception of the community, and incur positive sentiments from outsiders. That is, "noble works" would allow them to gain honour in the eyes of outsiders and present their religious message in a positive way (2:4), as exemplified in the past deeds of the sixty+ widow (5:9-10), the generosity of the wealthy (6:17–19), and nobly performed duties of men in leadership (3:4, 7, 12, 13; 5:17).[6]

The concern for visibility suggests that the whole community structure is in view in 5:24–25, including the age hierarchy of 1 Tim. 5:1–22; the leadership structure (3:1–13); the responsibilities of men and women (2:8–15), including those who are wealthy (6:17–19);[7] and the behaviour of the community generally (e.g., 2:1–3, 3:15), all with an eye to reputation. In this urban setting, such structures and honourable behaviours (or lack thereof) would not have been hidden (κρύπτω) for long.[8]

As noted earlier, the focus on age categories in 5:1–2 is the key to interpreting the rest of the chapter as a reflection of appropriate behaviour in the household of God (3:15). In fact, the section continues into 6:1–2 with an exhortation to slaves. At the end of this section of exhortation, the fictive Paul tells Timothy to "teach and urge these things" (6:2b), referring to all of the directives in 5:1–6:2a, including proper behaviour toward older men and women.

The fact that directions for slaves (6:1–2a) conclude the instructions starting in 5:1 confirms there is a loose resemblance to the *Haustafeln* (household codes) in 5:1–6:2a (e.g., Verner 1983; see also chapter 4). As in the traditional *Haustafeln*, the author of 1 Timothy was concerned to construct a model of household order that promoted proper order and proper behaviour. But whereas the typical *Haustafeln* governs relationships between a male head of the house and his wife, children, and slaves (e.g., Col. 3:18–24; Eph. 5:22–6:9), in 1 Tim. 5 it is adapted to feature age structure, with older men at the top of the hierarchy and an expectation that people of all age groups act appropriately. Older and younger men and women are characterized as members of a household in relation to Timothy (5:1–2), followed by specific problematic behaviours and solutions related to age (5:3–25), concluding with the behaviour of slaves (6:1–2a). Slaves could be any age and either sex, but as far as proper behaviour goes, obedience was most important for the reputation of the household.[9] Thus, the conclusion to this variation of the *Haustafeln* seems to be employed for apologetic purposes (Donelson 1986, 177–80; see also Balch 1981).

INTERGENERATIONAL DYNAMICS: A KEY TO 1 TIMOTHY

The letters to Timothy and Titus are commonly thought to focus on church leadership (hence the label "Pastoral Epistles"), characterized as "essentially manuals for church officers" that solidified "catholic organization" (Meeks 1972, 133).[10] Such a characterization anachronistically reflects later church manuals used for ecclesiastical discipline and behaviour (e.g., *Apostolic Constitutions*). More convincing characterizations of the three letters have focused on the community's identity in its late first-century context (e.g., Verner 1983, MacDonald 1996).

When we step back to view 1 Timothy on its own and as a whole,[11] we see that age structure actually permeates the rhetoric of this fictive "story," suggesting it is more important than previous studies have recognized.

The author's portrayal of Paul's relationship with young Timothy reflects typical Roman stereotypes of young men. He suggests that Timothy can rise above the usual vices of youth (4:12). His training (4:7) and Paul's example (1:16; 2:7) will lead him to behave properly (6:11), to keep himself pure (ἁγνὸν; 5:2, 22), and to teach others to do the same (4:11; 6:2b). Unlike the opposing teachers and the "wrongdoers" in 5:19, as a young man (νεότης; 4:12), the fictive Timothy exemplifies proper teaching and behaviour in four age-related relationships:

1. He behaves properly toward Paul. The fictive Paul addresses Timothy with the figurative language of a father to a son: "To Timothy, my legitimate child in faith [Τιμοθέῳ γνησίῳ τέκνῳ ἐν πίστει]" (1:2; also 1:18). The letter closes with language reminiscent of inheritance from a father to his son as Paul directs him to guard what (presumably) Paul has entrusted to him (6:20) and wants him to pass along to others in Paul's stead (3:14–15; 4:6).
2. He properly submits to the authority of other elders as well. He is living out his calling as a younger man because of the laying on of hands of the council of elders (4:14).
3. He displays proper behaviour toward the community, with its mix of ages. Paul anticipates "he will be a good servant/ *diakonos*" (καλὸς ἔσῃ διάκονος) who follows proper and noble

(καλῆς) teaching (4:6). Paul urges him to teach these proper teachings and model proper behaviour to others in the fictive community (4:11–16; 6:2b, 11–14, 20), in contrast to the opposing teachers (1:19–20; 4:1–5; 6:3–5, 21; cf. 1:3, 4:7) and in age-appropriate ways (4:11–14, 5:1–2).

4 He is expected to exemplify proper behaviour toward individuals as if they were close kin within a household. He is a young man whose elders are like fathers and mothers (5:1–2). He is to treat each appropriately according to their age and gender. Also, Timothy is expected to honour "real widows" who are older women (5:3) and to encourage others to provide worthy elders with tangible manifestations of honour ("double honour"; 5:17).

Thus, the "story" of Timothy in this letter illustrates themes that reflect intergenerational conflict and cooperation. In turn, these themes very likely signify that the difficulties of the real audience involved problematic intergenerational dynamics.

This brings us back to the setting of this letter, written to combat opposing teachings and to outline "proper" behaviour (3:15) at a time when the community's identity was uncertain. In Roman society at the time, age structure had been challenged by Augustus's rise to power as a young man (and probably many other smaller challenges), yet the traditional age hierarchy continued to be affirmed. If the author of 1 Timothy was influenced by the setting of Ephesus (though Ephesus is stated as the destination of the letter in 1:3, the question of authorship precludes certainty), then we could point to the social change occurring in the first and second centuries in that city. This included having recently become the capital of Asia under Augustus, notable growth in population and wealth as evidenced by the construction of many public buildings, and importance as a hub of communication, trade, and travel because of its strategic location (Treblico 2004, 13–18). Ancient Mediterranean evidence suggests that during times of major political change, elite youth publicly challenged the authority of their elders (see chapter 3). By analogy, during the profound time of social change represented in 1 Timothy, the author perceived young men (presumably non-elite) as important players in the direction of the community. They could either challenge the stability of the community by aligning with the opponents, or they could affirm the true inheritance – the "healthy" teaching. The author presents the young Timothy's calling (4:14, 6:20) and behaviour as an example for the younger men in his community.

There are additional clues in the letter that suggest age-related problems were very much on the author's mind. Perhaps most obvious are the highlighting of Timothy's youth (4:3) and submission to the elders (4:14); the mention of stories told by old women, presumably to influence the younger generation (4:7); and the references to the overseer and *diakonoi* having submissive children (3:4, 12). The latter are presumably not young children, but youth or adult children whose behaviour could either honour or shame their father. Honour, as we have seen, is an important cultural value in the Mediterranean, earned and maintained by having public regard through good reputation (chapter 2) – including proper respect from one's children, at least in the public eye. An explicit mention of outsiders is included in the attributes of an overseer: "he must be well thought of by outsiders [ἀπὸ τῶν ἔξωθεν], so that he may not fall into disgrace and the snare of the devil [or, the one who slanders; διαβόλος]" (3:7, NRSV). The other attributes required of an overseer also contribute to an honourable reputation in the public realm because they are typical virtues in ancient Greek and Roman cultures (3:2–5).[12] In three other instances, the author hints at the importance of outsiders' opinions with regard to the behaviour of subordinate members of the household. Slaves are exhorted to honour their masters for the sake of the community's reputation ("so that the name of God and the teaching may not be blasphemed"; 6:1). Also, the author recommends that young widows remarry, have children, and manage their households so that "the adversary" (the one who opposes; ἀντικείμενος) has no reason to scorn (λοιδορία) them (5:14). If "the adversary" is taken to be a person (see Marshall 1999, 604–5), the text likely refers to outsiders. Finally, young men threatening the traditional age structure entailed behaviour that would be seen as encroaching on the honour of the group, and thus be seen as public challenge, subject to outsiders' judgment of the community (5:19–20, 24). In the author's view, failing to live up to the accepted societal code of conduct would bring shame on the community, incurring ridicule from outsiders.

The obligation to defend and display honour in the perception of outsiders helped the author define the group. The distinct identity of the group is evident in the statement: "[God] desires everyone to be saved and to come to a knowledge of the truth. For there is one God; there is also one mediator between God and humankind, Christ Jesus, himself human, who gave himself a ransom for all" (2:4–6; NRSV). An evangelistic goal is suggested here as well, which might be more successful (at least for some converts) if the community appeared to be a culturally "normal" group. The author characterizes the basis of proper behaviour, namely, εὐσέβεια ("duty and devotion," chapter 5), as beneficial for the present situation as well as for the future (4:8–10, 6:19). In the context of instructions about proper behaviour, he hints that outsiders are part of the motivation: God is the "Saviour of all people" (4:10). The opinion of outsiders mattered to the author, but so did the distinct identity of the community. These were held in tension. If subordinate members of the community (including the young) were acting in ways that compromised their reputation, the honour of whole community was at stake. For the sake of honour, the author of 1 Timothy pressed for adhering to the norms of age hierarchy.

WRONGDOING AND AGE: 1 TIM. 1:9–10 AND 6:11

A closer look at the opening and closing of the letter, namely, the vice list in 1:9–10 and virtue list in 6:11, brings out a strong resemblance to some of the age-related issues described in other parts of the letter.

The author states that "the law is not laid down for a righteous person [δικαίῳ]" but for people known for their vices (1:9–10), which are listed. There is a rhetorical break in the list: the first eight categories of people are placed in pairs; each pair is connected with καὶ (1:9). The second set is a string of six words reflecting a more general list of vices ("murderers, sexually immoral [people]," etc.; 1:9b–10) that resembles other vice lists[13] but reflects activities that would threaten household order. The list concludes with a statement about anything opposing the "healthy teaching" (1:10). Interestingly, most of the terms in the καὶ pairs can be correlated with terms or ideas used for age-related issues elsewhere in 1 Timothy.

The first pair is "those who are lawless [ἀνόμοις] and insubordinate [ἀνυποτάκτοις]." Most terms related to νόμος are found in this section (1 Tim. 1:3–11), which describes those who "teach other things" (1:3) and are presumably upsetting age hierarchy.[14] The opposite of "insubordination" (ἀνυπότακτος) is "submission" (ὑποταγή), and can be found in the context of women who are to learn in submission (2:11) and an overseer's children, who should be submissive to their fathers (3:4), the latter a clear age-related behaviour.

The second pair is "those without duty and devotion [ἀσεβέσι] and wrongdoers [ἁμαρτωλοῖς]." The opposite of ἀσεβέσι is εὐσέβεια (and its cognates; see chapter 5). Though found in various contexts in 1 Timothy (e.g., 3:15, 6:5), in 5:4 it used as a description of the culturally dictated duty to care for parents and grandparents. "Wrongdoers" [ἁμαρτωλοῖς] are found (in the form of a participle cognate; τοὺς ἁμαρτάνοντας) in 5:20 describing young men disrespecting their elders (chapter 9). The related noun ἁμαρτίαι (wrongdoings) is used in 5:22 to discourage Timothy from participating in others' (assumedly his young peers') wrongdoings. In 5:24, ἁμαρτίαι are contrasted with "good works" (τὰ ἔργα τὰ καλά), a phrase also used for an overseer (3:1), the exemplary sixty+ widow (5:10), and those who have wealth (6:18). This contrast of wrongdoing and good works concludes the section on age issues (5:24–25).

The third pair is "unholy [ἀνοσίοις] and profane [βεβήλοις]." The opposite of unholy is found in 2:8 (ὁσίους) describing the hands that men are to lift up (and so not explicitly linked to age), but βεβήλοις is used of "profane" myths associated with old women (4:7; as well as the empty chatter of opponents in 6:20).

The final pair is "those who kill their fathers [πατρολῴαις][15] and those who kill their mothers [μητρολῴαις]," and while there are no verbal parallels, the contrast with placating older men as fathers and older women as mothers (5:1–2) that frames the whole argument of 1 Tim. 5 is striking.[16] While likely exaggerated for effect as one of the most heinous of vices, the idea points to parricide, used in comedy in the intergenerational conflict in ancient Greece and Rome, and thus suggests a clash between generations (chapter 4).[17]

These pairs of unsavoury labels are all set in contrast to the righteous person, who, by implication, is young Timothy. Near the close of the letter, a list of virtues outlines the model to be followed, personified by Timothy, who is to "pursue righteousness [δικαιοσύνην; also 3:16], duty and devotion [εὐσέβειαν], faithfulness [πίστιν], love [ἀγάπην], endurance and gentleness" (6:11). The first two terms (δικαιοσύνην and εὐσέβεια) are recognizable as opposites of two terms listed in 1:10, namely "lawless" and without duty and devotion (ἀνόμοις and ἀσεβέσι). The terms πίστις and ἀγάπη are to be cultivated and found in the children raised by the submissive woman in 2:15. Also, the terms and cognates of εὐσέβεια and πίστις are woven throughout 1 Timothy, with specific connotations related to age (see discussions in chapters 5 and 8).

The rhetorical clues about age in 1 Timothy, from the opening verses to the closing verses, suggest that age-related issues are key to understanding the situation to which the author is speaking. It is not surprising that 1 Tim. 5, with its focus on age-related problems, is the climactic moment of the letter. Here the author speaks most directly to the audience's issues and the deleterious effects of the opposing teachings: younger people neglecting their widowed mothers and grandmothers (5:4), middle-aged women neglecting the younger widows (5:16), and younger men rebelling against their elders (5:19–20). Those with wealth were especially at issue, for they needed to fulfill their filial and patron duties, being content with and thankful for what they had (4:4–5; 6:6–8) and focusing on others in their care (3:1–12; 5:3, 4, 16, 17; 6:17–19) rather than focusing on themselves (5:5), their appearance (2:9), or their ambition (3:6; 5:19). The community's reputation was at stake in the midst of a crisis of identity, and the author was convinced that a return to the foundation of proper age hierarchy would bring them through.

CONCLUSION

In the late first century, the author of 1 Timothy attempts to save the community's good reputation and restore its stability by putting forth the voice of Paul with the agenda of an older man who holds to traditional age-related behaviour. As the living voices of the founders of the community faded at the end of the first century, "other" teachings were threatening the stability of the community (1:3, 6:3). The crisis is characterized by insiders whose teaching has strayed from what the author deems "healthy." Instead, these opposing teachers promote behaviours that compromised the reputation of the community. Many of these behaviours are associated with age-related roles reflected in the ancient household. The "other" teachings especially affected middle-aged women and younger men (along with some slaves), causing ruptures in the usual functioning of age hierarchy. The author presents Paul and Timothy within an ideal intergenerational relationship. The voice of an older Paul admonishes a younger Timothy to model and teach behaviours that promote traditional age-related behaviours, demonstrating the conservative elements of the generational cycle. These behaviours especially include mentorship and benefaction of older women to younger women (including helping younger widows to remarry), filial piety (including children and grandchildren caring for their widowed mothers and grandmothers), and honourable intergenerational behaviour (including younger men having proper deference for their elders). By affirming the traditional behaviours of the household in the "household of God," especially the conservative age-related roles that display true "faithfulness" (πίστις) and duty and devotion to God and the ancestors (εὐσέβεια), any dishonourable conduct becoming noticeable to outside eyes would be overcome, thus restoring the reputation of the community as well as the "proper" legacy of Paul as the community sought to affirm its identity and direction.

11

The Visibility of Age

In this final chapter, I consider the implications of this study on age, namely, the importance of age in Christ groups and early Christianity more generally and why age matters when considering the social dynamics of early Christian communities.

I start by examining two scholarly debates related to age: parent-child relationships and the development of hierarchy in leadership. In both cases, I argue that even if age was not often explicitly referenced in the extant literature, the evidence from the ancient Mediterranean (with analogies from the modern Mediterranean) suggests age was always an important marker of social identity. It was so engrained in the cultural constructs of identity that it is often implicit, mentioned in passing, or not remarked on at all. The extant texts do suggest, however, that the *visibility* of age increased by the end of the first century. Age hierarchy was not a new phenomenon; rather the continuity of age structure became more worthy of note over time. Extant sources also suggest that the demography of early Christian communities likely reflected the demography of the surrounding society, and this was notable to outsiders, especially the activity and presence of women and younger men.

I conclude by suggesting how further studies might consider the implications of appreciating age as a critical part of social identity and as reflected in the social world of Christ groups and early Christians.

THE CONTINUITY OF AGE STRUCTURE

The model of generational stability and social change (chapter 2) suggests that the expectations related to age structure in the ancient Mediterranean were tenacious. Yet we observe conflicting messages with regard to age in early Christian texts. In the gospel accounts, Jesus both interrupts filial piety (e.g., Matt. 4:21–22) and affirms it (e.g., Matt. 15:4–6); Paul seems surprisingly silent about age, yet appeals to his old age to motivate Philemon (Philem. 1:9). Only in later texts does age structure appear to be explicitly affirmed (e.g., Col, 3:20–21) or enforced (e.g., Titus 2:1–8). These observations have not gone unnoticed by scholars. Relevant scholarship can be categorized under two broad topics that land squarely within the study of 1 Timothy: the relationship between adult children and their parents (addressed in 1 Tim. 5:4), and the role of elders (1 Tim. 5:17) in the development of church leadership. Scholarship in these two areas has broached issues regarding age in a way that reflects its importance but also highlights the need for a culturally sensitive interpretation of age structure and age-related roles. Some scholars have argued for a *resurgence* or *restoration* over time of age hierarchy (age-related roles that involved positions of higher or lower status on the basis of age, such as younger members deferring to their elders). However, it is most likely, considering this study of 1 Timothy, that age hierarchy in the early Christian communities was *intact* and *assumed* from the origins of the community, even if some aspects of age hierarchy were challenged within the community, especially in times of social change.

We begin by looking briefly at the discussion of parent-child relationships in early Christ groups. Here there are two areas of debate: the gospel record of Jesus's apparent rejection of family (parents in particular), and the apparent shift from egalitarian to hierarchical relationships in Pauline communities.

Early tradition depicts Jesus as (at times) rejecting the traditional household (e.g., Mark 3:31–35; Matt. 12:46–50; Luke 8:19–21; Q 12:51–53, from Micah 7:6; Luke 14:25–27; Matt. 10:37–39), including calling disciples away from their fathers (Matt. 4:21–22; Luke 5:11) and dismissing a potential disciple's worry about not burying his father (Q 9:60). These are radical sentiments in a set of cultures in which one was expected to honour one's parents, including with proper burial. They raise the question whether Jesus (or those who wrote about Jesus) challenged the cultural norm of filial duty.[1] They also raise the question about whether Paul (and communities associated with him) disregarded respect for parents as part of a rejection of social hierarchy (e.g., Gal. 3:28; Barclay 2007, 239–41).

Those who posit that the movement began with egalitarian ideals (including with respect to age) interpret the later visibility of age categories as a resurgence or restoration of age categories for later communities. Halvor Moxnes suggests that Jesus's countercultural message in Palestine was untenable for Paul and post-Pauline authors who were compelled to address concerns within family structure in urban Hellenistic settings (1997, 37). For Moxnes, how one acted toward one's parents in early Christian communities changed over time as age categories *reappeared*. Similarly, Barclay suggests age categories were disregarded by Jesus (and Paul), then *re-emerged* as the church developed out of its charismatic phase (1997, 72). He posits that Paul himself rejected age categories in his apocalyptic vision of Christian community, but that as time went on, these categories inevitably *reasserted* themselves as people grew older and the parousia did not occur (2007, 239–41). David G. Horrell (2001) ascribes the decline of sibling language in Pauline communities to a shift from egalitarian to hierarchical relationships.

There are similarities in discussions of the parent-child relationship in the Christian versions of the *Haustafeln* (household codes; e.g., Col. 3:20–21; Eph. 2:19; 1 Tim. 3:15; 1 Pet. 4:17). The *Haustafeln* reflected a traditional structure of authority in which relationships within the community functioned along the lines of an analogy of the Roman household, including age hierarchy (see chapter 4). Verner suggests the progression of the *Haustafeln* in the letters to Timothy and Titus involved a *resurgence* of age categories among non-kin who functioned in intergenerational relationships (1983, 83–106). However, the lack of evidence for age structure in Paul's letters does not necessarily mean that Pauline communities had little conscious age distinction.

Others posit that filial duty of an adult child to a parent was a continuing cultural norm that was challenged rhetorically rather than in reality. Stephen O. Barton posits that the "anti-family" material of the gospels may be "primarily a rhetorically powerful metaphorical way of calling for displacement of every obstacle to true discipleship of Jesus in the light of the imminent coming of the kingdom of God" (1997, 81). In this scenario, children would still be socially obligated to care for aging parents, unless this somehow usurped their religious commitments (see also Sapp 1987). This seems to be reflected in Mark when Jesus condemns the Pharisees for not honouring their parents (Mark 7:9–13; see also Matt. 15:4–6). Similarly, Peter Balla cites the Stoic Epictetus who placed philosophy above respect for parents (*Discourses* 3.3.5–6), yet listed the care of parents as a fundamental duty (3.7.25–8; 2003, 61). Balla's analysis of Pauline letters (undisputed and disputed) suggests that children's duty to parents followed societal norms – both in their behaviour and in their reasons for this behaviour (e.g., God's order, moral obligation). Paul's silence on the issue of "leaving parents" confirms for Balla that Jesus's words were not acted upon literally in these communities. For Reidar Aasgaard, parent-child language was often used in a metaphorical sense, especially in exhortations for loving one another as "children" of God and fellow Christian "siblings." His nuanced assessment of parent-child language in Paul's undisputed letters reflects the cultural realities of ancient Mediterranean family dynamics (2004, 285–95). He understands Paul's metaphorical use of the parent-child relationship as a strategy to assert authority within the realm of parental-type affection and love for the communities he founded. Aasgaard argues that the post-Pauline letters represent a time when the sibling metaphor of Paul was "toned down" (2004, 302–3), and Christian communities returned to the *language* of traditional family structures in the *Haustafeln*, especially with hierarchical elements related to age (as well as class and gender; 312). In a study of 1 Tim. 4:12, David W. Pao also argues for a continuity of age structure, which helps to place the reference to Timothy's age within its cultural context (2014, 753–4).[2] Warren Carter (2001) ambiguously notes that the New Testament offers two (assumedly equally valid) messages with regard to aging parents: rejection on the one hand and acceptance of hierarchical structure on the other.

I would concur with Aasgaard and Pao that a *continuity* of social hierarchy between parents and adult children seems to fit the ancient evidence most consistently when we consider age. Age nearly always had hierarchical connotations, whether in the family or the public realm, and the hierarchy functioned along gender lines. In general, older age was associated with greater status (combined with considerations of gender and social class). This is the reason Paul uses the rhetoric of age to engage Philemon, employing his status as an "old man" (Philem. 9) to appeal to Philemon's sense of honour in getting him to accept Onesimus back on Paul's terms (Hock 1995).

While Aasgaard emphasizes the transformation of community in Paul's day (necessitating the use of sibling language), I suggest that the next phase after Paul's time represented an even more profound social transformation. By the latter half of the first century, "new" converts continued to join the movement, at least sometimes apart from their households (1 Cor. 7:6–8; 1 Pet. 3:1), which may account for comments about rejected family. However, we can also imagine that by the 60s and 70s CE, the children who grew up in Christian families at this point were the first substantial age cohort to be socialized within the community. Such a cohort is in view in this late-first-century quotation in *1 Clem.* 23.3: "We have heard these things from the time of our parents, and look! We have grown old, and none of these things has happened to us" (AF 2003, 1:79). The various internal dynamics of children growing up within the community are implicated in the *Haustafeln* (MacDonald 2014, 33–107). Adult children who are part of the community with their parents may be assumed in 1 Tim. 5:4, since their actions of neglect are worse than those of an "unbeliever" (someone outside of the community; see also Barclay 2020, 274n21; chapter 8).

The second major area of scholarship that has engaged issues of age is the long-standing debate around the development of leadership, especially with regard to the role of elders (see chapter 9). At least some of the debate rests in the (largely Protestant) assumptions about a nascent Christian movement that was egalitarian but grew increasingly hierarchical, usually considered a degradation of Christian origins. In von Campenhausen's (1969) classic view of the development of church leadership, the church became less apocalyptic and more "institutionalized" in the late first century. Charismatic gifts that functioned in harmony within Pauline churches (as exemplified by travelling apostles and prophets) were replaced by offices of hierarchical leadership, including elders.[3]

The main debate around leadership is outlined in chapter 9, but here I point out that some scholars within this discussion have suggested that respect due to age was a hierarchical structure that was not part of the earliest manifestations of community; rather, it was *restored* over time. The evidence from my study of 1 Timothy suggests that even in the development of institutional structure in early Christianity, age hierarchy was constant, although the *visibility* of this aspect of age structure increased over time.

J. Gordon Harris assumes that traditional ideas around respect for elders and their leadership *resumed* when the church settled into a more family-centred phase after Paul's time (1987, 84–5). For James T. Burtchaell, Hellenistic Judeans used the term πρεσβύτερος (elder) for wealth and status instead of age, but later, second-century Christians "restored" the meaning of age, so that people like Papias and Irenaeus understood those who were "old" as people who provided a "living link" to the apostolic generation (1992, 276). The "living link" is suggestive, but it is difficult to imagine how, in Burtchaell's view, the term πρεσβύτερος could change so radically within such a short period of time (fifty years or so), especially if its original meaning appears to be "restored" at that time. John H. Elliott suggests that the πρεσβύτεροι in 1 Pet. 5:1–5 were not necessarily old in "natural age" but had seniority in the community. The νεώτεροι, whom Elliott understands to be recent converts rather than young men, were exhorted to submit to the elders (5:5) to keep "order" in the community so that they could remain *distinct* from the society around them and retain solidarity within (1981, 69, 139, 191; see also Elliott 1970, 390). Elliott's view is a kind of reinterpretation of age categories, though his later work affirms age hierarchy (2003, 6).

Others posit that age hierarchy was always a reality in the ancient Mediterranean (Harvey 1974; Campbell 1994; Malherbe 2008; Stewart 2014; Welborn 2018, 96–7) and that age would normally be part of seniority, as was the case in contemporary voluntary associations (Stewart 2014, 161–5).[4] Aasgaard (2004) convincingly argues that in the honour-based culture of the ancient Mediterranean, the concept of "egalitarianism" was virtually non-existent. Although he posits a return to traditional family structures in post-Pauline communities, Aasgaard maintains that the sibling language within Pauline communities was hierarchical, not "egalitarian," and even the use of sibling language did not promote egalitarianism but rather concord. Similarly, John S. Kloppenborg suggests that rather than compare modern "egalitarianism" to the situation of Pauline communities, voluntary associations provide a better ancient analogy (see also Stewart 2014, 161–5). He argues that like some associations, Pauline communities were "egalitarian" in that they accepted a variety of people into the group (i.e., men and women; slaves and free; people of different social status), but this variety did not negate the social differences between members. Hierarchy continued to be a reality, but tension was mediated, perhaps most strongly by sibling language (Kloppenborg 1996b, 252, 258–9). I would add that generational stability and age-related roles and expectations also naturally mediated these relationships. Because of the cultural value of deference to age, many older men and women in the Christ groups likely had some kind of social precedence from the beginning of the movement (e.g., 1 Thess. 5:12). In other words, while age hierarchies seem to have become more visible in the late first century, they could hardly have been irrelevant in the earlier phase of the movement.

In conclusion, taking a culturally sensitive view of age structure, it is unlikely that age hierarchy in intergenerational relationships and early church governance in early Christian communities was restored as early Christian communities evolved. Rather, it was likely always so much a part of the social structure that it was assumed at all stages of the development of these communities. Even as leadership structure developed over time, the expectations of age hierarchy would have remained intact. When the usual order was challenged, the conservative element of age hierarchy prevailed, so that over time there was a balance with younger people respecting their elders and older people maintaining precedence and caring for their juniors. Since age hierarchy was central in the household, the increased use of household and intergenerational language within early Christian communities likely reflected the value of maintaining appropriate age-related behaviour, especially in the face of questions about their reputation or increasing social persecution. It may be that some scholars perceive a restoration of age norms because they focus on the challenges to age hierarchy, but I would argue that, though the challenge may affect social change in some way, it never eliminates the basic tenet of age hierarchy and generational stability. There was a continuity of age norms from the beginning of the movement, but an increased *visibility* of issues related to age by the end of the first century.

TOWARD A DEMOGRAPHY OF EARLY CHRISTIAN COMMUNITIES

If early Christian communities in the first and second centuries functioned socially according to the age structure of the ancient Mediterranean cultures in which they developed, then the age range of members typically present in early Christian groups is worth considering. The evidence from sources we have already examined confirms what we might assume: communities contained a full range of ages. That is, the demography of early Christian communities probably paralleled society at large, with members representing a full range of ages. The *Haustafeln* demonstrate parents and children were part of the community together, and the letters to Timothy and Titus explicitly mention older and younger members, both male and female (most notably, 1 Tim. 5, 2 Tim. 1:5, Titus 2:1–8). Of course, as with the ancient world in general, the exact demographic situation of early Christian communities will always be uncertain, and specifics varied from place to place and through time. Specific statements about individual communities and regions would need more detailed analysis.

The fact that there was a full range of ages was, for the critics of the early Christians, worthy of note. It was not until the second century that we find extant writings of non-Christian writers observing (and criticizing) Christians from an outsider's perspective. As these sources are from different eras and regions, we can only take them as suggestive. However, it is apparent that age was noticeable to non-Christian critics of the movement: several of these critics explicitly mention age or age categories. The critics' comments and the evidence in 1 Timothy also suggest certain groups (namely, widows and younger men) seemed especially visible, indicating that they were either particularly attracted to the movement in the midst of social change or were more noticeable because of their particularly visible roles in the community.[5]

In his letter to the Emperor Trajan around the year 117 CE, Pliny the Younger explicitly mentions the age range of members within the Christian groups he observed in Bithynia. He asks for guidance in dealing with Christians whose movement apparently cleared the polytheistic temples – a political threat in Pliny's eyes. Pliny wonders if he should discriminate between the very young or more mature Christians (1969, 10.96.1), and was concerned with the great numbers of people who were of *every age* and rank and both genders (10.96.5). We can only assume that he meant to include young children, as well as young adults, mature adults, and the elderly. His inclusion of a statement on age is striking because it suggests that the age range of members was a notable, perhaps even surprising, element of the movement for Pliny. Also, his hesitancy to deal with all age groups in the same manner suggests that these distinctions made a difference in the public sphere. This reflects the private-public distinction between young and old age-related behaviour that is part of the cycle of generational stability and social change (chapter 2). For Pliny, this likely meant that how he normally treated an older man of high status would differ significantly from a child of low status (for example).

As a point of comparison, from a later era (early third century CE), the Christian apologist Minucius Felix wrote a dialogue between a Christian and polytheist critic of Christianity with a similar observation. He polemically describes a Christian feast (and orgy) that includes "all their children, sisters, and mothers, people of either sex and *every age*" (my emphasis, Tertullian, Minucius Felix 1931, 339, *Octavius* 9.6). Again, this suggests that a range of ages was a notable characteristic of the Christian community to an outsider.

Around 177 CE, Celsus, a staunch critic of Christianity, wrote a treatise entitled *On True Doctrine*, which only survives in part as cited by Origen of Alexandria in his *Contra Celsum* in the mid-third century CE. His detailed polemical description of the Christians highlights several elements of age:

> In private houses also we see wool-workers, cobblers, laundry-workers, and the most illiterate and bucolic yokels, who would not dare to say anything at all in front of their elders and more intelligent masters. But whenever they get hold of children in private and some stupid women with them, they let out some astounding statements as, for example, that they must not pay any attention to their fathers and school-teachers, but must obey them; they say that these talk nonsense and have no understanding, and that in reality they neither know nor are able to do anything good, but are taken up with mere empty chatter. But they alone, they say, know the right way to live, and if the children would believe them, they would become happy and make their home happy as well ... [and] they should leave their fathers and their schoolmasters, and go along with the women and little children who are their playfellows to the wooldresser's shop, or to the cobbler's or the washerwoman's shop, that they may learn perfection. And by saying this they persuade them. (Celsus in Origen, *Against Celsus*, 3.55; translated by Chadwick 1965, 165–6)

MacDonald has aptly explored how Celsus's ridicule of the Christians reflects cultural stereotypes about women, particularly the suspicion of their teaching in private spaces (1996, 29, 111–12). She argues that these observations from Celsus as an outsider also serve to demonstrate the power of women's positive shame (modesty), either embodying or decimating the honour of the community.

Celsus also has noteworthy observations related to age. He describes the perpetrators of the movement as "the most illiterate and bucolic yokels, who would not dare to say anything at all in front of *their elders* [πρεσβύτεροι] and more intelligent *masters* [δεσποτῶν]" (emphasis added). This description of the main evangelists suggests that they are younger men, since Celsus implies they would be stymied before their elders and masters[6] – by definition, men who are older than they are. If we take both elders and masters together, we have an image of older (and wiser) men who, according to cultural norms, should have precedence and a certain amount of control over these evangelists because of their younger age and (in some cases) lower status. The description reflects the stereotypes of foolish and rebellious youth, young men who are pliable, gullible, and railing against authority (chapter 9).[7] Celsus portrays them as luring their vulnerable prey back to their places of work or to women's spaces,[8] another clue to the youth of Celsus's evangelists since older (honourable) men would be unlikely to occupy explicitly female spaces.

Celsus appears to be using an age-based stereotype to illustrate his negative view of the Jesus movement, namely, the foolish ambition of younger men (chapter 9). While Celsus's comments are polemical, they do suggest that young men (and perhaps slaves) were an observable, and possibly influential, part of the Christian group at this time – at least more visible and/or influential than Celsus seems to think is proper. Celsus's comments have some parallel to my reading of the behaviour of younger men in 1 Tim. 5:17–20 as well as in *1 Clement* (see discussion in chapter 9).[9] In all three cases, the behaviour of foolish younger men is perceived as capable of severely affecting the group's reputation.

Also of note is Celsus's focus on the vulnerability of παῖδες (children) who are usurping proper age hierarchy.[10] Twice he states that these young people are convinced by the Christians to ignore and leave their father (the Greek is singular) and schoolteachers. To an outsider, this would be shameful behaviour indeed.

In sum, with regard to age, Celsus highlights younger men and children in particular, whose age-related behaviour should reflect deference to their elders, masters, fathers, and school-teachers, but does not. The younger men, whom he associates with base professions and women's spaces, have thwarted any sense of age hierarchy and convinced their young victims to do the same in their brazen persuasion toward disobedience against those who are directly above them in the social hierarchy.

Finally, Lucian of Samosata presents a satirical story of Peregrinus, who is clearly someone who thwarts the norm of age hierarchy by killing his father, "unable to tolerate his living beyond sixty years" (1936, 11, *The Passing of Peregrinus*, 10). Having fled to escape justice, he swindles a group of Christians by pretending to be one of them and becomes a revered leader (11). As a younger man (he was not older than about forty because of his father's age), he sought renown (δοξοκοπία; 12) and found it (as well as financial gain), for a time, among the gullible Christians.[11] His leadership role among the Christians may be a critique on Lucian's part of younger men taking positions of influence in the movement.

In addition, in one scene, Peregrinus has been imprisoned. The Christians kept him company, "and from the very break of day aged widows and orphan children could be seen waiting near the prison" (1936, 13, *The Passing of Peregrinus*, 12). MacDonald notes that the phrase γράδια χήρας better captures the derogatory tone if translated "old hags called widows" (1996, 74). She posits that old women perhaps provided prisoners with resources or prayer, or served as look-outs. If old women were usually ignored in public, they might have been the logical choice for such activities. However, using the negative stereotype of older women, Lucian mentions old widows in this role to ridicule the Christians, so that they became "a graphic image of credulity, shamelessness, and transgression" (82).

Along with aged widows, Lucian notes the presence of "orphan children." A child whose father had died would be considered an orphan, though the prevalence of adoption in Roman society meant that this situation may be remedied by an adopting father. Nevertheless, in Lucian's story, the older widows and orphan children together illustrate a picture of some of the most marginalized people in society – women and children who sat outside the kin structure. However, in this tale, they are portrayed as part of an early Christian community – a surrogate family. Even if they are depicted as helping out a fellow Christian, Lucian sees them, along with the whole group they represent, as duped by Peregrinus. Thus, for Lucian, they represent the group's lack of honour.

Observations of the Critics

These critics have some striking observations related to age. Pliny and Minucius Felix both distinctly remark on the range of ages among the Christians. It may seem obvious from this end of history that the groups they encountered would have members who range from old to young. This internal evidence certainly suggests that the range of ages (implied in 1 Timothy and many other texts) is likely to be common in Christ groups. But the fact the critics point it out with some *surprise* is worth pondering.

One important group to consider is the very young. Parkin estimates that children ages fifteen and younger (slave and free) comprised one-third of the population (2013, 42; see also MacDonald 2014). Yet, their presence in this group was noteworthy to their opponents: Pliny and Minucius Felix observed "every age" in the group; Celsus emphasized children's vulnerability to the teachings of the Christ followers; and Lucian included an observation of "orphan children" with the widows who visited the imprisoned Peregrinus.

The description from Celsus and Lucian of younger men thwarting the system and rebelling bears a striking resemblance to my reading of 1 Tim. 5:17–20 (also Young 1994b, 107) as well as the situation in *1 Clement* (Welborn 2018). In the model of generational stability and social change, such challenges to the system are part of its elasticity, especially during times of social change. Perhaps some young men were attracted to the movement because they saw opportunities for prestigious positions of honour (like those found in voluntary associations). According to demographic data of the population of the Roman Empire, there were many more young men in the population than there were older men (Parkin 2003, 51). As I argue in chapter 9, any detectable tension between old and young men in a movement already seen as suspicious would make their behaviour more visible and further suspect, such as in the critique of Celsus and in Lucian's story of the young Peregrinus. Challenges to age hierarchy tended to prompt this kind of conservative reaction – a reaction that serves to affirm age hierarchy, including having younger men in a position of deference.

Though whole families were present in early Christian communities (e.g., 1 Tim. 3:2–5, 12), not everyone joined with their households. In Corinth, some men and women joined the Pauline church without their marriage partners (1 Cor. 7:10–13), and 1 Pet.

3:1 focuses on married women who joined the movement apart from their husbands (MacDonald 2003). In 2 Tim. 1:5 the author portrays Timothy as influenced by his mother and grandmother, with no mention of his father or grandfather.[12] Celsus highlights women as actively instructing initiates, perhaps in their own homes and/or shops (MacDonald 1996, 111–12). These various scenarios might suggest something about the age of such women. If such a woman did have young children, she might bring them along, which is the implication of 1 Cor. 7:13–14 (see also Lührmann 1981). If a young mother was busy with domestic or non-domestic labour, a grandmother or other female kin might bring children along. A woman past menopause would be less suspect leaving her home than a woman of childbearing years.

Widows, especially old widows, may have been particularly visible as evidenced by Lucian's comment about widows and orphans as well and the extended discussion involving widows in 1 Tim. 5. Both suggest the potentially deleterious effect of visible widows on the reputation of the group. It is also possible there was a higher proportion of women, perhaps especially widows, in the community than one would expect given the demography of the ancient Mediterranean. Given the relatively high proportion of permanent widows (widows who did not remarry) in the general population, some widows, especially widows without children or kin (like the "real widows" of 1 Tim. 5:3, 5, 16), might have been attracted to Christian communities for financial support (Bremmer 1995, 49) and/or for emotional or social support. These may not all have been old widows, for some vulnerable young widows might have sought social protection if they could not find it in their natal or marital families. Though we cannot take the account of the nascent Jesus movement in Acts at face value, it suggests that early Christ followers may have taken a special interest in caring for needy widows from its beginnings. Luke's late first-century or early second-century account of widows' meals (Acts 6:1) and Tabitha's care for widows (9:39) reflects a particular interest in widow care roughly contemporary with 1 Timothy. The reliance on the Septuagint as sacred writings in early Christian communities may form some background to early Christian care for widows and orphans (e.g., Deut. 10:18, 24:19–21, 26:12–13; also James 1:27). It appears that the author of 1 Timothy accepts their prayer (5:5) as reciprocity for their financial support (5:16), suggesting that they are not just receiving from but also giving to the community. However, not all widows would need financial assistance. Especially if they had married *sine manu* and managed their own inherited property, some may have found Christ groups worthy of their benefaction. In Lucian's story, widows have access to and are helping prisoners, perhaps either because they were inconspicuous as marginalized persons or because they had the means to do so. The visibility of women, especially women not associated with husbands or households within the movement and/or widows in particular, suggests there may have been proportionately more women and widows in the movement than in the population at large.

Finally, there were certainly older people in the group, as Pliny noted. Since those over sixty comprised 5 to 10 percent of the general population (Parkin 2003, 49–50, 224), we can surmise that the number within the movement who attained "old age" was small but not insignificant. Elderly people would *not* have constituted a distinct group. However, we find clues about the roles of some older people in 1 Timothy: elders who shepherd well (5:17), elders who preach and teach (5:17), widows who are not less than sixty (5:9), real widows (who must be older because they are not remarrying; 5:3, 5, 16), and widows with family (who likely must be older because they did not remarry; 5:4). Elsewhere in early Christian literature, individuals may be designated as "old," such as Luke's characters of Elizabeth, Zechariah (Luke 1:7, 18, 36), and Anna (Luke 2:37), and Polycarp, who attained old age as a life-long Christian (e.g., *Martyrdom of Polycarp* 9.3). The critics of early Christianity do not comment specifically on older men within the group, likely because those in positions of deference (i.e., women and younger men; Welborn 2018, 28–9, 147–8) had more potential to be visible in a way that shamed the community. Of course, we have plenty of indications of the importance of older active men (elders) in the movement (see chapter 9).

These observations suggest that, even as the composition of each community was in flux as individuals grew up and grew older, and as adherents came and went, the demography of early Christian communities might be characterized (in a very general sense) as comprising a full range of age groups, including children, generally reflecting the demographic range of ages found in society at large. This meant there was a stable number of young and mature adult men and women, and relatively few, but still present, elderly people, with a significant presence of older women (perhaps a good number of whom were widows), and many children. The proportion of older men was probably similar to the general Roman population. Older men would have drawn less comment from critics since older men regularly joined associations and fulfilled public roles. Given their visibility, it is possible that there was a more obvious presence of younger men and a higher representation of women, particularly widows, in early Christian communities than in the general non-elite populace. Women's involvement might suggest something about the continuity of the movement since mothers usually outlived fathers, and mothers may have had significant influence in keeping their children in the movement.

AGE AND SOCIAL IDENTITY

In many ways, the experience of aging in the ancient Mediterranean world would have been radically different from the modern Western experience. Although people did not expect to die young, demographic realities meant that death was not primarily associated with old age.[13] Most would have experienced the passing of siblings and playmates in childhood, the early death of one or both parents by young adulthood, the grief of watching infants and children die, and the loss of adult spouses, siblings, kin, and friends who succumbed to infection or disease (see also Osiek and MacDonald 2006, 78–82). The kin universe for most people would often have been in flux, having to negotiate shifting relationships with the realities of marriage, widowhood, remarriage, care of or from extended family, shifting household responsibilities, and the possibility of involvement with fictive kin, especially among women's networks. Yet, those who survived the perils of childhood and became adults lived their life course as it unfolded, usually connecting families through marriage and having children and a household of their own. The presence of elders (both men and women) was normal and important. And the generational cycle remained stable over time.

In very general terms, descriptions of modern Mediterranean expectations of the trajectory of the life course are similar to what can be understood from the ancient Mediterranean. A man would emerge from his "foolish" youth to marry, be productive in public or vocational life, provide for his children, and begin to relinquish active responsibilities as he moved into old age. In contrast, a woman's identity was derived from biological and social factors, namely, marital status, motherhood, and child-rearing, her social standing increasing with age. The family or household formed the basis of a typical life course. One's position in the household was a critical factor in determining its basic facets. How individuals were viewed and how they behaved depended on cultural expectations of certain chronological ages and/or social ages (Harlow and Laurence 2002, 17). There was a strong contrast between stages of life (especially childhood, youth, adulthood, and old age). Age-appropriate behaviour was strongly gendered. Men were expected to behave and age in a "masculine" way; women were expected to behave and age in "feminine" ways over the life course.

As it is in all times and cultures, age mattered as part of social identity in the ancient Mediterranean world. In that context, it was at least as important as gender and social status. Age affected what kinds of roles one might play in the family and in society during the life course. Age-related behaviour mattered for honourable reputation. How younger people behaved in public, including how they treated their elders, reflected on and affected the reputation of the group. Older men and older women also had certain gendered roles to fulfill in their responsibilities toward those younger than themselves. The designation of "young" and "old" was fluid, depending on context. Group dynamics in the private realm were affected by whether members conformed or rebelled against age-related norms. Although the author of 1 Timothy tends to see intergenerational relationships as working toward *generational stability*, there may be other early Christian texts that demonstrate ways that intergenerational dynamics tend toward *social change*.

These nuances and complexities of age and demography, as well as generational stability and social change, provide background for considering the lives of the early Christ followers and early Christians. Finding clues about age and understanding it in the context of the ancient Mediterranean may not always be as straightforward as finding evidence about other social markers (like gender or social status). Many characters and figures are seemingly ageless – but of course they were not. However, the importance of age for social identity provides an impetus to consider its implications. Being cognizant of age as part of social identity is part of an informed imagination as we read early Christian texts and try to understand the social universe they assume.

SOME SUGGESTIONS FOR FUTURE RESEARCH

This study looks at 1 Timothy through a culturally sensitive lens focused on age as a critical aspect of social identity, finding new possibilities to explain the social situation and rhetoric of this letter. Given the importance of age structure as part of social dynamics, I offer a few suggestions for further study in the area of age dynamics in early Christianity.

The author of Luke-Acts seems particularly interested in age; he refers to specific ages and stage of the life course more frequently than other canonical gospel writers. Luke is the only gospel to tell the story of Elizabeth and Zechariah, who were too old to have children when they miraculously conceive John the Baptist (Luke 1:7, 18, 36), for example.[14] In fact, Luke-Acts has a curiously high number of chronological age references. For instance, Luke reports that Jesus was twelve when he stayed behind at the Temple (2:42), and around thirty when he began his ministry (3:23). Anna, the Judean widow and prophet of Luke's birth narrative, was purportedly eighty-four (2:37). Jesus heals a girl who is twelve years old (8:42; also Mark 5:42; Matthew skips this detail). Jesus heals a woman whose body was disfigured for eighteen years (Luke 13:11, 16); Peter heals a man lame from birth (Acts 3:2) who was over forty years old (4:22). As least some of these ages are symbolic or highlight age-related roles. Examining the author's interest in age-related roles may provide more nuanced readings of the stories and characters in Luke-Acts.

How old was the adult Jesus presented in the canonical gospels? This may seem to have a straightforward answer. According to Luke, Jesus was around thirty when he began his ministry (3:23), but this stated chronological age may be more about the maturity of the character of Jesus in Luke's gospel story than about the age of the historical person of Jesus when he began his public appearances (see chapter 1, note 11 and chapter 6, note 7). The only other early reference to Jesus's age is in the Gospel of John where the Judeans question Jesus, saying he is "not yet fifty years old" (8:57), perhaps meaning he was not yet old enough to have the authority or wisdom he displayed (*m. Aboth* 5.21, age fifty is when one is able to "counsel"). This reference may tell us more about age assumptions than about Jesus's age per se.[15] In his late second-century treatise *Against Heresies*, Irenaeus suggests Jesus was closer to fifty when his ministry ended, having passed through all the stages of life so as to relate to all people (2.22.4–6). This is a theological statement, not a historical or demographic one, and may simply take John's reference at face value, but it does cause one to wonder about Jesus's age (both historically, and within the gospel stories).

I have argued that older women had significant roles connected to their age, marital status, and social standing in early Christian communities (suggested also by Osiek and MacDonald 2006, 13). As we have seen, older women were viewed not only as influential teachers of younger women (Titus 2:3–5) but of children as well (2 Tim. 1:5), and old widows are presented as models of behaviour and legacy (1 Tim. 5:9–10). On the other hand, old women are also prone to negative sentiment ("old wives' tales" 1 Tim. 4:7) and stereotypes (Titus 2:3). It is worth considering the ages of women like Phoebe (Rom. 16:1–2), Priscilla (Rom. 16:3; 1 Cor. 16:19; 2 Tim. 4:19; Acts 18:2, 18, 26), Junia (Rom. 16:7), Tabitha (Acts 9:36–41), Lydia (Acts 16:13–15), and Grapte (who is granted the authority to instruct widows and orphans with the same teachings as the men [and presumably their wives] would receive from the elders; *Shepherd* of Hermas, Visions 8.3. Their prominence, independence, and authority suggest that they are likely to be older women. E.P. Sanders comments on the paucity of information on Mary Magdalene, humorously suggesting, "For all we know, on the basis of our sources, she was eighty-six, childless, and keen to mother unkempt young men" (1995, 75). Perhaps he is more correct than one might think, in contrast with the popular notions of Mary Magdalene as a *young* (often seductive) woman that emerge from later (especially Western Catholic and Protestant) traditions.

Age is implicated in understanding certain images connected to particular stages or moments of the life course. The "bride" of Christ (Rev 21:2, 9; 22:17) would have been understood as a young woman, with all of its implications. The word "bride" (νύμφη) is translated elsewhere as "daughter-in-law" (Q 12:53, an allusion to Micah 7:6), which has particular social implications within ancient Mediterranean social contexts.

Assumptions about age in the ancient Mediterranean are not necessarily obvious to modern readers. Age could be a factor in how conflict played out between individuals, for instance. Perhaps there was an age element to the conflict between Paul and Peter if a younger Paul confronted Peter as someone older than himself (Gal. 2:11–14).[16]

With the potential consequences of private and public confrontation between generations, there may be more to consider with regard to intergenerational relationships, such as the tension between younger and older men in the community in 1 Peter (5:5; see Welborn 2018, 89), and the conflict between Hermas and his adult children in the *Shepherd* of Hermas (Visions 3.1). First John is couched in intergenerational terminology (e.g., "my little children," 2:1), and 2 and 3 John are written by someone who calls himself a πρεσβύτερος, that is, an elder or old man (verse 1 in both texts).

This study on age structure provides a foundation for culturally sensitive work on old age in early Christianity (Carter 1995), including demographic realities (chapter 1), and considerations of how positive and negative stereotypes, idealization, gender differences, and expected roles affect characterizations and rhetoric around old age and elderly people in early Christian texts.

Considerations of age as a social category in texts originating in Second Temple Judaism would help to gain a clearer sense of Judean/Jewish understandings of age leading up to the first century. The possibilities are many. The wisdom sayings of Sirach (e.g., 3:12–16, 25:3–11), the stories of older people, like Eleazar in Maccabees (2 Macc. 6:18–31; 4 Macc. 6:1–30), and the stories of younger people, like the apparently young, brave, honourable widow Judith, the impropriety of the elders toward Susanna (Book of Susanna), and the young hero Daniel (Daniel 1:3–7; Book of Susanna 1:45), are but a few.

Further studies in the Apostolic Fathers, the New Testament Apocrypha, and early Patristic writers would also yield considerations of varying attitudes with regard to age among the diversity of Christianities in the first few centuries.

CONCLUSION

While the experience of aging is constantly in flux through time, age structure is a relatively constant, stable force that helps to govern social relationships. How people perceive, experience, and live out that age structure and its expectations varies according to cultural and social norms, as well as individual, communal, and historical experiences.

Examining dynamics of age in 1 Timothy has allowed us to consider age and age structure in early Christianity, how they affected intergenerational relationships, development of leadership roles and other responsibilities among men and women, and behaviour related to the honour and reputation of the community. Among the Christ-followers, the age of individuals was always fluid as children grew up, adults grew older, and the generational cycle continued. Texts typically represent snapshots, and the best we can do is compare these moments in time. Still, it is possible to detect patterns of age structure and age-related expectations and behaviour, comparing the texts with demographic, epigraphical, and literary data from the ancient Mediterranean world, as well as drawing on analogies from modern traditional Mediterranean patterns and norms. Age structure and age-related roles, though regularly challenged, remained stable. As an important part of social identity, age shaped how one behaved in one's family, in one's community, and in society. It was an important component of how a person interacted in every relationship they had.

Honouring age as a crucial social category and an embodied reality in the ancient Mediterranean alerts us to its constancy and importance. It may also prompt us to consider our own experiences of age – in all their varieties – with new appreciation. After all, all human beings share the experience of an aging body, intergenerational relationships, and age cohort effects, even as we each understand age through our individual life experiences, and cultural, historical, and spatial contexts. Indeed, we all age. The social dynamics of age and aging, however, are remarkably variable across time and cultures and worthy of closer examination.

Notes

CHAPTER ONE

1 In the undisputed Pauline letters, for example, Paul often refers to men and women, and to slavery or wealth (e.g., Gal. 3:28; 1 Cor. 7:1–40, 11:1–14), but there is a distinct dearth of references to age or age structure (Barclay 2007, 225). A lack of reference, however, does not mean age was not important to Paul (*contra* Barclay 2007, 240–1). Marianne Bjelland Kartzow points out the importance of age as a social category, especially reflected in the letters to Timothy and Titus (2009, 22).

2 The use of the word "Christian" for the earliest groups of followers of Jesus is anachronistic; the term is never used by Paul, and the Greek equivalent (χριστιανός) is found only three times in the New Testament (Acts 11:26, 26:28; 1 Pet. 4:16). Phrases like "Christ followers" or "Christ groups" are becoming more common in scholarship to describe Pauline and other early groups. However, the communities of the late first and early second centuries CE (like the one represented by 1 Timothy) point toward a more legitimate use of the phrase "early Christian," given the increased use of χριστιανός within the movement at that time (for example, Ignatius, *Rom.* 3.2, AF 2003, 1:272; *Poly.* 7.3, AF 2003, 1:318; *Didache* 12.4, AF 2003, 1:436; and *Epistle to Diognetus* 4.6, AF 2003, 2:138).

3 I use the term "modern" strictly as a means of contrasting my contemporary world with the "ancient" peoples in and behind the texts; thus, I am not using "modern" in a philosophical sense. I use the phrase "modern Western" to define the prominent twenty-first century social, economic, and political structures of the dominating culture found in Canada (and elsewhere) that tends toward an individualist worldview. My primary motive is to contrast this individualist, technologically advancing

worldview with the ancient Mediterranean world in which the early Christians lived, and which tended toward a collectivist way of thinking and being (e.g., Malina 2010, 17–28). My own worldview derives from twenty- and twenty-first-century "Western" experience, having been born and raised in western Canada, with English-speaking Anglo-Protestant and Ukrainian Orthodox ancestors, all of whom migrated from Europe several generations before me. I have now lived for over two decades in southern Ontario on the traditional territory of the Anishnaabe, Haudenosaunee, and Neutral (Indigenous) peoples. I have chosen not to use the term "Global North" because many people groups (like Indigenous nations and many who have immigrated "north" from around the world) within the Global North have collectivist worldviews. In acknowledging the variety of worldviews within the groups who reside on Turtle Island, I also acknowledge that "Western" colonial structures and intellectual paradigms have usurped other ways of knowing in public and academic discourse. My own worldview is the primary lens through which I read the text, even as I seek to be influenced by and in dialogue with other ways of knowing, such as the decolonializing perspectives of Néstor Medina, Alison Hari-Singh, and HyeRan Kim-Cragg (2019), Fernando F. Segovia (2000), and R.S. Sugirtharajah (1995).

4 Roman historians draw on several types of data. (1) *Census data* from Roman Egypt in the first three centuries CE (Bagnall and Frier 1994) provides a good starting point, but this is fragmentary, sometimes deliberately misrepresentative, and geographically unique to Egypt (Scheidel 2001b, 12–14). (2) *Funerary inscriptions* (epigraphy) commemorate household members after their deaths (Shaw 1991; Hope 2007), but ages are not always included (Hope 2007, 111–12), and some are rounded (Duncan-Jones 1977). Also, they represent only a portion of the population, namely, those who could afford public commemoration (Hopkins 1966, 246; Parkin 1992, 6–19; Saller 1994, 15–19). (3) *Model life tables* provide a statistical framework that extrapolates ancient population patterns by using known (modern) population patterns (tables) of mortality and fertility (Parkin 1992, 72, 79–90; Bagnall and Frier 1994, 34–5; Woods 2007). Model life tables provide the most popular demographic tool used by historians of the ancient Roman world, with the caveat that they are meant to be generalizations. They are also subject to significant revision (Woods 2007) and do not account for geographically specific disease and climate variations (Scheidel 2001a, 34–5; 2001b, 5–11, 15–19; 22, 25) or migration. Recent work with osteological data (human skeletal remains) is still developing (MacKinnon 2007; Gowland 2007, 165–8; see

also Marklein, Leahy, and Crews 2016), but it has similar limitations to funerary inscriptions since burial is culturally determined and does not account for all individuals in a population (Parkin 1992, 41–58; Saller 1994, 18–19; Scheidel 2001b, 11).

5 Because of the nature of the evidence, I discuss life expectancy at birth in the Roman world around the two centuries before and after the beginning of the Common Era in a general sense. My goal is to sketch a broad understanding of age structure, especially in contrast to my contemporary context. Studies related to the social world of specific Christ groups and early Christian communities would benefit from finding demographic data related to life expectancy for particular moments in time and particular geographical regions, if possible.

6 Though many would argue that socio-economic status (education, income, occupation) is "one of the strongest predictors of health and mortality among all variables used in social science" (Lynch 2008, 127), disease, climate, and the urban-rural divide were likely more of a measure in the ancient Roman Empire. See discussion and sources in Scheidel (2001b); see also Sallares (2002). For recent surveys on Roman demography see Scheidel (2012) and Hin (2013). For similar anthropological discussions, see Weiss (1981, 27–50), Amoss and Harrell (1981, 2), and Crew (1990, 16–18).

7 There is no way to calculate the average with certainty because we do not possess enough data from the ancient Mediterranean world. However, the range of twenty to thirty years is the "standard view" (Saller 1994, 20). Tim G. Parkin argues that a range of twenty to thirty years allows for changes over time (1992, 84). Roger S. Bagnall and Bruce W. Frier's study of Egyptian census returns leads them to suggest the lower twenties, namely, twenty-two to twenty-five years (1994, 109–10). Given the nature and paucity of the data available, Walter Scheidel insists that a range of twenty to thirty years is as precise as we can be (the range of climates and environments throughout the Roman Empire would change the average from place to place) (2001a, 20–5). With his revision of the use of model life tables for ancient demography, Robert Woods suggests "upper twenties or low thirties" (2007, 394).

8 Following Robert Woods (2007), Tim G. Parkin estimates infant mortality (up to age one) to be approximately 200 of every 1000 births and early childhood mortality (up to age five) to be approximately 350 in every 1000 births (2011, 185). These are revised from Parkin's previous studies, namely, infant mortality of 300 per 1000 infant births and early childhood mortality of 450 per 1000 births (Parkin 2003, 48–9, 280; also

Harlow and Laurence 2002, 10). The debate regarding infant mortality rates in ancient Rome centers around the difficulties of using model life tables. The fact remains, however, that infant and child mortality were comparatively very high.

9 Woods (2007) proposes that more younger adults died than Parkin's figures suggest. Woods's revised use of model life tables (which has become standard in the field; see Parkin 2011, 185), may change these figures slightly, but the general pattern remains illustrative.

10 As an analogy from isolated communities in the south Pacific islands, Dorothy Ayers Counts and David R. Counts observe that low average life expectancy at birth in these communities was not relevant to the physical or mental state of community members. They suggest that "the process and duration of physical aging are everywhere the same" (1985, 7).

11 Censorinus reports that Varro, for example, lists *adulescens* from fifteen to thirty and *iuvenis* from thirty to forty-five (*The Natal Day*, 14.2). Others listed age twenty-eight as the beginning of male adulthood (for sources, see Laes and Strubbe 2014, 26–7). Luke's statement that Jesus was "about age thirty" (ὡσεὶ ἐτῶν τριάκοντα; 3:23) is likely signifying male adult maturity, not the latter stage of life (*contra* Rohrbaugh 1996, 5).

12 For example, among the !Kung prior to 1950, whose average life expectancy at birth was estimated to be thirty years (on par with the ancient figures), old age was always a "regular and unremarkable phenomenon" (Biesele and Howell 1981, 82).

13 Similarly, Ray Laurence argues that the numbers of epitaphs dedicated to children in Pompeii "highlights a sense of bereavement amongst the adults who cremated and buried their loved ones" because, despite the demographic realities and experience of high child mortality, parents expected their children to outlive them (2007, 103).

14 Saller suggests three scenarios (1994, 48–65): one "ordinary" (assuming a non-elite woman married at twenty, a non-elite man married at thirty, both with a life expectancy at birth of twenty-five years), and two "senatorial" (assuming earlier marriage and arguably higher life expectancy for the elite; but see Scheidel [1999]). I summarize figures from the "ordinary" simulations for men. In fact, there are a number of problematic assumptions about the simulation, including the static age of marriage. While the simulation for men has some suggestive qualities, the simulation for women is unusable. For example, the percentages of married women in their fifties are much too high (e.g., 93 per cent at age fifty-five). Jens-Uwe Krause argues that 40 per cent of women between the ages of thirty and fifty, and 30 per cent of all adult women at any given

time, were widows (1994, 73). Thomas McGinn suggests these estimates are too high (1999, 631), but they are likely closer to reality than Saller's numbers are.

15 For evidence from inscriptions regarding a gap in age of five to ten years in a first marriage, see Shaw (1987, 43; see also Saller 1987). For evidence from Roman Egypt, see Bagnall and Frier (1994, 118–19). Mary Harlow and Ray Laurence outline three marriage scenarios: (1) The marriage of a twenty-five-year-old male to a fifteen-year-old female linked three generations and a long, stable marriage was expected (2002, 97). (2) A forty-year-old bridegroom might prefer a young bride because older women might be more powerful and more assertive due to their higher status after having children (85, 90). In this case, the groom and his father-in-law would be of similar ages, creating an alliance through the young bride (see also chapter 8, note 33). This scenario would be especially important for a man who needed heirs (97–8). (3) Occasionally, an old man (say about sixty) might marry a young virgin, but this marriage was usually ridiculed because it "subvert[ed] the normal life course" (98–9). On old age in the ancient Roman world, see Parkin (1998, 2003) and Cokayne (2003).

16 Colloquially, age cohorts are often referred to as "generations." Popular terms like the "Baby Boomer Generation" (understood to refer to people born between 1946 and 1964) or "Generation X" (born between 1965 and 1980) are actually describing birth cohorts (people born at or around the same time). The word "generation" most accurately describes kin relationships; at the most basic level, a parent and child are in different generations. For example, I am in the same generation as my sibling and first cousins, even if some of my cousins are closer in age to my mother. My mother, aunts, and uncles are all in the same generation, even if some of my aunts and uncles are closer in age to my paternal grandmother. By and large, the term "age cohort" is a more accurate representation of a group of people born around the same time, though there is some debate about the terminology (e.g., Alwin and McCammon 2003).

17 Johnson finds the majority opinion untenable and argues for Pauline authorship, "convinced that the position now in favor is deeply flawed and in need of re-examination" as "an assumed and unexamined verity" (1996, 3) and, primarily on the basis of ancient evidence, Towner agrees (2006, xv, 5–15). Johnson does consider 1 Timothy the "most difficult of the three letters to defend as authentic" (106; see also 67). Friedrich D.E. Schleiermacher (1807) was the first critical scholar to question whether 1 Timothy was written by Paul. Interestingly, he did not question 2 Timothy or Titus, though within a few years, F.C. Baur (1835) argued for the unity

of 1 Timothy, 2 Timothy, and Titus, and thus pseudepigraphy (or heteronymity, see below) for all three. For a good discussion of the history in scholarship, see Jens Herzer (2008, 547–55). In addition to Johnson and Towner, there are other notable contemporary scholars who advocate Pauline authorship, such as C. Spicq (1947) and George W. Knight III (1992).

18 I use the term "overseer" for ἐπισκόπος to avoid the anachronistic connotations of the usual translation "bishop," except in direct quotations of others (see also Campbell 1994, 179n11). The word διακόνος literally means "servant" but can refer to an "attendant or official in a temple or religious guild" (LSJ 1940, 398). In the undisputed letters, Paul uses it of himself and others, like Apollos (e.g., 1 Cor. 3:5; 2 Cor. 3:6, 6:4) and Phoebe (Rom. 16:1), but also uses it in a more general sense (e.g., Rom. 13:4). The term later came to be known as an official title in the Christian church: "deacon." To avoid the potentially anachronistic sense of the English rendering "deacon," I retain the transliterated Greek word (*diakonos*) because it distinguishes the distinct role assumed in 1 Tim. 3:8–13 from other words that could also be translated as "servant" or "attendant." The word is also used for Timothy himself (1 Tim. 4:6); it is not found in 2 Timothy or Titus.

19 This is a term coined by Harold Remus (personal communication). See also I. Howard Marshall's use of the term "allonymity"; he posits that the letters were written by someone "other" (ἄλλος) than Paul shortly after Paul's death, with no intention of deceit (1999, 84).

20 Paul Treblico cites a list of people who are associated with Ephesus and "the Pastorals" (2004, 206–7). Most of the names, however, are associated with 2 Timothy, not 1 Timothy, so this cannot prove definitively that 1 Timothy was destined for Ephesus.

21 Marshall advocates an early date of 70–80 CE, shortly after the death of Paul (1999, 92), positing an author who promotes the same core theology as Paul (102; also Pietersen 2004, 138). This early date is plausible but does not easily account for what appear to be social developments in the letter. Most other commentators suggest a range of dates for all three letters to Timothy and Titus, either 80 to 100 CE (e.g., Treblico 2004, 204) or 100 to 140 CE (e.g., MacDonald 1988, 3–4; Hanson 1966, 7–8), increasingly favouring the former. Others are more vague, dating them in the first, possibly second century (e.g., Young 1994b, 5). I consider a late date less plausible because 1 Timothy had to have been written early enough that people would accept it as part of the Pauline corpus. Other letters purportedly written by Paul were clearly rejected in the second

century (e.g., *3 Corinthians*; Johnson 1996, 23). Jerome D. Quinn and William C. Wacker point out that "if the [Pastoral Epistles] originated in the second century, it is striking that they, intent on transmitting the Pauline heritage, do not quote the apostle's own words," especially since other authors like the author of *1 Clement* (96 CE) and Ignatius (110 CE) do quote Paul's letters (2000, 19; e.g., Ignatius, *Eph.* 8.2, citing Rom. 8:5). In addition, the letter implies movement toward greater community structure (e.g., choosing overseers; 3:1–7), but not necessarily the more advanced structure evident in the second century, such as Ignatius's (110 CE) recognition of overseers as leaders in many locations (*Eph.* 4.2).

22 For challenges to this concept see, for example, Michael Prior (1989), Jerome Murphy-O'Connor (1991), Johnson (1996, 22), LaFosse (2001), Williams A. Richards (2002), Michel Gourgues (2009, 39–41), Alistair C. Stewart (2014), and especially Herzer (2007; 2008). Abraham J. Malherbe also endorsed a methodological approach to 1 Timothy, 2 Timothy, and Titus that treats each letter on its own terms (personal communication). Johnson, who advocates Pauline authorship, asserts that the majority opinion of heteronymity assumes the unity of all three letters, so that if 2 Timothy was shown to be Pauline (for example), the entire theory would collapse (1996, 7–8, 22; also 19–26). See also Towner (who seems unaware of Richards's study) for an insightful discussion on the unity and individuality of these letters (2006, 27–30).

23 There is debate over how to translate the term Ἰουδαῖος (and cognates), given that it is a term that denotes identity with the land, people, and God of Ἰουδαία (Judaea). "Judean" may be preferred over "Jew" in this respect (Elliott 2007), though generally the convention continues to be "Jew" (see Mason 2007). I tend to use Judean, but sometimes use both terms to cover both accuracy and clarity.

24 *Contra* Dibelius and Conzelmann who argue that "if all these sections are interpreted as referring to the same heresy, and a distinction is made only between the seducers and the seduced, a comparatively clear picture can be attained" (1972, 65). In this typical view, taking all three letters together (e.g., Marshall 1999, 44–6), the following attributes are apparently discernible: In addition to their apparent Judean teaching and mythology (1 Tim. 1:7; Titus 1:14), they encouraged asceticism, prohibiting marriage (1 Tim. 4:3; also 1 Tim. 2:15, 5:14 and Titus 2:4) and promoting abstinence from foods (1 Tim. 4:3; 1 Tim. 5:23). They "spiritualized" the resurrection, saying it had already happened (2 Tim. 2:18). Their influence was widespread but had a special appeal for women, captivating weak women by infiltrating households (2 Tim. 2:6), deceiving women

(resembling the deception of Eve; 1 Tim. 2:14), and leading them astray (like the young widows; 1 Tim. 5:15). Doctrinally, they may have rejected the idea that all people can be saved by God (1 Tim. 2:4–6, 4:10), and perhaps questioned the humanity of Jesus (1 Tim. 2:5, 3:16). Notice that these characteristics of the opponents are drawn from various parts of the three letters, conflating them as if they were one text. Taking 1 Timothy as a letter on its own terms shifts (and I think clarifies) the picture of the opponents (see chapter 3).

25 See also Herzer (2007), where he outlines a theory for different authors and the literary dependence of 1 Timothy upon 2 Timothy and Titus.

26 David G. Horrell encourages modern readers of 1 Timothy "to read the author's rhetoric (and every author's rhetoric!) with a degree of suspicion, and to resist taking (often stereotypical) polemic at face value" (2008, 112; see also Zamfir 2013, xvii).

27 Peter G. Bush deems this "properly conducted order" (1990, 156) in the community. See discussion in Annette Bourland Huizenga (2013, 301n41).

28 It is not a general letter of traditional material (as touted by Dibelius and Conzelmann 1972, 8–9), a view that has generally been rejected in scholarship (e.g., Verner 1983, 3–26; Donelson 1986, 2; Towner 2006, 37–53).

CHAPTER TWO

1 The subfield of the anthropology of aging has slowly grown in importance since the 1980s (Kertzer and Keith 1984, 13–14). Nearly three decades ago, Lawrence Cohen noted that while anthropologists have lamented the paucity of attention paid to age and aging, there are, in fact, numerous monographs and articles that do focus on age (Cohen 1994, 18–19). At that time, he was critical of this subfield because it did not often consider the insights of the self-reflective, postmodern anthropology of the late twentieth century, especially the biases of the anthropologist, ageist language, and other hegemonic effects of the researcher's perspective of the elderly. He lauded the efforts of Barbara Myerhoff (1979), who donned gardening gloves and heavy shoes in regular daily activities to try to experience some of the physical efforts of her elderly informants (Cohen 1994, 18–19). Another example of self-reflective research is the fieldwork of David and Dorothy Counts (1996), who travelled for a year in their own RV (recreational vehicle), exploring the subculture of older people who form transient RV communities in the United States.

2 As a historian, I approach these texts as data to help explain the communities they represent. On one level, I am using the anthropological

comparison to better understand the text, but ultimately, I am interested in using the text to better understand history, namely, the history of Christ groups and early Christians in their ancient Mediterranean settings. Yet, I suspect all historical study has some element of implicit comparison to one's own time and place.

3 There has been important debate around the terminology and use of "models" in studying the early Christian texts (e.g., Garrett 1992, 97; Horrell 1996, 9–18; Esler 1998; Horrell 2000; Esler 2000). I have been influenced by, and have gratefully been a part of, the Context Group, whose members have typically strongly endorsed the use of models. However, I also agree with those who are concerned about the static or rigid use of models; who emphasize the need for nuance and recognition of variation, the necessity of review and of revision; and who warn of the dangers of misrepresenting the data through abstraction (e.g., Horrell 1999, 14–15; Garrett 1992, 93; Chance 1994; Meggitt 1998). I, therefore, attempt to construct and use my "models" in a heuristic way that opens up new questions and possibilities to be explored with comparative ancient data rather than dictating what age structure should look like (cf. Horrell 1999, 11).

4 Discussed in Horrell (1999, 10). In his critique of the field many decades ago, E.A. Judge warned, "A 'religious' history that settles for a predetermined pattern of explanation, be it ecclesiastical or sociological, disqualifies itself from discovering how things were" (1980, 217, see also 210; in addition, see Rodd 1981, 95–106).

5 For example, in one Greek community in the mid-twentieth century, reputable women who were over sixty would bake the bread for Easter (Campbell 1964, 290). Their age might be a direct application of 1 Tim. 5:19 where widows who are over sixty are highlighted for their pious contribution to the community. Or the age of sixty could reflect a general Mediterranean notion of age that was adapted differently by both the textual reference in 1 Timothy and the Greek Orthodox bread-baking privilege. Or the age of sixty might just be coincidental. The twentieth-century bakers tell us nothing directly about the early Christians, but the two references to a specific age might prompt us to search the ancient literature for similar references to women over sixty.

6 For example, Elizabeth Schüssler Fiorenza's groundbreaking work in feminist hermeneutics (*In Memory of Her*, 1983) remains foundational for establishing a new lens through which to view early Christian studies. In my estimation, it has moments that betray reading the values of the late twentieth century into her historical reading of the text. For instance, she

finds "equality" in a culture that rarely, if ever, tolerates such a concept (see Kloppenborg 1996b and discussion in chapter 11). I acknowledge that my historical reading is one way of reading and engaging the biblical texts among many, but I believe it is valuable and useful, both for understanding the text in its own context and for further interpretation.

7 Where appropriate, I refer to Mediterranean "cultures" rather than "culture" since the cultures of the Mediterranean region vary (Fry 1980, 8–9; Herzfeld 1980).

8 Contact with modernized cultures is itself an agent of culture change, but the change may come in the shape of an impetus to retain or revive traditional ways.

9 Renée B. Hirschon's study within a Greek city (1983), Neni Panourgiá's ethnography of death in Athens (1995), and several essays from J.G. Peristiany's edited volume *Mediterranean Family Structures* (1976) in Turkish cities are particularly helpful. Panourgiá discusses the historical distance between ancient Athens and the modern city in its European context (1995, 36–40).

10 I use the terms "polytheistic" and "polytheism" rather than "pagan" or "paganism" to denote Roman religious practice, following the suggestion of Harold Remus (2004). As he notes, all terms have their problems, but "polytheism" is closer to the mark and less anachronistic. It also lessens confusion around modern movements and practice that use the term "pagan" today.

11 Thus, when I refer to "Roman" I am not referring to citizenship or the city of Rome itself (cf. Winter 2003, 5). I largely avoid the term "Greco-Roman" even though there is some cultural continuity between the Greek and Roman civilizations.

12 In the New Testament, this includes most of the undisputed and disputed Pauline letters, 1 Peter, the Johannine literature, Revelation, possibly Luke-Acts, and non-canonical texts, including the letters of Ignatius and Polycarp, the Montanist fragments, and many others.

13 David Magie demonstrates that Romans resided in many cities in Asia Minor and set up additional Roman settlements, modelled on those in Italy, beginning with Julius Caesar and continuing with Augustus (1950, 415). The people of Asia Minor originated the imperial cult, demonstrating their general loyalty to Rome (406–7, 447–8, 452). The inscriptions found on tombs and sarcophagi discovered in Ephesus by John Turtle Wood (1975 [1877]) demonstrate a mix of Latin and Greek, with a good number of Roman names. Clifford Ando suggests that the peace in the Roman Empire that followed Augustus's victory allowed for the

perception of consensus in the provinces through granting citizenship, promoting the emperor cult, circulating imperial art and monuments, and sharing a common calendar. This perceived unification promoted loyalty to Rome and adoption of Roman legal and political ideas (2000, 1–15). Bruce W. Winter argues that such "Romanization" extended also to social ideas and behaviour through the promotion of Roman values in the provinces (2003, 2–6).

14 In their study of the Roman life course, Mary Harlow and Ray Laurence suggest that perceptions and beliefs about age and age-related behaviour might be similar across different social positions in the ancient Mediterranean world (2002, 146). Following the methodology of Malherbe (1986, 11–15), Korinna Zamfir also argues that elite views can illuminate "contemporary norms" (2013, 63) and reflect the environment in which early Christianity operated (xvii, 37–8, 68–9). One must still exercise due caution on a case-by-case basis for application to the non-elite population.

15 Similarly, Cicero's personal letters provide "our most intimate evidence for day-to-day experiences of Roman families" (Saller 1994, 2). This is not to say their experiences would always reflect those of the non-elite since their economic and social worries would differ significantly (see MacMullen 1974, 88–120).

16 Plays written in the prolific period of the Athenian fifth century BCE, such as those by Aristophanes (e.g., *Wasps*, *Clouds*) and Sophocles (e.g., *Oedipus at Colonus*; see Bertman 1976; Parkin 2003), are popular choices for Classical scholars studying age. Roman audiences would have been familiar with such plays, and, at times, Roman playwrights adapted themes from the great Greek plays to suit their own audiences (e.g., the *Oedipus* of Seneca written in the first century CE).

17 For example, Papyrus Michigan 322 (46 CE) is a legal document that outlines how a married couple in their sixties wished to distribute their wealth to their children while ensuring their care in old age and proper burial. See Jane Rowlandson (1998) for this source as well as caches of family letters. It is worth noting that the geographical and cultural specificity of inscriptions and papyri can limit their value. Papyri, for example, were mostly preserved in Roman Egypt.

18 Among anthropologists, the original conception of this cultural value was highly gendered (Peristiany 1976, Pitt-Rivers 1977), where honour was associated with men and shame with women. More recent presentations of this cultural value may simply call it "honour" (e.g., Rohrbaugh 2010), which takes into account more developed ideas about honour in the

anthropological literature (e.g., Delaney 1987, Wikan 1984). See my explanation of modesty and shame below.

19 Following Abu-Lughod (1993, 22), I tend to prefer the term "modesty" rather than "shame" when labelling the deferential behaviour of women to men, young people to their elders, and those of lower status or social position to their superiors. In this way, modesty is an expression of honourable behaviour.

20 Importantly, women are not simply passive preservers of shame, and neither are the young (see below).

21 The patron-client relationship is a particular form of social and economic interaction that is found in most Mediterranean cultures but is rather foreign to contemporary Western society (Elliott 1996, 146). A person of higher status (the patron) forms an informal, reciprocal relationship with a person (or a group) of lower status (the client). Each party benefits from the other. The patron assists the client with financial aid, legal support, career advancement, lodging, protection, and other favours that his or her influence can afford. The client returns the patron's favours with loyalty, praise for the patron's generosity, and public support (such as voting for the patron in political contests), thereby strengthening the patron's social prestige and influence. The relationship is voluntary because it is not legally binding, but the continual cycle of reciprocal obligations means it is typically long-term. Scholars use this cultural phenomenon as a model to consider social dynamics that might otherwise make little sense within a Western worldview that emphasizes egalitarianism. For further detail, see Saller (1982) and John H. Elliott (1996, 144–56). For examples of patronage in the New Testament, see Alicia J. Batten (2010), Zeba A. Crook (2004), and John K. Chow (1992). On women as patrons, see Carolyn Osiek and Margaret Y. MacDonald (2007, 194–219), and Osiek (2009).

22 For general discussions on "honour" as relevant to Christ groups and early Christian texts, see, for example, Halvor Moxnes (1996, 19–40), Malina (2001, 27–57), and Richard L. Rohrbaugh (2010).

23 In Milocca, people expect a daughter will share the reputation of her mother, whether positive or negative (Chapman 1971, 85, 96). Muriel Dimen notes that, in Greece, the reputation of a married woman is based on that of her mother-in-law (1986, 64). Campbell also suggests that moral attributes pass from parents to children, as expressed by the saying (which is not unfamiliar in its English parallel) "The apple will fall under the apple tree" (*to milo apo kat'ap'ti milia tha pesi*; 1964, 166–7). Peristiany states that a woman must defend her chastity within marriage "in order not to dishonour her own children" (1976, 12).

24 Michael Herzfeld recommends carefully defining honour according to emic categories (how people within a culture perceive themselves), since "the precise interpretation of moral-value terms requires a clear perception of their linguistic and social context in each community" (1980, 347–8).
25 Similarly, Cool and McCabe observe that in the Lebanese community they studied, the father-son relationship is pivotal in the male life course, especially between the father and son or sons who will inherit the father's property (1983, 65).
26 The household (οἶκος) refers to the space and the people associated with the family domicile. We might be tempted to equate οἶκος with "family," but "the Roman family is an ambiguous concept and defies easy definition" (Bradley 1991, 5; see also Osiek 2011). The differentiation of the Latin terms *domus* and *familia* is helpful. The Roman *domus* denoted the typical domestic unit (often meaning household or living unit). It included those related by blood or marriage as well as others (slaves and domestic servants) within the household, with the husband, wife, and children as the typical core unit. The Roman *familia*, by contrast, referred to those under the power of the *paterfamilias*, by nature (primarily children and descendants through the male line), or by law (such as adopted children and slaves, who were part of the *familia* whether or not they resided in the *domus*). One's *familia* identity was important for legal matters, but the *domus* was the focus of social interaction, and thus of the experience of the life course. The Latin *domus* approximates the semantic domain of the Greek οἶκος (normally translated "household"). The Roman definitions for family and household are illustrative for considering the life course of the early Christ followers. Moxnes distinguishes between family (encompassing kinship grouping, as well as certain symbols, values, and meaning), household (a residence unit in one location that was task-oriented and functional), kinship (the larger network of relatives based on birth and marriage, which may involve political power), and family history (a process through which the family interacts with external society and wider kin; 1997, 16–17).
27 The centrality of family identity over individual identity is crucial in considering age structure, as exemplified in Ray Laurence's study of inscriptions on *columellae* in Pompeii. The inscriptions seldom mention age, but for those that do, more than half are for females aged eighteen to thirty-two, and the majority are for males from zero to seven years old. Such a small sample of ages does not reflect demographic realities or the life course of an individual; instead, Laurence surmises, the inscription

represents the person's *familia* identity. When a young woman dies, her kin publicly mourn the loss of new *familia* (the connection to her husband's family), as well as potential descendants that she could have birthed. A male child's death threatens the loss of the entire *familia* (2007, 109).

28 Paul, for example, uses familial language in his letters, most notably the term ἀδελφοί (literally "brothers" or "brothers and sisters," depending on context), but also father-child language (e.g., 1 Thess. 2:9–12; Aasgaard 2004, 85–95). Most importantly for my study, the family and the household continued to provide metaphors for the self-conception and social interaction of early Christian communities in the late first and early second centuries (e.g., Eph. 2:19; Heb. 3:6; 1 Pet. 4:17; Osiek and Balch 1997, 215). The author of 1 Timothy, for example, explicitly conceives of the community as "the household of God" (1 Tim. 3:15; also Eph. 2:19, 1 Pet. 4:17). The household metaphor "shapes" the content and character of the letter (Horrell 2008; see also Verner 1983).

29 Paul highlights the household of Stephanus (1 Cor. 16:15) and mentions several families in Rom. 16:10–11. According to Acts, Cornelius and his whole household became Christ followers (Acts 10:2, 24, 44; 11:14); likewise, Lydia and her household (16:15) and the jailer and his household (16:33) all joined the Christ group.

30 Slaves might attain some status, but they were in the lowest social position in society. While their sex (male or female) may be clear, they did not have "gender"; that is, they did not have the responsibilities or rights of a free man or free woman (Osiek and MacDonald 2007, 96). They could neither legally marry nor call their offspring their own children. They either lived servile lives from childhood or became slaves at some point in the life course due to conquest. Some slaves were manumitted after a certain number of years of service or in old age (when they were no longer productive). Slaves within the early Christ groups did not differ in legal status from slaves in society at large, and there is no clear evidence that greater numbers of slaves were manumitted by Christ followers or within Christ groups (MacDonald 2014, 33–65; Bartchy 2003[1973]; Glancy 2002; Osiek 2003). In fact, early Christian texts indicate that although slaves were baptized alongside freepersons and considered to be co-heirs of the promises of Christ (Gal. 3:28; Col. 3:11, 24), their social status was not altered: they were still slaves. For example, 1 Tim. 6:1–2 indicates that slaves should behave properly by honouring their masters, serving them with respect. The author of Ephesians says plainly, "Slaves, obey your earthly masters with fear and trembling" (6:5, NRSV; also Col. 3:22–4:1, Titus 2:9–10, 1 Pet. 2:18–21). In short, as in society at large, slaves in

Christ groups were in a different social category from free men and women. On the presence of slaves in the household, especially among children, see MacDonald (2014, 33–65).

31 Harlow and Laurence define the "life cycle" as a "cumulative patterning of life courses [which] is the life cycle of a society" reproduced from generation to generation (2002, 4). The phrase "generational cycle" emphasizes the family-orientation (rather than individual) nature of the cycle.

32 An elder brother has precedence over a younger brother or sister. Among the Bedouin, an older sister has precedence over a younger brother in childhood, but as adults, the brother would have precedence (Abu-Lughod 1986, 80–2). In rural Turkey, if there are disputes among brothers in a patrilocal household before the father dies, it is not about questioning "pecking order," but "how hard the pecking should be" (Stirling 1965, 133). These relationships are further complicated in that setting by the commonality of half-brothers, due to premature death and remarriage (106).

33 In Friedl's analysis, intergenerational relationships are the quintessential example of hierarchical relationships in Mediterranean cultures (1962, 88); that is, the behaviour of the young toward their elders is the fundamental cultural representation of deference that *helps to define* women's behaviour toward men. "The strength of the conceptual difference of men and women in the village may be judged from the expectation that the women will give men the kind of deference the young give the old" (1962, 90). Women and "young people" (I am not sure if she means children or youth or young adults) share (perceived?) characteristics of modesty, greater emotion, a longer struggle for self-control, less rationality, greater vulnerability, and a need for assistance from mature men or the supernatural (90). Chapman uses age groups in the household as a comparison for economic relationships outside the household that involve the cooperation of different social classes (1971, 144–5; see also Abu-Lughod 1986, 81–2).

34 For example, a wife, daughter, and daughter-in-law are normally subordinate in the private realm, but in urban Turkey, they are treated according to their rank within the company in the world of work, even having authority over men in some cases (Fallers and Fallers 1976, 246–55).

35 Egyptian Bedouin women do not defer to younger men (even if they are dependent on them). Neither do they defer to men who are their husband's clients. Abu-Lughod reasons that if a person has witnessed someone dominated by others, she or he does not show deference to that individual. "People feel embarrassed in front of their elders not just because the latter

control resources and currently have authority, but also because the elders may have known them in an earlier state of extreme weakness and exposure. By the same token, individuals do not feel fear or shame in front of anyone they have seen exposed or vulnerable" (1986, 113). Concomitantly, women and young people are socially segregated from older men because, as vulnerable persons, they are uncomfortable around those more powerful (116).

36 These modern Greek kinship terms are specified by John Andromedas (1975, 1086–7). According to M. Miller, ancient Greek kinship terminology was similar (1953, 47, 49). Grandfather is πάππος; grandmother could be μαῖα and μάμμη (both terms could also be used for mother; the latter occurs in 2 Tim. 1:5), or at times, τέθη, τέθις, ἄννις, or νίννη. Uncle is θεῖος, and aunt is θεία (perhaps father's brother and sister). Aunt could also be νάννα, νίννιον, τέθη or τέθις (note the last two terms are the same as grandmother). These kinship terms are rare in early Christian literature. The term μάμμη in modern Greek evolved to mean "midwife."

37 In a Turkish village, older women are also called by a kinship term out of respect for their age (Stirling 1965, 174). Likewise, in Sicily, Chapman notes a great respect for old age demonstrated in the term *Vossia*, used "for anyone whose age status or relationship to the speaker commands respect" (1971, 51). This term is considered the highest honour. If an older person has a good reputation, even his peers may call him *Vossia*.

38 I say this strictly in the context of ancient and modern traditional Mediterranean cultural norms, in which gender is understood in rigid terms. In my own context in contemporary Canada, by contrast, one's gender identity may change over time and be expressed in multiple ways.

39 Dimen suggests that, for a man, the household is the repository of pride, self-esteem, and security. The private sphere offers a place to "reconstruct" his sense of self, which is "damaged" by personal and social expectations that he faces in the public realm, enabling him to resume his duties the next day (1986, 62). Whether this is an emic or etic assessment, and whether it is an ideal or a reality, is hard to ascertain, but it suggests the kind of "safety" the domestic context may provide to its members. Panourgiá comments on the tension between individuality and emotional support found in modern Athenian families (1995, 72).

40 Brandes notes that this folktale is found in other parts of the world as well, including Japan and northern Europe (1995, 27n1).

41 Older people are not passive in securing care, even when they are dependent. Brandes suggest that in Iberia, parents traditionally controlled property in order to secure care in old age, but in recent times adult children

rely more on urban work than on rural inheritance. Older parents have less economic influence but may offer their social security to a care-giving son or daughter and/or other incentives to encourage them to care for them in old age (1995, 22–6). Likewise, an elderly informant in northwest Spain expresses how dismal it is for old people without children to care for them. Even so, they actively seek ways to be sure they have what they need, even if that means entering a nursing home, however foreign to their experience and desires (Lisón-Tolosana 1976, 309).

42 In urban Athens, inheritance continues to be of utmost importance. According to Panourgiá, after her grandfather's death in 1986, friends and relatives came to see him laid out in his home, and someone asked, "Had he divided the property among his sons before he died?" (1995, 112).

43 In Spain, inheritance patterns can vary within one fairly homogeneous area (Lisón-Tolosana 1976, 305). One child may inherit all or the majority of the estate and be solely responsible for caring for aging parents, or the inheritance may be split between the sons, or sons and daughters (equally or not), and children expected to rotate care for elderly parents (Brandes 1995, 15–24).

44 Peter Benedict observes that in Turkey only about a quarter of households at any given time conform to the ideal of the patrilineal joint household due to the early death of the father, disputes among brothers, or the desire for autonomy over time and resources (1976, 220, 222). This may be analogous to typical ancient Roman experience, given their demographic realities (see chapter 1).

45 Jill Dubisch reminds us that how Westerners perceive power may not be how someone in another culture perceives power, particularly since Westerners tend to emphasize economic control as power (the power most associated with older men). "Overemphasis on material factors as the root of power, then, may lead to neglect of other possible sources of power" (1986a, 23).

46 The life course approach has been used in classical studies, pioneered by Harlow and Laurence, who explore an "age-based approach" in their study of Roman social life (2007, 23–4). They propose a "framework for the study of temporal experience in the Roman world" (147). Their focus is "underlying codes of behaviour or the expectations of others when viewing the actions of a person according to their age" with awareness of "variation in the life course" (1).

47 Renée B. Hirschon is careful to note that "the study of social change must be firmly grounded in long-term empirical study in order to avoid the uncritical imposition of our own culturally biased preconceptions and

assumptions" (1983, 128). David I. Kertzer and Jennie Keith warn of two problematic theoretical assumptions: (1) the "life course fallacy" in which differences between age cohorts are attributed to life course changes rather than the experience and character of the cohorts themselves, and (2) the "cohort fallacy" in which differences between age cohorts are attributed to different slices of history when there is actually a change as people age and move through the life course (1984, 34). The unique nature of social change in the form of modernization should make us wary of the cohort fallacy. Anthropological fieldwork and early Christian texts both reflect a moment in time – a snapshot – of a particular culture, which makes it easy to miss the shifts that occur because of life course changes, thus falling into the cohort fallacy.

48 Sociological theories of social change are of little help here, except perhaps by way of contrasting typical Mediterranean responses to change. Age stratification theory, for example, suggests that the social system determines behaviour in age-related roles, but in turn, the uniqueness of an age cohort in its historical context influences changes in the social system (Riley, Johnson, and Foner 1972). According to Kertzer and Keith's age stratification theory, intensely hierarchical relationships based on age in the private sphere primarily manifest "in conflicts of authority, succession and inheritance," especially in time of rapid social change and more obvious power differential such that peers become more important than family (1984, 40). The theory assumes the kind of rapid change from generation to generation that occurred in twentieth-century American society but does not necessarily apply universally. The traditional Mediterranean family forms one's primary identity, and one's primary loyalty always belongs to the family. Those of a particular age group may share similar interests and be at ease with one another, but they do not "unite" in extra-familial causes as equals against their own families (Chapman 1971, 49; Stirling 1965, 119, 224). Peer friendships exist outside the family (even complaining about some aspects of their family), but family members would not risk the family's honour and reputation, except in extraordinary circumstances. Finally, modernization theory focuses on how the status of the elderly declines when modernization influences a traditional culture (Cowgill and Holmes 1972). The studies that support this hypothesis often fail to look at whether the elderly continue to have lower status in a succession of several generations after modernization.

49 Similarly, Kertzer and Keith suggest that in developing theory about age norms, we "need to take account of differentiation in at least two social arenas, the domestic and the public." However, they ask, "When is the

egalitarian face of age dominant, as opposed to its hierarchical and more conflictual potential?" (1984, 40). In this question, they assume that hierarchy necessarily produces conflict without accounting for *cooperation* between age groups – a common feature in the Mediterranean family. They also assume that age groups outside the household are more likely to be egalitarian and cooperative, which is also not the case in the Mediterranean. For example, men who are equal in age compete for honour, and family honour takes precedence over relationships outside the family. A man does not want to appear to be subordinate to anyone among his peers (Kenna 1976, 348), but this does not manifest as egalitarian cooperation.

CHAPTER THREE

1 David W. Pao examines 1 Tim. 4:12 in the context of honour-shame language, arguing that this verse subverts the usual age hierarchy of the time (2014, 750–1; see also Barclay 2007). Christopher Roy Hutson argues that the letter was written to youthful leaders rather than the church community as a whole (1998, 10). In my view, the rhetoric between the "old" Paul and the "young" Timothy is central, but the letter addressed the whole community, at times focusing on various groups in the community.
2 According to narrative criticism, the implied audience (the audience presumed by the author) is not the same as the "real" audience, who may or may not read or receive the text in the way in which the author intends the implied audience to react (Powell 1990, 19–21). This notion helps get at even more complexity in the layers of this heteronymous letter (see chapter 1), but I proceed on the assumption that when I discuss the "real" audience, I am often engaging the implied audience because everything we read in the letter is filtered through the perception of the author. Further study on this letter with such concepts borrowed from narrative criticism may be fruitful, but see my discussion of grammar (pages 75–7).
3 All translations of 1 Timothy are mine unless otherwise noted.
4 I prefer the terms "opponents" or "opposing teachers" to "false teachers" because the Greek phrasing in 1:3 and 6:3 reflects the notion of "teaching *different* things [ἑτεροδιδασκαλεῖν]," a compound word using ἕτερος ("different") rather than ψευδής ("false"). "False" does not capture the internal struggle this community must have faced. The two rival factions had disparate teaching resulting in different behaviour displayed by community members; the two vied for followers in their way of behaving and thinking

(LaFosse 2018). Neither the author nor his opponents knew that his letter would become part of "orthodox" Christianity. In contrast, several decades later Polycarp used the term ψευδοδιδασκαλίαι (false teachings, *Phil.* 7.2, AF 2003, 1:342), along with ψευδαδέλφοι (false brothers; *Phil.* 6.3, AF 2003, 1:342). The "different" teaching in 1 Timothy does not appear to be "heretical" or "heterodox" in a clear doctrinal sense (see discussion in Zamfir 2013, 165–78). Rather, the author focuses on the behaviours that result from this teaching, which is probably an ascetic interpretation of Pauline thought, especially as found in 1 Cor. 7 (194), which is discussed below.

5 The critique of how one displays wealth, especially in a self-indulgent way, was a common rhetorical trope against an opponent (Zamfir 2013, 152–8, 366–7).

6 Zamfir notes that the language used for the opponents is clearly polemical, meant to shame them and damage their reputation and credibility (2013, 33–6, 124).

7 *Contra* Dibelius and Conzelmann, who assert this section "intersperses a general teaching about duties with instructions for specific classes within the congregation" (1972, 73). The details in the text refer to a specific situation, and a particular solution. Though some sections are based on traditional lists or formulae (e.g., 1:8–11; 2:1–7), they serve a distinct purpose in the context of the letter (for example, see chapter 10). The author specifies the expected behaviour of adult children toward their parents (5:4, 8). He describes and repudiates specific behaviour of women (2:9–15) and younger widows (5:11–15). These hardly seem like standard exhortations in a general situation. Rather, they address concrete present problems, even if we possess few details about the nature of these problems.

8 See, for example, Marshall (1999, 42–3) and Dibelius and Conzelmann (1972, 135).

9 Placing the letters as late as Marcion's controversy (early second century CE) is a laudable project (Collins 2011), but (in my opinion) places them too late.

10 *The Acts of Paul and Thecla* is found in the *Acts of Paul* (section 3). but it is also sometimes published on its own. I employ the standard numbering found in J.K. Elliott (1993, 364).

11 MacDonald suggests 2 Tim. 3:6 confirms the influence of opponents' teaching on women (1988, 179–80).

12 Asceticism may have been desirable to the opponents due to a "combination of influences" (Marshall 1999, 535), perhaps including abstinence for ritual or reasons of purity (like the Essenes); as a manifestation of the

"kingdom of God" in the present world (Mat. 19:12); as an expression of superior morality or spirituality (as seems to be the case in 1 Cor. 7) or contempt for the material world as in the story of Thecla (*Acts of Paul and Thecla* 3.6). See discussion in Marshall (1999, 533–5).

13 Towner's view is conveniently made clearer by combining information in 1 Timothy with that found in 2 Timothy. Specifically, Towner's description of a "spiritualized Christianity" relies on clues from both 2 Timothy (the opponents taught that the resurrection had already happened; 2 Tim. 2:18) and 1 Timothy (the opponents' ascetic tendencies; 1 Tim. 4:3). Towner views the letters to Timothy and Titus as separate but posits that the author indirectly addressed the same community in the two letters directly addressed to Timothy. For Towner, 2 Timothy apparently represents a later time (2006, 41).

14 There is a long history of this motif. For example, in late eighth or early seventh century BCE, Hesiod laments that in the age of iron, there would be discord between children and parents; children would dishonour their parents, rebuking them and refusing to support them in old age (*Works and Days* 174–89, especially 180–7; Reinhold 1970, 350). See also chapter 5.

15 As Barclay argues, the designation of young and old tended to be fluid in antiquity (2007, 227–32).

16 Eyben detects intergenerational conflict from the time of the early Republic, but an intensification as the Republic came to an end (1993, 52–6).

17 The *Lex Plaetoria* (ca 200 BCE) legally protected a person under age twenty-five against financial exploitation. The *Lex Villia annalis* (180 BCE) established the minimum age for public office at thirty. (Augustus later reduced the age to twenty-five for quaestorship.) According to Eyben, elders used these laws as "the creation of a new sub-category or age-group, the 'real' youth" and as protection against the assertiveness of the younger generation in public law (1993, 7–8).

18 *Contra* Eyben, who suggests that Rome's extravagance probably did not affect non-elite youth as much because they had little chance for education or leisure at this age (1993, 22).

19 After Augustus, young emperors included Nero (emperor at seventeen), Commodus (at nineteen), Elegabalus (at fourteen), Carcalla (at twenty-three), and Alexander Severus (at thirteen). They were not always well received, at least in part because they introduced too many innovations (Eyben 1993, 67–8).

20 Cicero was elected for each position at the minimum age allowable: quaestor at thirty, praetor at thirty-nine, consul at forty-two.

21 Augustus lowered the age of quaestor from thirty to twenty-five, when he himself was thirty-four, making the magistrates some nine or ten years younger than those in the same positions in the Republic. He also essentially dropped the age of incoming senators, patterned after his own experience, and passed legislation that encouraged senators' sons to follow in their fathers' footsteps, particularly sons of patrician families (versus plebeian and "new men," *novi homines*) who held political office at younger ages than their Republican counterparts (Harlow and Laurence 2002, 104–16).

22 From the time of Augustus, the state issued laws to encourage the elite of Rome to have more children because of the low birth rate and high mortality rate, and it began to appoint political positions to elite men from the provinces. Perhaps the ages for public office were also lowered to encourage the traditionally political families to involve their sons (Osiek and Balch 1997, 92). Senator positions had become de facto hereditary (Eyben 1993, 70), but senatorial families were not reproducing. Over two-thirds of senatorial families were replaced every generation despite adoption and freedom to give three-quarters of the patrimony to whomever one wished (Saller 1994, 162).

23 Not all men joined the military. In Rome, men had to be strong, healthy citizens to join (Phang 2008, 18), though in the provinces auxiliary soldiers could be noncitizens (Southern 2006, 131, 133). Probably most young men in the Roman East entered trades (on apprenticeship, see Hübner 2009, 75) or were unskilled labourers or merchants. Nevertheless, the Roman military was a prominent element of life in the Roman Empire as demonstrated by the presence of Roman soldiers in the gospel stories (e.g., Q 7:1–10; Mark 15:16; Luke 23:36, 47; John 19:2, 23, 24, 34), and Acts (e.g., 12:4–6, 21:32), as well as military imagery found in New Testament letters (e.g., 2 Tim. 2:3–4; Eph. 6:10–17; 1 Thess. 5:8).

24 On specific ages for military duty, see Parkin (2003, 95–6).

25 Valerie M. Hope's study of first-century CE military inscriptions in Britain demonstrates that the army could function as a "pseudo-family" in setting up commemorations for soldiers who did not die in the battlefield but must have found the military base their home (2007, 115–16; see also Saller and Shaw 1984, 133–4). The distribution of age at death, ranging from twenties to sixties (and a few older), represented mostly men in their twenties and thirties (around two-thirds), and about 20 percent in their forties (2007, 117).

26 Publius Cornelius Scipio Africanus the Elder was born in 236 BCE and known especially for fighting Hannibal in the Second Punic War (Briscoe 2003, 398).

27 When he became consul a few years later, Scipio came into conflict with an older man, Fabius Maximus, who called him "a foolhardy young man [ἀνὴρ ἀνόητος καὶ νέος]" (Plutarch 1916, 190–1, *Fabius Maximus* 25.2; Eyben 1993, 48–9).
28 Similarly, 2 Tim. 2:3–4 reads, "Share in suffering like a good soldier [στρατιώτης] of Christ Jesus. No one serving in the army [στρατευόμενος] gets entangled in everyday affairs; the soldier's aim is to please the enlisting officer" (NRSV). This text serves to define Christ followers as separate from the people around them (as soldiers are separate from civilians) and identifies military hierarchy as an analogy. In some English translations (e.g., NRSV, NASB) both 1 Tim. 1:18 and 6:12 are translated "fight the good fight"; however, 6:12 uses a different analogy: "struggle with the good contest of the faith [ἀγωνίζου τὸν καλὸν ἀγῶνα τῆς πίστεως]." The word ἀγών (along with its cognates) has a strong sense of athletic competition, but also a general notion of "a struggle against opposition" (BDAG 2000, 17). Although the cognate ἀγώνισμα is used by Herodotus to connote "brave deeds" in battle (LSJ 1940, 18; see Herodotus, *The Persian Wars* 8.76), it is not primarily a military image. A third related analogy is found in 1 Tim. 4:7, which introduces the physical training of an athlete (who competes) compared to training in godliness (εὐσέβεια; also 2 Tim. 2:5). Victor Pfitzner argues that all three metaphors are intimately related in Paul and in the letters to Timothy and Titus (1967, 157–71), but they clearly refer to a range of (male) experiences and contexts.
29 Several distinct organizations in the ancient Mediterranean world have been proposed as possible models or analogies for Christ groups: philosophical schools, synagogues, mystery cults, voluntary associations, and political associations (Ascough 1998, 9, 21; Stegemann and Stegemann 1999, 273), all of which have particular aspects that help to explain the character of Christ groups (Ascough 1998, 95–7).
30 In the first and second centuries, ease of travel and movement due to trade, slavery, and veterans settling in provinces created a need to replace kin and village social structures (Kloppenborg 1996a, 17–18). On travel and the spread of religious cults, see Meeks (1983, 16–19).
31 There were some rare exceptions, such as the North African farmer's son who rose from poverty to become a wealthy city senator (*CIL* 8.11824).
32 They were "mainly social clubs which perhaps on rare occasions flexed some political muscle" (Kloppenborg 1996a, 22). An association could be connected to civic or imperial politics through benefactors (e.g., a Roman senator). Associations connected to services regulated by the state, like the grain trade, could mediate between the non-elite and elite in cities (27).

Associations could be perceived as threatening if they moved beyond the local level, but public duty and loyalty to the state (expressed as *pietas* or εὐσέβεια) were not usually compromised (Wilson 1996, 3; Walker-Ramisch 1996, 134–6). The term "voluntary associations" covers a wide range of associations in the ancient world, but "private" associations (as opposed to government-sanctioned associations; Kloppenborg 1996a, 16) are the most pertinent analogy for Christ groups. On voluntary associations as they pertain to Christ groups, see, for example, Kloppenborg and Wilson (1996), Harland (2003), and Ascough, Harland, and Kloppenborg (2012).

33 This kind of continuity was likely quite important in a context where fathers often died when their sons were becoming adults (see chapter 1). Sometimes sons were forced to grow up faster than they expected. Eusebius notes that when disease took great numbers of people of all ages in third-century Alexandria, "the youngest in appearance have become, as it were, of equal age with those who formerly were the oldest" (*Ecclesiastical History* 7.21.9–10). This probably means that younger men had to step up to positions of authority and responsibility before the usual time because so many of their elders had died. Although Eusebius offers an extreme example, demographic realities suggest that some young men throughout Roman history had such experiences.

34 Lucian of Samosata's main character in his fictional *The Death of Peregrinus* illustrates a younger man who charms his way into leadership among a group of Christians by duping them (11; see chapter 11).

35 For example, a person who was twenty years old in 50 CE (a time when the community in Ephesus might have been well established) would be fifty years old in 80 CE, sixty years old in 90 CE, and seventy years old in 100 CE. In a stable population with a life expectancy at birth of twenty-five, a person at twenty would have an average life expectancy of another 31.3 years. After the age of sixty, life expectancy dropped significantly and few people lived into their seventies and eighties (Parkin 2003, 49–50).

36 Whether or not this can be taken as historical is debatable, but it does demonstrate the value of the oral story and the need to record it in writing before it was lost. For the importance of orality in early Christianity and Christian origins, see, for example, Holly E. Hearon and Phillip Ruge-Jones (2009), Pieter J.J. Botha (2012), and David Rhoads, Joanna Dewey, and Donald Michie (2012).

37 The date of Luke-Acts is not certain, except that it was written after Mark (probably after 70 CE). Commonly dated at the end of the first century (ca 90 CE), recent assessments lean toward the first quarter of the second century. For example, Richard I. Pervo bases his dating of 110–120 CE, or

more precisely, 115 CE, in part on the kind of formal organization of leadership he parallels with 1 Timothy, 2 Timothy, and Titus, as well as *1 Clement* (2006, 343–4). Pervo's assumptions about the well-established nature of leadership structure in these documents is more confident than is warranted. Joseph B. Tyson (2006) argues that the final form of Luke and Acts was written in part to combat the influence and teachings of Marcion ca. 120–25 CE.

38 On the importance of living witnesses and oral tradition, see Bauckham (2006, 21–30).

39 Worded slightly differently, Jerome also quotes Papias: "For books that can be read are less useful to me than a living voice that resounds through authorities still alive in our own day" (AF 2003, 2:106–7, frag. 5, Jerome, *Lives of Illustrious Men* 18).

40 It is commonly thought that his use of the aorist εἶπεν indicates that the first list of Jesus's disciples (Andrew, Peter, etc.) were dead, and the present tense λέγουσιν indicates that Aristion and John the Elder were still alive in Papias's day. Yet, if Papias wrote between 110 and 140 CE (see Ehrman in AF 2003, 2:87) it would be very unlikely or impossible for any of Jesus's disciples to still be alive. Bauckham convincingly argues that Papias refers to an earlier time when he collected his information, perhaps in 80–90 CE when Aristion and John the Elder, who knew Jesus, were still alive, and Papias was perhaps twenty to thirty years old (2006, 19).

41 As an analogy, we might consider our own living link to the men and women who fought and served in the First World War or Second World War and survived. The last surviving veteran who fought in the First World War died on 4 February 2012. See http://www.bbc.com/news/uk-england-norfolk-16929653 (accessed 5 August 2015). The few living veterans who served in the Second World War are now very elderly. Their direct memories, recounted in Remembrance Day services, for example, will soon no longer be readily available. We have films, history books, and YouTube videos to allow us to continue to learn about the events and people associated with the Second World War, but the living connection has significant impact of a different kind.

42 The concern about continuity of knowledge from Jesus's disciples was solved in the subsequent centuries in the orthodox church by "apostolic succession" – the notion that authority vested in the apostles by Jesus was handed down to successive leaders (usually bishops), symbolized by the laying on of hands. In this discussion, I am concerned only about the slice of history at the end of the first century and beginning of second century, when it is yet not clear how the teachings of Jesus and his disciples would

be disseminated when those who knew them were dead or old and near death. There is an early suggestion of apostolic succession in *1 Clem.* 44.1–3.

43 This is perhaps similar to Plutarch's praise of older men in Lacedaemon who not only "oversee public affairs" and teach young men, but get to know their interests (e.g., sports), and in so doing "enhance and encourage the decorum and innate nobility of the young without arousing their envy" (1936, 143, *Moralia* 10:796A).

44 Lewis R. Donelson argues that the idea of succession in the letter to Timothy makes the author's "fiction" successful (1986, 164).

45 Some suggest 2 Timothy functions in a similar way, as a "testament," though this is debated. See discussion, for example, in Luke Timothy Johnson (2001, 320–2) and Michael Prior (1989).

46 Donelson argues that the author creates the concept of Pauline tradition as he presents the tradition as a "trust" (1986, 163–9). Malherbe suggests the author is setting up an image of "the old man who is concerned about the future of the church" (1994, 201). While there is some element of forward thinking in bequeathing an inheritance and in teaching the young, I am convinced that the ancient Romans were generally past-oriented (see Malina 1989, whose initial evaluation of time orientation is suggestive for future work on this theme; see also Bettini 1991). Thus, the author's primary concern is about solidifying tradition from the past and addressing the present problems of the community to ensure the younger generation would adopt the "right" teaching and behaviour as they matured. Joseph H. Hellerman highlights the past orientation of Roman culture as exemplified by their concern for ancestors (2001, 51–5). He then suggests that inheritance is important for the *future* of the kin group (55), yet his definition of ancestors and inheritance emphasizes the continuity of family patrimony rather than the future. Inheritance is associated with "passionate preoccupation with ancestral origins." Furthermore, "personal honour is strongly dependent on one's ancestral lineage. Inheritance [is] understood collectively – it belongs to the patriline as a whole and must be preserved as such" (57). For the author of 1 Timothy, concern for future generations is not nearly as important as the current need to secure healthy teaching (in the name of Paul) in what he saw as a present crisis.

47 The historical Paul assigned Timothy to work with churches in Thessalonica (1 Thess. 3:1–10), Corinth (1 Cor. 4:17, 16:10–11), and presumably Philippi (Phil. 2:19–24). Timothy is listed as co-author in four of Paul's undisputed letters (2 Cor. 1:1, Phil. 1:1, 1 Thess. 1:1, Philem. 1:1), and two disputed letters (Col. 1:1, 2 Thess. 1:1). Timothy also offers a

greeting as Paul's co-worker in Rom. 16:21. While its historicity is not certain, according to Acts, Timothy was from Lystra and had a good reputation among the Christians there (16:1–3). His mother was Judean, his father was Greek (meaning he was a polytheist), and Paul had Timothy circumcised to bolster his reputation among the Judeans as they travelled together. See also Malina (2008).

48 Zamfir also suggests that the letters to Timothy and Titus are written in reaction to a time of social change, namely, the delayed parousia (2013, xi, 58, 69), which I am increasingly convinced is not the primary motivation for re-evaluating the identity of the community at the end of the first century CE (a question posed by Margaret Y. MacDonald, personal communication).

49 See Hellerman for a description of Mediterranean family structure, especially patrilineal kinship. He argues that the Christ groups provided a new "surrogate family" in place of natural family, which was particularly attractive for urbanites (2001, 25). Hellerman discusses the Jesus movement, Pauline communities, and second-century Asian and North African communities, but curiously skips over the letters to Timothy and Titus.

50 Of course, the household was more than a metaphor because the household was also a physical setting for early Christian communities (see chapter 1). Zamfir argues that the household (*oikos*) provided the metaphor for fictive kin and combined with the city (*polis*) as a metaphor for the kind of structure (and "offices") that is idealized in the letters to Timothy and Titus, including discouraging women from speaking publicly (2013, xvi, 2; *passim*).

51 This use of the first person to address the community does not occur in 2 Timothy or Titus, making it a unique feature of 1 Timothy among the three letters.

52 William A. Richards finds that in 1 Timothy, twenty-seven of every one thousand words is an imperative, compared with 2 Timothy, also at twenty-seven per one thousand, and Titus at twenty-one per one thousand (2002, Appendix C). Ray Van Neste notes the concentrated use of the second-person singular imperative in 4:1–6:2 (2004, 134).

53 There are thirty-seven imperatives in 1 Timothy, twenty-four of which are second person and thirteen of which are third person. The list of third-person imperatives is surprisingly extensive compared to the one use of the third-person imperative in 2 Timothy (2:19, "let everyone abstain from unrighteousness") and two uses in Titus (2:15, "do not let anyone despise you" and 3:14, "let our people learn to engage in good works").

54 One could argue for the translation "must learn." Schuyler Signor prefers "should" (1999, 62n317).

CHAPTER FOUR

1 Contrast Titus 2:2, where "Paul" directs "Titus" to tell the older men, older women, and younger men what kinds of behaviours they should display. See LaFosse (2017a).
2 For references to fluid definitions of νεώτερος and πρεσβύτερος in Classical Greek literature, see Reinhold (1970, 353, 356). For example, in political rhetoric, νεώτερος could be used as a label of imprudence for someone who is in an older generation.
3 The *Haustafeln* were used in early Christian texts to address real social needs. James E. Balch (1981), for instance, understands the codes in 1 Peter as used apologetically to demonstrate that early Christians were of solid social repute. David Crouch (1973) considers the codes in Colossians to have a paranaetic function; namely, they offered conservative directives to subdue deviant enthusiasts in the movement. John H. Elliott (1981) argues that the author of 1 Peter employed the *Haustafeln* because the group's internal solidarity was threatened, but also to establish the group as distinct from its polytheist neighbours.
4 For thorough summaries, see Crouch (1973) and Balch (1981).
5 Some scholars prefer to use the phrase "station codes" for this adaptation of the household codes (Verner 1983, 90, 92; Zamfir 2013, 6n7).
6 The theme of household hierarchy continues in 1 Tim. 6:1–2a with instructions to slaves and masters. See also Zamfir (2013, 138–45).
7 Zamfir argues that the household metaphor is an interplay between the private and public realms with a cosmic dimension as the "household *of God*" (2013, 70–85). While Zamfir focuses on roles in voluntary (religious) associations which replicate the *polis* (city), I focus here on fictive kin roles.
8 Creating non-kin networks in the form of wedding sponsors and godparents (baptism sponsors) is common in modern Greece and Italy (e.g., Friedl 1962, 72; Chapman 1971, 115–20). Such relationships are considered binding and permanent. They involve expectations of reciprocity and restrictions regarding eligible marriage partners that are similar to biological kin. In modern Athens, non-kin can have the "status of family members through the love, support and affiliation they have exhibited toward the family throughout the years" (Panourgiá 1995, 99). This status includes practical assistance in crises, such as providing a funeral meal (118), as well as affection (76). Italian immigrants in New York create fictive kin (*compari*) in the absence of biological kin (Johnson 1983, 94). However, it is worth noting that on the Greek island of Nisos, intense

competition between families means that cooperation and trust resides primarily in the family household. Any cooperation outside of the family must be "phrased in the idiom of family and backed by moral sanctions," such as wedding and baptism sponsors (Kenna 1976, 351).

9 In Greek thought, Aristotle reflects similar sentiments. Note that age differences between the young and old are not defined, except by contrast of age status. "For the male is by nature better fitted to command than the female (except in some cases where their union has been formed contrary to nature) and the older and fully developed person than the younger and immature [τὸ πρεσβύτερον καὶ τέλειον τοῦ νεωτέρου καὶ ἀτελοῦς] ... The rule of the father over the children on the other hand is that of a king; for the male parent is the ruler in virtue both of affection and of seniority [πρεσβείαν] ... For though in nature the king must be superior, in race he should be the same as his subjects, and this is the position of the elder in relation to the younger and of the father in relation to the child" (1932, 58–9, 1.5.2, [Bekker's numbering] 1259b).

10 Note that although English derives the word "adolescent" from the Latin *adulescentis*, the Latin term denotes a young man typically up to about the age of thirty (again, depending on context). See chapter 1, note 11.

11 For example, Prov. 23:22 states, "Listen to your father who begot you, and do not despise your mother when she is old" (NRSV; also Mic. 7:6), suggesting that filial respect was not always the behavioural norm, even if it was ideal (Mal. 4:6).

12 LSJ defines πρεσβεῖον as "a gift of honour," often with the sense of "privilege of age" or "right of the eldest," such as in the right to inheritance. It can also refer to "old age" in general (1940, 1462). This exact term is not found in early Christian literature, but it is in the same semantic domain as πρεσβύτερος (elder).

13 Classicists have a variety of opinions. Thomas M. Falkner and Judith de Luce assert that the treatment of the elderly was a measure of morality (1992, 8). Harlow and Laurence disagree: "Only in the mythical golden age of the past were the elderly respected for their years" (2002, 118). Karen Cokayne argues that attitudes toward the elderly were ambiguous: "only the strong and feisty, those who were still contributing to society, were admired and shown the traditional reverence; only those who were still fit and active, whether in public life or through the subsequent pursuit of intellectual studies, had respect and status. The old and weak were tolerated at best, and often viewed with contempt or ridicule" (2007, 209; also de Luce 1993b). Aspects of all three opinions are found in the ancient evidence. Meyer Reinhold suggests that respect for parents rose in the

Hellenistic era because of a restoration of hierarchy after the rebellious uprising of youth in Greek city-states (1970, 361–2). However, the Roman evidence suggests otherwise because respect for age was not entirely automatic.

14 In the ancient Roman world, the *puer senex* (a young man with the maturity of an old man) was also an exception to the rule, esteemed because of his unusual maturity (Eyben 1993, 10). The prominent example in the Roman world was Augustus (see Eyben 1993, 262n29).

15 For example, Josephus tells of how a respectable self-made man named Joseph sent his son Hyrcanus to pay homage to the ruler Seleukos (king of Syria). Joseph's steward *rebuked* [ἐπιπλήσσω] Hyrcanus, who wanted more money than the steward (a slave) thought was prudent. Hyrcanus used his rightful power as master to throw the slave in prison for his rebuke. Cleopatra, who liked the steward, said she would *rebuke* [ἐπιπλήσσω] the child (Hyrcanus) for his action (*Antiquities* 12.204). Diodorus Siculus (90–30 BCE) provides another example, recounting the tale of a king named Philip who jeered at his captives in a drunken state. Demedes, one of the captives who was an orator, *rebuked* [ἐπιπλήσσω] him, shaming him into behaving with more dignity. Philip released Demedes and gave him honours, demonstrating perhaps that Philip recognized Demedes' social power in the situation (*The Library of History*, 16.87.2).

16 There were several exceptions, namely, beating slaves (who had no honour), corporal punishment of soldiers, and subjugation of people from the provinces who did not have citizenship (Saller 1994, 137–41). Livy recounts a story about an old man, a former centurion who fought honourably for Rome. After all his inherited property had been destroyed by enemies, the state demanded taxes anyway. His debt forced him into slavery. The sight of his recent beatings incited the crowd, prompting the first plebeian secession (*History of Rome* 2.23.7). The historical accuracy of the story is uncertain, but Livy's readers evidently would have found the violence done to this old man deplorable enough to justify prompting a major historical reform (Saller 1994, 141).

17 In modern Greece, "the idea of an adolescent or adult son striking his father is almost unthinkable. Only slightly less serious is swearing at or insulting a father. Both are acts of insolent and wanton violence ... To curse or strike a father is, also, a grave sin (*hamartia*) for it is an act which upsets a part of the absolute order of life instituted and sanctioned by God. The misfortunes of a person guilty of such acts are always considered to be punishments from God" (Campbell 1964, 160–1). Personal

sins against the family include maltreatment of aged parents, striking a parent, and public insult of a parent by son or daughter (324).

18 This parable is often given the title "The Prodigal Son." I prefer "The Lost Son" because it is the last of three parables in Luke 15. The first two feature a lost sheep (15:3–7) and a lost coin (15:8–10), and the third logically follows with a lost son. Also, the word "lost" is in the text itself (15:24, 32), and "prodigal" is not. Furthermore, the phrasing allows for the ambiguity in the story regarding the two brothers, highlighting the possibility of both sons being "lost."

19 Interestingly, in the instances of παρακαλέω cited above, most involve a person of greater authority (e.g., king, father) making peace with a subordinate whom they have wronged, though the use in 1 Cor. 4:13 suggests otherwise. It is possible that the author of 1 Timothy is subtly poking at the ambitious younger men seeking power (see argument in chapter 9) by showing them how such power is actually supposed to be used – to make peace rather than problems in the community.

20 Brothers and sisters were depicted as emotionally close in ancient literature, perhaps retaining a lifelong bond even though a sister's marriage may diminish their contact (Aasgaard 2004, 64–5). In the classic Greek play, Antigone proclaimed loyalty and affection toward her brother over husband and children (Sophocles, *Antigone* 909–12). Martial, a first-century poet, condemns a mother and son whose affection leads them to call each other brother and sister: "Oh, how affectionate you are to your mother, Ammianus, and how affectionate your mother is to you! She calls you 'brother' and is called 'sister.' Why do naughty names attract the two of you? Why aren't you happy to be what you are? Do you imagine this is just innocent fun? Not so. A mother who wants to be a sister is not happy to be either mother or sister" (1993, 133, 2.4). Reidar Aasgaard argues that this odd situation highlights the normality of brother-sister affection (2004, 64–5, 107–8).

CHAPTER FIVE

1 The prominence of women in 1 Timothy, particularly in 2:11–15 and 5:3–16, is striking. Linda M. Maloney comments, "Here, almost alone among Christian Testament writings, women actually take center stage from time to time" (1994, 361). Similarly, J.L. Houlden points out that there is more space given to widows than any other group in 1 Timothy; they were a notable, and in his opinion, the most troublesome, group in the community (1976, 91).

2 Having studied this text for over two decades, Jouette M. Bassler states, "The more one ponders the text, the more the questions proliferate." She suggests that an "aggressive interpretation" and an "imaginative historical reconstruction" are needed (2003, 122).

3 Thomas A.J. McGinn suggests that χήρα could also refer to a woman who was not yet married (1999, 631). Barclay and others (see chapter 7, note 1) have made this suggestion for the younger widows in 1 Tim. 5:11–15, citing Ignatius, who refers to households of men with their wives and children and the "virgins who are called widows" (*Smyr.* 13.1, AF 2003, 309) as a separate group (Barclay 2020, 280). I am hesitant to read Ignatius's second-century comment back onto 1 Timothy, especially if asceticism in 1 Timothy is based on the opponents' (perceived) interpretation of Paul's views on marriage expressed in 1 Cor. 7 (see chapter 3), because Paul clearly distinguishes between χήρα (women no longer married) and παρθένος. Paul used the latter term for young women who are not yet married (1 Cor. 7:25–38).

4 The prevalence of divorce, especially among the non-elite, is more difficult to assess than the prevalence of widowhood. Demography provides some quantifiable measurement of probable death rates for women's husbands, and inscriptions tend to reveal more information about widows than about divorcées (Treggiari 1991, 482). Bagnall and Frier find that divorce "was not rare among the general population of Egypt" (1994, 123), but how reflective this is of the rest of the Roman world is unknowable.

5 Men divorced women more often than women divorced men for sexual indiscretion, but either spouse could initiate divorce because of adultery (proven or suspected). By the first century CE, women were able to divorce their husbands on their own initiative (Treggiari 1991, 443–6). Women might also initiate divorce for a husband's physical violence. An amicable divorce for practical reasons was possible: "Gifts are allowed between husband and wife in the case of divorce. This often happens because the husband enters the priesthood or because of sterility" (*Digest* 24.1.60, Justinian 1998, 2:255) "or where marriage is no longer appropriate because of old age, illness, or military service" (2:255, 24.1.61) "so the marriage is dissolved by agreement" (2:255, 24.1.62). Incompatibility was not a culturally acceptable reason for divorce. A young male character in Terence's play remarks, "It would be insulting [*superbus*] to return a bride to her father when there's no fault you can allege in her" (*The Mother-in-Law* 1.154–55, Terence 2001, 160–1; Treggiari 1991, 461–5).

6 Polycarp's division of wives and widows as separate groups may indicate different life stages (Polycarp, *Phil.* 4.2–3, AF 2003, 1:338). The directives for wives include affection for their husbands and disciplining children in the φόβος (fear) of God, which correlates with the childbearing phase of a woman's life (see the νέας [young women] in Titus 2:4–5). The directives for widows in Polycarp's letter are suggestive of older women: they are to be in prayer, as the "real widows" are in 1 Tim. 5:5. They are not to be slanderous, an instruction given to older women in Titus 2:3. They are to be self-controlled (σωφρονέω), a virtue the older women are to teach the younger women (Titus 2:4–5) and respectable women are to possess (1 Tim. 2:9). On the other hand, in the *Shepherd* of Hermas, Grapte was to admonish the widows and orphans separate from Hermas, who was to read his revelation with the elders of the church (Visions 8.3). The "orphans" may be the widows' own young children, or they may be orphans with neither biological parent living (AF 2003, 2:193).
7 In pre-industrial societies, older women always outnumber old men, especially widows (Cowgill and Holmes 1972, 322).
8 McGinn points out that Krause does not distinguish between a woman whose husband has died and a woman who is divorced (1999, 631). Krause's lack of definition may compromise his arguments for the proportion of women whose husbands had died.
9 McGinn disagrees with Krause's suggestion that free women in the population were not significantly outnumbered by men. McGinn argues that exposure of female newborns (resulting in infanticide or slavery) was prevalent enough that the numbers of women who were eligible for marriage was less than Krause estimates. Thus, the proportion of widows was probably not as high as Krause suggests (McGinn 1999, 618–19).
10 Saller concludes from inscriptions in the Western Roman Empire that non-elite women married at about age twenty (1994, 37). There is no compelling reason to think that his findings would not be broadly applicable to the East, such as in Asia Minor.
11 Bagnall and Frier find that "long-term stable marriages are ubiquitous" in their study of Egyptian census returns (1994, 122). They suggest remarriage may have been less frequent after about the age of thirty-five (127–8; also Hopkins 1980, 334, see his figure 5). This may be a regional variation unique to Roman Egypt (Parkin 1992, 196n196), but the pattern is suggestive for other parts of the Roman world.
12 In the Augustan marriage laws (*Lex Julia et Papia Poppaea*), women were no longer required to remarry at the age of fifty in order to inherit property. The age of fifty was considered the time when women would reach

menopause and thus no longer be fertile (Harlow and Laurence 2002, 127). For more on menopause in the Roman world, see chapter 6.
13 In Roman Egypt, women owned land, collecting rent from tenants (e.g., *P.Oxy.* 33.2680), and bequeathing it as they wished (e.g., *P.Köln* 2.100). For further examples of women's property ownership and translations of these papyri, see Rowlandson (1998, 218–45).
14 Elizabeth Fernea describes a family of women, a local schoolteacher who lived with her mother and two adult sisters, who did not fit this pattern. The schoolteacher earned money for the family, and one man stated, "They have no man to protect them, but their good reputation is protection enough." They were known to be pious and conservative (1965, 53).
15 Krause argues that Christian asceticism altered the motivation to remarry very little, both because material need and social pressure motivated widows to remarry throughout antiquity and because the prevalence of asceticism is overestimated (1995, 109).
16 The adverb ὄντως means "really" or "truly." The fact the author uses this adverb with widow(s) three times suggests that he is labelling a specific group of widows, whom he clearly defines in 5:5. The wording suggests that these are widows who will never be in the second or fourth categories outlined here: they will never have children or grandchildren (like the widows with family; 5:4), and they will never remarry (like the younger widows; 5:14), probably due to their age.
17 This is a perfect passive participle; the sense is that when she lost her husband, she was and continues to be bereft of that primary relationship (and by extension, the support it provided).
18 An alternative reading suggests that the plural verb (care for) refers to the widows caring for their dependents (e.g., Bassler 1996, 94–6), but such a reading does not logically reflect the expectation of filial piety in the ancient Mediterranean, as I argue in this chapter. See also Barclay (2020, 272n10).
19 There have been many interpretations of the kinds of widows in 1 Tim. 5:3–16. Horrell's perspective is fairly typical. He posits two categories following "two patterns of sanctioned cultural practice" (2008, 124). On the one hand, there are the "genuine," enrolled widows (as defined by 5:3, 5, 16 conflated with 5:9–10 in Horrell's assessment). They were old and qualified for support from their fictive household, that is, the church (124). He suggests that "very large numbers of widows" would not be considered "genuine [real] widow[s]" (118–19). The remaining widows "should be reintegrated into actual households, whether this involves their children and grandchildren showing the appropriate care to members of their οἶκός (v. 4)

or their integration into a new household through marriage (v. 14)" (124). While the categories are concise and not without merit, especially the second category, this interpretation does not seriously account for age or demographics, or for widows who do not fit into these categories (e.g., a widow under sixty with no children). See discussion in chapter 6.

20 One might argue that the advice on familial care (5:4, 8) reflects a rather generic set of instructions typical of the author's traditional stance on age-related behaviour. However, as the section progresses, conceiving of a specific situation better explains the cryptic nature of the text.

21 In this chapter I focus on the adult children (5:4), and in chapter 8 I focus on the believing woman (5:16).

22 The word is used for the Septuagint (LXX) version of Exod. 20:12: "honour your father and mother," which is quoted in several New Testament texts (Matt. 15:4, 19:19; Mark 7:10, 10:19; Luke 18:20; Eph. 6:2).

23 Although the notion of "honour" (τιμάω, τιμή) is used in three distinct sections in this part of 1 Timothy, Towner is right to emphasize the "range of meanings" (2006, 337; see also Fee 1988, 115). In 5:3 "honour" is a verbal command; the other two instances are noun phrases: "double honour" (διπλῆς τιμῆς) for elders in 5:17 and "all honour" (πάσης τιμῆς) for slaves' own masters in 6:1. Honour for elders appears to be associated with an honorarium (5:17; Malherbe 2008). The honour due to masters is specifically directed at slaves and comprises respect and service (6:1–2).

24 For example, Pliny praises his young wife for her devotion to him, especially in her encouragement of his writing as he grew old: "she does not love me for my present age nor my person, which must gradually grow old and decay, but for my aspirations to fame" (*Letters* 4.19, Pliny 1969, 299).

25 Jan N. Bremmer argues that when the Hebrew Bible advocates for widows, it "strongly suggests that human care was rather deficient" (1995, 31). Whether the directives about caring for widows are prescriptive because of neglect or descriptive of common activity is debatable and would require further study.

26 The cognate noun εὐσέβεια is often translated "godliness" or "godly" (2:2; 6:3, 5, 6; NRSV, NIV, NASB; also 3:16, NIV, NASB, CEB; 4:7, 8 and 6:11, NRSV, NIV, NASB), and occasionally "religion" (3:16, NRSV; also GNT), "holy life" (4:7, CEB) or "holy living" (4:8, 6:11; CEB). The verb εὐσεβέω, however, has a range of translations: "religious duty" (NRSV), "put religion into practice" (NIV), "practice piety" (NASB), and "respect" (CEB). See also D'Angelo (2003) and Hoklotubbe (2017).

27 Filial duty was also important to Judeans (first-century Jews). Josephus summarizes that according to Hebrew Law, parents should be honoured

immediately after God himself, and young men should respect every elder because God is the oldest of all beings (*Against Apion* 2.28; see also Balla 2003, 91–2). David Noy suggests that Judeans might have treated the elderly with special care. He found proportionately more Judean than Roman epitaphs dedicated to the elderly (2007, 92–4). It is possible that the epitaphs reflect less about the treatment of the elderly and more about making sure the person who arranged for the inscription appears to honour their parents in death, and so procure social and divine approval for this tangible sign of filial duty (gaining or maintaining honour in the view of his peers). Noy's study does confirm that the fulfillment of filial duty was a strong cultural value for Judeans of the Diaspora.

28 BDAG defines εὐσεβέω as a "sense of awesome obligation arising within a system of reciprocity in which special respect is showed to those who have the greater investment in one's well-being, such as deities and parental figures" (2000, 413).

29 From his description of the excesses in the city of Rome in the first century CE, Sallust would seem to agree, relating a picture of people who, instead of using their wealth respectably, squandered it with immoral and selfish activities and no thought of the future (*Cataline* 13:2–5).

30 Aristotle's sentiments about affection for parents reflect the hierarchical nature of the parent-child relationship as well as the positive emotional and social relationship (*Nicomachean Ethics* 8.12.5). These ideas are echoed in the second century by Hierocles, who considers children friends, comrades, helpers, and allies in all situations; they participate in their parents' joy and offer sympathy in sorrow (*On Duties* 4.25.53; 4.22.21–4; see Malherbe 1986, 91, 101; also Plato, *Laws* 6.754B).

31 Campbell reports that in the modern Mediterranean, an old Sarakatsan mother receives unconditional devotion and care from her children because of her love and sacrifice for them. "One cannot abandon an old mother because 'she brought me into the world' (*me ephere sto kosmo*)" (1964, 164–5). In such patriarchal and patrilocal cultures, sons often support their aging parents because of their ability to provide economically, though, in practice it is the daughter-in-law who does most of the physical care, like food preparation, clothes washing, and personal care (Brandes 1995, 17; also Campbell 1964, 166; Lisón-Tolosana 1976, 309).

32 For example, about half of the male population may have had a living mother when they reached age thirty (46 per cent), but only about a quarter (28 per cent) may have had a living father (Saller 1994, 52). Also, because women married at a younger age than men (as noted above), on

average, a person could expect their mother to outlive their father (Harlow and Laurence 2002, 97–8).

33 In fact, natural affection of a child for her or his parent may take priority over obedience to authority (Saller 1994, 110). In the first of his *Controversies*, Seneca the Elder details arguments for and against a man who was caught between his father and his uncle, brothers who did not get along. When the young man supported his uncle against his father's wishes, his father disinherited him. He was adopted by the uncle, who became rich through an inheritance. Later, when the father was in need, the youth helped him against his uncle's wishes, only to be disinherited by his uncle. One participant in the discussion names nature and duty as motivators in the young man's actions: "Nature moved me, piety [*pietas*] moved me, and the mutability of human fortune, so clearly exemplified. Fortune seemed to stand before my eyes and say: 'Those who do not support [*alo*] their own go hungry'" (1.1.16, Seneca the Elder 1974, 46–7). This reveals the reciprocal nature of *pietas*, the notion that it is "natural," and also the idea that whether or not a person fulfills his filial duty will affect their fate.

34 Malherbe (2006) makes a similar argument for 2:1–2 and 2:9–15. He posits that the repetition of particular words in the exhortation for women to be modest and submissive demonstrates what the author thinks is proper to live a quiet and peaceable life.

35 A similar sentiment was expressed by Aristotle (*Nicomachean Ethics* 9.2.8). Aeneas cares for his father Anchises in Virgil's *Aeneid* (2.707–48, 3.480, 6.110-14). Cicero ranked duty to parents only after following one's duty to gods and country. Duty to dependents, namely, children, the whole family (*domus*), and kin, were lower on the list (*On Duties* 1.45.160; see also 1.17.58). Similarly, Hierocles stated, "After discussing the gods and the fatherland, what person should be mentioned before our parents?" (*On Duties* 4.25.53; translated by Malherbe 1986, 91).

36 Old age was a time of anxiety and vulnerability for elite and non-elite alike because (as with old age everywhere, especially before modern health care) health and physical frailty were concerns. For example, Pliny praises the healthy and active senator Spurinna, who was seventy-six (*Letters* 3.1), and bemoans the plight of Domitius Tullus, a wealthy man who physically deteriorated in his old age so that servants had to feed him and clean his teeth (*Letters* 8.18).

37 For a discussion of children's duty to parents in ancient Roman culture, see Parkin (2003, 205–16). Parkin discusses the scope of children's

38 responsibilities, the lack of Roman laws regarding filial duty, and the limits of *patria potestas* for other elderly members of the family.
38 Seneca the Elder states, "Children must support their parents or be imprisoned [*liberi parentes alant aut vinciantur*]" (*Controversiae* 1.1, 1974, 26–7; 1.7, 1974, 150–1). The verb *alo* can mean to nourish, sustain, or support, and in the first of the *Controversies* clearly means to feed, or provide food (1.1.16–20, Seneca the Elder 1974, 47–53).
39 This papyrus and a translation can be found at Papyri.info, https://papyri.info/ddbdp/p.mich;5;322a (also labelled P.Mich.inv. 967).
40 Campbell's argument is unconvincing for two main reasons. First, he wants to equate the use of οἰκεῖος in other letters associated with Paul (Gal. 6:10, Eph. 2:19) to 1 Tim. 5:8 as "an established piece of jargon among Pauline Christians" (1995, 158). However, two instances, both of which qualify the word οἰκεῖος with a genitive phrase ("household of believers [οἰκείους τῆς πίστεως]," Gal. 6:10; "household of God [οἰκεῖος τοῦ θεοῦ]," Eph. 2:19), hardly constitute "established ... jargon." Second, Campbell translates μάλιστα as "in other words" rather than "especially." He translates μάλιστα οἰκείων as "in other words, members of God's household" or fellow believers. Campbell follows Hanson (1982, 92, 101, 175), who follows T.C. Skeat (1979, 173–7), in translating μάλιστα this way "wherever it occurs in the Pastorals" (Campbell 1995, 200). However, Hong Bom Kim convincingly demonstrates that each instance of the word must be carefully evaluated in the letters to Timothy and Titus (2004, 360–8). As Kim points out (364), Skeat himself does not consider the use of μάλιστα in 1 Tim. 5:8 in his argument, and probably considered it an example of its traditional meaning, "especially" (1979, 174n1).
41 Campbell argues that rendering "the members of the household" as the community of believers would not disqualify unbelieving family members because Paul's injunction in 1 Cor. 7:14 makes all of one's relatives "somehow included among the people of God" (1995, 160). However, Campbell does not adequately justify using Paul's idea that an unbelieving wife or husband is made "holy" by the believing spouse, thereby making the children "holy." Campbell would apply this to all relatives, but the husband-wife bond is different from other familial relationships. It is based on reproduction (Cicero, *On Duties* 1.17.53) and represents a bond between families that compete for honour. Paul's concern is primarily for the children in 1 Cor. 4:17, whereas in 1 Tim. 5:8, the author is concerned for widowed mothers and grandmothers. As we have seen, duty to parents ranks above duty to children and other kin (Cicero, *On Duties* 1.45.160).

42 Whether parent-child relationships continued in multi-generational households (Carter 2001, 45) is debated in current scholarship on Roman family structure. Saller suggests that most households would have been made up of the nuclear family only (1994, 96; see also Saller and Shaw 1984). Bagnall and Frier's work on Egypt census data indicates that the majority of households would not be multi-generational, but some were when the necessity arose (1994, 59–74). The nature of change within families over time suggests that multi-generational households existed especially when aging parents were in need of care (Bradley 1991, 4; Harlow and Laurence 2002, 23, 31–3).

43 This contrasts with the Greeks, who had laws to regulate filial support. In the Greek city-states, a law prescribed children's obligations to provide food, lodging, and burial to their parents. Solon introduced legislation in the early sixth century BCE specifying that unless sons had not learned a trade, they had to fulfill their filial duty, and those who did not have a trade were disgraced (Plutarch, *Solon* 2.2-3; see also Parkin 1997, 126–7, Berkel 2020, 125-8). Also, a law at Delphi reads, "If anyone does not feed his father and mother, when this is reported to the council (βουλὰ [sic]), if the council shall find the person guilty, they shall bind him and conduct him to civic jail" (Lerat 1943; translated by Reinhold 1970, 352).

44 Parents may have encouraged their children to care for them with the power they had to disinherit them (Parkin 2003, 210–11). For those sons who still had a living father, the inheritance could be a source of tension (Saller 1994, 131), and a source of control for a father who could threaten to disinherit his son (Harlow and Laurence 2002, 119). Though a mother might have some property to bequeath, she probably had less economic leverage than a father, so this aspect of motivation is less important for the situation in 1 Tim. 5.

45 Legal discussions in the *Digest* (Justinian 1998) feature the following similar cases: 31.87.4, Paulus (a father gave one son his inheritance before his death, specifying that the son give half to his sister, which he did not); 32.37.3, Scaevola (a father gave his entire property except two slaves to his son, stipulating that it should be returned if he later wished it to be returned); 34.4.23, Papinian (a man divided his goods among his sons, with the stipulation that a sum of money be given to his daughter; he subsequently used the money to purchase property, so that the sons had to sell property to recover the sister's money); 41.10.4.1, Pomponius (a general scenario of a father dividing his estate before his death).

46 Saller notes that "some fathers partially forfeited their power by transferring their property before their death," an arrangement that assumed that

the child could refuse to provide for his aged parents (1994, 131). On the other hand, it suggests that a father had reason to trust in his children's care without having to dangle their inheritance in front of them to force them to comply. Or perhaps he had reason to trust in his children's sense of honour.

47 In 138 CE, a seventy-five-year-old widower named Kronion divided his property between two sons and a granddaughter. To Kronion junior, the father bequeathed only forty drachmas of silver because he "has suffered many wrongs at his hands in the course of his life." In essence, he publicly declares that he has disinherited his son for improper behaviour toward his father. Kronion senior specified that until he died, he would "have complete control of his affairs, to manage as he chooses" (*P.Mil.Vgl.* 84 = *P.Kronion* 50; translation in Lewis 1983, 72). Unlike the couple in *P.Mich.* V 322, Kronion had little trust in his children's ability to care for him and his affairs.

48 Those who took Jesus's comments to "let the dead bury their own dead" (Q 9:60), and "hate your father and mother" (Luke 14:26; *Gospel of Thomas* 101; see also Matt. 10:37) literally would have been subject to social sanction. It is possible that such sayings had some influence on the "different teaching" in 1 Timothy that manifested in children not caring for their widowed mothers, prompting the author's directives in 1 Tim. 5:4, 8.

CHAPTER SIX

1 The reference is singular ("a widow should be put on the list"), but the fact there is a list suggests a group of widows rather than just one. Also, the lack of a definite article suggests the author expects more than one widow to be enlisted.

2 Older women in the modern Mediterranean are known for inappropriate behaviour like lewd talk or drunkenness, which are usually excused by younger people on account of their age (Chapman 1971, 46; Fernea 1965, 147; Cool and McCabe 1983, 67). For instance, McCabe witnessed young people dismissing the shameful behaviour of a seventy-two-year-old woman. The woman mocked the immodest dress of younger women by lifting her skirt and exposing her underwear; the young people were embarrassed but dismissed the behaviour because "she is an old woman" (Cool and McCabe 1983, 66).

3 In Julian Pitt-Rivers's conception of honour and shame, he described men as defenders of honour and protectors of women's shame, and women as

passively embodying shame (1977, 20–4). But, as noted in chapter 2, women are far from passive in defending their modesty in Mediterranean cultures. For example, according to Fernea, a good Iraqi woman is hard working, devoted to family, domestically competent, quiet and obedient to her husband, has a stainless reputation, and wields significant influence over her husband and sons, helping to make decisions involving such important matters as marriage and the schooling of her children (1965, 56). Dubisch asserts that, operating within certain cultural restrictions, women try to accomplish their goals and sometimes even succeed in altering the social system. In some ways they support the system, in other ways they attempt to "get around" it, and at some level they often find contentment within it (1986a, 29, 35). On ancient Mediterranean women in Christ groups in cultural context, see MacDonald (1996).

4 Modern traditional Greek women are also thought to have to redeem their sexuality because of their association with Eve, who, according to Christian tradition, was the primeval woman who brought sin into the world (Genesis 2–3). A woman may work to overcome this "moral disability" through a "redeeming archetype," namely, by exemplifying the Orthodox Christian concept of the Mother of God (*Panagia*; Hirschon 1983, 117).

5 According to Campbell, a Sarakatsan woman is beyond sexual activity when she is over sixty or when her husband dies. At this time, she is said to have a "clean soul" (*kathari psychi*); thus "the prestige of some old women is considerable" (1996, 290). (The specificity of sixty may be coincidence, or cultural continuity from a notion of sixty as old from the ancient Mediterranean world, or a reflection of tradition that emerged from 1 Timothy as sacred text.) Yewoubedar Beyene finds that Greek women are sexually active after menopause (1989, 124) and may certainly continue to be into their sixties. The perception that they are no longer sexual is likely a male notion, or an assumption.

6 On third-person imperative use in 1 Timothy, see chapter 3.

7 Dio Cassius reports a speech by Agrippa specifying that a man could not become praetor until the age of thirty because before this age, he was not considered trustworthy to manage private or public affairs (*History of Rome* 74.20.1). According to the Dead Sea Scrolls, a man could participate in lawsuits and judgments at the age of thirty (*The Messianic Rule*, 1QSa=1Q28a 1.13–14).

8 While Collins has no comment about the widows of 1 Tim. 5:9 being at least sixty, he does use Philo's age divisions (*On the Creation* 35[104]) to envision younger men/women as being in their twenties and older men/

women as in their fifties in 1 Tim. 5:1–2 (134; also on Titus 2:3–5, 2002, 343). Of course, the community involved people of other ages as well, which Collins does not account for. Also, Philo's age categories are for men, not women. Marshall suggests the age of forty as the "rough division" between young and old (1999, 239, 593). Since what constituted "young" and "old" was contextual, these chronological ages are not necessarily helpful.

9 On 5:9–10, Collins states, "The Pastor's use of the technical term 'enrolled' suggests that there was a well-defined group of *real widows* in the community" (2002, 139, my emphasis). Quinn and Wacker "presume" these widows are alone and without support (2000, 437). Dibelius and Conzelmann state the real widow "is *probably* the same as" the widow in 5:9 (1972, 74, my emphasis). Marshall acknowledges that the terminology is different, but still equates the two: "In the light of vv.4–6 it can be *assumed* that the generic χήρα here [in 5:9] by implication excludes those who have a family to look after them or are morally unworthy and is now tantamount to 'genuine widow'" (1999, 591, my emphasis).

10 On the "order of widows," see below.

11 Though Guthrie rightly reasons that it would be "inconceivable" for the church to limit aid for needy widows based on an "arbitrary age," he subsequently suggests that a small group of widows who received aid were privileged with special duties, and 1 Tim. 5:9–10 is an official recognition of these women (1990, 114).

12 Barclay admits this age is "surprisingly high" given the demographic realities (2020, 278).

13 The fourth-century *Apostolic Constitutions* specifies that widows must be at least sixty (quoting 1 Tim. 5:9) to be part of the "order of widows" so that they were beyond the time of life when they would want to marry again. "Choose your 'widows not under sixty years of age,' that in some measure the suspicion of the second marriage may be prevented by their age." Remaining unmarried was a "gift" (3.1.1; Coxe 1994 [1886], 426). They were called "true widows" (αἱ ἀληθιναὶ χῆραι) – a similar but different phrase from the one found in 1 Tim. 5 (τὰς ὄντως χήρας, 5:3, 16; ἡ ὄντως χήρα 5:5). They received financial assistance from the church (3.1.7). They were expected to pray and to refrain from teaching or baptizing, and their status as the "altar of God" meant they were not mobile (3.1.6; see Osiek 1983). This fourth-century text is clearly an interpretation of 1 Tim. 5:3–16 applied to a developed "order of widows." The number of people who belonged to the church at that time was much greater than at the end of the first century, so there would be proportionately more women who would fit

the parameters of the "order of widows" as presented by the *Apostolic Constitutions*. Given the demography of the late first century CE, the membership of the community that received the letter to Timothy at the end of the first century would have had relatively few widows over the age of sixty.

14 An "office of widows" is argued on the basis of several details in the text. Thurston, for example, interprets "honour" (5:1) as payment for service, καταλέγω (5:9) as an introduction to regulations for the "order," and the so-called "vow" (πίστις) associated with the younger widows (5:14) as a vow of celibacy (1989, 44–5; also Verner 1983, 164). Thurston recognizes that separately each of these points is refutable but argues that together "they make a good case" (46).

15 Gustav Stählin posits that the real widow chooses to be "alone" in order to function in a ministry that includes prayer (1979, 456). This interpretation seems to lack insight into cultural norms and social realities of widows in the late first century CE.

16 Zamfir notes this is a "rather high" age limit given life expectancy at birth in the ancient Mediterranean (2013, 359).

17 Verner, who argues that 5:9 begins a new section, suggests the author wants only elderly women to qualify for office. He posits that some of the younger widows in 5:11–12 were formerly enrolled in the office of widows, but because of their problematic behaviour, the author is limiting the office to elderly women (1983, 165). As with the argument for restricting aid (above), an interpretation that involves the term παραιτοῦ (usually rendered "deny," 5:11) is problematic because this word does not have a clear sense of "un-enrolling" widows (see also chapter 7).

18 As noted above, by the time of the *Apostolic Constitutions* in the late fourth century, a formal order of widows was in place (3.1.1, 2), but we have earlier evidence in Tertullian (160–220 CE). He clearly names an order of widows alongside the offices of bishop (overseer), presbyters (elders), and *diakonoi* (*On Monogamy* 11.1), and mentions an age preference for older women in the order: "I know of a virgin somewhere who was placed among the order or widows before she was twenty" (*On the Veiling of Virgins* 9.2, Dunn 2004, 109). He refers to the statement of a one-husband woman from 1 Tim. 5:9 (*To His Wife* 1.7.4), and possibly refers to a widow's office in a list of roles that includes widow and virgin alongside bishop and deacon (and doctor) (*Prescription Against Heretics* 3.5; Rankin 1995, 176). Tertullian's evidence is not early enough (and is arguably too idiosyncratic) to be applied to 1 Timothy, however.

19 J.N.D. Kelly suggests that the "duties" in 5:10 are similar to the responsibilities of the overseer (1963, 117), but as Gordon Fee points out,

giving primacy to the duties themselves does not accurately reflect the meaning of the text. Fee also emphasizes that "this list reflects a reputation *already gained* through these kinds of good deeds" rather than a list of current duties (1988, 125, emphasis added).

20 The Greek word in 3:11 is γυναῖκας (plural of γυνή), meaning either "women" or "wives." In this context it is ambiguous: it could refer to female *diakonoi* or the wives of *diakonoi*.

21 Although polygamy occurs in the Hebrew Scriptures (e.g., Jacob married both Leah and Rachel [Gen. 29]; David had multiple wives [1 Sam. 18:27, 25:42–43; 2 Sam. 3:5, 11:27], and Solomon is recorded as having seven hundred wives plus concubines [1 Kings 11:3]), monogamy was the moral and cultural norm at the time of the Roman Empire (Treggiari 1991, 229–61).

22 The word φιλόξενος (3:2) is an adjective that is derived from the words for love or friend (φίλος) and stranger or guest (ξένος), with a sense of being a person who "lov[es] strangers" (i.e., outsiders or non-kin; LSJ 1940, 1938). The verb ξενοδοκέω (5:10) means to "entertain hospitably" (1938), demonstrating hospitality (which is, by definition, for "strangers," that is non-kin) in action (BDAG 2000, 684).

23 Namely, young people needed to respect their elders (5:1), adult children needed to care for their aging mothers and grandmothers (5:4), young widows needed to remarry (5:14), elders needed to have compensation (5:17–18), young men needed to refrain from accusing elders (5:19–20; see chapter 9), and slaves needed to respect their masters (6:1–2). I do not consider the description of "elders" (5:17–18) to be parallel or related to the qualifications in 3:1–13 (see chapter 9).

24 Osiek and Balch posit that the author "lays down procedures for the acceptance of widows into something that must have looked like a women's service organization that accepted women of proven virtue who qualified by also being in need" (1997, 166). Knight suggests that the church was committed to providing support for these widows, but that they in turn performed special tasks from time to time (1992, 223).

25 The phrase τοὺς βεβήλους καὶ γραώδεις μύθους refers to myths (μύθους) that are unholy (βεβήλους) and associated with old women (γραώδεις). "Old wives' tales" were synonymous with "nonsense," reflecting the idea that old women were susceptible to *superstitio*. In Latin literature, "it is therefore not surprising to see the twice-marginal *anus* ([because she is a] woman and old) associated with the humbler aspects of folk religion and with magic" (Rosivach 1994, 112–13). The phrase could also be used literally, since old women were "story-tellers *par excellence*" (Bremmer

1987, 200–1; also Kartzow 2009, 138). For a modern example of old women as storytellers, see Abu-Lughod (1993). In 1 Timothy, the author contrasts the proper behaviour of εὐσέβεια with the improper implications of stories that promote unhealthy teaching, some of which are associated with older women (see also the potential role of oral tales in the development of *The Acts of Paul and Thecla* in MacDonald 1983). Old women could be seen as a bad influence on their younger counterparts so that some thought it was best not to encourage them to visit (e.g., second-century poet Naumachios, quoted by Stobaeus 4.23.7; Treggiari 1991, 197).

26 Women working together may threaten men's power. David D. Gilmore describes men's experience of women in modern Andalusia: wives working with their mothers can form a formidable team, so mothers-in-law are threatening figures (1990, 960–1).

27 Kevin Madigan and Carolyn Osiek offer helpful distinctions between office, role, and special status (2005, 18), the last of which fits this context rather well. In the case of these chosen widows, perhaps "special status" is a suitable label, but not in the sense of an official, set role.

28 Cornelia (mother of the Gracci, see below) states, "Therefore when a maiden's toga gave way to the nuptial torch, and a different headband caught up to bound my hair, I was wedded to your couch, Paullus, destined so to leave it that on this stone I shall be recorded as married to one man alone … Upon the lustre of such grand trophies Cornelia brought no tarnish: rather was she an example to be followed in that noble house" (Propertius, *Elegies* 4.11.33–6, 43–44; 1990, 385).

29 Humbert found fifty inscriptions that praised marital faithfulness, and only five that explicitly praised a woman who did not remarry after her husband died (1972, 73). In the *Laudatio Murdiae* (CIL 6.10230), an inscription erected in the first century BCE, a son honoured his mother who married twice, once to his father and then to another man. She was faithful in both marriages, and fairly distributed her property to her children of both marriages. Her son from her first marriage (the testator) received what her first husband had wished his son to have. Her son praises her, declaring, "the provisions of her will proved both her gratitude and devotion towards her husbands, her impartiality towards her children and her sincere righteousness" (translated by Wiedemann and Gardner 1991, 132–3).

30 For example, in one inscription, Fabia, who died leaving three children, was only twenty-three years old (CIL 6.31711), and Aurelia, a freedwoman of Augustus, was thirty-six years old (CIL 6.31711). On the other hand, someone like Negelia, at forty-two years old, having been married

for twenty-four years, was fortunate to be called a *univira* since her husband outlived her (CIL 5.7763).
31 Valerius Maximus recounts a story of a guest staying at Cornelia's home. She showed Cornelia her fine jewelry. "Cornelia kept her in talk until her children came home from school, and then said, 'These are *my* jewels'" (2000, 385, 4.4 [preface]).
32 On childbearing (1 Tim. 2:15, 5:14) and childrearing (5:10) as synonymous in an ancient Mediterranean context, see discussion in Zamfir (2013, 261–3).
33 Equating the sixty+ widows with the real widows (who have no children to care for them; 5:5), MacDonald suggests that she may not have raised her own children, but foundlings (1996, 226). Bremmer suggests that in ancient Greece, old women were typically nurses of children (1987, 192, 193, 200) and would come upon foundlings because young women were not free to move around (192). While old women may have raised others' children at times, this would not preclude their own children. Many children died before they reached adulthood (see chapter 1; as mentioned above, Cornelia had three surviving children out of twelve; Plutarch, *The Life of Tiberius Gracchus* 1.5). More importantly, if we do not equate the real widow (who is alone) with the sixty+ widow, there is no logical barrier in positing that the sixty+ widows raised their own children.
34 It is also reminiscent of the Johannine story of Jesus washing his disciples' feet (John 13). We cannot know for certain the extent to which different communities knew or used this as a symbolic act by the end of the first century. See also the suggestion below on death rituals.
35 It is difficult to assess what the meaning of "saint" was at the end of the first century. In the mid-second century, Polycarp refers to saints (*sancta*) in a sense that may not refer to all believers: "and may [God] grant you the lot and portion to be among his saints [*inter sanctos*] – and to us as well with you" (*Phil.* 12.2, also 11.2, AF 2003, 1:348–9). I recognize that this is not conclusive evidence. Much later usage designated "saints" as particular individuals who had lived pious lives (there were further developments on who could be called a "saint"). As a matter of speculation, I wonder if here "saints" could refer to travelling apostles of Paul's era. Washing the feet of the founders of the community could then refer to a tangible, or symbolic, connection women of this age would have had with these important people when they were younger, with implications of their role as eyewitnesses to the founding of the community (for the important role of "eyewitnesses," see Bauckham 2006 and chapter 3). Another possibility is an allusion to women's roles in death rituals (see below).

36 On women as ideally hidden from public view (and scrutiny), see Zamfir (2013, 128–37). Reit van Bremen argues that women honoured with statues and inscriptions for their public benefaction represented their family's honour rather than their own (1993, 236; 1996, 108).

37 Spicq cites the *Apostolic Constitutions* (3.1.1) to support this notion, contrasting the younger women of 5:11 who wanted to remarry (1947, 171). However, as noted above, this fourth-century textual interpretation of 1 Tim. 5:9–10 is an anachronistic application from a later, evolved Christian community; the author of 1 Timothy has more interest in the community's reputation than in remarriage per se.

38 In the Mishnah, an old woman was defined in terms of menopause (cessation of menstruation) (*Niddah* 1:5).

39 Lesley Dean-Jones notes that Greek medical writers were not concerned about the mechanics or symptoms of menopause, though they were aware of it and considered older women "dry" (1994, 106–7). For a range of ancient sources, see Darrel W. Amundsen and Carol Jean Diers (1970).

40 Judith K. Brown agrees that "menopause is typically unmarked by ritual and therefore remains unreported by ethnographers. Also the perimenopausal period in a woman's life tends to be briefer than middle age." She suggests that the term "middle age" is more accurate for the stage of life at which women are typically most powerful, attaining relative leisure and authority. The cross-cultural evidence suggests power typical in this stage of life for many women (1992, 18). In her ethnography of her own family in modern Athens, Panourgiá recalls that she told her mother her concerns about baking the Eucharist bread for the Orthodox church while she was menstruating. (Even though she is not personally religious, she found the ritual important, particularly since it related to her dying grandfather.) Officially, a woman is not allowed to touch the bread if she is menstruating. Her mother scoffed at the idea that menstruation affected the bread and told her to take it in proudly (1995, 100–1). Of course, no one but Panourgiá and her mother would know the difference.

41 Similarly, Harlow argues that men became less interested in women as they aged (except if they had wealth), especially as they became less associated with fertility. Male authors often seem interested in inheritance issues when writing about women's betrothal and marriage, production of children, and the end of marriages due to death or divorce (2007, 196–7).

42 Vincent Rosivach comments that "if men are not interested in having sex with older women, then from the male perspective older women should not be interested in having sex; and if they are interested – again from the male perspective – they deserve to be ridiculed" (1994, 111). Bremmer

(1987, 206) and Parkin (2003, 246–7) go further to say that old women were past their usefulness, and this is why they were portrayed so negatively. Among modern Egyptian Bedouin, old women and remarriage are the object of joking because marriage is associated with sex, and old women are not supposed to be sexually active (Abu-Lughod 1993, 82–4); see also Panourgiá 1995, 203).

43 This may be what Anthony Tyrell Hanson is implying when he states that "sixty" creates "an obvious solution" where the experiment of enlisting young widows was tried and failed, though he does not elaborate (1982, 99).

44 In his comments about the sixty-year-old women involved in funerals (see below), Bremmer equates the age of sixty and the evident freedom for women this age in this context with menopause (1987, 192), still leaving a gap of at least a decade if menopause typically occurred around age fifty.

45 Dionysius of Halicarnassus states, "Now we assume [Dinarchus] returned from exile at the age of seventy, as he himself says when he calls himself an old man [γέροντα]; since it is from this age onwards that we most commonly call men at this time of life old" (1985, 260–2, *Dinarcus* 4; Parkin 2003, 16; see also Harlow and Laurence 2002, 118). Judith de Luce posits that women were considered old at age forty, and men at age fifty (1993a, 230–1; see also 1993b, 41). She chooses age forty for women as "old" on the basis of ancient physician reports of when a woman would reach menopause, but she does not consider the range of ages that ancient sources report (see Amundsen and Diers 1970).

46 For various scholars' interpretations of when old age begins, see Parkin (2003, 312nn3–4). Parkin uses sixty as the "minimum age to qualify as old" as a matter of convenience (2003, 36).

47 Spicq does cite several important instances of women specified as sixty, which I explore below.

48 This explanation makes more sense than applying reproductive limitations to men (mentioned by Cokayne 2003, 122).

49 At the age of sixty, a man was no longer eligible to serve in the military and therefore could no longer vote in the *comitia centuriata*, an assembly in the Roman Republic that decided on laws, magistrate positions, war, and judgment upon citizens. This institution was based on wealth (such that those with more wealth had more influential votes) and age, since the vote was split between those who were seventeen to forty-six and those who were forty-six and older. The older contingency was a much smaller group and so had less power in the vote (Momigliano and Cornell 2003, 372). Maintaining this balance of power might be the meaning behind the

phrase "sixty year olds over the bridge" (Parkin 2003, 264) or "hurling sexagenarians from the bridge [*sexagenrios de ponte*]" (Macrobius 2011, 48–9, *Saturnalia* 1.5.10) since the "bridge" led to the voting space.

50 Plato specifies that the interpreters also should be the same age (not less than sixty), but their position is for life (*Laws* 6.759E). Earlier he specifies that the guardian of the law must be at least fifty years old when elected and can remain in the position for twenty years. If a person is elected at sixty, he would hold the post for only ten years, if he lives that long (*Laws* 6:755A). Thus, sixty appears to denote the last stage of life for Plato.

51 Also, Philo mentions the age of sixty as it relates to Lev. 27:7 and the monetary worth of male and female slaves at different ages. He points out that there is no distinction made between physical attractiveness or height, just distinctions in sex and age. Women and men are worth differing amounts beyond age sixty, but the age at which they are "old" (πρεσβύτος / πρεσβύτιδος) is the same (1937, 326–7, *Special Laws* VII, 2.32–34 [Colson's numbering]).

52 On religious functions of old women in ancient Greece, see Bremmer (1987, 198). See also discussion in van Bremen (1996) of women in public religious roles in the Greek East of Hellenistic and Roman times.

53 A Roman festival for the dead involved an old woman surrounded by maidens offering a sacrifice (Ovid *Fasti* 2.571; Bremmer 1987, 199). On insights about Christian women in the first few centuries related to death rituals and catacombs, see Denzey (2007; on burial ritual and mourning, see, for example, xii–xiii, 98).

54 I know of no research on this specific possibility to date. John 12:3 indicates that Mary, the sister of Lazarus, anoints Jesus's feet for his burial, though in the parallel story in Mark (14:3–9) and Matthew (26:6–13) an unnamed woman anoints his head (with connotations of anointing a Messiah). Luke's radically different version of the story does not allude to Jesus's death (Luke 7:38, 44–46). The nature of the activities of the women at the tomb of Jesus (Mark 16:1, Matt. 28:1, Luke 23:55–24:1, John 20:1) are not entirely clear (nor are their ages) but would have involved at least lament. On women and death rituals in early Christianity, see Kathleen Corley (2010) along with Nicola Denzey Lewis (2012).

55 BDAG suggests the definition "to make a selection for membership into a group," with the passive translated either generally as "be selected" or specifically as "be enrolled" (2000, 529). Johnson suggests "register certain persons as widows" (2001, 264), Guthrie prefers "reckon" (1990, 114), and Dibelius and Conzelmann propose "to regard as" (1972, 75n14),

apparently on the basis of Plato *Laws* (6.763A). However, all of these suggestions seem to be conflating "real" widows with the sixty+ widows.

56 This translation and the Greek text are found in Kloppenborg and Ascough (2011, 251) in their note on lines 39–40 of *IG* II² 1368: The Rule of the *Iobakchoi*.

57 I am grateful for John Kloppenborg's assistance in translating and providing context for this as well as the next two inscriptions.

58 On the importance of women's public service for family reputation (as opposed to individual honour), see van Bremen (1996, 83–108).

59 Some association lists include fathers and sons. For example, *IG* II² 1335 includes at least one father and son, and *IG* II² 2358 includes at least three father-son pairs). See also van Bremen (1996, 83–108).

60 Other inscriptions list both men and women (e.g., *IG* II² 2354), sometimes with a mix of various social rank and status (e.g., *IG* II² 2358, *SEG* 36:228).

61 I am not aware of any direct evidence of inscriptions by Christians as early as the late first or early second century, but a list could have been recorded in some other medium, such as parchment or vellum. The early Christians used such materials for letter writing and other documents. For example, the author of 2 Timothy has Paul ask Timothy to bring his "books and especially the parchments [τὰ βιβλία μάλιστα τὰς μεμβράνας]" (2 Tim. 4:13). Hermas writes his visions in little books (βιβλαρίδια) which are read to the churches (*AF* 2003, 2:192, *Shepherd* of Hermas, Visions 8.3).

62 On καλῶς see chapter 9.

63 On εὐσέβεια and its cognates in 1 Timothy, see chapter 5.

64 For ἀνέγκλητος, see 1 Tim. 3:10 (of *diakonoi*); Titus 1:6–7 (of elders).

65 Van Bremen points out that women who took public religious offices tended to be focused on ritual, and they held office for a limited period of time. Unlike men, whose public positions contributed to civic careers built over a lifetime, women did not pursue political careers; instead, they held temporary positions for the honour of their families (1996, 85). Van Bremen's assessment of the sources is that women normally took office only once (86).

66 Since there is no other indication of fictive kin language in the inscription, Euaxis is probably the true (biological?) mother of Metrodora rather than a fictive mother. If so, celibacy would not have been a stipulation for the position of priestess. It was not uncommon, according to van Bremen, for euergetism and support of public projects (which were connected to office, like the priesthood) to continue over several generations of the same family (1996, 97–100; 108–10).

67 According to T. Christopher Hoklotubbe, visual reminders of idealized female virtues in the form of imperial women's images (on coins, reliefs, and statues) and honorary inscriptions among voluntary associations were ubiquitous, especially in Asia Minor (2017, 84–5, 111–25; also 135–7 for further inscriptions for patrons, including women).

68 Kloppenborg and Ascough argue that the threat to refuse to bestow honours (indicated in an earlier part of the inscription) would be as potent as a fine would be in persuading them to follow the rules (2011, 174).

69 Paul does name specific women at times (e.g., Phoebe commended as patron in Rom. 16:1–2). Comparatively, the author of 2 Timothy mentions Timothy's mother, Eunice, and grandmother, Lois (1:5), highlighting the passing down of "sincere faith" through the generations. Unlike 1 Timothy, 2 Timothy more closely approximates Paul's letters by including greetings to Prisca and Claudia (among others) in his closing remarks (4:19, 21).

70 In 1 Corinthians, Paul makes suggestions using third-person imperatives (e.g., 7:2, 3, 12, 18, 20), comparisons to his own unmarried state (7:7, 8), and differentiation between his own advice and directives of "the Lord" (7:10, 12, 25), and occasionally second person imperatives (7:5, 27). The author of 1 Timothy uses second-person imperatives more frequently as Paul directs Timothy (e.g., 5:1, 3, 7, 11, 19, 20, 22), and third-person imperatives with some frequency (e.g., 5:4, 9, 16, 17). See chapter 3.

71 See also van Bremen's case studies of women honoured with public inscriptions, such as Publia who was praised for "the impeccability of her character and manners as well as 'nourisher' and 'founder'" (1996, 103); and Plancia, who held positions of religious office and was (arguably) about sixty when she was honoured for having a gate complex built in the city of Perge (106).

72 Though he equates the sixty+ widow with the real widows, Barclay would concur that the sixty+ widow is a model "for others to emulate" (2020, 278).

CHAPTER SEVEN

1 Recently, scholars have begun to consider the possibility that the "younger widows" (5:11) are actually women who have never been married (see for example Collins 2011; Tsuji 2001, 101; Barclay 2020, 278–9, and see 279n46 for other sources). They argue that these younger women have *chosen* to be celibate due to the influence of the opposing teachers.

However, 5:12 states they *do* want to marry. Whether they are women who have been previously married or have never married only affects the argument insomuch as the challenges of providing dowries and finding husbands for women whose first husbands have died or divorced them are likely greater than they would be for a first marriage. Zamfir argues designating χῆραι as "virgins" is "difficult to prove" in 1 Timothy (2013, 357).

2 The literature is vast. There is much discussion around the younger widows following the opposing teachers in desiring an ascetic life (e.g., Thornton 2016) and Paul's assumed directive that restricts them from being in an "office" of widows because of their age and/or problematic behaviour (e.g., Tsuji 2001; Thurston 1989, 44–53; Verner 1983, 165). I address many of the assumptions behind these arguments in chapters 7 and 8.

3 See chapter 8 for further explanation of this translation.

4 It is curious that no children are mentioned among the younger widows, except the future children of the younger widows' second marriages. It may be assumed that any children from a first marriage would be with the widow's husband's family or were simply to be incorporated into the new arrangement. The younger widows in the real community may also have been widowed before they had any children, or this scenario may exclude children for the sake of the rhetorical argument that focuses on taking care of the younger widows.

5 The "adversary" is unlikely to be one of those who teaches different things (1:3); the author is more likely to have an outsider in mind. These opposing teachers are depicted as insiders over whom Paul has authority (i.e., Paul hands two of them over the Satan so they will learn not to slander; 1:20), whereas the adversary has the power to criticize them, presumably as a community.

6 On women's public speech as inappropriate, see Zamfir (2013, 180–94).

7 This phrase likely means that the author identifies some younger women as having followed the opponents' teachings because he associates specific opposing teachers with Satan (1:20). This is the only other mention of "Satan" in 1 Timothy. Both have to do with problematic speech; the younger widows are "saying things that are not necessary" (5:13) and in 1:20, Paul removes (hands over to Satan) two named men, Hymenaeus and Alexander, with the purpose of having them learn not to slander. "Slander" indicates a problem with reputation, which is also the case with the mention of "the adversary" in 5:14 (see note 4 above). The use of "Satan" in 5:15 implies that the younger widows were particularly vulnerable to the *effects* of the opposing teachings (1:3, 6:3).

8 On why this text is not about women spreading heresy, see Zamfir (2013, 182–8).
9 In general, the genitive is "the case of qualification (or limitation as to kind) and (occasionally) separation" (Wallace 1996, 77). The genitive here appears to be an "ablatival genitive" or "genitive substantive," which is defined as "that from which the verb or sometimes head noun is separated" (107). Though not common in the New Testament, here "it is used to indicate the point of departure" (107). This use of the genitive can denote either progressive separation ("movement away from, so as to become separated") or static separation ("in a separated state"), with an emphasis on the result or the cause (107). Similar use of the genitive can be found in Acts 15:29 and Eph. 2:12 (107). Here in 1 Tim. 5:12, it denotes movement away from Christ, with emphasis on the cause, which is (perceived) wanton behaviour.
10 We could point to analogies of the opposite notion, that women were desperate to marry. In modern Sicily, marriage is a duty for a man, but "marriage is represented as the ardent desire of every woman" (Chapman 1971, 89). Songs, proverbs, and legends suggest that because of sexual desire women are more interested in marriage itself than in any particular man (1971, 89–90). This is more likely the perception of men than the reality of women themselves.
11 She may have had the right to continue living in the marital house, for example. If she received an inheritance as a widow and then remarried, she may have brought the new husband to live in the house. In one legal example, a woman even brought along her father-in-law (Justinian 1998, 7.8.4.1). Her children, freedmen, and parents may also have resided with her (7.8.6).
12 The situation would be somewhat different in the case of divorced women but would likely still be fraught with suspicion and questions of identity.
13 In the modern Mediterranean, a Sarakatsan widower would marry non-virgins, or "used women" (honourable widows and dishonoured maidens; Campbell 1964, 83, 128, 159, 304). In this way, such women were fitted into normal categories of family and marriage so that they would not have the shame of "remaining" (304; see also Stirling 1965, 111, 196). In Sicily, "except for house-nuns, who have taken vows of chastity, unmarried women are regarded as not responsible for their condition and are not blamed" (Chapman 1971, 89), but there is a general suspicion of women who live alone, and the slightest blunder produces gossip about them (108). Another potential avenue of honourable status is religious devotion, but in Marjo Buitelaar's cross-cultural study of

widows, this is usually reserved for the elite (1995, 13). Those who argue that the younger widows were pursuing celibacy might find this compelling, but the young widows were not elite, and the "first faith" is not necessarily a chosen vow of celibacy (as argued below).

14 Abu-Lughod (1986) and Mari H. Clark (1983) both comment on their experiences as female ethnographers who did not have children of their own. They occupied a liminal status while doing their fieldwork because they were not considered girls, but not really considered women either, since in those settings, having children is "one of the most defining characteristics of women" (Abu-Lughod 1986, 17; Clark 1983, 123–5).

15 I disagree with commentators who suggest this has the same force as imperatives in the letter (e.g., Van Neste 2004, 135n202, and others discussed below). In total, the author uses the first-person indicative eighteen times in 1 Timothy. Three times he indicates an attribute of Paul's identity: "I myself was entrusted [with the gospel] (1:11); "I myself am among the foremost of sinners" (1:15); "I myself was made a herald and an apostle" (2:7). Five times he denotes his own actions in the present: "I give thanks to Jesus Christ" (1:12); "I am telling the truth" (2:7); "I am not lying" (2:7); "I permit no woman to have authority over a man" (2:12); "I write these things" (3:15). Three times he denotes actions: two in the past, one passive ("I was shown mercy," 1:16), and one active ("I have turned over [Hymenaeus and Alexander] to Satan," 1:20), and one action is in the future: "until I come" (4:13). Twice he addresses Timothy in a neutral sense: "I encouraged you to remain in Ephesus" (1:3); "I entrust this commandment to you, Timothy [my] child" (1:18). Twice he uses strong directives: "I charge [you] before God" (5:21); "I command you before God" (6:13). Three times he makes a request of community members (2:1, 8, 5:14; discussed below). Among this range of uses of the first person, his use of "I wish" (βούλομαι) seems rather muted.

16 In a third request of community members, Paul urges (παρακαλῶ) that prayers be made on behalf of all humanity (2:1). Note that requests of community members are unique to 1 Timothy when compared to 2 Timothy and Titus. In 2 Timothy there are twenty-three uses of first-person indicative, with one indication of Paul's identity (1:11), and three instances of directives to Timothy (1:6; 2:7; 4:1), but mostly referring to Paul's current or past actions (1:3 [x2], 12; 2:9, 10; 3:11; 4:6, 7, 12, 13, 17, 20) or his current or past state of mind (1:3, 4, 5, 12 [x4]). The latter is not used in 1 Timothy or Titus. Titus has only five instances of first-person indicative: three are actions (past [1:5; 3:12] and future [3:12]), one is a directive to Titus (3:8), and one is related to Paul's identity (1:3).

17 One could argue that the use of βούλομαι in Titus 3:8 is a fairly "strong directive," meaning, "I want you to speak confidently." But here Paul addresses concerns for Titus himself rather than for others as in 1 Tim. 2:8 and 5:14.
18 For example, he strongly directs Timothy twice using first-person indicative: "I charge [you] before God" (5:21) and "I command you before God" (6:13). In 5:20, Paul uses second-person imperative to direct Timothy to "rebuke [ἔλεγχε] those who continue to sin in front of everyone so that the others might also have fear" (Titus 1:1 and 2:15 are similar; see chapter 9). Just before his description of the young widows, the author uses a strong imperative, "command these things [ταῦτα παράγγελλε]," (5:7), referring to two sets of people: on the one hand, children and grandchildren to take care of their widowed mothers and grandmothers (5:4; Marshall 1999, 589), and on the other hand, the woman who was living luxuriously, and thus behaving badly (5:6; see chapter 8). Paul does use a second-person imperative to introduce the problematic younger widows (5:11), but, as discussed below, translating παραιτοῦ as "deny" or "avoid" makes little sense in the context of Paul "desiring" (βούλομαι) young women to embrace culturally appropriate domestic roles.
19 See similar conclusions in Huizenga, who primarily comments on Titus 2:3–5 (2013, 258, 265, 271–2, 285; for a discussion of the scholarship, see 265n20).
20 Similar to the rhetoric of 1 Timothy, the author of Titus takes on the voice of Paul. Whether the same author wrote 1 Timothy and Titus cannot be assumed. See discussion in chapter 1.
21 The word πρέπω is also used in 1 Tim. 2:10 to contrast fancy adornment with "that which is suitable [πρέπει] for women who profess devotion to God [θεοσέβειαν], through good works [δι' ἔργων ἀγαθῶν]." That which is "suitable" is implicitly contrasted with the opposing teachings and paired with the devotion or duty owed to God (θεοσέβειαν is a cognate of εὐσέβεια, chapter 5).
22 Whereas 1 Tim. 5:1–2 uses the comparative adjectives "older" and "younger" for men and women (see chapter 4), Titus 2:3 uses the noun form for all except "younger men" (which uses the comparative adjective).
23 Also, as in 1 Tim. 5:1–6:2a, slaves make up the final category of people addressed (Titus 2:9–10; 1 Tim. 6:1–2a). See the discussion of the *Haustafeln* (household codes) in chapter 4.
24 The author uses the infinitive (εἶναι) in apposition to the pronoun in 2:1: "*these things* [ἅ] that are suitable for healthy teaching" in the sense of defining such things (Wallace 1996, 607). Thus, old men "are to be

[πρεσβύτας ... εἶναι]" identified with the list of things that define what is suitable for healthy teaching. This infinitive construction and meaning is borrowed for the old women ("likewise old women [πρεσβύτιδας ὡσαύτως]" are to be identified by the list of things defining what is suitable for healthy teaching). When the author gets to "younger men," he shifts the grammar, using an imperative and infinitive of indirect discourse ("likewise exhort the younger men to behave sensibly [τοὺς νεωτέρους ὡσαύτως παρακάλει σωφρονεῖν]," 2:6).

25 Similarly, Horrell points out that the author of *1 Clement* does not directly address the women or the young people (1.3, 21.6–8; 1996, 269–70).

26 By teaching "noble" things (καλὰ) or being noble teachers (the Greek is ambiguous here), they would be contributing to what was "suitable for healthy teaching" (πρέπει τῇ ὑγιαινούσῃ διδασκαλίᾳ, 2:1) rather than the problematic teaching of opposing teachers (2:11). In du Boulay's study of a modern, traditional Greek village, if a woman was considered "good" (she illustrates with the modern Greek word *kalē*, derived from its ancient form), with a connotation of being "chaste," this was exhibited in her diligent domestic behaviour (1974, 131).

27 Fallers and Fallers go so far as to suggest that the women of Turkey are more independent than Western women because they function within their own sphere, outside the sphere of men. "The women's world has a complex structure of its own, quite apart from the occupational roles filled by some women in the public sphere. Women organize, conduct and participate in a wide range of work activities, sociability and ceremonies at a distance from the world of men. To it they bring their own leaders, skilled specialists and loyal followers. The separate structure allows freedom of action, away from men" (1976, 53).

28 If marriage is arranged, a woman is not as invested in a romantic and emotional way with her husband as in typical modern Western marriages; however, her daily contact with the women of the family into which she marries is very significant. At a Turkish wedding in Erdemit, the bride is surrounded by women for three days, she dances with the groom's sister, and the mother-in-law presents a gift (Fallers and Fallers 1976, 253).

29 Chapman describes how kin and neighbours assist one another, maintaining daily contact and cooperation, including small economic exchanges of goods and services; cooperating in activities like bread making, setting up a loom; or sharing leaven, coal, or even a sewing machine; and aiding one another in emergencies. Children play together outside, and women gather informally, bringing their sewing, spinning, baking, etc. (1971, 129, 131, 135).

30 Linda Cool and Justine McCabe note that female solidarity contributes to a positive experience of women's aging process (1983, 67). This seems overly positive about networks of women since a certain amount of intergenerational and interfamilial conflict is inevitable.
31 For both men and women, age and life experience bring increased responsibility and social value in middle age, followed by a decline in old age (Chapman 1971, 49, 217).
32 A Sarakatsan woman is considered "old" after her eldest son marries (Campbell 1964, 290).
33 While Egyptian Bedouin women cooperate and defend other women from the criticisms of men, there is a clear age hierarchy. Women defend their female kin against male kin, but the older women would complain among themselves about the lack of modesty in young women (Abu-Lughod 1993, 50).
34 Nicola Denzey points out that even inscriptions and commemorations about women were generally written by men for a male public to view and evaluate (2007, 21).
35 James LaGrand (1998) questions the assumption that Simeon is an old man, since the text is not explicit about his age.
36 Although Sudan is not part of the Mediterranean, the urban patterns of Sudanese female networks provide an image of how unrelated women in Greco-Roman cities may have survived and thrived in a subculture largely unimportant to men (see LaFosse 2017a). While female kin are still important, networks of unrelated women who live in the same area of the city fulfill kinship roles, functioning as female kin did in traditional situations (visiting, preparing for rites of passage, aiding one another in various tasks). For older women, their age affords them more flexibility and influence: their children are grown, they have more experience, and they have more access to resources. Thus, they can offer support to younger women in an informal system (Kenyon 1998, 20).
37 Aristophanes's play *Assemblywomen* illustrates women's hierarchy and age roles, with comedic twists (877–1111). An old woman done up with makeup and a party dress (which would not be suitable for a woman of her age) argues with a young woman about who will sleep with the old man they are expecting. When a young man arrives, he desires to sleep with a young woman but is told that it has been decreed that he must sleep with the old woman first (*Assemblywomen* 1015–20). The girl quips that the old woman is the age of the man's mother, alluding to Oedipus (1038–42). Two other old women come to take him away. The older women clearly have authority over the younger woman.

38 They would learn their duties for ten years, serve for ten years, then teach other younger virgins for ten years (*Life of Numa Pompilius* 10). A girl was chosen to be a Vestal Virgin between the ages of six and ten (Aulus Gellius, *Attic Nights* 1.12). Therefore, she would be trained up to the age of sixteen or twenty, serve until she was between twenty-six and thirty, and train others until she was between thirty-six and forty.

39 See examples in van Bremen of older women (potentially widows) using inherited wealth (often with male guardianship) to benefit their communities and especially their families (1996, 231–7, 256–61, 301–2). She comments on women's use of wealth: "Freedom to act appears more often connected to a woman's age and familial circumstances" (236).

40 *Contra* Winter, who posits that the instructions for the "believing woman" in 5:16 were "an innovation which had neither legal nor ecclesiastical precedent" (1988, 94). Far from being an innovation, it was an expectation, and the precedent was a social one.

CHAPTER EIGHT

1 Barclay rightly notes that only the real widows are "supported directly by the church *qua* church" (2020, 276).

2 As the penultimate specific item in the list before the more general notion of "pursuing every good work," the author gives this action some emphasis.

3 The same verb is used of overseers who have children who are submissive (τέκνα ἔχοντα ἐν ὑποταγῇ; 3:4) and widows who have (ἔχει) children and grandchildren who should take care of them (5:4).

4 The NRSV has a rather confusing translation: "If any believing woman has relatives who are *really widows*, let her assist them; let the church not be burdened, so that it can assist those who are real widows [my emphasis]." The phrase "really widows" is the translation used for τὰς ὄντως χήρας in 5:3. The NRSVUE (Updated Edition) has rightly eliminated "really" in 5:16.

5 Some interpreters assume that in 5:16 the author is returning to the subject in 5:4, where children and grandchildren are directed to care for their older female relatives (e.g., Knight 1992, 230), but this interrupts the flow of thought.

6 Van Neste observes clear parallels in subject matter and ethics in 2:1–3:13 and 5:1–6:2 (2004, 144).

7 Those who connect the letters to Timothy and Titus more closely than I do (see chapter 1) often cite 2 Tim. 3:6–7 and Titus 1:11, which indicate that opposing (perhaps travelling) teachers worm their way into households,

with vulnerable women as their particular victims (2 Tim. 3:6–7). See, for example, Barclay (2020, 282). These texts need not dictate the scenario imagined for 1 Timothy 5:3–16. Within the context of 1 Timothy, I see the middle-aged women as being more convinced by the opposing teachers than younger women are, but the effects of the teaching influence the perceived behaviour of the younger women because of the middle-aged women's neglect.

8 The textual variants for this phrase are (1) "believing woman [πιστή]," (2) "believing man [πιστός]," and (3) "believing man or woman [πιστός ἢ πιστή]" (Aland 2001, 720). The first variant has the strongest evidence. The variant of "believing man" may have arisen if later interpreters of the text assumed that a father should be responsible for his widowed daughter(s). Guthrie prefers the variant "believing man" because he (erroneously, in my view) concludes, "it is difficult to believe that the exhortation to relieve the church of its responsibility to care for widows would be confined to women" (1990, 117).

9 What follows is not a comprehensive list but gives a sense of the range.

10 The author also uses the phrase πιστὸς ὁ λόγος (1:15, 3:1, 4:9), meaning "the word/saying is trustworthy."

11 Interestingly, the female *diakonoi* (or wives of *diakonoi*) are also associated with "faithfulness in everything" (πιστὰς ἐν πᾶσιν; 3:11).

12 For discussion on the first half of this verse, see chapter 7.

13 For example, Ignatius suggests there are young women in Smyrna who are celibate with his phrase "virgins who are called widows" (*Smyr.* 13.1, AF 2003, 309). In the apocryphal *Acts of Paul and Thecla*, Thecla is a young virgin who chooses not to marry. In the third-century interpretation of 1 Tim. 5:3–16, the *Apostolic Constitutions* suggest that younger widows could not be part of the "order of widows" because of the temptation to marry a second time. A second marriage would not be a problem in itself but would be considered immoral if a widow promised to remain unmarried (3.1.2).

14 Treggiari notes one instance of a woman called *perpetua virgo* by Pliny the Elder (*Natural History* 35.147; 1991, 83n2).

15 However, if a young widow was actually sexually promiscuous, as Winter suggests, I find it hard to believe she would be easily able to remarry with such a tainted reputation.

16 Plutarch states, "A wife ought not to make friends of her own, but to enjoy her husband's friends in common with him. The gods are the first and most important friends. Wherefore it is becoming for a wife to worship and to know only the gods that her husband believes in, and to shut

the front door tight upon all queer rituals and outlandish superstitions. For with no god do stealthy and secret rites performed by a woman find any favour" (1928, 111, *Advice to the Bride and Groom* 19, *Moralia* 2:140D [Stephanus's numbering]).

17 On the complexities of women who belong to Christ groups and are married to polytheist men in the first century, especially the restrictions and suspicion they drew, see MacDonald (2003, 14–28). For an interesting (but problematic) analysis of how women marrying polytheistic men helped the movement to grow, see Rodney Stark (1996, 111–15). Harlow and Laurence note that in the case of Pudentilla's remarriage (see chapter 6), the fact that Apuleius was an outsider provoked suspicion (2003, 89).

18 E.g., Tacitus, *Annales*, 15.44; Suetonius, *Life of Nero* 16; Pliny, *Letters to Trajan* 10.96. See also MacDonald (1996).

19 The word "first" (πρῶτος) might also have been used by the opposing teachers. It is used three other times in the letter, twice in Paul's assertion of his identity as the "first" among sinners (1:15, 16), and once in the justification of why women should not have authority over a man/husband ("Adam was created first," 2:13). It is possible that the term "first" (πρῶτος) denoted some kind of superiority of teaching promoted by the opposing teachers that the author was using against them in this rhetoric.

20 Barclay suggests the author is not opposing the young women's desire to marry (which would be inconsistent with the author's desire in 5:14 for them to marry); rather, he finds their "oath or pledge" not to marry problematic, not least because of their economic dependence on the church. Barclay's argument is that the young women have never been married, having renounced human marriage to be devoted to Christ in place of marriage (2020, 279–81). However, the fact that the author of 1 Timothy clearly states that they "want to marry" (5:12) is not adequately addressed in this scenario.

21 In 1 Maccabees, in a letter confirming their alliance with Rome, certain Judean leaders agreed: "To the enemy that makes war they shall not give or supply [οὐ δώσουσιν οὐδὲ ἐπαρκέσουσι] grain, arms, money, or ships, just as Rome has decided; and they shall keep their obligations without receiving any return" (8:26, NRSV). The word ἐπαρκέω may imply having sufficient means from which to provide aid, as the root of the verb ἀρκέω entails having enough or being satisfied, as in 1 Tim. 6:8: "if we have food and clothing, we will be satisfied with these things [τούτοις ἀρκεσθησόμεθα]."

22 Brown points out that male ethnographers may attribute decision-making about marriage to men when in fact women are the most influential figures in the process (1982, 144). A mother-in-law in Iraq, for example, may play a key role in choosing her daughter-in-law (Fernea 1965, 164).
23 Addressing a young woman, Catullus describes a mother's role in her daughter's marriage choice: "And you, maiden, strive not with [do not resist] such a husband; it is not right to strive with him to whom your father himself gave you, your father himself with your mother, whom you must obey. Your maidenhead [virginity] is not all your own; partly it belongs to your parents, a third part is given to your father, a third part to your mother, only a third is yours; do not contend with two, who have given their rights to their son-in-law together with the dowry" (1913, 91, 62.59–65).
24 Perhaps it should be noted that mothers often wept for their daughters who left them (Virgil, *Aeneid* 7.357).
25 In modern Sicily, Chapman notes that while parents usually arrange marriages, an old woman (or man) may encourage a marriage "for the benefit which she may derive from its successful conclusion" (1971, 95, 99), by which I assume she means a financial reward.
26 *Contra* Winter, who presupposes that all young widows had dowries and legal support and thus were denied support from the church (1988, 97). Also, *contra* Winter who later suggests that the believing woman is to aid only widows who are her kin (since the community is caring for the real widows with no kin; 1994, 71). The distinction for the author in 5:16 is not between kin or non-kin; rather it is a distinction of age, as the widows under the care of the believing woman are the younger ones, that is, the ones still able to bear children and who should be, according to the author, getting remarried.
27 She had no children herself (2.31), so she proposed that her husband marry a younger woman to beget children, and she would act as a sister and mother-in-law (2.34–35). But he evidently did not marry again (at least while his first wife was alive).
28 Zamfir argues that the letters to Timothy and Titus (1 Timothy in particular) restrict the public roles of women more than Roman society did, since some women were appointed to roles in polytheistic religious offices (for the public benefit of their families; also van Bremen 1993, 236; 1996, 108) and honoured for their benefaction (Zamfir 2013, 289–391). The female *diakonoi* are a possible exception (350–2). My view of the evidence is that in fact there are older women that the author of 1 Timothy understood to

be honoured in a public way. The idealized sixty+ widow demonstrated this kind of honour (5:9–10) as examples of how older women were expected to behave. More specifically, older women were to be benefactors in a way that contributed to the honour of the community by supporting the younger women (financially and otherwise) to marry (or remarry).

29 Treggiari notes, "When a woman reached marriageable age or was divorced or widowed while still reasonably young, it was natural and usual that suitors would present themselves" (1991, 126), but the search for suitable marriage partners, at least among the elite, was often "tedious and complicated" (127). In addition, if she had children, their interest in her inheritance might be threatened by a new husband (Harlow and Laurence 2003, 89), as was the case in Pudentilla's marriage to Apuleius (see chapter 6).

30 A young widow might be able to return to her father's home with hope of remarrying. If she had children, she might remain widowed and raise her children; if she remarried she may raise the children with a stepfather, or they may be raised by paternal kin. A wealthy widow had more choices than a poor one (Harlow and Laurence 2003, 89).

31 Plutarch describes a recently divorced woman, Valeria, flirting with Sulla, recently widowed. After checking into her family and past, Sulla sought to marry her. Plutarch does not find Valeria's actions questionable but does comment that Sulla allowed his passions to guide him like a young man would (*The Life of Sulla* 35.3–5).

32 Roman mothers were influential in their sons' lives (Dixon 1988, 168–202), just as they are in the modern Mediterranean (Kiray 1976, 263–5; Campbell 1964, 165–6). According to Cool and McCabe, sons are emotionally reliant on their mothers and may seek their advice and approval for marriage (1983, 65–6).

33 Harlow and Laurence suggest that the status of a father-in-law was important for a bridegroom who was striving for heightened status (2003, 95–8). If a man married at the age of twenty-five, his father would likely be in his late fifties, the age at which his public life (or life course) might be drawing to a close. If he married a woman who was fifteen, his father-in-law might be in his late forties, a time of life at which he was particularly powerful in public life. If a man was around forty when he married (for the second time) a woman of twenty, his father-in-law may be at a similar stage of life and might provide a suitable peer alliance. A prospective groom might also be interested in a woman's brothers or other male kin for social or political alliances.

34 Among the Sarakatsani, there is little prestige in marrying a widower, but for non-virgins (honourable young widows and young women with tainted reputations), marrying a widower might be their only choice to avoid the shame of being unmarried (Campbell 1964, 83, 128, 159, 304).
35 Demographically, many men and women married after their father's death (Saller 1994, 229).
36 Young women may have had some personal choice, especially in a second or subsequent marriage (Treggiari 1991, 134–5).
37 Huizenga argues that older women were role models for younger women in 1 Timothy and Titus just as they were in the Pythagorean letters (2013, 322–3). There are also some similarities here with Osiek and MacDonald's models of "mothering" in early Christian communities based on an older woman teaching a younger woman as in Titus 2:4–5. They suggest an older woman could be an indirect role model, a role model who offered financial support for widows living in their own homes, or a woman who took women into her own home, as reflected in 1 Tim. 5:16 (2006, 77).
38 On the importance of rejecting self-indulgence, sharing wealth, and using it for good, according to Greek and Roman moral philosophers, see Malherbe (2011, 79–88). Malherbe argues that the directives of 6:17–19 are intended to promote "socially responsible actions" instead of "self-centeredness" (90). The motivation for sharing wealth is not for personal gain or honour, but for the enjoyment that comes from a "socially responsible use of wealth" (94), which "God intends in providing richly" (92–3).
39 This is the term used in Titus 2:1 to describe the "healthy teaching" (see chapter 7).
40 In 1 Timothy, the similar phrase ἔργος κάλος is used of "noble work(s)" that matters for public reputation (3:1, 5:10, 5:25, 6:18; see chapter 9). The phrases of "good work(s)" do not appear to be strongly patterned in 2 Timothy or Titus, though they are important phrases in those letters as well.
41 In chapter 9, I argue for a similar subject shift in 5:20, where there are accusations against an elder (singular), and those who continue to sin (i.e., the accusers, plural) should be rebuked before everyone.
42 The base sense of this verb is "to bear or beget children," but several commentators suggest that it could mean to raise or rear children, with a focus on women's *roles* because of their ability to give birth rather than the act of childbirth itself (Moo 1981, 205; 1980, 72; Spicq 1947, 73; see also Marshall 1999, 468–70). Stanley E. Porter rejects this interpretation (1993, 95), but suggests the possibility of interpreting διά in a temporal

sense, rendering the meaning "during the time of childbearing." He settles on an instrumental sense, "by means of childbearing" (97). Kenneth L. Waters (2004) suggests that it is an allegory; the "children" are actually virtues which, if cultivated, will provide salvation. The translation of διά is particularly difficult here. The sense that seems to fit best is "with the accompanying circumstances of" (BDAG 2000, 224). See also Hubbard (2012).

43 The phrase "purity with self-control" (ἁγιασμῷ μετὰ σωφροσύνης; 2:15) reflects two items the older women were to teach the younger women in Titus 2:5.

44 Malherbe argues that the literary context of the discussion on wealth in 1 Tim. 6 is the whole of 1 Tim. 5:1–6:21, which lends some support to my argument about the middle-aged female patrons as central to the problems being addressed (2010, 287).

45 On social death in cross-cultural perspective, see Counts and Counts (1985).

46 This is even worse than the fate of Hymenaeus and Alexander, who are said to be handed over by Paul to Satan to learn not to slander (1:20).

47 These are placating others of the older generation and same generation (5:1-2); honouring the real widow (5:3); caring for widowed family members (5:4); providing for one's own (5:8); enlisting the sixty+ widow (5:9); interceding for the younger widows (5:11); caring for [younger] widows (5:16), and/or not burdening the community (5:16).

48 Interestingly, the same phrase is used of the opponents and their wayward thinking just after the section on elders and slaves: "if someone teaches other things [εἴ τις ἑτεροδιδασκαλεῖ καὶ]" (6:3, cf. 1:8). It is also used in the context of overseers: "If someone aspires [to be] an overseer, he wants a good work [εἴ τις ἐπισκοπῆς ὀρέγεται, καλοῦ ἔργου ἐπιθυμεῖ]" (3:2), and "if someone does not know how to manage his own household [εἰ δέ τις τοῦ ἰδίου], how will he take care of the church?" (3:5).

CHAPTER NINE

1 Since the late nineteenth century, but even as far back as the seventeenth century (Stewart 2014, 2), the development of "offices" (leadership positions) in the early church has received much attention in historical scholarship, often strongly influenced (however implicitly) by scholars' diverging Protestant and Catholic views of leadership (see discussions in Burtchaell 1992; Campbell 1994, 11–17).

2 I use the term "overseer" for ἐπίσκοπος to avoid the anachronistic connotations of the usual translation "bishop," except in direct quotations of others (see also Campbell 1994, 179n11).
3 As part of unfinished business, Titus is left on Crete to "appoint elders [older men] in every town" (Titus 1:5). In Titus 1:6–9 there are two lists of qualifications reminiscent of those found in 1 Tim. 3, one linked to elders (1:6) and one clearly for overseers (1:7–9). There are clear linguistic parallels to elements in the leadership attributes in Titus that are found in 1 Tim. 3:1–5.
4 For von Campenhausen (1969), the roles of "bishop" and "deacon" derived from Pauline communities (mentioned in Phil. 1:1), while the role of elder derived from the Judean/Jewish synagogue. The earliest instance of this grouping appears to be penned by Ignatius (110 CE): "I urge you to hasten to do all things in the harmony of God, with the bishop [τοῦ ἐπισκόπου] presiding in the place of God and the presbyters [τῶν πρεσβυτέρων] in the place of the council of the apostles and the deacons [τῶν διακόνων], who are especially dear to me, entrusted with the ministry [διακονίαν] of Jesus Christ" (*AF* 2003, 1:246–7, *Mag.* 6.1) While Ignatius offers analogies for the three titles of overseer, elder, and *diakonos* together, their functions are not clear or developed, nor can this grouping be considered normative in this period. The three titles are not normally seen together in other proto-orthodox literature of that time. For example, the *Didache* directs the community to "elect for yourselves bishops and deacons [χειροτονήσατε ἑαυτοῖς ἐπισκόπους καὶ διακόνους]" (*AF* 2003, 1:440–1, 15.1). This is the same pairing that is found – with no elaboration – in Paul's letter to the Philippians (1:1). A unique pair is found in the *Shepherd* of Hermas: "overseers and those who are hospitable [ἐπίσκοποι καὶ φιλόξενοι]" (*AF* 2003, 2:452–3, Parables 104). In his *Letter to the Philippians*, Polycarp directs his listeners to "be subject to the elders and deacons [ὑποτασσομένους τοῖς πρεσβυτέροις καὶ διακόνοις]" (*AF*, 1:340–1, 5.3).
5 Examining 1 Pet. 5:1–5, Elliott asserts that the terms νεώτεροι and πρεσβύτεροι both imply an "intermingling" of age and office or rank (1970, 377), arguing that νεώτεροι could refer to new members (as opposed to an age designation; 381). In his more recent comments from a social-scientific perspective, however, Elliott refutes this, arguing that "office" is not an appropriate term for Christian social structure in the first two centuries CE (2003, 6).
6 With the majority of scholars, Campbell understands the role of elders to be continuous from the Judean and Greco-Roman social roots of

Christianity to the emergence of the proto-orthodox Christian community leadership structure in the late first and early second centuries. Like Harvey, Campbell argues that overseer and elder were not mutually exclusive categories because leaders in specific roles (e.g., overseer) were chosen from among the elders.

7 Towner suggests that the term πρεσβύτεροι mainly "denoted status or prestige rather than function," on the basis of "age, family, and probably also social standing as heads of households" (2006, 245). However, like the majority of scholars, he understands elder and overseer to be equivalent, as two "aspects of the reality of leadership" (686), where elder refers to prestige and overseer to function (247).

8 Stewart translates the phrase "generous with their support," focusing on their role as patrons (2014, 147).

9 Grammatically, the plural πρεσβύτεροι could refer to old men, or a mix of old men and women, but is unlikely to include women in this context. The author is not keen on women teaching in the public forum (2:12), which is characterized as constituting improper behaviour. Osiek and MacDonald argue that women were much less likely to preach and teach in mixed company than they were to act as patrons (benefactors) and hosts of the Lord's Supper (2006, 161–2). In chapter 8, I argue that that patronage is at issue in 1 Tim. 5:3–16 among the older and younger women.

10 The genitive is used in *Shepherd* of Hermas, Visions 8.3. Hermas is told to read his visions to the community (τῆς ἐκκλησίας; genitive) "with the elders who shepherd the community [μετὰ τῶν πρεσβυτέρων τῶν προϊσταμένων τῆς ἐκκλησίας]" (my translation).

11 Occurring directly after 5:16, this word may suggest a contrast with the middle-aged women who are not properly performing their duties (i.e., the believing woman, 5:16) and/or a comparison with the sixty+ widows who are "well attested for [their] noble works [ἐν ἔργοις καλοῖς μαρτυρουμένη]" (5:10; see chapters 6 and 8).

12 The fourth instance of καλῶς is also associated with the *diakonoi* who were "serving well [καλῶς διακονήσαντες]" (3:13). The related adjective καλός is also associated with honourable service in 1 Timothy: the person who aspires to be an overseer wants a "noble work [καλοῦ ἔργου ἐπιθυμεῖ]" (3:1); the sixty+ widow is "well attested for her noble works [ἐν ἔργοις καλοῖς μαρτυρουμένη]" (5:10); the wealthy should be "rich in noble works [πλουτεῖν ἐν ἔργοις καλοῖς]" (6:18); if Timothy brings Paul's teaching to the community, he "will be a noble servant [καλὸς ἔσῃ διάκονος] of Christ Jesus" (4:13).

13 The analogy between a person's literal household and the metaphorical household of God (3:15) helps to link the two terms προΐστημι (3:4, 5:17) and ἐπιμελέομαι (3:5). Both terms represent a combination of supervisory responsibilities and benevolent care. The verb ἐπιμελέομαι is widely attested in association inscriptions, and the cognate noun ἐπιμελήται is used for supervisory roles in the Attic associations of the imperial era. The title was borrowed from the ancient civic offices in Athens (see Kloppenborg and Ascough 2011, 37). Often several ἐπιμελήται are honoured or listed in an inscription (*IG* II² 1327, *IG* II² 1256). The functions of the ἐπιμελήται normally included financial and cultic responsibilities (e.g., offering sacrifices, financing, and leading processions; *IG* II² 1261, *IG* II² 1324, *IG* II² 1290, *IG* II² 1262, *SEG* 2:9), in accordance with the ancestral customs (*IG* II² 1277). They often functioned as benefactors for the association (*IG* II² 1301.3-8, *IG* II² 1324, *IG* II² 1327.26–27; *IG* II² 1361.16). This helps to support Stewart's claim that officers were chosen from among the honoured patrons of the community (2014, 167; so also Zamfir 2013, 44–59; see also 283–6).
14 The word κοπιάω (grow tired or weary) is also found in 1 Tim. 4:10 as a description of how both Paul and Timothy "toil and struggle [κοπιῶμεν καὶ ἀγωνιζόμεθα]" for the sake of the healthy teaching.
15 Polycarp condemns the love of money (*avaritia*) with regard to a presbyter (a term denoting an office? Latin: *presbyter*) who had embezzled from the church (11.1–2, *AF* 2003, 346), and lists the opposite, "free from the love of money" (ἀφιλάργυροι), as a trait necessary to be a *diakonos* (5.2, 338–9). It would be tempting to parallel this situation with the one in 1 Timothy by considering the wrongdoers in 1 Tim. 5:20 as elders who have fallen into this kind of avarice, associated with the opposing teachers (6:3–10), but as I argue below, the model of generational stability and social change suggests otherwise.
16 Plato suggest that among the pursuits one should have, money should come last after the soul and the body (*Laws* 5.743E).
17 For a summary of theories and interpretations of this phrase, see Marshall (1999, 612–15).
18 The *gerousia* were apparently common in the Greek cities of the Roman period (we only have evidence in papyri that were preserved from Alexandria and Oxyrhynchus). They may have been public associations with religious functions, or social organizations with no official or public function. Either way, men applied to join, and to receive benefits, namely, to be maintained at the public expense (e.g., *P.Oxy.* 3099, 3101).

However, the minimum age required is unknown (mid-fifties perhaps), and financial support appears to have required proof of social status based on birth rather than financial need (El-Abbadi 1964, 168; Parkin 2003, 171–2).

19 In fact, this was a way to secure "liquidated" wealth for those who owned property. Their wealth also gave them the right to take loans or material favours based on their ability to pay it back, namely, their ownership of property (e.g., olive trees, farmland).

20 Modern analogy would suggest that as men aged, they had fewer active duties, no longer able to do the work of younger men (Campbell 1964, 83; Chapman 1971, 47) but still able to direct active sons (Stirling 1964, 224; Chapman 1971, 47; Campbell 1964, 163). An older man may be "mostly idle" (Chapman 1971, 74), chatting with other old men (47; see also Stirling 1965, 223–4) and joking about his age (Clark 1983, 122; Campbell 1964, 286). He may drink too much (though this is a common stereotype), spend more time in religious pursuits (Chapman 1971, 47; Hirschon 1983; Abu-Lughod 1986, 90–1), or concern himself with his grandchildren (Campbell 1964, 164). Growing old is a process, so the onset of this stage varies with health, resources, and inclination (Stirling 1965, 223–4). An older man's inactivity often correlates with a loss of his former authority and status, though remnants of his status remain. Perhaps because of his years of experience (or his increasing interest in religious matters; Hirschon 1983), in a moral crisis, his opinion may be important (Campbell 1964, 106, 286). He may be able to retain an advisory role, offering advice or mediation (Chapman 1971, 47; Cool and McCabe 1983, 65; Stirling 1965, 95, 224). He still acts as the formal head of the household at weddings, and the marriages of his children require his consent. However, his day-to-day influence may wane with time (Campbell 1964, 286). Widowers tend to find another wife to depend on in the domestic sphere (Chapman 1971, 110).

21 As he does in 5:16, the author chooses to use a third-person imperative in 5:17. He tends to use this verbal structure in the letter in order to address third parties whose behaviour is problematic (see chapter 3).

22 It is possible these false accusations are related to the slander or disrespectful talk (βλασφημέω) of Hymenaeus and Alexander (1 Tim. 1:20). The fictive Paul has squarely punished them by handing them over (παραδίδωμι) to Satan (1:20), and he contrasts them with his faithful child, Timothy (1:18).

23 There are two other cognates in 1 Timothy: ἁμαρτωλός (one who does wrong; 1:9, 15) and ἁμαρτία (wrongdoing; 5:22, 24). In 1 Tim. 1:9, the

fictive Paul speaks against the opposing teachers who wish to be teachers of the "law" (νόμος). He says the "law" is not for the righteous, that is, those who already live correctly (δίκαιος), but for those who are without a law (ἄνομος). What follows is a rather lengthy list of people who are labelled by their wrongdoing (see chapter 11). The list begins with those who neglect duty and devotion (ἀσεβέσι) and those who do wrong (ἁμαρτωλοῖς; 1:9). The use of this cognate in 1:9 is comparable to the seriousness of the wrongdoing in 5:20. But in 1:15, Paul refers to himself as the greatest example of receiving salvation, naming himself as the worst of the wrongdoers [ἁμαρτωλούς], for whom Christ Jesus came into the world, implying that there is a way back to being upright. See below for a discussion of 5:22, 24.

24 A few commentators argue that the phrase refers to wrongdoers in general, who would be rebuked before the whole congregation (e.g., Guthrie 1990, 118), but it is difficult to justify the shift in topic here from elders to the community at large (Meier 1973, 331–2).

25 The term ἔλεγχε also indicates a correction of wrongdoing in Titus 1:9 and 1:13 with regard to rebuking opponents; the purpose is to bring them around to "healthy" teaching (1:13; see also Titus 2:15). In James 2:9 and Jude 1:15, the word is associated with wrongdoing (ἁμαρτία). In Rev. 3:19, it is paired with discipline (παιδεύω; see below).

26 In Turkey, "to disagree publicly with his father is a declaration of rebellion" (Stirling 1965, 224). Campbell observes that young Sarakatsan men rarely made their differences with their father public (Campbell 1964, 159–63).

27 Verner recognizes that the section on elders "deals with behaviour toward elders rather than elders' behaviour" (1983, 101), yet he reverts to the typical interpretations for the wrongdoers: "5:20 envisions either guilty elders being convicted in the presence of the presbytery or sinners in general being convicted in the presence of the congregation" (156).

28 Similarly, in Egyptian Bedouin society, the "code of modesty," often used to describe women's behaviour toward men, also applies to the behaviour of younger members of the group toward their elders (Abu-Lughod 1986, 99). Willingly submitting to elders is honourable; being coerced into subordination is shameful.

29 To illustrate the point in a rather graphic (and androcentric) way, Plutarch says that a man who gives up public service to take up work in the marketplace is "like stripping a freeborn and modest woman of her gown, putting a cook's apron on her, and keeping her in a tavern" (1936, 89, 10:785D).

30 The modern Olympic games is helpful analogy. When an athlete from our nation wins a gold medal, her victory is not hers alone, but "ours." She represents and demonstrates our success as a nation to, and in the midst of, the other nations; she desires victory for more than just herself, but for also her team and her nation.

31 According to J.G.F. Powell, Cicero was sixty-two when he wrote his treatise on old age (Cicero 1988, 2), and Plutarch was over fifty, perhaps over sixty, when he wrote *Whether an Old Man Should Engage in Public Affairs* (Jones 1966, 74). Even at forty-four or forty-five years old (Pelling 2003, 1348), Sallust would have been considered a mature man, and thus "older" when he wrote *Catiline*.

32 In a study of upper-class Roman men, Cokayne describes the desire of old men to retain status in society as "competitive and status-conscious" (2007, 210). Boasting was a way to "re-assert their status and overcome the fear that they might be overlooked or neglected" (210). She argues that old men feared marginalization because of physical decline. Inactivity was considered weakness (215). Plutarch argues this point throughout his treatise.

33 Similar age structures are found in many traditional cultures. In his novel *Things Fall Apart* (1958), Chinua Achebe illustrates the breakdown of such structure in late nineteenth-century Nigeria. The influence and prestige that an older man spent his lifetime building became meaningless in the face of radical social change. Younger men gained positions of power under a different worldview because of the introduction of European Christianity. With no support from the younger generation, the old worldview collapsed, and with it the social structure that upheld the social power of older men.

34 The word πρεσβύτεροι in *1 Clement* appears to be used for an age designation in some contexts, and for a leadership role in others. I accept the ambiguity here and assume some connotation of age in all instances.

35 The mention of "jealousy and envy" (ζῆλος καί φθόνος; AF 2003, 1:42-3, *1 Clem.* 4.7, 5.2) as a root of the problem is reminiscent of Plutarch's rhetoric about the "envy or jealousy" of young men (1936, 100-1, *Moralia* 10:787F; see above), although *1 Clement* focuses on jealousy (ζῆλος; AF 2003, 1:42-5, 4.1-5.7).

36 Hans Lietzmann argues that the conflict in *1 Clement* is between the young and old, finding an analogy with voluntary associations. He suggests that the young wanted elections for office as it was "everywhere customary" in religious organizations, so that they had a chance for office (1961, 1:192). Harry O. Maier suggests that young against old was one

manifestation of conflict; factions among women were another form of conflict. But the "precise difficulty" is more complicated (1991, 89–90).

37 The Greek word for "respecting" is αἰδέομαι (AF 2003, 1:74–5, *1 Clem.* 21.6), which means to have shame and fits the classic framework of honour and shame. It can mean to be ashamed or to have shame (in the positive sense); the latter is best translated "to revere" or "to respect." It can also mean to reconcile. Perhaps Clement uses this word deliberately to give some nuanced shades to the necessity of exhibiting proper modest behaviour before leaders, that is, respecting them, as well as being reconciled with (or under) them.

38 This list provides some parallels to 1 Timothy that suggest similarities in values between the two communities: an overseer, who has a leadership role, is to be respectable (3:2), women are to be devoted and submissive wives (2:9–15, 5:14), ideal relationships between different age groups are to be preferred (e.g., 5:1–2), and children are to display honourable behaviour (2:15, 3:4, 12).

39 There are two other instances in which he addresses Timothy in the first person, but in a neutral sense: "I encouraged you to remain in Ephesus." (1:3); "I entrust this commandment to you, Timothy [my] child" (1:18), which parallels 6:13–14.

40 The parallel in 6:13 contains the same phrasing as that found in 5:21, but with elaborations describing God and Jesus: "*in front of God* who gives life to all *and Christ Jesus* who presented the noble confession before Pontius Pilate."

41 Brian Irwin outlines a number of possibilities from the Hebrew Bible for what "laying on of hands" could have meant. He rightly observes that this mode of "appointment" of elders is not attested elsewhere (2008, 126). However, his conclusion that "laying on of hands" was related to a "public accusation" (128–9) assumes that *elders* were being publicly rebuked (1 Tim. 5:20), which I argue is not the case. He moves in the right direction to acknowledge that "deference to elders" (129) and caution about how they are treated is important for understanding this text.

42 This may suggest that the older men had significant influence in choosing the leaders (perhaps *diakonoi*, as Timothy himself is called a *diakonos* [servant]; 4:6) of the community, though in the fiction of the letter Timothy, who is "young" but exemplary, has been granted this authority (5:22), presumably by the elders (4:14).

43 This is similar to the directive in 2 Tim. 2:2 in which Paul tells Timothy to entrust what he has taught him to those will be able to teach others (Hutson 2013, 82).

44 If female *diakonoi* (or wives of *diakonoi*; see chapter 6, note 20) are in view in 1 Tim. 3:11, we may include them here, though given the gendered nature of age hierarchy, this section is likely about men. Would men appoint women to such positions? If the wives of *diakonoi* are in view in 3:11, their appointment would likely be part of their marriage obligations.

45 John P. Meier suggests that these are the wrongdoings committed before ordination (1973, 333), but there is no evidence within 1 Timothy for associating laying on of hands with remission of wrongdoings. As a verbal parallel to Titus 1:5, Meier cites *1 Clem*. 54:2, "the presbyters who have been appointed" (καθεσταμένων). In the established community of Corinth, Meier assumes that some older men were "ordained"; others were not (343). The verb καθίστημι could have many possible connotations and need not be defined here as ordination to an office.

46 *Contra* Hutson, who sees this moderation as important for Timothy as he rebukes *older men* in 5:17–22 (2013, 91).

CHAPTER TEN

1 In this sense, I agree with Barclay's assessment that "1 Tim. 5:3–16 offers, in fact, a rare glimpse into early Christian economics in the selective allocation of resources" and the "intersection of gender, household, and the material support offered by the church" (2020, 269). I would add that the section highlights particular members of the community who have economic responsibilities, particularly the middle-aged women who should support the younger widows (5:16) and the older men who should be honoured for their patronage (5:17).

2 Female *diakonoi* (or wives of *diakonoi*, see chapter 6, note 20) in 3:11 also appear to have some influence, being singled out amidst the qualifications of male *diakonoi*.

3 Whether this is someone in her own literal household or whether it refers to the "household of God" (3:15) is debatable (see discussion in chapter 8). Perhaps the author meant to be ambiguous on this point.

4 Though not with the same argument, Pao pairs youth (i.e., young men) and widows as marginalized groups featured in 1 Timothy (2014, 753–4).

5 I employ here the suggestion from Osiek and MacDonald that both men and women should be included when encountering male plural words (here: "to the rich [τοῖς πλουσίοις],") unless there is good reason to favour only one gender (2006, 6–7). The evidence from my reading of 1 Timothy suggests that women are among those who are wealthy patrons and benefactors (see chapter 8).

6 So also 1 *Clement* promotes this ideal: conduct that is noble (καλός) and pleasing to God is associated with "harmony" and proper order (AF 2003, 1:74-5, 21.1).
7 Malherbe argues that though some see the paraenesis to those who are wealthy in the community as oddly placed in 6:17–19, it is "more reasonable to read these verses as directives to persons who have not yet been identified explicitly in the letter as wealthy" (2011, 75).
8 There may be a connotation here of God's judgment when hidden things (κρυπτά) are brought to light (1 Cor. 4:5, also Mark 4:22), but the historical Paul also suggests that "hidden things" can be associated with shame (αἰσχύνη), which is related to reputation (2 Cor. 4:2).
9 The role of slaves within this section of the letter deserves more attention but is outside the scope of the present study.
10 In the second edition of *The Writings of St. Paul*, Meeks no longer characterizes the letters as a "church manual," presumably recognizing that "more elaborate church organization" did not necessarily constitute a "manual" as such (Meeks and Fitzgerald 2007, 122–3).
11 It is worth reiterating that though 1 Timothy has evident literary connections to 2 Timothy and Titus, I do not assume all three are written for one audience and with a common purpose. Rather, I focus on 1 Timothy on its own terms (see chapter 1).
12 For example, in *On Choosing a General*, Onasander states, "I believe, then, that we must choose a general, not because of noble birth as priests are chosen, nor because of wealth as the superintendents of the gymnasia, but because he is temperate [σώφρονα], self-restrained, vigilant, frugal [ἀφιλάργυρον], hardened to labour, alert, free from avarice, neither too young nor too old, indeed a father of children if possible, a ready speaker, and a man with a good reputation" (*Aeneas Tacticus, Asclepiodotus, Onasander* 1928, 375, 1.1; Dibelius and Conzelmann 1972, 158).
13 For example, in Pauline writings, similar lists can be found in 1 Cor. 6:9–10, Gal. 5:19–21, Rom. 1:29–31; other lists include those in Mark 7:21–22, 1 Pet. 4:3, 15, 2 Tim. 3:2–5, and perhaps Titus 3:3, which just mentions disobedience. These lists are not identical, suggesting that authors adapted the lists according to their rhetorical needs and context.
14 Though a verbal cognate is found in 6:5 (νομιζόντων) describing those who have different teachings, there is no explicit connection to age.
15 The phrase πατραλοίαν ἢ μητραλοίαν is also found in Lysias's *Against Theomnestus*: "For I presume, Theomnestus, you would not go so far, while expecting to get satisfaction from a man who called you a

father-beater or mother-beater [πατραλόιαν ἢ μητραλοίαν] as to consider that he should go unpunished for saying that you struck [ἔτυπες] your male or female parent, because he had spoken no forbidden word!" (1930, 201–3, 1.8). See also Plato, *Phaedo* 114A. Josephus uses the term πατραλόιας for parricide in *Antiquities* (16.356). Quinn and Wacker note that the word πατρολῴας is derived from πατήρ and ἀλοάω (ἀλοιάω), meaning "father" and "to thrash," respectively, and thus "to thrash one's father" (2000, 87). Aristophanes employed this term in his play *Clouds* in the context of the son striking (τύπειν) his father (lines 1327, 1331; cf. 911; see also comments in chapter 4 on 1 Tim. 5:1). It is ironic that in Seneca's *Controversies*, the Latin verb used for supporting, or literally "feeding," parents is *alo* – an opposite meaning of the Greek word ἀλοάω (to thrash) – both of which are related to the treatment of parents.

16 In the vice list of Rom. 1:29–31, Paul includes rebelling against parents. In 2 Tim. 3:2–5, disobedience to parents is listed (see Balla 2003, 160–2, 200).

17 Quinn and Wacker emphasize the "dramatic" nature of the list, citing Greek drama, such as Aeschylus's fifth-century Greek play *Libation Bearers*, in which Orestes kills his mother as revenge for her murder of his father (2000, 96; see also 87) The quintessential story of parricide is Oedipus's unintentionally killing his father and marrying his mother (97). These were popular stories among both Greek and Roman playwrights (Brown 2003, 1062). According to Lucian of Samosata's satirical version of the story of Peregrinus, he joined a group of Christ followers just after he killed his own father (*The Passing of Peregrinus*, 10–11; see also chapter 11). Lucian's mockery of Christ followers includes their ignorance of the fact that Peregrinus had committed the most heinous crime of patricide. Actual parricide was probably rare, representing a potential but unlikely outcome to intergenerational tension (Foner 1984, 126, 229). Some commentators consider this list an inversion of the Decalogue of the Hebrew Bible (Ex. 20:2–17; Quinn and Wacker 2000, 98–9; also Spicq 1947, 27) so that the terms for patricide and matricide represent disobeying the commandment to honour one's father and mother (Ex. 20:12, Lev. 19:3; Marshall 1999, 380). However, Dibelius and Conzelmann consider the list "a Hellenistic transformation of Jewish ethics" rather than a reference to the Decalogue (1972, 23). It is possible that the opposing teachers might have advocated Jesus's teachings regarding "hating your father and mother" (e.g., Luke 14:26) above his teachings to "honour your father and mother" (e.g., Mark 7:10–11).

CHAPTER ELEVEN

1 This is exemplified in the Decalogue in the Torah: one should obey one's parents (Ex. 20:12; Lev. 19:3; Prov. 19:26, 28:24). Filial duty, however, appears to be a pan-Mediterranean expectation in ancient times.
2 Pao assumes Pauline authorship and thus a mid-first century setting (2014, 743–4).
3 Campbell traces this Protestant-driven dichotomy between charisma and office to Rudolph Sohm (1892) who characterized it as the "decline" from Pauline spirit-filled communities to church organization and structured leadership positions (1994, 3). Elizabeth Schüssler Fiorenza's (1983) classic work on women in the New Testament also conceived of the origins of the Christian movement as "egalitarian." The movement then grew increasingly hierarchical, like the society around it, thus *restoring* some kinds of social structure and interaction.
4 While Gerd Theissen's foundational work on love-patriarchalism in the Pauline letters does not deal particularly with age, it is suggestive. Love-patriarchalism refers to the notion that mutual love and respect ruled relationships, but also recognizes that those who were "strong" (that is, those with higher social class and status, and likely older) continued to have precedence over the "weak." Love-patriarchalism reflects ancient social norms (1982, 8), and assumes a "willing acceptance of given inequalities," but promotes "love" as a mediating factor (14, an idea derived from Troeltch), which of course assumes there was friction between the "strong" and the "weak," and by extension, the old and the young.
5 This section is inspired by MacDonald's (1996) use of early Christian critics to illuminate insights about women in the early church.
6 The term δεσπότης can mean the master or lord of the household or a master of slaves.
7 Eyben suggests that the young (elite) were thought to be particularly attracted to philosophy, religion, and mystery cults (1993, 176); clearly, the elite are not in view in Celsus's exposition, but stereotypes about youth probably also applied to the non-elite (Harlow and Laurence 2002, 1).
8 MacDonald notes that women were active participants in Celsus's description (1996, 111–12). The word γυναικωνῖτις (Chadwick: "washerwoman's shop") may more accurately be translated as "women's apartments," highlighting this is women's space (LSJ 1940, 363). Though younger people (and slaves) could be male or female, it is likely that Celsus has young men (and perhaps male slaves) in mind since the recipients of the teachings are women

and children, and young (or enslaved) females in such a position would likely receive special comment. Perhaps he has in mind young apprentices or helpers (in the professions of "wool-workers" or "cobblers").

9 In 1 Tim. 5:17, elders (πρεσβύτεροι) should receive "double honour" (διπλῆς τιμῆς; 5:17; see chapter 9) and slaves should give their own masters "all honour" (πάσης τιμῆς; 6:1; see chapter 10). Taken together, the two phrases exemplify the opposite to this expected behaviour that is portrayed in the critique of Celsus involving young men and slaves.

10 The word παῖς must be understood contextually, since it can refer to age (someone in childhood), to condition in life (e.g., a slave may be called a παῖς), or to descent (to demonstrate someone is a son or daughter of his or her father) (LSJ 1940, 1289). Perhaps the most obvious meaning in Celsus's writing relates to an expectation of subservience (whether that of a child, slave, or a son) that is being thwarted.

11 Lucian's story begins with a critique of Peregrinus's decision (as an old man) to die by jumping on a pyre, which some deemed a noble death. Lucian is adamant, however, that Peregrinus was always looking only for his own glory (δόξα; *The Passing of Peregrinus* 1).

12 Lois would most likely be Timothy's maternal grandmother, since a maternal grandmother was more likely to be alive than a paternal grandmother (Parkin 2003, 52). Only a quarter of twenty-year-old males were likely to have a living grandparent. According to Saller's simulations (which demonstrate generalities rather than specifics, see chapter 1; 1994, 47), 17 per cent would have a living maternal grandmother, and 5 per cent a living paternal grandmother. A decade later, at thirty years of age, only 6 per cent of men would have a living grandparent, 5 per cent maternal, 1 per cent paternal (48–65).

13 Leo W. Simmons asserts the dearth of old people in pre-industrial societies meant that death was not primarily associated with old age, and death was not seen as normal or natural. The sudden and unexpected death of youth and vigorous adults was often considered a result of magic and sorcery (1970 [1945], 217–18; also Counts and Counts 1985, 150).

14 This is an allusion to the old age of Abraham and Sarah when they bore Isaac (Gen 17:1, 17, 24; 21:5). Interestingly their ages are specified whereas those of Elizabeth and Zechariah are not.

15 Mark J. Edwards (1994) suggests that the Johannine reference to Jesus being "not yet fifty" relates to the period of time between Jubilees (an interval of fifty years), but this view has been refuted by George Wesley Buchanan (1995).

16 Suggested by Michel Desjardins (personal communication).

References

Aasgaard, Reidar. 2004. *"My Beloved Brothers and Sisters!" Christian Siblingship in Paul*. London and New York: T & T Clark.

Abu-Lughod, Lila. 1986. *Veiled Sentiments*. Berkley and Los Angeles: University of California Press.

– 1990. "The Romance of Resistance: Tracing Transformations of Power through Bedouin Women." *American Ethnologist* 17, no. 1: 41–55.

– 1993. *Writing Women's Worlds: Bedouin Stories*. Berkeley: University of California Press.

Achebe, Chinua. [1958] 1967. *Things Fall Apart*. London: Heinemann Educational Books.

Aeneas Tacticus, Asclepiodotus, Onasander. 1928. *Aeneas Tacticus, Asclepiodotus, and Onasander*. Translated by Illinois Greek Club. Loeb Classical Library 156. Cambridge: Harvard University Press.

Aland, Barbara, et al., eds. 2001. *The Greek New Testament*. 4th ed. Stuttgart: Deutsche Bibelgesellschaft and United Bible Societies.

Alwin, Duane F., and Ryan J. McCammon. 2003. "Generations, Cohorts and Social Change." In *Handbook of the Life Course*, edited by Jeylan T. Mortimer and Michael J. Shanahan, 23–49. New York: Kluwer.

Amoss, Pamela T., and Stevan Harrell, eds. 1981. *Other Ways of Growing Old : Anthropological Perspectives*. Stanford: Stanford University Press.

Amundsen, Darrel W., and Carol Jean Diers. 1970. "The Age of Menopause in Classical Greece and Rome." *Human Biology* 42: 79–86.

Ando, Clifford. 2000. *Imperial Ideology and Provincial Loyalty in the Roman Empire*. Berkley, Los Angeles, and London: University of California Press.

Andromedas, John. 1957. "Greek Kinship Terms in Everyday Life." *American Anthropologist* 59, no. 6: 1086–8.

Angel, J. Lawrence. 1972. "Ecology and Population in the Eastern Mediterranean." *World Archaeology* 4: 88–105.
The Apostolic Fathers. 2003. Vol. 1, *I Clement. II Clement. Ignatius. Polycarp. Didache.* Edited and translated by Bart D. Ehrman. Loeb Classical Library 24. Cambridge: Harvard University Press.
– 2003. Vol. 2, *Epistle of Barnabas. Papias and Quadratus. Epistle to Diognetus. The Shepherd of Hermas.* Edited and translated by Bart D. Ehrman. Loeb Classical Library 25. Cambridge: Harvard University Press.
Appian. 2020. *Roman History,* Vol. 5, *Civil Wars, Books 3–4.* Edited and translated by Brian McGing. Loeb Classical Library 543. Cambridge: Harvard University Press.
Aristotle. 1926. *Nicomachean Ethics.* Translated by H. Rackham. Loeb Classical Library 73. Cambridge: Harvard University Press.
– 1932. *Politics.* Translated by H. Rackham. Loeb Classical Library 264. Cambridge: Harvard University Press.
– 2020. *Art of Rhetoric.* Translated by J.H. Freese. Revised by Gisela Striker. Loeb Classical Library 193. Cambridge: Harvard University Press.
Arjava, Antti. 1996. *Women and Law in Late Antiquity.* Oxford: Clarendon Press; New York: Oxford University Press.
Ascough, Richard S. 1998. *What Are They Saying about the Formation of the Pauline Churches?* New York: Paulist.
Ascough, Richard S., Philip A. Harland, and John S. Kloppenborg. 2012. *Associations in the Greco-Roman World: A Sourcebook.* Waco: Baylor University Press.
Badian, Ernst. 2003. "Sergius Catalina, Lucius." In *Oxford Classical Dictionary,* edited by Simon Hornblower and Antony Spawforth, 1393. 3rd ed. Oxford: Oxford University Press.
Bagnall, Roger S., and Bruce W. Frier. 1994. *The Demography of Roman Egypt.* Cambridge: Cambridge University Press.
Balch, David. 1981. *Let Wives Be Submissive: The Domestic Code in 1 Peter.* Chico, CA: Scholars Press.
Balla, Peter. 2003. *The Child-Parent Relationship in the New Testament and Its Environment.* Peabody, MS: Hendrickson.
Barclay, John M.G. 1997. "The Family as the Bearer of Religion in Judaism and Early Christianity." In Moxnes, *Constructing Early Christian Families,* 66–80.
– 2007. "There Is Neither Old Nor Young? Early Christianity and Ancient Ideologies of Age." *New Testament Studies* 53: 225–41.
– 2020. "Household Networks and Early Christian Economics: A Fresh Study of 1 Timothy 5:3–16." *New Testament Studies* 66: 268–87.

Barrett, C.K. 1963. *The Pastoral Epistles*. Oxford: Clarendon.

Bartchy, S. Scott. 2003 [1973]. *[Mallon Chrēsai], First-Century Slavery and the Interpretation of 1 Corinthians 7:21*. Eugene, OR: Wipf and Stock Publishers. Previously published by Society of Biblical Literature.

Barton, Stephen O. 1997. "The Relativisation of Family Ties in the Jewish and Graeco-Roman Traditions." In Moxnes, *Constructing Early Christian Families*, 81–100.

Bassler, Jouette M. 1984. "The Widows' Tale: A Fresh Look at 1 Timothy 5.3–16." *Journal of Biblical Literature* 103: 23–41.

– 1996. *1 Timothy, 2 Timothy, Titus*. Abingdon New Testament Commentaries. Nashville: Abington.

– 2003. "Limits and Differentiation: The Calculus of Widows in 1 Timothy 5:3–16." In Levine, *A Feminist Companion*, 122–46.

Batten, Alicia J. 2010. *Friendship and Benefaction in James*. Blandford Forum, UK: Deo Publishing.

Bauckham, Richard. 2006. *Jesus and the Eyewitnesses: The Gospels as Eyewitness Testimony*. Grand Rapids: Eerdmans.

BDAG = Bauer, Walter, Frederick William Danker, W.F. Arndt, and F.W. Gingrich, eds. 2000. *A Greek-English Lexicon of the New Testament and Other Early Christian Literature*. 3rd ed. Chicago and London: University of Chicago Press.

Baur, Ferdinand Christian. 1835. *Die sogenannten Pastoralbriefe des Apostels Paulus aufs neue kritisch untersucht*. In der J.G. Cotta'schen Verlagshandlung.

Benedict, Peter. 1976. "Aspects of the Domestic Cycle in a Turkish Provincial Town." In Peristiany, *Mediterranean Family Structures*, 219–41.

Berkel, Tazuko Angela van, 2020. *The Economics of Friendship: Conceptions of Reciprocity in Classical Greece*. Leiden: Brill.

Bertman, Stephen, ed. 1976. *Conflict of Generations in Ancient Greece and Rome*. Amsterdam: B.R. Grüner.

Bettini, Maurizio. 1991. *Anthropology and Roman Culture: Kinship, Time, Images of the Soul*. Translated by John Van Sickle. Baltimore: Johns Hopkins University Press.

Beyene, Yewoubdar. 1989. *From Menarche to Menopause: Reproductive Lives of Peasant Women in Two Cultures*. New York: State University of New York Press.

Biesele, Megan, and Nancy Howell. 1981. "'The Old People Give You Life': Aging among !Kung Hunter-Gatherers." In Amoss and Harrell, *Other Ways of Growing Old*, 77–98.

Bornkamm, G. 1964. "πρέσβυς." In *Theological Dictionary of the New Testament*, edited by Gerhard Kittel, vol. 6, 651–83. Translated by Geoffrey W. Bromiley. Grand Rapids: Eerdmans.

Botha, Pieter J.J. 2012. *Orality and Literacy in Early Christianity*. Eugene, OR: Cascade Books.

Bowe, Barbara Ellen. 1988. *A Church in Crisis: Ecclesiology and Paraenesis in Clement of Rome*. Minneapolis: Fortress.

Bradley, Keith R. 1991. *Discovering the Roman Family: Studies in Roman Social History*. Oxford: Oxford University Press.

Brandes, Stanley. 1995. "Kinship and Care for the Aged in Traditional Rural Iberia." In *Aging and Intergenerational Relations over the Life Course: A Historical and Cross Cultural Perspective*, edited by Tamara K. Hareven, 13–29. Berlin: Walter de Gruyter.

Bremmer, Jan N. 1987. "The Old Women of Ancient Greece." In *Sexual Asymmetry: Studies in Ancient Society*, edited by Josine Block and Peter Mason, 191–215. Amsterdam: Gieben.

– 1995. "Pauper or Patroness: The Widow in the Early Christian Church." In *Between Poverty and the Pyre*, edited by Jan N. Bremmer and Lourens van den Bosch, 31–57. London and New York: Routledge.

Briscoe, John. 2003. "Cornelius Scipio Africanus (the elder), Publius." In Hornblower and Spawforth, *Oxford Classical Dictionary*, 398

Brooks, James A., and Carlton L. Winbery. 1979. *Syntax of New Testament Greek*. Lanham, MD: University Press of America.

Brown, Andrew L. 2003. "Oedipus." In Hornblower and Spawforth, *Oxford Classical Dictionary*, 1061–2.

Brown, Judith K. 1982. "Cross-Cultural Perspectives on Middle-Aged Women." *Current Anthropology* 23, no. 2: 143–56.

– 1992. "Lives of Middle-Aged Women." In *In Her Prime: New Views of Middle-Aged Women*, edited by Virginia Kerns and Judith K. Brown, 17–30. 2nd ed. Urbana and Chicago: University of Illinois Press.

Buchanan, George Wesley. 1995. "The Age of Jesus." *New Testament Studies* 41, no. 2: 297.

Buitelaar, Marjo. 1995. "Widows' Worlds: Representations and Realities." In *Between Poverty and the Pyre*, edited by Jan N. Bremmer and Lourens van den Bosch, 1–18. London and New York: Routledge.

Burtchaell, James Tunstead. 1992. *From Synagogue to Church: Public Services and Offices in the Earliest Christian Communities*. Cambridge and New York: Cambridge University Press.

Bush, Peter G. 1990. "A Note on the Structure of 1 Timothy." *New Testament Studies* 36: 152–6.

Campbell, J.K. 1964. *Honour, Family and Patronage*. New York and Oxford: Oxford University Press.
Campbell, R. Alastair. 1994. *The Elders: Seniority within Earliest Christianity*. Edinburgh: T&T Clark.
– 1995. "ΚΑΙ ΜΑΛΙΣΤΑ ΟΙΚΕΩΝ – A New Look at 1 Timothy 5:8." *New Testament Studies* 41: 157–60.
Campenhausen, Hans von. 1969. *Ecclesiastical Authority and Spiritual Power in the Church in the First Three Centuries*. Stanford: Stanford University Press.
Caraveli, Anna. 1986. "The Bitter Wounding: The Lament as Social Protest in Rural Greece." In Dubisch, *Gender and Power in Rural Greece*, 169–94.
Carney, T.F. 1975. *The Shape of the Past: Models and Antiquity*. Lawrence, KS: Coronado.
Carter, Warren. 1995. "A Survey of Recent Scholarship on the New Testament and Aging and Suggestions for Future Research." *Journal of Religious Gerontology* 9, no. 2: 35–50.
– 2001. "Adult Children and Elderly Parents: The Worlds of the New Testament." *Journal of Religious Gerontology* 12, no. 2: 45–59.
Catullus, Tibullus. 1913. *Catullus. Tibullus. Pervigilium Veneris*. Translated by F.W. Cornish, J.P. Postgate, J.W. Mackail. Revised by G.P. Goold. Loeb Classical Library 6. Cambridge: Harvard University Press.
Chance, John K. 1994. "The Anthropology of Honor and Shame: Culture, Values and Practice." *Semeia* 68: 139–51.
Chapman, Charlotte Gower. 1971. *Milocca: A Sicilian Village*. Cambridge, MA, and London: Schenkman.
Chow, John K. 1992. *Patronage and Power: A Study of Social Networks in Corinth*. Sheffield, England: JSOT Press.
Cianca, Jenn. 2018. *Sacred Ritual, Profane Space: The Roman House as Early Christian Meeting Place*. Montreal & Kingston; London; Chicago: McGill-Queen's University Press.
Cicero. 1913. *On Duties*. Translated by Walter Miller. Loeb Classical Library 30. Cambridge: Harvard University Press.
– 1923. *On Old Age. On Friendship. On Divination*. Translated by W.A. Falconer. Loeb Classical Library 154. Cambridge: Harvard University Press.
– 1958. *Pro Caelio. De Provinciis Consularibus. Pro Balbo*. Translated by R. Gardner. Loeb Classical Library 447. Cambridge: Harvard University Press.

– 1988. *Cato Maior de Senectute*. Translated and edited by J.G.F. Powell. Cambridge: Cambridge University Press.

Clark, Mari H. 1983. "Variations on Themes of Male and Female: Reflections on Gender Bias in Fieldwork in Rural Greece." *Women's Studies* 10, no. 2: 117–33.

Cohen, Lawrence. 1994. "Old Age: Cultural and Critical Perspectives." *Annual Review of Anthropology* 12: 137–58.

Cohick, Lynn H. 2009. *Women in the World of the Earliest Christians: Illuminating Ancient Ways of Life*. Grand Rapids: Baker Academic.

Cokayne, Karen. 2003. *Experiencing Old Age in Ancient Rome*. London and New York: Routledge.

– 2007. "Age and Aristocratic Self-identity: Activities for the Elderly." In Harlow and Laurence, *Age and Ageing in the Roman Empire*, 209–20.

Collins, Adela Yarbro. 2011. "The Female Body as Social Space in 1 Timothy." *New Testament Studies* 57: 155–75. doi:10.1017/S0028688510000305.

Collins, Raymond F. 2002. *1 & 2 Timothy and Titus: A Commentary*. Louisville and London: Westminster John Knox.

Cool, Linda, and Justine McCabe. 1983. "The 'Scheming Hag' and the 'Dear Old Thing': The Anthropology of Aging Women." In *Growing Old in Different Societies: Cross-Cultural Perspectives*, edited by Jay Sokolovksy, 56–71. Belmont, CA: Wadsworth.

Corley, Kathleen E. 2010. *Maranatha: Women's Funerary Rituals and Christian Origins*. Minneapolis: Fortress Press.

Counts, Dorothy Ayers, and David R. Counts. 1985. "Introduction: Linking Concepts of Aging and Gender, Aging and Death." In *Aging and Its Transformations: Moving Toward Death in Pacific Societies*, edited by Dorothy Ayers Counts and David R. Counts, 1–24. Lanham, MD: University Press of America.

– 1996. *Over the Next Hill: An Ethnography of RVing Seniors in North America*. Peterborough, ON: Broadview Press.

Cowgill, D.O., and L.D. Holmes. 1972. *Aging and Modernization*. New York: Appleton-Century-Crofts.

Coxe, A. Cleveland, ed. 1994 [1886]. *Ante-Nicene Fathers*. Vol. 7. American edition. Originally edited by Alexander Roberts and James Donaldson. Peabody, MA: Hendrickson.

Crew, Douglas E. 1990. "Anthropological Issues in Biological Gerontology." In *Anthropology and Aging: Comprehensive Reviews*, edited by Robert L. Rubinstein, 11–38. Dordrecht; Boston; London: Kluwer Academic Publishers.

Crook, Zeba A. 2004. *Reconceptualising Conversion: Patronage, Loyalty, and Conversion in the Religions of the Ancient Mediterranean.* Berlin; New York: W. de Gruyter.

Crouch, James E. 1973. *The Origin and Intention of the Colossian Haustafeln.* Göttingen: Vandenhoeck & Ruprecht.

Danforth, Loring M. 1982. *The Death Rituals of Rural Greece.* Princeton: Princeton University Press.

D'Angelo, Mary R. 2003. "Εὐσέβεια: Roman Imperial Family Values and Sexual Politics in 4 Maccabees and the Pastorals." *Biblical Interpretation* 11, no. 2: 139–65.

Dean-Jones, Lesley. 1994. *Women's Bodies in Classical Greek Science.* Oxford: Clarendon.

Delaney, Carol. 1987. "Seeds of Honor, Fields of Shame." In *Honor and Shame and the Unity of the Mediterranean*, edited by David D. Gilmore, 35–48. Washington: American Anthropological Association.

De Luce, Judith. 1993a. "Quod Temptabam Scribere Verus Erat: Ovid in Exile." In *Aging and Gender in Literature: Studies in Creativity*, edited by Anne M. Wyatt-Brown and Janice Rossen, 229–41. Charlottesville and London: University Press of Virginia.

– 1993b. "Ancient Images of Aging: Did Ageism Exist in Greco-Roman Antiquity?" *Generations* 17 (2): 41–5.

Demosthenes. 1939. *Orations*, Vol. 5, *Orations 41–49: Private Cases.* Translated by A.T. Murray. Loeb Classical Library 346. Cambridge: Harvard University Press.

Denzey, Nicola. 2007. *The Bone Gatherers: The Lost Worlds of Early Christian Women.* Boston: Beacon Press.

Dibelius, Martin, and Hans Conzelmann. 1972. *The Pastoral Epistles.* Translated by Philip Buttolph and Adela Yarbro. Philadelphia: Fortress.

Dimen, Muriel. 1986. "Servants and Sentries: Women, Power and Social Production in Kirovrisi." In Dubisch, *Gender and Power in Rural Greece*, 53–67.

Dionysius of Halicarnassus. 1950. *Roman Antiquities*, Vol. 3, *Books 11–20*. Translated by Earnest Cary. Loeb Classical Library 388. Cambridge: Harvard University Press.

– 1985. *Critical Essays*, Vol. 2, *On Literary Composition. Dinarchus. Letters to Ammaeus and Pompeius.* Translated by Stephen Usher. Loeb Classical Library 466. Cambridge: Harvard University Press.

Dixon, Suzanne. 1988. *The Roman Mother.* Norman and London: University of Oklahoma Press.

– 1992. *The Roman Family*. Baltimore and London: Johns Hopkins University Press.
– 1999. "Conflict in the Roman Family." In *The Roman Family in Italy: Status, Sentiment and Space*, edited by Beryl Rawson and Paul Weaver, 149–67. Oxford and New York: Clarendon.
Donelson, Lewis R. 1986. *Pseudepigraphy and Ethical Argument in the Pastoral Epistles*. Tübingen: J.C.B. Mohr (Paul Siebeck).
Dubisch, Jill. 1986a. "Introduction." In Dubisch, *Gender and Power in Rural Greece*, 3–41.
– 1986b. "Culture Enters Through the Kitchen: Women, Food, and Social Boundaries in Rural Greece." In Dubisch, *Gender and Power in Rural Greece*, 195–214.
– ed. 1986. *Gender and Power in Rural Greece*. Princeton: Princeton University Press.
Du Boulay, Juliet. 1974. *Portrait of a Greek Mountain Village*. Oxford: Clarendon Press.
– 1986. "Women: Images of Their Nature and Destiny in Rural Greece." In Dubisch, *Gender and Power in Rural Greece*, 139–68.
Duncan-Jones, Richard P. 1977. "Age-Rounding, Illiteracy and Social Differentiation in the Roman Empire." *Chiron: Mitteilungen Der Kommission für Alte Geschichte und Epigraphik des Deutschen Archäologischen Instituts* 7: 333–53.
Dunn, Geoffrey D. 2004. *Tertullian*. London and New York: Routledge.
Easton, Burton Scott. 1947. *The Pastoral Epistles*. New York: Scribner.
Edwards, Mark J. 1994. "'Not Fifty Years Old': John 8:57." *New Testament Studies* 40, no. 3: 449–54.
Eisen, Ute E. 2000. *Women Officeholders in Early Christianity: Epigraphical and Literary Studies*. Translated by Linda M. Maloney. Collegeville, MN: Liturgical.
El-Abbadi, M.A.H. 1964. "The *Gerousia* in Roman Egypt." *Journal of Egyptian Archaeology* 50: 164–9.
Elder, Glen H., Jr, Monica Kirkpatrick Johnson, and Robert Crosnoe. 2003. "The Emergence and Development of Life Course Theory." In *Handbook of the Life Course*, edited by Jeylan T. Mortimer and Michael J. Shanahan, 3–19. New York: Kluwer Academic/Plenum.
Elliott, J.K. 1993. *The Apocryphal New Testament*. Oxford: Oxford University Press.
Elliott, John H. 1970. "Ministry and Church Order in the NT: A Traditio-Historical Analysis (1 Pt 5,1–5 & plls.)." *Catholic Biblical Quarterly* 32: 367–91.

– 1981. *A Home for the Homeless: A Sociological Exegesis of I Peter, Its Situation and Strategy*. Philadelphia: Fortress.
– 1996. "Patronage and Clientage." In *The Social Sciences and New Testament Interpretation*, edited by Richard L. Rohrbaugh, 144–56. Peabody, MA: Hendrickson.
– 2003. "Elders as Honored Household Heads and Not Holders of 'Office' in Earliest Christianity." Book review of *The Elders: Seniority within Earliest Christianity*, by R. Alastair Campbell. *Biblical Theology Bulletin* 33, no.2: 77–82.
– 2007. "Jesus the Israelite Was Neither a 'Jew' Nor a 'Christian': On Correcting Misleading Nomenclature." *Journal for the Study of the Historical Jesus* 5: 119–54.
Epictetus. 1925. *Discourses, Books 1–2*. Translated by W.A. Oldfather. Loeb Classical Library 131. Cambridge: Harvard University Press.
Esler, Philip F. 1998. Review of *The Social Ethos of the Corinthian Correspondence: Interests and Ideology from 1 Corinthians to 1 Clement* by David G. Horrell. *Journal of Theological Studies* 49, no. 1: 253–60.
– 2000. "Models in New Testament Interpretation: A Reply to David Horrell." *Journal for the Study of the New Testament* 78 (June): 107–13.
Evans-Grubbs, Judith. 2007. Review of *The Age of Marriage in Ancient Rome* by Arnold A. Lelis, William A. Percy, and Beert C. Verstraete. *Mouseion: Journal of the Classical Association of Canada* 7, no. 1: 67–71. https://doi.org/10.1353/mou.0.0011.
Eyben, Emiel. 1993. *Restless Youth in Ancient Rome*. London and New York: Routledge.
Falkner, Thomas M., and Judith de Luce. 1992. "A View from Antiquity: Greece, Rome and the Elders." In *Handbook of Humanities and Aging*, edited by Thomas R. Cole, David D. Van Tassel, and Robert Kastenbaum, 33–29. New York: Springer.
Fallers, Lloyd A., and Margaret C. Fallers. 1976. "Sex Roles in Edremit." In Peristiany, *Mediterranean Family Structures*, 243–60.
Fatum, Lone. 2005. "Christ Domesticated: The Household Theology of the Pastorals as Political Strategy." In *The Formation of the Early Church*, edited by Jostein Ådna, 175–207. Wissenshaftliche Monographien zum Alten und Neuen Testament 183. Tübingen: Mohr Siebeck.
Fee, Gordon. 1988. *1 and 2 Timothy, Titus*. New International Biblical Commentary. Peabody: Hendrickson.

Fernea, Elizabeth Warnock. 1965. *Guests of the Shiek: An Ethnography of an Iraqi Village*. Garden City, NY: Doubleday.

Fiorenza, Elisabeth Schüssler. 1983. *In Memory of Her: A Feminist Theological Reconstruction of Christian Origins*. New York: Crossroad.

Foner, Nancy. 1984. *Ages in Conflict: A Cross-Cultural Perspective of Inequality between Old and Young*. New York: Columbia University Press.

Friedl, Ernestine. 1962. *Vasilika: A Village in Modern Greece*. New York: Holt, Rinehart and Winston.

Frier, Bruce W. 1994. "Natural Fertility and Family Limitation in Roman Marriage." *Classical Philology* 89, no. 4: 318–33.

Fry, Christine L. 1980. "Toward an Anthropology of Aging." In *Aging in Culture and Society: Comparative Viewpoints and Strategies*, edited by Christine L. Fry, 1–20. New York: J.F. Bergin.

Garnsey, Peter, and Richard P. Saller. 1987. *The Roman Empire: Economy, Society and Culture*. London: Duckworth.

Garrett, Susan R. 1992. "Sociology of Early Christianity." In *Anchor Bible Dictionary*, edited by David Noel Freedman, vol. 6, 89–99. New York: Doubleday.

Geertz, Clifford. 1976. "'From the Native's Point of View': On the Nature of Anthropological Inquiry." In *Meaning in Anthropology*, edited by Keith H. Basso and Henry A. Selby, 221–37. Albuquerque: University of New Mexico Press.

Gehring, R.W. 2004. *House Church and Mission: The Importance of Household Structures in Early Christianity*. Peabody, MA: Hendrickson.

Gilmore, David D. 1986. "Mother-Son Intimacy and the Dual View of Woman in Andalusia: Analysis through Oral Poetry." *Ethos* 14, no. 3: 227–51.

– 1990. "Men and Women in Southern Spain: 'Domestic Power' Revisited." *American Anthropologist* 92, no. 4: 953–70.

Glancy, Jennifer A. 2002. *Slavery in Early Christianity*. Oxford; New York: Oxford University Press.

Gourgues, Michel. 2009. *Les Deux Lettres à Timothée. La lettre à Tite*. Commentaire biblique: Nouveau Testament, 14. Paris: Les Éditions du Cerf.

Gowland, Rebecca. 2007. "Age, Ageism and Osteological Bias: The Evidence from Late Roman Britain." In Harlow and Laurence, *Age and Ageing in the Roman Empire*, 153–69.

Guthrie, Donald. 1990. *The Pastoral Epistles*. Rev. ed. Grand Rapids: Wm. B. Eerdmans.

Hanson, Anthony Tyrell. 1966. *The Pastoral Letters*. Cambridge: Cambridge University Press.
– 1982. *The Pastoral Epistles: Based on the Revised Standard Version*. Grand Rapids: Wm. B. Eerdmans.
Hareven, Tamara K. 1982. "The Life Course and Aging in Historical Perspective." In *Aging and Life Course Transitions: An Interdisciplinary Perspective*, edited by Tamara K. Hareven and Kathleen J. Adams, 1–26. New York: Guildford.
– 1994. "Aging and Generational Relations: A Historical and Life Course Perspective." *Annual Review of Sociology* 20: 437–61.
– ed. 1996. *Aging and Generational Relations over the Life Course: A Historical and Cross-Cultural Perspective*. Berlin and New York: W. de Gruyter.
– 2001. "Historical Perspectives on Aging and Family Relations." In *Handbook of Aging and the Social Sciences*, 5th ed., edited by Robert H. Binstock and Linda K. George, 141–59. San Diego and London: Academic Press.
Harland, Philip A. 2003. *Associations, Synagogues, and Congregations: Claiming a Place in Ancient Mediterranean Society*. Philadelphia: Fortress.
Harlow, Mary. 2007. "Blurred Visions: Male Perceptions of the Female Life Course – the Case of Aemilia Pudentilla." In Harlow and Laurence, *Age and Ageing in the Roman Empire*, 195–208.
Harlow, Mary, and Ray Laurence. 2002. *Growing Up and Growing Old in Ancient Rome: A Life Course Approach*. London and New York: Routledge.
– 2003. "Old Age in Ancient Rome." *History Today* 53, no. 4: 22–7.
– 2007. "Introduction: Age and Ageing in the Roman Empire." In Harlow and Laurence, *Age and Ageing in the Roman Empire*, 9–24.
– eds. 2007. *Age and Ageing in the Roman Empire*. Journal of Roman Archaeology Supplementary Series, 65.
Harris, J. Gordon. 1987. *Biblical Perspectives on Aging and the Elderly*. Philadelphia: Fortress.
Harrison, P.N. 1921. *The Problem of the Pastoral Epistles*. London: Oxford University Press.
Harvey, A.E. 1974. "Elders." *Journal of Theological Studies* 25, no. 2: 318–32.
Hearon, Holly E., and Philip Ruge-Jones, eds. 2009. *The Bible in Ancient and Modern Media: Story and Performance*. Vol. 1, Biblical Performance Criticism. Eugene, OR: Cascade Books.

Hellerman, Joseph H. 2001. *The Ancient Church as Family*. Minneapolis: Fortress.

Herodotus. 1921. *The Persian Wars*, Vol. 2, Books 3–4. Translated by A.D. Godley. Loeb Classical Library 118. Cambridge: Harvard University Press.

Herzer, Jens. 2007. "'Das Geheimnis der Frömmigkeit' (1 Tim. 3,16): Sprache und Stil der Pastoralbriefe im Kontext hellenistich-römischer Popularphilosophie – eine methodische Problemanzeige." *Theologische Quartalschrift* 187, no. 7: 309–29.

– 2008. "Rearranging the 'House of God': A New Perspective on the Pastoral Epistles." In *Empsychoi Logoi – Religious Innovations in Antiquity: Studies in Honour of Pieter Willem van der Horst*, edited by Alberdina Houtman, Albert de Jong, and Magda Misset-Van de Weg, 545–66. Leiden and Boston: Brill.

Herzfeld, Michael. 1980. "Honour and Shame: Problems in the Comparative Analysis of Moral Systems" *Man* 15, no. 2: 339–51.

Hin, Saskia. 2013. *Demography of Roman Italy: Population Dynamics in an Ancient Conquest Society 201 BCE–14 CE*. Cambridge; New York: Cambridge University Press.

Hirschon, Renée B. 1983. "Women, the Aged and Religious Activity: Oppositions and Complementarity in an Urban Locality." *Journal of Modern Greek Studies* 1, no. 1: 113–29.

Hock, Ronald F. 1995. "A Support for His Old Age: Paul's Plea on Behalf of Onesimus." In *The Social World of the First Christians: Essays in Honor of Wayne A. Meeks*, edited by L. Michael White and O. Larry Yarbrough, 67–81. Minneapolis: Augsburg Fortress.

Hoklotubbe, T. Christopher. 2017. *Civilized Piety: The Rhetoric of Pietas in the Pastoral Epistles and the Roman Empire*. Waco: Baylor University Press.

Holleran, Claire, and April Pudsey. 2016. "Introduction: Studies in Ancient Historical Demography." In *Demography and the Graeco-Roman World: New Insights and Approaches*, edited by Claire Holleran and April Pudsey, 1–13. Cambridge; New York: Cambridge University Press.

Hope, Valerie M. 2007. "Age and the Roman Army: The Evidence of Tombstones." In Harlow and Laurence, *Age and Ageing in the Roman Empire*, 111–29.

Hopkins, Keith. 1966. "On the Probable Age Structure of the Roman Population." *Population Studies* 18: 309–27.

– 1980. "Brother-Sister Marriage in Roman Egypt." *Comparative Studies in Society and History* 22, no. 3: 303–54.

Hornblower, Simon, and Antony Spawforth, eds. 2003. *Oxford Classical Dictionary*. 3rd ed. Oxford: Oxford University Press.

Horrell, David G. 1996. *The Social Ethos of the Corinthian Correspondence: Interests and Ideology from 1 Corinthians to 1 Clement*. Edinburgh: T & T Clark.

– 2000. "Models and Methods in Social-Scientific Interpretation: A Response to Philip Esler." *Journal for the Study of the New Testament* 22, no. 78: 83–105. https://doi.org/10.1177/0142064X0002207805.

– 2001. "From ἀδελφοί to οἶκος θεοῦ: Social Transformation in Pauline Christianity." *Journal of Biblical Literature* 120, no. 2: 293–311.

– 2008. "Disciplining Performance and 'Placing' the Church: Widows, Elders and Slaves in the Household of God (1 Tim. 5,1–6,2). In *1 Timothy Reconsidered*, edited by Karl P. Donfried, 109–34. Leuven: Peeters.

– ed. 1999. *Social-Scientific Approaches to New Testament Interpretation*. Edinburgh: T. & T. Clark.

Horsley, G.H.R. 1981. *New Documents Illustrating Early Christianity*. North Ryde, Australia: Macquarie University, Ancient History Document Research Centre.

– 1987. *New Documents Illustrating Early Christianity: A Review of the Greek Inscriptions and Papyri Published in 1979*. Vol. 4. North Ryde, Australia: Macquarie University, Ancient History Document Research Centre.

Houlden, J.L. 1976. *The Pastoral Epistles*. Pelican New Testament Commentaries. Middlesex, England: Penguin.

Hubbard, Moyer. 2012. "Kept Safe through Childbearing: Maternal Mortality, Justification by Faith and the Social Setting of 1 Timothy 2:15." *Journal of the Evangelical Theological Society* 55, no. 4: 743–62.

Hübner, Sabine R. 2009. "Callirhoe's Dilemma: Remarriage and Stepfathers in the Greco-Roman East." In *Growing Up Fatherless in Antiquity*, edited by Sabine R. Hübner and David M. Ratzan, 61–82. Cambridge: Cambridge University Press.

Huizenga, Annette Bourland. 2013. *Moral Education for Women in the Pastoral and Pythagorean Letters: Philosophers of the Household*. Leiden; Boston: Brill.

Humbert, Michel. 1972. *Le remariage à Rome: Étude d'histoire juridique et sociale*. Milano: A. Giuffrè.

Hurtado, Larry W. 2014. "Oral Fixation and New Testament Studies? 'Orality,' 'Performance' and Reading Texts in Early Christianity." *New Testament Studies* 60: 321–40. doi:10.1017/S0028688514000058.

Hutson, Christopher Roy. 1998. "My True Child: The Rhetoric of Youth in the Pastoral Epistles." PhD dissertation. Yale University.

– 2013. "'A Little Wine': 1 Timothy 5:23 and Greco-Roman Youth." *Lexington Theological Quarterly* 45, nos 3/4: 79–98.

Irwin, Brian P. 2008. "The Laying On of Hands in 1 Timothy 5:22: A New Proposal." *Bulletin for Biblical Research* 18, no. 1: 123–9.

Jeremias, Joachim. 1949. *Die Briefe an Timotheus und Titus*. Göttingen: Vandenhoeck & Ruprecht.

Johnson, Colleen Leahy. 1983. "Interdependence and Aging in Italian Families." In *Growing Old in Different Societies: Cross-Cultural Perspectives*, edited by Jay Sokolovsky, 92–103. Belmont, CA: Wadsworth.

Johnson, Luke Timothy. 1996. *Letters to Paul's Delegates: 1 Timothy, 2 Timothy, Titus*. Valley Forge, PA: Trinity Press International.

– 2001. *The First and Second Letters to Timothy: A New Translation with Introduction and Commentary*. New York and Toronto: Doubleday.

Johnson, Paul, and Patricia Thane, eds. 1998. *Old Age from Antiquity to Post-Modernity*. London and New York: Routledge.

Jones, C.P. 1966. "Toward a Chronology of Plutarch's Works." *Journal of Roman Studies* 56: 61–74.

Judge, E.A. 1980. "The Social Identity of the First Christians: A Question of Method in Religious History." *Journal of Religious History* 11, no. 2: 201–17.

Justinian. 1998. *The Digest of Justinian*. Translated by Alan Watson. Rev. ed. 4 vols. Philadelphia: University of Pennsylvania Press. https://doi.org/10.9783/9780812205527.

Kartzow, Marianne Bjelland. 2009. *Gossip and Gender: Othering of Speech in the Pastoral Epistles*. Berlin and New York: Walter de Gruyter.

Kelly, J.N.D. 1963. *A Commentary on the Pastoral Epistles*. London: A & C Black.

Kenna, Margaret E. 1976. "The Idiom of Family." In Peristiany, *Mediterranean Family Structures*, 347–62.

Kennedy, Robinette. 1986. "Women's Friendships on Crete: A Psychological Perspective." In Dubisch, *Gender and Power in Rural Greece*, 121–38.

Kenyon, Susan M. 1991. *Five Women of Sennar: Culture and Change in Central Sudan*. Oxford: Clarendon.

– 1998. "Gender and Alliance in Southern Sudan." In *Women among Women: Anthropological Perspectives on Female Age Hierarchies,* edited by Jeanette Dickerson-Putman and Judith K. Brown, 15–29. Urbana and Chicago: University of Chicago Press. Originally published in 1994 in *Journal of Cross-Cultural Gerontology* 9, no. 2.

Kerzter, David I., and Jennie Keith, eds. 1984. *Age and Anthropological Theory*. Ithaca and London: Cornell University Press.

Kidd, Reggie M. 1990. *Wealth and Beneficence in the Pastoral Epistles*. Atlanta: Scholars.

Kim, Hong Bom. 2004. "The Interpretation of ΜΑΛΙΣΤΑ in 1 Timothy 5:17." *Novum Testamentum* 46, no. 4: 360–8.

Kiray, Mübeccel. 1976. "The New Role of Mothers: Changing Intrafamilial Relationships in a Small Town in Turkey." In Peristiany, *Mediterranean Family Structures*, 261–71.

Kloppenborg, John S. 1996a. "Collegia and *Thiasoi*: Issues in Function, Taxonomy and Membership." In Kloppenborg and Wilson, *Voluntary Associations in the Graeco-Roman World*, 16–30.

– 1996b. "Egalitarianism in the Myth and Rhetoric of Pauline Churches." In *Reimagining Christian Origins: A Colloquium Honoring Burton L. Mack*, edited by Elizabeth A. Castelli and Hal Taussig, 247–63. Valley Forge, PA: Trinity Press International.

Kloppenborg, John S., and Richard S. Ascough. 2011. *Greco-Roman Associations: Texts, Translations, and Commentary: Attica, Boeotia, Macedonia, Thrace*. Berlin and New York: Walter de Gruyter.

Kloppenborg, John S., and Stephen G. Wilson, eds. 1996. *Voluntary Associations in the Graeco-Roman World*. Hoboken: Routledge.

Knight, George W., III. 1992. *The Pastoral Epistles: A Commentary on the Greek Text*. Grand Rapids: Eerdmans.

Kongar, Emre. 1976. "A Survey of Familial Change in Two Turkish *gecekondu* Areas." In Peristiany, *Mediterranean Family Structures*, 205–18.

Kraemer, Ross S., ed. 1988. *Maenads, Martyrs, Matrons, Monastics: A Sourcebook on Women's Religions in the Greco-Roman World*. Philadelphia: Fortress.

Krause, Deborah. 2004. *1 Timothy*. London: T & T Clark.

Krause, Jens-Uwe. 1994. *Witwen und Wissen in Römischen Reich*. Vol. 1. Stuttgart: F. Steiner.

– 1995. *Witwen und Wissen in Römischen Reich*. Vol. 4. Stuttgart: F. Steiner.

Laes, Christian, and Johan Strubbe. 2014. *Youth in the Roman Empire: The Young and the Restless Years?* Cambridge; New York: Cambridge University Press.

LaFosse, Mona Joy. 2001. *Situating 2 Timothy in Early Christian History*. MA thesis. Wilfrid Laurier University.

LaFosse, Mona Tokarek. 2017a. "Age Hierarchy and Social Networks among Urban Women in the Roman East." In *Mediterranean Families in Antiquity: Households, Extended Families, and Domestic Space*, edited by Sabine R. Huebner and Geoffrey Nathan, 204–20. Chichester, UK: Wiley-Blackwell.

– 2017b. "Women, Children and House Churches." In *The Early Christian World*, edited by Philip F. Esler, 385–405. 2nd ed. London; New York: Routledge.

– 2018. "Those Who Hear: The Power of Learners in 1 Timothy." In *Religion and Education in Antiquity: Essays in Honour of Michel Desjardins*, edited by Alexander Damm, 147–70. Leiden: Brill.

LaGrand, James. 1998. "Luke's Portrait of Simeon (Luke 2:25–35): Aged Saint or Hesitant Terrorist?" In *Common Life in the Early Church*, edited by Julian V. Hills, 175–85. Harrisburg, PA: Trinity Press International.

Lane, William L. 1965. "1 Tim. IV.1–3: An Early Instance of Over-Realised Eschatology." *New Testament Studies* 11, no. 2: 164–7. doi.org/10.1017/S0028688500017628.

Lassen, Eva Marie. 1997. "The Roman Family: Ideal and Metaphor." In Moxnes, *Constructing Early Christian Families*, 103–20.

Laurence, Ray. 2007. "Gender, Age, and Identity: The Female Life Course at Pompeii." In Harlow and Laurence, *Age and Ageing in the Roman Empire*, 95–110.

Lelis, Arnold A., William A. Percy, and Beert C. Verstraete, 2003. *The Age of Marriage in Ancient Rome*. Lewiston, NY: Edwin Mellen.

Lerat, L. 1943. "Un loi de Delphes sur les devoirs des enfants envers leurs parents." *Revue de Philologie* 17:62–86.

Levine, Amy-Jill, ed. 2003. *A Feminist Companion to the Deutero-Pauline Epistles*. Cleveland: Pilgrim.

Lewis, Naphtali. 1983. *Life in Egypt under Roman Rule*. Oxford: Clarendon.

Lewis, Nicola Denzey. 2012. Review of *Maranatha: Women's Funerary Rites and Christian Origins*, by Kathleen Corley. *Catholic Biblical Quarterly* 74, no. 3: 594–6.

LSJ = Liddell, Henry George, Robert Scott, and Henry Stuart Jones. 1940. *A Greek-English Lexicon*. Oxford: Clarendon.

Lietzmann, Hans. 1961. *A History of the Early Church*. 4 vols. Translated by Bertram Lee Wolf. Cleveland and New York: World Publishing Company.

Lightman, Marjorie, and William Zeisel. 1977. "Univira: An Example of

Continuity and Change in the Roman Empire." *Church History* 46, no. 1: 19–32.

Lindsay, Hugh. 2004. "The 'Laudatio Murdiae': Its Content and Signficance. *Latomus* 63, no. 1: 88–97.

Lisón-Tolosana, Carmelo. 1976. "The Ethics of Inheritance." In Peristiany, *Mediterranean Family Structures*, 305–15.

Livy. 2018. *History of Rome*, Volume 11, *Books 38–40*. Edited and translated by J.C. Yardley. Loeb Classical Library 313. Cambridge: Harvard University Press.

Lucian. 1936. *The Passing of Peregrinus. The Runaways. Toxaris or Friendship. The Dance. Lexiphanes. The Eunuch. Astrology. The Mistaken Critic. The Parliament of the Gods. The Tyrannicide. Disowned.* Translated by A.M. Harmon. Loeb Classical Library 302. Cambridge: Harvard University Press.

Lührmann, Dieter. 1981. "Neutestamentliche Haustafeln und antike Ökonomie." *New Testament Studies* 27: 83–97.

Lynch, Scott M. 2008. "Race, Socioeconomic Status, and Health in Life-Course Perspective: Introduction to the Special Issue" *Research on Aging* 30, no. 2: 127–36.

Lysias. 1930. *Lysias*. Translated by W.R.M. Lamb. Loeb Classical Library 244. Cambridge: Harvard University Press.

MacDonald, Dennis Ronald. 1983. *The Legend and the Apostle: The Battle for Paul in Story and Canon*. Philadelphia: Westminster.

MacDonald, Margaret Y. 1988. *The Pauline Churches: A Socio-historical Study of Institutionalization in the Pauline and Deutero-Pauline Writings*. Cambridge: Cambridge University Press.

– 1996. *Early Christian Women and Pagan Opinion: The Power of the Hysterical Woman*. Cambridge: Cambridge University Press.

– 2003. "Early Christian Women Married to Unbelievers." In Levine, *A Feminist Companion*, 14–28.

– 2014. *The Power of Children : The Construction of Christian Families in the Greco-Roman World*. Waco: Baylor University Press.

MacKinnon, Michael. 2007. "Osteological Research in Classical Archaeology." *American Journal of Archaeology* 111, no. 3: 473–504.

MacMullen, Ramsey. 1974. *Roman Social Relations: 50 B.C. to A.D. 284*. New Haven and London: Yale University Press.

Macrobius. 2011. *Saturnalia*, Vol. 1, *Books 1–2*. Edited and translated by Robert A. Kaster. Loeb Classical Library 510. Cambridge: Harvard University Press.

Madigan, Kevin, and Carolyn Osiek, ed. and trans. 2005. *Ordained*

Women in the Early Church: A Documentary History. Baltimore: Johns Hopkins University Press.

Magie, David. 1950. *Roman Rule in Asia Minor to the End of the Third Century after Christ*. 2 vols. Princeton: Princeton University Press.

Maier, Harry O. 1991. *The Social Setting of Ministry as Reflected in the Writings of Hermas, Clement and Ignatius*. Waterloo, ON: Wilfrid Laurier Press.

Malherbe, Abraham J. 1980. "Medical Imagery in the Pastoral Epistles." In *Texts and Testaments: Critical Essays on the Bible and Early Church Fathers*, edited by Wallace Eugene March and Stuart Dickson Currie, 19–35. San Antonio: Trinity University Press.

– 1983. *Social Aspects of Early Christianity*. 2nd ed. Philadelphia: Fortress.

– 1986. *Moral Exhortation: A Greco-Roman Sourcebook*. Philadelphia: Westminster.

– 1994. "Paulus Senex." *Restoration Quarterly* 36, no. 4: 197–207.

– 2006. "The Virtus Femiarum in 1 Timothy 2:9–15." In *Renewing Tradition: Studies in Texts and Contexts in Honor of James W. Thompson*, edited by Mark W. Hamilton, Thomas H. Olbricht, and Jeffrey Peterson, 45–65. Eugene, OR: Pickwick.

– 2008. "How to Treat Old Women and Old Men: The Use of Philosophical Traditions and Scripture in 1 Timothy 5." In *Scripture and Traditions: Essays on Early Judaism and Christianity in Honor of Carl R. Holladay*, edited by Patrick Gray and Gail R. O'Day, 263–90. Leiden and Boston: Brill, 2008.

– 2010. "Godliness, Self-Sufficiency, Greed, and the Enjoyment of Wealth: 1 Timothy 6:3–19 Part I." *Novum Testamentum* 52: 376–405.

– 2011. "Godliness, Self-Sufficiency, Greed, and the Enjoyment of Wealth: 1 Timothy 6:3–19 Part II." *Novum Testamentum* 53: 73–96.

Malina, Bruce J. 1989. "Christ and Time: Swiss or Mediterranean?" *Catholic Biblical Quarterly* 51: 1–31.

– 2001. *The New Testament World: Insights from Cultural Anthropology*. 3rd ed. Louisville: Westminster John Knox.

– 2008. *Timothy: Paul's Closest Associate*. Collegeville, MN: Liturgical.

– 2010. "Collectivism in Mediterranean Culture." In *Understanding the Social World of the New Testament*, edited by Dietmar Neufeld and Richard E. DeMaris, 17–28. London, New York: Routledge.

Malina, Bruce J., and Jerome H. Neyrey. 1996. *Portraits of Paul: An Archaeology of Ancient Personality*. Louisville: Westminster John Knox.

Maloney, Linda M. 1994. "The Pastoral Epistles." In *Searching the Scriptures*. Vol. 2, *A Feminist Commentary*, edited by Elizabeth Schüssler Fiorenza, 361–80. New York: Crossroad.

Marklein, Kathryn E., Rachael E. Leahy, and Douglas E. Crews. 2016. "In Sickness and in Death: Assessing Frailty in Human Skeletal Remains." *American Journal of Physical Anthropology* 161, no. 2: 208–25. https://doi.org/10.1002/ajpa.23019.

Marshall, I. Howard. 1999. *The Pastoral Epistles*. The International Critical Commentary. Edinburgh: T & T Clark.

Marshall, John W. 2008. "'I Left You in Crete': Narrative Deception and Social Hierarchy in the Letter to Titus." *Journal of Biblical Literature* 127, no. 4: 781–803.

Martial. 1993. *Epigrams*, Vol. 1, *Spectacles, Books 1–5*. Edited and translated by D.R. Shackleton Bailey. Loeb Classical Library 94. Cambridge: Harvard University Press.

Mason, Steve. 2007. "Jews, Judaeans, Judaizing, Judaism: Problems of Categorization in Ancient History." *Journal for the Study of Judaism in the Persian, Hellenistic and Roman Period* 38: 457–512.

McGinn, Thomas A.J. 1999. "Widows, Orphans and Social History." *Journal of Roman Archaeology* 12: 617–32.

Medina, Néstor, Alison Hari-Singh, and HyeRan Kim-Cragg, eds. 2019. *Reading In-Between: How Minoritized Communities Interpret the Bible in Canada*. Eugene, OR: Pickwick.

Meeks, Wayne A. 1983. *The First Urban Christians: The Social World of the Apostle Paul*. New Haven: Yale University Press.

– ed. 1972. *The Writings of St. Paul: A Norton Critical Edition*. New York: W.W. Norton and Company.

Meeks, Wayne A., and John T. Fitzgerald, eds. 2007. *The Writings of St. Paul: A Norton Critical Edition*. 2nd ed. New York: W.W. Norton and Company.

Meggitt, Justin J. 1998. "Review of *The Social World of Jesus and the Gospels*." *Journal of Theological Studies* 49, no 1: 215–19.

Meier, John P. 1973, "*Presbyteros* in the Pastoral Epistles." *Catholic Biblical Quarterly* 35, no. 3: 323–45.

Miller, M. 1953. "Greek Kinship Terminology." *Journal of Hellenic Studies* 73: 46–52.

Minois, Georges. 1989. *History of Old Age: From Antiquity to the Renaissance*. Translated by Sarah Hanbury Tenison. Chicago: University of Chicago Press.

The Mishnah. 1933. Translated by Herbert Danby. Oxford: Clarendon Press.

Mitchell, Stephen. 2003. "Asia Minor." In Hornblower and Spawforth, *Oxford Classical Dictionary*, 190–1.

Momigliano, Arnaldo, and Tim. J. Cornell. 2003. "Comitia." In Hornblower and Spawforth, *Oxford Classical Dictionary*, 372–3.

Moo, Douglas J. 1980. "1 Timothy 2:11–15: Meaning and Significance." *Trinity Journal* 1: 62–83.

– 1981. "The Interpretation of 1 Timothy 2:11–15: A Rejoinder." *Trinity Journal* 2: 198–222.

Moxnes, Halvor. 1996. "Honour and Shame." In *Social Sciences and New Testament Interpretation*, edited by Richard L. Rohrbaugh, 19–40. Peabody, MA: Hendrickson.

– 1997. "What Is Family? Problems in Constructing Early Christian Families." In Moxnes, *Constructing Early Christian Families*, 13–41.

– ed. 1997. *Constructing Early Christian Families: Families as Social Reality and Metaphor*. London: Routledge.

Munck, Johannes. 1959. "Presbyters and Disciples of the Lord in Papias: Exegetical Commentary on Eusebius, *Ecclesiastical History* III.39." *Harvard Theological Review* 52, no. 4: 223–43.

Murphy-O'Connor, Jerome. 1991. "2 Timothy Contrasted with 1 Timothy and Titus." *Revue Biblique* 98, no. 3: 403–18.

Myerhoff, Barbara. 1979. *Number Our Days*. New York: Dutton.

Nash, June C. 2007. *Practicing Ethnography in a Globalizing World: An Anthropological Odyssey*. Lanham, MD: AltaMira.

Noy, David. 1990. "Matchmakers and Marriage-Markets in Antiquity." *Echos du monde classique/Classical Views* 9: 375–400.

– 2007. "The Life Course of Jews in the Roman Empire." In Harlow and Laurence, *Age and Ageing in the Roman Empire*, 82–94.

Origen. 1965. *Contra Celsum*. Translated by Henry Chadwick. Cambridge: Cambridge University Press.

Osiek, Carolyn. 1983. "The Widow as Altar: The Rise and Fall of a Symbol." *Second Century* 3: 159–60.

– 2003. "Female Slaves, *Porneia*, and the Limits of Obedience." In *Early Christian Families in Context: An Interdisciplinary Dialogue*, edited by David L. Balch and Carolyn Osiek, 255–74. Grand Rapids: WB Eerdmans.

– 2009. "The Politics of Patronage and the Politics of Kinship: The Meeting of the Ways." *Biblical Theology Bulletin* 39, no. 3: 143–52. https://doi.org/10.1177/0146107909106758.

– 2011. "How Much Do We Really Know about the Lives of Early Christ

Followers?" HTS *Teologiese Studies/Theological Studies* 67, no. 1. https://doi.org/10.4102/hts.v67i1.841.

Osiek, Carolyn, and David Balch. 1997. *Families in the New Testament: Households and House Churches*. Louisville: Westminster John Knox.

Osiek, Carolyn, and Margaret Y. MacDonald, with Janet H. Tulloch. 2006. *A Woman's Place: House Churches in Earliest Christianity*. Minneapolis: Fortress.

Panourgiá, Neni. 1995. *Fragments of Death, Fables of Identity: An Athenian Anthropology*. Madison: University of Wisconsin Press.

Pao, David W. 2014. "Let No One Despise Your Youth: Church and the World in the Pastoral Epistles." *Journal of the Evangelical Theological Society* 57, no. 4: 743–55.

Parkin, Tim. G. 1992. *Demography and Roman Society*. Baltimore and London: Johns Hopkins University Press.

– 1997. "Out of Sight, Out of Mind: Elderly Members of the Roman Family." In *The Roman Family in Italy: Status, Sentiment, Space*, edited by Beryl Rawson and Paul Weaver, 123–48. New York: Oxford University Press.

– 1998. "Aging in Antiquity: Status and Participation." In *Old Age: From Antiquity to Post-Modernity*, edited by Paul Johnson and Pat Thane, 19–42. London and New York: Routledge.

– 2003. *Old Age in the Roman World: A Cultural and Social History*. Baltimore: Johns Hopkins University Press.

– 2011. "From the Margins to the Centre Stage: Some Closing Reflections on Ancient Historical Demography." In *Demography and the Graeco-Roman World*, edited by Claire Holleran and April Pudsey, 181–5. Cambridge: Cambridge University Press.

– 2013. "The Demography of Infancy and Early Childhood in the Ancient World." In *The Oxford Handbook of Childhood and Education in the Classical World*, edited by Judith Evans Grubbs and Tim G. Parkin, 40–61. New York: Oxford University Press.

Parkin, Tim. G., and Arthur John Pomeroy. 2007. *Roman Social History: A Sourcebook*. London and New York: Routledge.

Pelling, C.B.R. 2003. "Sallust." In Hornblower and Spawforth, *Oxford Classical Dictionary*, 1348–9.

Peristiany, J.G., ed. 1976. *Mediterranean Family Structures*. Cambridge: Cambridge University Press.

Pervo, Richard I. 2006. *Dating Acts: Between the Evangelists and Apologists*. Santa Rose, CA: Polebridge.

Pfitzner, Victor C. 1967. *Paul and the Agon Motif*. Leiden: Brill.
Phang, Sara Elise. 2008. *Roman Military Service: Ideologies of Discipline in the Late Republic and Early Principate*. Cambridge ; New York: Cambridge University Press.
Philo. 1937. *On the Decalogue. On the Special Laws, Books 1–3*. Translated by F.H. Colson. Loeb Classical Library 320. Cambridge: Harvard University Press.
– 1939. *On the Special Laws, Book 4. On the Virtues. On Rewards and Punishments*. Translated by F.H. Colson. Loeb Classical Library 341. Cambridge: Harvard University Press.
Pietersen, Lloyd K. 2004. *The Polemic of the Pastorals: A Sociological Examination of the Development of Pauline Christianity*. London and New York: T & T Clark.
– 2007. "Women as Gossips and Busybodies? Another Look at 1 Timothy 5:13." *Lexington Theological Quarterly* 42, no. 1: 19–35.
Pitt-Rivers, Julian. 1977. *The Fate of Shechem or the Politics of Sex: Essays in the Anthropology of the Mediterranean*. Cambridge: Cambridge University Press.
Plato. 1926. *Laws*, Vol. 1, *Books 1–6*. Translated by R.G. Bury. Loeb Classical Library 187. Cambridge: Harvard University Press.
Plescia, Joseph. 1976. "*Patria Potestas* and the Roman Revolution." In *Conflict of Generations in Ancient Greece and Rome*, edited by Stephen Bertman, 143–69. Amsterdam: B.R. Grüner.
Pliny the Younger. 1969. *Letters*, Vol. 1, *Books 1–7*. Translated by Betty Radice. Loeb Classical Library 55. Cambridge: Harvard University Press.
Plutarch. 1916. *Lives*, Vol. 3, *Pericles and Fabius Maximus. Nicias and Crassus*. Translated by Bernadotte Perrin. Loeb Classical Library 65. Cambridge: Harvard University Press.
– 1917. *Lives*, Vol. 5, *Agesilaus and Pompey. Pelopidas and Marcellus*. Translated by Bernadotte Perrin. Loeb Classical Library 87. Cambridge: Harvard University Press.
– 1920. *Lives*, Vol. 9, *Demetrius and Antony. Pyrrhus and Gaius Marius*. Translated by Bernadotte Perrin. Loeb Classical Library 101. Cambridge: Harvard University Press.
– 1926. *Lives*, Vol. 11, *Aratus. Artaxerxes. Galba. Otho. General Index*. Translated by Bernadotte Perrin. Loeb Classical Library 103. Cambridge: Harvard University Press.
– 1927. *Moralia*, Vol. 1, *The Education of Children. How the Young Man Should Study Poetry. On Listening to Lectures. How to Tell a Flatterer from a Friend. How a Man May Become Aware of His Progress in*

Virtue. Translated by Frank Cole Babbitt. Loeb Classical Library 197. Cambridge: Harvard University Press.

– 1928. *Moralia*, Vol. 2, *How to Profit by One's Enemies. On Having Many Friends. Chance. Virtue and Vice. Letter of Condolence to Apollonius. Advice about Keeping Well. Advice to Bride and Groom. The Dinner of the Seven Wise Men. Superstition*. Translated by Frank Cole Babbitt. Loeb Classical Library 222. Cambridge: Harvard University Press.

– 1936. *Moralia*, Vol. 10, *Love Stories. That a Philosopher Ought to Converse Especially with Men in Power. To an Uneducated Ruler. Whether an Old Man Should Engage in Public Affairs. Precepts of Statecraft. On Monarchy, Democracy, and Oligarchy. That We Ought Not to Borrow. Lives of the Ten Orators. Summary of a Comparison between Aristophanes and Menander*. Translated by Harold North Fowler. Loeb Classical Library 321. Cambridge: Harvard University Press.

Polybius. 2010. *The Histories*, Vol. 2, *Books 3–4*. Translated by W.R. Paton. Revised by F.W. Walbank, Christian Habicht. Loeb Classical Library 137. Cambridge: Harvard University Press.

– 2011. *The Histories*, Vol. 3, *Books 5–8*. Edited by W.R. Paton. Revised by F.W. Walbank, Christian Habicht. Loeb Classical Library 138. Cambridge: Harvard University Press.

Porter, S.E. 1993. "What Does It Mean to Be 'Saved by Childbirth?' (1 Timothy 2:15)." *Journal for the Study of the New Testament* 49: 87–102.

Powell, Mark Allen. 1990. *What Is Narrative Criticism?* Minneapolis: Fortress.

Prior, Michael. 1989. *Paul the Letter-Writer and the Second Letter of Timothy*. Journal for the Study of the New Testament Supplement Series 23. Sheffield: JSOT.

Propertius. 1990. *Elegies*. Edited and translated by G.P. Goold. Loeb Classical Library 18. Cambridge: Harvard University Press.

Quinn, Jerome D., and William C. Wacker. 2000. *The First and Second Letters to Timothy*. Eerdmans Critical Commentary. Grand Rapids, MI and Cambridge, UK: William B. Eerdmans.

Rankin, David Ivan. 1995. *Tertullian and the Church*. Cambridge and New York: Cambridge University Press.

Rawson, Beryl. 2003. *Children and Childhood in Roman Italy*. Oxford and New York: Oxford University Press.

Reckford, Kenneth J. 1976. "Father-Beating in Aristophanes' *Clouds*." In

The Conflict of Generations in Ancient Greece and Rome, edited by Stephen Bertman, 89–118. Amsterdam: B.R. Grüner.

Reinhold, Meyer. 1970. "The Generation Gap in Antiquity." *Proceedings of the American Philosophical Society* 114, no. 5: 347–65.

Remus, Harold. 2004. "The End of 'Paganism'?" *Studies in Religion* 33, no. 2: 191–208.

Rhoads, David, Joanna Dewey, and Donald Michie. 2012. *Mark as Story: An Introduction to the Narrative of a Gospel*. 3rd ed. Minneapolis: Fortress.

Richards, William A. 2002. *Difference and Distance in Post-Pauline Christianity: An Epistolary Analysis of the Pastorals*. New York: Peter Lang.

Riley, Matilda White, Marilyn Johnson, and Anne Foner. 1972. *Aging and Society*. Vol. 3, *A Sociology of Age Stratification*. New York: Russell Sage Foundation.

Rodd, Cyril S. 1981. "On Applying a Sociological Theory to Biblical Studies" *Journal for the Study of the Old Testament* 19: 95–106.

Rohrbaugh, Richard L. 1996. Introduction. In *The Social Sciences in New Testament Interpretation*, edited by Richard L. Rohrbaugh, 1–15. Peabody, MA: Hendrickson.

– 2010. "Honor: Core Value in the Biblical World." In *Understanding the Social World of the New Testament*, edited by Dietmar Neufeld and Richard E. DeMaris, 109–25. London and New York: Routledge, 2010.

Rosivach, Vincent. 1994. "*Anus*: Some Older Women in Latin Literature." *Classical World* 88, no. 2: 107–17.

Rowlandson, Jane, ed. 1998. *Women in Society in Greek and Roman Egypt: A Sourcebook*. Cambridge: Cambridge University Press.

Sacks, Karen Brodkin. 1992. "Introduction: New Views of Middle-Aged Women." In *In Her Prime: New Views of Middle-Aged Women*, edited by Virginia Kerns and Judith K. Brown, 1–6. 2nd ed. Urbana and Chicago: University of Illinois Press.

Salamone, S.D., and J.B. Stanton. 1986. "Introducing the *Nikokyra*: Ideality and Reality in Social Process." In *Gender and Power in Rural Greece*, edited by Jill Dubisch, 97–120. Princeton: Princeton University Press.

Sallares, Robert. 2002. *Malaria and Rome: A History of Malaria in Ancient Italy*. Oxford and New York: Oxford University Press.

Saller, Richard P. 1982. *Personal Patronage under the Early Roman Empire*. Cambridge: Cambridge University Press.

– 1987. "Men's Age at Marriage and Its Consequences in the Roman Family." *Classical* Philology 82, no. 1: 21–34.

– 1994. *Patriarchy, Property and Death in the Roman Family.* Cambridge: Cambridge University Press.

Saller, Richard P., and Brent D. Shaw. 1984. "Tombstones and Roman Family Relations in the Principate: Civilians, Soldiers and Slaves." *Journal of Roman Studies* 74: 124–56.

Sallust. 2013. *The War with Catiline. The War with Jugurtha.* Edited by John T. Ramsey. Translated by J.C. Rolfe. Loeb Classical Library 116. Cambridge: Harvard University Press.

Sanders, E.P. 1995. *The Historical Figure of Jesus.* London; New York: Penguin Books.

Sanders, Karl Olav. 1997. "Equality within Patriarchal Structures." In Moxnes, *Constructing Early Christian Families*, 150–65.

Sapp, Stephen. 1987. *Full of Years: Aging and the Elderly in the Bible and Today.* Nashville: Abington.

Scheidel, Walter. 1999. "Emperors, Aristocrats and the Grim Reaper: Towards a Demographic Profile of the Roman Elite." *Classical Quarterly* 49: 254–81.

– 2001a. "Problems and Progress in Roman Demography." In *Debating Roman Demography*, edited by Walter Scheidel, 1–81. Boston: Brill.

– 2001b. "Roman Age Structure: Evidence and Models." *Journal of Roman Studies* 91: 1–26. https://doi.org/10.2307/3184767.

– 2012. "Epigraphy and Demography: Birth, Marriage, Family, and Death." In *Epigraphy and the Historical Sciences*, edited by John Davies and John Wilkes, 101–29. Oxford: Oxford University Press.

Schleiermacher, Friedrich. 1807. *Über den sogenannten ersten Brief des Paulos an den Timotheos: ein kritisches Sendschrieben an J.C. Gass.* Berlin: Realschulbuchhandlung.

Schöllgen, Georg. 1989. "Die διπλῆ τιμή von 1 Tim. 5,17." *Zeitschrift für die Neutestamentliche Wissenschaft* 80: 232–9.

Segovia, Fernando F. 2000. *Decolonizing Biblical Studies: A View from the Margins.* Maryknoll, NY: Orbis Books.

Seneca. 1932. *Moral Essays*, Vol. 2, *De Consolatione ad Marciam. De Vita Beata. De Otio. De Tranquillitate Animi. De Brevitate Vitae. De Consolatione ad Polybium. De Consolatione ad Helviam.* Translated by John W. Basore. Loeb Classical Library 254. Cambridge: Harvard University Press.

Seneca the Elder. 1974. *Declamations*, Vol. 1, *Controversiae, Books 1–6.* Translated by Michael Winterbottom. Loeb Classical Library 463. Cambridge: Harvard University Press.

Shaw, Brent D. 1987. "The Age of Roman Girls at Marriage: Some Reconsiderations." *Journal of Roman Studies* 77: 30–46.
– 1991. "The Cultural Meaning of Death: Age and Gender in the Roman Family." In *The Family in Italy: From Antiquity to the Present*, edited by David I Kertzer and Richard P. Saller, 66–90. New Haven and London: Yale University Press.
Sigismund-Nielsen, Hanne. 2013. "Slave and Lower-Class Children." In *The Oxford Handbook of Childhood and Education in the Classical World*, edited by Judith Evans Grubbs and Tim Parkin, 286–301. New York: Oxford University Press.
Signor, Schuyler. 1999. "The Third Person Imperative in the Greek New Testament." MA thesis, Abilene Christian University.
Simmons, Leo W. 1970 [1945]. *The Role of the Aged in Primitive Society*. Archon Books.
Skeat, T.C. 1979. "'Especially the Parchments': A Note on 2 Timothy IV.13." *Journal of Theological Studies* 30: 173–7.
Southern, Pat. 2006. *The Roman Army*. Santa Barbara, CA: ABC Clio.
Spicq, C. 1947. *Saint Paul: Les Épitres pastorales*. Paris: Librairie Lecoffre.
Stählin, Gustav. 1979. "χήρα." In *Theological Dictionary of the New Testament*, edited by Gerhard Kittel, vol. 9, 440–65. Translated by Geoffrey W. Bromiley. Grand Rapids: Eerdmans.
Stark, Rodney. 1996. *The Rise of Christianity*. San Francisco: HarperCollins.
Stegemann, Ekkehard W., and Wolfgang Stegemann. 1999. *The Jesus Movement: A Social History of Its First Century*. Translated by O.C. Dean Jr. Edinburgh: T & T Clark.
Stewart, Alistair C. 2014. *The Original Bishops: Office and Order in the First Christian Communities*. Grand Rapids: Baker Academic.
Stirling, Paul. 1965. *Turkish Village*. New York: John Wiley and Sons.
Sugirtharajah, R.S. 1995. *Voices from the Margin: Interpreting the Bible in the Third World*. Maryknoll, NY: Orbis/SPCK.
Terence. 2001. *Phormio. The Mother-in-Law. The Brothers*. Edited and translated by John Barsby. Loeb Classical Library 23. Cambridge: Harvard University Press.
Tertullian, Minucius Felix. 1931. *Apology. De Spectaculis. Minucius Felix: Octavius*. Translated by T.R. Glover, Gerald H. Rendall. Loeb Classical Library 250. Cambridge: Harvard University Press.
Theissen, Gerd. 1982. *The Social Setting of Pauline Christianity: Essays on Corinth*. Translated by John H. Schultz. Philadelphia: Fortress Press.
Thornton, Dillon T. 2016. "'Saying What They Should Not Say':

Reassessing the Gravity of the Problem of the Younger Widows (1 Tim. 5:11–15)." *Journal of Evangelical Theological Studies* 59, no. 1: 119–29.

Thurston, Bonnie Bowman. 1989. *The Widows: Women's Ministry in the Early Church*. Minneapolis: Fortress.

– 2003. "1 Timothy 5:3–16 and Leadership of Women in the Early Church." In Levine, *A Feminist Companion*, 159–74.

Towner, Philip H. 2006. *The Letters to Timothy and Titus*. New International Commentary on the New Testament. Grand Rapids: Eerdmans.

Treblico, Paul. 2004. *The Early Christians in Ephesus from Paul to Ignatius*. Grand Rapids, MI, and Cambridge, UK: William B. Eerdmans.

Treggiari, Susan. 1991. *Roman Marriage: Iusti Coniuges from the Time of Cicero to the Time of Ulpian*. Oxford: Clarendon Press.

– 2005. "Putting the Family Across: Cicero on Natural Affection." In *The Roman Family in the Empire: Rome, Italy and Beyond*, edited by Michele George, 9–35. Oxford and New York: Oxford University Press.

Tsuji, Manabu. 2001. "Zwischen Ideal und Realität: Zu den Witwen in 1 Tim. 5.3–16." *New Testament Studies* 47: 92–104.

Tyson, Joseph B. 2006. *Marcion and Luke-Acts: A Defining Struggle*. Columbia: University of South Carolina Press.

Valerius Maximus. 2000. *Memorable Doings and Sayings*, Vol. 2, Books 6–9. Edited and translated by D.R. Shackleton Bailey. Loeb Classical Library 493. Cambridge: Harvard University Press.

Van Bremen, Riet. 1993. "Women and Wealth." In *Images of Women in Antiquity*, edited by Averil Cameron, 223–42. Detroit: Wayne State University Press.

– 1996. *The Limits of Participation: Women and Civic Life in the Greek East in the Hellenistic and Roman Periods*. Amsterdam: J.C. Gieben.

Van der Toorn, Karel. 1995. "The Public Image of Widow in Ancient Israel." In *Between Poverty and the Pyre*, edited by Jan N. Bremmer and Lourens van den Bosch, 19–30. London and New York: Routledge.

Van Neste, Ray. 2004. *Cohesion and Structure in the Pastoral Epistles*. London and New York: T & T Clark.

Verner, David C. 1983. *The Household of God: The Social World of the Pastoral Epistles*. Chico, CA: Scholars Press.

Walker-Ramisch, Sandra. 1996. "Graeco-Roman Voluntary Associations and the Damascus Document: A Sociological Analysis." In Kloppenborg and Wilson, *Voluntary Associations in the Graeco-Roman World*, 128–45.

Wallace, Daniel B. 1996. *Greek Grammar beyond the Basics*. Grand Rapids: Zondervan.

Waters, Kenneth L. 2004. "Saved through Child-Bearing: Virtues as Children in 1 Timothy 2:11–15." *Journal of Biblical Literature* 123, no. 4: 703–35.
Weiss, Kenneth M. 1981. "Evolutionary Perspectives on Human Aging." In Amoss and Harrell, *Other Ways of Growing Old*, 25–58.
Welborn, L.L. 2018. *The Young against the Old: Generational Conflict in First Clement*. Lanham: Lexington Books/Fortress Academic.
Whitaker, Ian. 1976. "Familial Roles in the Extended Patrilineal Kin-Group in Northern Albania." In Peristiany, *Mediterranean Family Structures*, 195–203.
Wiedemann, Thomas E.J., and Jane F. Gardner. 1991. *The Roman Household: A Sourcebook*. London; New York: Routledge.
Wikan, Unni. 1984. "Shame and Honour: A Contestable Pair." *Man* 19, no. 4: 635–52.
Wilson, Stephen G. 1996. "Voluntary Associations: An Overview." In Kloppenborg and Wilson, *Voluntary Associations in the Graeco-Roman World*, 1–15.
Winter, Bruce W. 1988. "Providentia for the Widows of 1 Timothy 5:3–16." *Tyndale Bulletin* 39: 84–99.
– 1994. *Seek the Welfare of the City: Christians as Benefactors and Citizens*. Grand Rapids, MI: Eerdmans.
– 2003. *Roman Wives, Roman Widows: The Appearance of New Women and the Pauline Communities*. Grand Rapids, MI: Eerdmans.
Wistrand, Erik. 1976. *The So-Called Laudatio Turiae: Introduction, Text, Translation, Commentary*. Lund: Acta Universitatis Gothoburgensis.
Wood, John Turtle. 1975 [1877]. *Discoveries at Ephesus including the Site and Remains of the Great Temple of Diana*. Hildesheim and New York: Georg Olms Verlag.
Woods, Robert. 2007. "Ancient and Early Modern Mortality: Experience and Understanding." *Economic History Review* 60, no. 2: 373–99.
Yarbrough, O. Larry. 1993. "Parents and Children in the Jewish Family of Antiquity." In *The Jewish Family in Antiquity*, edited by Shaye J.D. Cohen, 39–59. Atlanta: Scholars.
Young, Frances M. 1994a. "On ΕΠΙΣΚΟΠΟΣ and ΠΡΕΣΒΥΤΕΡΟΣ." *Journal of Theological Studies* 45, no. 1: 142–8.
– 1994b. *The Theology of the Pastoral Epistles*. Cambridge: Cambridge University Press.
Zamfir, Korinna. 2013. *Men and Women in the Household of God: A Contextual Approach to Roles and Ministries in the Pastoral Epistles*. Göttingen and Bristol, CT: Vandenhoeck and Ruprecht.

Index

accusation. *See* elders
Acts of Paul and Thecla, 58, 170, 171, 186, 284n10, 285n12, 309n25, 323n13
age: chronological, 113, 117, 261; gap between husband and wife, 8, 9, 269n15; and life stages, 114, 159; in Luke-Acts 261; and material culture, 25; of men, 6, 62, 217, 261, 268n11, 285n20, 286n21, 293n10, 313n50; and seniority, 30–2, 68, 86–7, 89, 198, 250; social, 113–14; as social identity, 3, 11, 17, 18, 22, 245, 259–60, 263; visibility of, 245–59. *See also* sixty; thirty
age categories, 802, 83–92, 162, 199, 292n2, 293n9
age cohort, 9–10, 269n16
age hierarchy, 40, 44–5, 49, 83–92, 239, 246–9; among men, 60–8, 198, 212–17, 222; among women, 17, 149, 162–71, 192, 321nn33, 37; in 1 Timothy, 4, 11, 14, 36, 40, 54, 78
age status, 29–30, 45
age stratification theory, 282n48

age structure, 13, 16–18, 19, 24, 28, 36, 267n5, 273n3; in 1 Timothy, 31, 80, 93, 148, 198, 209–10, 221, 227, 234, 237–8; challenges to, 74, 218, 239–40; definition of, 10–11, 227n27; and implications for Christ groups, 251, 261, 263–4, 267n5; resilience of, 38–45, 48–9, 60–8, 245–7. *See also* model
aid (ἐπαρκέω), 324n21; for real widows, 99, 118–21, 151, 154; for younger widows, 149, 176–8, 185, 188–9, 196–7, 231
anachronism, 19, 199, 238, 265n2, 279n18, 274n10, 311n37, 329n2
ancestors, 27, 101–2, 244, 290n46. *See also mos maiorum*
anthropology, 16, 19–21, 51, 174, 267n6, 272nn1–2, 275n18, 282n47. *See also* ethnography
Apostolic Constitutions, 120, 238, 306–7n13, 307n18, 311n37
asceticism, 158, 235, 316n2, 301n35; associated with

opponents, 58–9, 78, 218, 271n24, 284n4, 284–5n12, 296n3
Asia Minor, 13, 24, 71, 202, 225, 274n13, 297n10, 315n67
audience. *See* implied audience; real audience
Augustus: age, 62–3, 72, 239, 285n17, 285n19, 286n21, 294n14; benefaction, 24, 188; political stability, 24, 239, 274n13, 286n22, 274n13; traditional values, 63–4, 95
authorship of 1 Timothy, 11–13, 14, 272n25

believing woman (πιστή), 149, 171, 176–97, 232; pivotal role, 178–9, 185, 196; responsibilities of, 98, 129, 154, 171, 175, 189, 231, 235; textual variants of, 323n8; and widows she "has," 119, 322n3, 325n26. *See also* faith/faithfulness; middle-aged women
benefaction: for community, 24, 236, 243; from elders, 207, 209, 218, 336n1; for individuals 83, 100, 187, 315n29; from older women, 115, 187–8, 229–30, 244, 274, 311n36, 325–6n28, 328n44, 330n9, 336n5; and patron-client relationship, 276n21; and voluntary associations, 67, 139, 142, 202, 204, 287n32, 331n13
bishop. *See* overseer
brothers and sisters. *See* siblings

celibacy, 58–9, 182, 184, 314n66, 318n13, 323n13. *See also* asceticism
character. *See* Paul; Timothy
charity. *See* aid
chastity, 26, 91, 114, 126–7, 132, 155, 160, 186–7, 276n23
childbearing, 42, 58, 63, 126, 156, 168, 182, 297n6; and childrearing, 129, 167, 192, 310n32; and remarriage, 94–5, 98, 102, 231; and women "saved through," 192, 327–8n42
children: in Christ groups, 249, 252, 254–9; guardian of, 41; and honour, 27, 194, 276n23; virtue of, 129, 192; as vulnerable, 254–6. *See also* death; father-son relationship; filial duty; inheritance; mothers; parent-child relationship; parents
Cicero: on intergenerational relationships, 85–6, 105–6, 187, 215; on marriage, 27, 187; on obligation to parents, 105–6, 301n35; on old age, 7, 24, 63, 210, 275n15, 285n20; as an older man, 62, 63, 334n11; on rashness of youth, 63, 210, 215
collectivism, 11, 12, 14, 27, 170, 183, 241, 266n3, 334n30
collegia. *See* voluntary associations
communal identity. *See* collectivism
concord, 75, 89, 91–2, 131, 227, 250
conflict. *See* intergenerational conflict
conservative element (of model of generational stability and social

change), 49–51, 63–4, 72, 244, 251, 256
conservative stance (of author of 1 Timothy), 54, 74, 77, 78–9, 98, 198, 226, 234
cooperation. *See* intergenerational relationships
Cornelia (mother of the Gracci), 128, 129, 159, 309n28, 310nn31, 33
council of elders. *See* elders
crisis: of identity in 1 Timothy, 14, 49, 51, 54, 68–74, 78–9, 198, 211, 226, 234, 243, 290n46; and social change, 53, 60, 61–2
critique of Christ groups: Celsus, 253–7, 339n7, 339–40n8, 340nn9–10; Lucian of Samosata, 255–7; Minucius Felix, 253, 256; Pliny the Younger, 252–3
cultural sensitivity, 3, 17, 20, 46, 51, 202, 217, 233, 246, 251, 261, 263
cultural values, 36–7, 38, 46, 51, 87
cursus honorum, 62, 63, 67

date of 1 Timothy, 13, 14, 270nn19, 21, 24
daughter-in-law, 166, 262, 279n34, 300n31, 325n23
deacon. See *diakonoi*
death: and burial, 66, 110, 136, 246, 267n5, 303n43, 313n54; of father, 7, 105, 288n33; and funeral, 107, 137, 292n8; and funerary inscriptions, 127, 266n4, 267n5; and funerary rites, 107, 135–6; of husband, 94–5, 121, 127; of infants and children, 5–6, 267–8n8, 268n13, 286n22; of loved one, 166, 259, 279n32; not associated with old age, 259; rate (mortality), 5, 266n4, 267n6; ritual, 136, 313n53; as "social death," 117, 191, 328n44. *See also* funerary rites; parents
decolonization, 20, 266n3
deference: of children to parents, 30; in Christ groups, 246, 251; and modesty, 26; to older men 207, 210, 214, 217, 235, 244, 254, 256; to older women, 167–8; of women to men, 276n19, 279nn33, 35; of young to elders, 4, 29–39, 49–51, 61, 85–8, 112, 226–7, 258. *See also* older men; older women; younger men
demography, 4–9, 19, 63, 68, 72, 263, 266–7n4, 267nn6–7, 288n33; of Christ groups, 245, 251–9, 267n5, 307n13; related to parents; 106, 110, 300–1n32, 327n35; related to widows, 94, 296n4, 297nn8–9
denial. See younger widows
diakonoi, 180, 221–2, 238–9, 270n18, 277n26, 330n12, 331n15; female or wives of (ambiguous), 55, 121, 129, 145, 180, 200, 308n20, 323n11, 336n44. *See also* overseer and *diakonoi*
disease, 5–6, 266n4, 267n6
divorce (divorcée), 93–4, 127, 296nn4–5, 297n8, 317n12

domestic realm. *See* household
dowry, 47, 95, 185–90, 197, 229, 235, 316n1, 325n26
duty and devotion (εὐσέβεια, εὐσεβέω), 12, 17, 54, 56, 66, 102, 103–5, 180, 205, 241–2, 288n22; definition of, 299n26, 300n28; as honourable behaviour, 111, 188, 191–2, 195, 228, 241, 244, 319n21; opposite of, 205, 212, 242, 333n23; as reciprocity, 105–7, 111; as traditional value, 63, 106, 288n32, 301n33

elders, 4, 16, 17, 83, 198–224, 232–4; in *1 Clement*, 219–20, 334n34; accusation against, 17, 32, 34, 81, 211–12, 217, 218, 224, 332n22; challenges to, 40–5, 60–8, 74, 90; council of, 66, 72, 80, 88, 221, 238, 335n42; disrespect toward, 77, 89, 223, 242–3, 253–4; leadership role for, 199–205, 334n34; "namely [μάλιστα] those who toil," 206; respect for, 29–32, 36, 85–8, 221–2, 232–5, 308n23; scholarship on, 200–2, 249–51; seniority (in the modern Mediterranean), 30, 42–3, 48; who shepherd (leadership and care), 203–6, 236, 258; teaching by, 209. *See also* deference; honour; older men
enlisted. *See* list
Ephesus, 13, 55, 119, 124, 239, 270n20, 274n13, 288n35
ethnocentrism, 4, 19–21, 46

ethnography, 16–17, 38, 40, 44, 46, 48, 169, 311n40, 325n22; use of, 20–3, 29, 38, 51, 60, 165. *See also* anthropology
exemplary widow. *See* sixty+ widow

faith/faithfulness (πίστις): children's, 192; of the community, 163, 188, 244; denial of, 4, 108, 111–12, 179, 195–6, 232;· "first," 181–4, 197, 231, 318n13, 324n19; and identity, 163, 180, 192; marital, 119–20, 127–8, 309n29; obligations of, 180, 181; and opposing teachers, 181, 232, 324n19; range of meaning of, 179–84; as rhetoric ("the faith"), 12, 56, 111, 183, 229; sincerity of, 105, 315n69; someone without, 102, 180, 184, 228, 230; as struggle, 59, 287n28; of Timothy, 105, 181, 332n22; of women, 163, 177, 181, 190, 229–30, 323n11. *See also* believing woman
false teachers. *See* opponents
family, 7, 9, 11, 260, 277n26, 277–8n27; culturally central, 46–9, 95, 166–7, 169, 282n48; as distinguished from community, 108; female honour, 115, 155, 158, 160, 171; as framework for other relationships, 30, 38; and honour, 27, 35, 39, 42, 51, 83–6, 283n49; and marriage, 185; as metaphor, 63–4, 278n28; rejection of, 246–9; and shame, 109–10; and women's power,

167–8. *See also* household; widows with family
father-son relationship, 27, 39, 41, 48, 61, 67, 277n25, 286n21; age gap, 9, 259; and duties of son, 84; in voluntary associations, 67, 138, 314n59. *See also* deference; household codes; parent-child relationship; parents; parricide; *paterfamilias*
feminist critique, 173–4
fertility, 5–6, 63, 96, 131, 266n4, 311n41
fictive kin. *See* kin
fictive narrative, 15–16, 72. *See also* letters to Timothy and Titus
filial duty, 17, 103–11, 247–8, 301nn35, 37; Judean expressions of, 299–300n27, 339n1; and laws in ancient Greece, 303n43; neglect of, 36, 41, 77, 98, 107, 109–11, 156, 179, 194–5, 236, 285n14; as obligation, 35, 101–2, 111, 171; as reciprocity, 104–7, 301n33; and social sanction, 109–11. *See also* duty and devotion
first faith. *See* faith/faithfulness
folklore. *See* myths
forebearers. *See* ancestors
funerary rights. *See* death

gender, 3, 18, 28, 36, 45, 55, 260, 280n38. *See also* hierarchy
generational cycle, 16, 29, 36–8, 51, 107, 279n31. *See also* model
gerousia, 206, 331n18
grammar. *See* rhetoric
grandchildren, 30, 36, 97, 101–2, 195, 228, 235–6, 298n19, 319n18
grandmother(s), 13, 17, 36, 101–2, 105, 124, 129, 132, 280n36, 340n12. *See also* widows with family
grandparents, 9, 10, 101–2, 106, 242
Greek words: βούλομαι (desire). *See* younger widows
ἐπιπλήσσω (jab at). *See* older men
ἐπαρκέω. *See* aid
ἐπίσκοπος. *See* overseer
ἔργα καλά. *See* noble works
εὐσέβεια, εὐσεβέω. *See* duty and devotion
καταλέγω (put on a list). *See* list
μάλιστα (especially/namely). *See* elders; household
οἶκος. *See* household
παραιτοῦ (intercede for). *See* younger widows
παρακαλέω (make peace with). *See* older men
πιστή. *See* believing woman
πίστις. *See* faith/faithfulness
σωφροσύνη. *See* self-control/moderation
group-orientation. *See* collectivism

Haustafeln. *See* household codes
heteronymity, 12–13, 15, 71, 270n17
hierarchy: in community, 11, 16, 38, 50, 75; in household, 4, 30, 48, 74. *See also* age hierarchy
historical circumstances, 38, 45, 46, 49–50, 51–2, 53, 59, 64
honour: active maintenance of, 33,

115–16, 171; affront to, 89–90, 98, 110, 255; and age, 32, 209–11, 214, 293n12; attained by young (dependents), 33, 66, 87, 256; of the community, 45, 57, 110–11, 236, 326n28; cultivation, 92; definition of, 25–9, 36, 99, 191, 198, 275n18, 276n22, 277n24, 299n23; as "double honour" (for elders), 36, 206, 207, 209; for elders, 204–10, 214–18, 224, 239, 260, 299n23, 333n28; of family, 39, 41, 48–51, 83–5, 158, 160, 167; and generational stability, 48–51, 83; and honour challenge, 91, 302n41; and hospitality, 128, 130; and marriage, 42; for parents, 106–7, 109–10, 240, 246; public recognition of (on a list), 137–46; and reciprocity, 35, 209; restoration of, 91, 224; threat to, 115, 221–3, 240–1; visibility of, 236; in voluntary associations, 67–8, 202; and widows, 32, 97–9, 100–1, 128, 152–3, 228; and women, 33, 104, 132, 181, 227, 254, 305–6n3. *See also* shame

hospitality, 35, 36, 39, 77, 129, 308n22

household (οἶκος): definition of, 27–8, 82, 260, 277n26; "especially [μάλιστα] one's own," 108–9; familial roles in, 30, 72, 108, 170, 303n42; hierarchy in, 4, 74, 247, 251; and honour, 25–32, 137, 218; ideal, 75, 77; as locus for social change, 38, 49–51; men's roles in, 43, 203–4, 206–7, 217, 328n48, 331n13; in Paul's letters, 28, 278nn28–29; separated from, 249, 256–8; and threat of opponents, 218, 322n7; and traditional roles, 59, 189; and women's activity, 38, 156, 159–63, 177–8, 185, 197. *See also* family

household codes, 82, 90, 236, 247, 292n3

household of God: community of 1 Timothy as, 28, 31, 51, 53, 66, 75, 78, 93; hierarchy of, 75, 145, 213, 227, 292n6; individual households within, 108–10, 336n3; as metaphor, 45, 64 74–5, 78, 82–3, 108, 188, 225, 278n28, 291n50; proper behaviour in, 17, 54–7, 75, 80–92, 103, 144, 197, 221, 226, 232; reputation of, 240; social order within, 4, 92, 771, 218, 224, 237, 241; younger widows in, 148, 189, 240

identity. *See* age; crisis; faith/faithfulness; marriage; mothers; thirty

implied audience, 76–7, 101, 283n2

individualism, 11, 20, 27, 181, 183, 265n3

inheritance, 25, 27, 36, 39, 43, 72, 277n25, 281nn41–43, 290n46, 294n16, 301n33; bequeathed before death, 107, 303–4n46, 304n47; and legal discussions, 63, 159, 303n45; as metaphor, 71–2, 146, 238–9; and reputation, 115; threat of

disinheritance, 131, 303n44, 304n47, 326n29; of women, 95, 115, 131, 303n44, 322n39; for women, 95, 124, 129, 158, 187, 258, 297n12, 317n11
intergenerational conflict, 39–45, 55, 60–4, 68, 78, 225–35, 242, 285n16
intergenerational relationships, 3, 13, 16–18, 25, 54, 60–8, 111, 279n33, 290n43; as ideal and idealized, 72–4, 80–1, 83–92; in the modern Mediterranean, 30–1, 34; and power dynamics, 38, 43–5, 63. *See also* father-son relationship; model; mothers: and daughters; parent-child relationship; parents

Jews. *See* Judeans
Judeans, 14, 24 55, 58, 271n23, 291n47

kin, 7, 30–6, 269n16, 277n26; female, 175, 188, 231, 257, 259, 321n36; fictive, 35, 66, 82–3, 92, 227, 239, 286n25, 287n30, 291n50, 292–3n8, 314n66; and marriage, 42, 278n27; relationships among, 100–1, 109, 155, 166, 168, 223, 269n16, 320n29; terms for, 35, 280nn36–37
kin universe, 7, 259, 268n14

Laudatio Murdiae, 188, 309n29
Laudatio Turiae, 103, 127, 188, 325n27
leaders. *See* elders; overseer and *diakonoi*

leadership, scholarly debate: 245, 249–51, 328n1
learning, 55, 76, 102, 156–7, 172
letters to Timothy and Titus, 13–14, 57–8, 319n2
life course, 9–11, 16, 22, 28, 39, 81, 259–60, 262
life course approach, 45–6, 59, 281n46
life cycle. *See* generational cycle
life expectancy, 5–6, 19, 267n5, 268n10; average, 6, 267n7, 268n12
list (καταλέγω, put on a list): as enrollment in voluntary associations, 138–43; as intergenerational honour, 138–41, 143–5; as public honour, 138–45; of sixty+ widow, 17, 137–45
living memory, 54, 60, 68–74, 78
luxurious living. *See* self-indulgence (luxurious living)

marital residence: neolocal, 170; patrilocal, 166, 168, 281n44
marriage: age of, 7–9, 10–11, 94, 217, 269n15, 297n11; arranged, 320n28, 325n25; and benefit for parents, 30, 42, 325n23; challenge to status quo, 42, 47, 59; and children and household, 161; desired by women, 158, 317n10; discouraged for men, 190, 231; as expectation for women, 58, 95, 132, 158, 160; and family honour, 158, 232, 259, 277n26; and father's death, 39, 327n35; fidelity in, 126–7, 309n29; forbidden by opponents, 56, 58, 180, 183–4, 189,

234; and historical Paul, 146, 296n3; and men's leadership roles, 197, 217; and men's status, 189, 326n33; monogamous, 308n21; mother's role in, 114, 115, 186–7, 326n32; older women's role in, 170–1, 175–6, 185, 189, 190, 197; with polytheist, 182; and procreation, 95, 131; and women's chastity, 160, 187; and women's identity, 95, 159, 259; and women's networks, 187; and women's transition to adulthood, 60, 94

matchmaking, 42, 185, 188, 325n25

matron. *See* older women

menopause, 115, 124, 311n40; perceptions of, 131–2, 298n12

middle-aged women: as a believing woman, 176–97, 232; as benefactors, 187; comparison with sixty+ widow, 178, 191–2, 196–7, 230, 235, 330n11; definition of, 168, 171, 311n40; and elders, 210; influence of, 149, 171, 179, 194, 229; judging younger widows, 184, 231–2; as models of virtue (ideally), 126, 190–5, 232; and neglect of duties, 17, 195–6; and the opponents, 149, 177, 231; pivotal role of, 190; and responsibility for younger women; 17, 149, 162, 171, 173, 175–6, 220, 232; and self-indulgence, 190–5

military, 10, 62, 63, 64–6, 286nn23–25; images in 1 Timothy, 66, 287n28

model life tables, 7, 266n4, 267nn7–8, 268n9

model: application of, 83, 107, 110, 209, 221, 223, 225, 253, 256, 260; of age status and the generational cycle, 16, 36–7, 53, 83; development of, 16–17, 19, 23, 53, 273n3; of generational stability and social change, 16, 46, 49–54, 59, 60, 64, 78, 246, 331n15;

moderation. *See* self-control/moderation

modernization and cultural change, 22, 46–9, 274n8

modern Mediterranean cultures (traditional), 19, 20, 23, 26,

modern Western cultures: assumptions from, 50, 173–4, 276n21; contrasted with ancient Mediterranean, 5, 9, 19, 20, 46, 259, 274n9, 281n45; definition of, 265–6n3; and theories of age, 282n48. *See also* individualism

modesty: and appearance, 55, 104, 191; behaviour of younger widows (immodest), 154–61, 181, 197; definition of, 26, 276n19; and maintaining group honour, 26, 92, 305n3; as modelled by older women, 171, 190, 192; and self-control, 191; and sexuality, 27, 181; as submission to elders, 27, 333n28, 335n37; of women, 75, 103–4, 155, 179, 191, 232, 254; of young, 33, 86–7, 92, 209, 224, 335n37. *See also* shame

mortality. *See* death

mos maiorum, 67, 102, 127. See also ancestors
mothers, 10, 13, 32, 58, 280n36; affection for, 105; age, 101, 229; arranging marriages, 186–7; as continuity of community, 259; and daughters, 143–5, 170, 186–7, 189, 311n40, 314n66, 324nn23–24; identity as, 96, 129, 159, 300n31; outliving fathers, 7, 259, 300–1n32; power and influence of, 124–5, 171, 259–60; and sons, 104–5, 132, 166–7, 159, 189, 295n20, 309n29, 315n69, 326n32; surrogate, 170, 228, 327n37; with young children, 257. See also Cornelia; filial duty; inheritance; parents; parricide; widows with family
mothers-in-law, 41, 132, 167, 168, 276n23, 309n26, 325n22
myths: and folklore, 40–1; of old women, 42, 54, 76, 104, 125, 172, 242, 308n25; of opponents, 41–2, 55;

noble works (ἔργα καλὰ), 122, 223, 235–7, 238–9, 320n26, 330n12; of elders, 204; for the sake of reputation, 163, 327n40; of sixty+ widow, 97, 117, 128–30, 137, 330n11
non-elite, 61–2, 107, 259, 268n14, 275nn14–15, 296n4, 301n36, 339n7; men as, 210, 217; sources for, 24–5, 51, 127; women as, 94–5, 101, 158–9, 169; in voluntary associations, 67–8, 287n32

occasion of 1 Timothy, 178–9, 284n7. See also social change
office: history of interpretation, 328n1; leadership defined as, 198, 199, 336n45
old age, 16, 24, 268n12, 312n45; behaviour in, 87–8, 132, 293n13; and care from younger kin, 30, 43, 106, 110, 275n17, 280–1n41, 285n14; in Christ groups, 258, 263; expectation of achieving, 6; frailty in, 106, 121, 301n36, 321n31; and life-long reputation, 115; and physical appearance, 25, 132; respect for, 85–8, 89, 214, 293–4n13; as shameful, 203, 214; sixty as threshold of, 133–4, 136–7, 146, 312n46; slaves freed in, 278n30; virtue in, 126, 129, 130, 137; vulnerability in, 99–100, 132, 301n36. See also elders; older men; older women
older men: authority of, 207, 209, 334n33; in Christ groups, 245; decline in activity of, 88, 207, 259, 332n20, 334n32; honour for, 32, 202, 209; influence of, 24, 203, 210, 214, 216, 335n42; jab at (ἐπιπλήσσω), 80, 89, 210, 212, 227, 294n17; make peace with (παρακαλέω), 80, 89, 91–2, 210, 212, 227, 295n19; mistreatment of, 89–90, 294–5n17; with perceptions of younger men, 24, 214, 216, 233; precedence of, 31, 62, 86–7, 209, 210, 237, 334n32; with reliance on younger men, 217; remarriage of, 100, 269n15; reputation of,

210, 224, 258–9; responsibilities of, 203, 210, 214; stereotypes of, 205, 331n14; threatened by younger men, 61, 68, 214, 216, 217, 234. *See also* elders; old age

older women: authority of, 114, 124–5, 129, 132, 168, 171, 262, 321n37; as bad influence, 309n25; as benefactors, 171, 188, 244, 326n28; and children, 310n33; in Christ groups, 258, 262; deference to, 30–1, 33, 91; definition of (stage of life), 114, 321n32; freedom of, 100, 124, 167, 170, 321n36; as ideal, 114–15, 126, 128, 178; involved in marriage decisions, 42, 168, 170, 185, 187, 189–90; make peace with, 99–100, 227; as models of virtue, 190; remarriage of, 95, 100, 127; reputation of, 115, 145; with responsibility for younger women, 4, 32, 34, 92, 162–5, 168, 175, 229, 260; sexuality of, 133, 305n5, 311–2n42; stereotypes of, 114–16, 125, 130, 255; as storytellers, 308–9n25; as teachers, 162–5; treatment of, 91; visibility of, 130. *See also* middle-aged women; mothers; old age; sixty+ widow; widows with children

old wives' tales. *See* myths

opponents: authors' rhetoric for, 183–4, 195, 197, 232; character of, 104, 218, 283n4, 316nn5, 7, 328n46; influence of, 11, 38, 56, 75, 77–8, 102, 189, 234, 243, 323n7; and "learning," 102; in letters to Timothy and Titus, 13–14, 271–2n24; at odds with Paul, 33, 43, 66; proper behaviour as solution to, 17, 33–4, 57, 71; and reputation, 11, 197; teachings of, 4, 15, 38, 41–2, 51, 55–9, 74, 77–8, 104, 284n4, 316n7; terminology for, 283–4n4. *See also* asceticism

orality, 22, 58, 69–70, 288n36, 289n38. *See also* living memory

order of widows, 119, 121–6, 298n16, 305n14

orphans, 257, 296n6

outsiders: adversary as, 316n5; distrust of, 26; judgment from, 45, 111, 196, 210, 223, 236, 231–3; love of, 308n22; observations of age from, 245, 252–9; opinion of, 57–8, 79, 98, 105, 175, 235–6, 240–1; sensitivity to, 14, 17, 27, 77, 92, 218, 221, 223, 228

overseer (ἐπισκόπος), 88, 199, 202, 204, 206, 218, 222, 240, 335n38; succession of, 289n42; terminology of, 270n18, 329n2

overseer and *diakonoi*, 4, 12, 31, 42, 189, 204, 236, 270n18, 271n21, 314n64; children of, 58, 110, 123, 217–18, 240; compared with widows, 121–4, 242, 330n12; and elders, 199–201, 329n4; gendered expectations of, 55; marriage of, 42, 58, 122, 197; maturity of, 31, 217, 234

paganism. *See* polytheism

parent-child relationship, 16, 27, 35–6, 43–4, 49–50, 61, 269n16,

276n23; debate in scholarship about, 245–9
parents: affection for, 104–5, 300n30, 301n33; death of, 7, 43, 227, 259, 281n44, 300n27, 303n45, 327n35; emotional needs of, 107; as image of the divine, 106; obedient to, 82, 301n33; and reliance on children, 30–1; respect for, 30, 38, 110, 124; rhetoric of rejection of, 247–8. See also father-son relationship; mothers
parricide, 90, 242, 337–8n15, 338n17
Pastoral Epistles. See letters to Timothy and Titus
past-orientation, 290n46
paterfamilias, 27, 61, 109, 169, 204, 207, 277n26
patrilocal. See marital residence
patron, patronage. See benefaction
Paul: authority of, 15, 31, 57; character of (in 1 Timothy), 4, 15–16, 40, 53–72, 225–6; as a historical person, 11–12, 13, 14, 57–9, 69, 83, 270–1n21, 290–1n47, 315n7, 337n8; as an older man (rhetoric), 4, 31, 45, 53–4, 71; rival interpretations of, 57, 58–9, 180
peers: and honour, 26, 91, 109, 207, 280n37, 282n48, 283n49, 300n27; and politics, 63, 326n33; and Timothy, 35, 80, 91, 221, 234, 242
pietas. See duty and devotion
Plutarch: age of 334n11; on cultivated virtue, 88, 128, 129, 138; on older men, 24, 203, 205, 210,

217, 333n29, 334n32; on respect for parents/elders, 85, 87–8, 214–15
polytheism, 24, 103, 136, 182, 274n10, 291n47, 324n17
poverty, 62, 67, 95, 99–100, 120, 287n31
power: in intergenerational dynamics, 38–40, 49–52, 89, 171; in later life, 159–60, 167, 175, 214, 229; modern Western conception of, 281n45; of parents/elders, 48, 62, 68, 217, 303n44; of *paterfamilias*, 61, 207, 277n26; of women, 33, 115, 118, 121–6, 146, 168, 188, 254, 309n26, 311n40; of younger men, 48, 61–3, 74, 198, 215–16, 219, 233–5, 239, 295n19, 334n33
presbyter. See elders; older men
pseudepigraphy. See heteronymity
public and private realms: age structure in, 7, 40, 44–5, 49, 252–3; conflict in, 60–1, 78; and honour, 27, 36, 40, 49–51, 77, 86; women in, 155, 160
public behaviour. See reputation
public honour. See list
purity: and Timothy, 180, 222, 234, 238; and younger women, 91, 163, 328n43

real audience, 4, 15–16, 53, 71–2, 98, 116, 146, 181, 198, 224, 228, 283n2; behaviour of, 54–6, 74–8, 93, 154, 178, 203, 235, 239
real widow, 17, 32, 91, 129, 177–8, 207; aid for, 119, 189, 228; contrasted with other

women, 118–21, 152–3, 194–6, 229; definition of, 94, 97–100, 119, 298n16
rebuke, 212, 218, 221, 294n15, 333n25
reciprocity, 32, 35, 66; of children to parents, 102–3; lack of (as social death), 194; of the patron-client relationship, 276n21; and the prayer of real widows, 100; of wedding/baptism sponsors (in the modern Mediterranean), 292–3n8.
remarriage: Augustan laws, 131, 134–5, 159, 297n12; with children, 188, 316n4, 326nn29–30; discouragement of, 93–4, 184, 271n24; of men, 189; as norm for childbearing women, 96, 126, 181; parents' involvement with, 188–90; reasons against, 100, 127–8, 131, 133, 323n13; reasons for, 96, 159, 317n13, 327n34; for younger widows, 120, 121, 158–9, 182–3, 188
reputation, 4, 11, 17, 26, 27, 35, 39, 40 49, 79, 276n23; of the community, 176; and female sexuality, 95; of Paul, 57; and remarriage, 96; of Timothy, 291n47. *See also* honour; older men; older women; younger men; younger women
respect. *See* deference
rhetoric, 3, 11, 18, 31, 45, 53–4, 71–8, 68, 74–8, 272n26; of 1 Timothy, 97–8; and anxiety, 198; of comparison of widows, 151–3; and fictional narrative, 97–8; of first person indicative, 75–6, 161, 220, 291n51, 318n15, 319n18; of grammatical shift from singular to plural, 100, 192, 213, 327n41; and Paul's authority, 98, 145–6; of second-person imperative, 76, 291n52, 319n18; of third-person imperative, 76–7, 116, 123, 203, 291n53, 332n21; on women, 145–6
rites of passage: ancient, 83, 169–70; modern, 38, 129, 136, 165–6, 168–9, 321n36
Roman: definition of, 24, 274n11

Scipio, 65, 286n26, 287n27
self-control/moderation (σωφροσύνη): and men, 194, 207, 210, 214, 222; and women, 114, 125, 130, 163, 191, 194, 297n6, 328n43
self-indulgence (luxurious living), 104, 190–5, 194–5, 229, 319n18
seniority. *See* age; elders
servant. *See diakonoi*
shame: definition of, 26, 58, 155–6, 276n19, 275n18, 335n37. *See also* modesty
shame (negative): of behaviour of women, 58, 86, 148, 158, 227, 231, 255; of behaviour toward elders, 86, 90, 233, 254; of being unmarried, 94, 317n13, 327n34; of old age, 214, 304n2; as public humiliation, 89, 212, 223, 240
shame (positive): embodied by community, 194, 254, 181, 258; and hidden things, 337n8; and

respect for leaders, 27, 335n37; sensitivity to, 89, 195, 335n37
shaming: as corrective, 47, 145, 181, 212, 224, 229, 294n15. See also social sanction
siblings: death of, 259; hierarchy among, 30, 91, 279n32; language for, 82, 247–51, 278n28; relationships of, 82, 295n20
sin. See wrongdoing
sixty: in *Acts of John*, 124; life expectancy at, 6, 117, 120, 228n35, 307n13; and military roles, 65, 312n49; and parricide, 134, 255; and public roles, 48, 134, 135, 137; as rhetoric, 131; and the saying "sixty over the bridge," 134, 313n49; and slaves, 313n51; as threshold of old age, 133–6, 146, 258, 312n46, 313n50; women at the age of, 113, 269n15, 273n5, 305n5, 306n13, 312n44, 315n71. See also sixty+ widow
sixty+ widow, 113–47; as exemplary, ideal model, 145–6, 192, 196–7, 232, 236, 326n28; and funerary rites, 135–6; on a list (honoured), 137–45; and noble deeds, 117, 122–3, 127–30, 137, 330nn11–12; not an "office," 121–3, 151, 306n13; as not a real widow, 119–21, 152, 310n33; and parallels to 1 Tim. 2:9–15, 191–2; and past deeds (witnessed by others), 121, 123, 126–30, 147, 178, 230, 236–7;
slaves: in household, 82–3, 189, 237, 277n26, 278–9n30, 292n6, 319n23, 337n9; life course of, 28, 313n51; and obedience, 55, 180; and reputation, 240, 254, 299n23, 339–40n8, 340n9
social change: in ancient Greece, 60–1; in ancient Rome, 61–4, 239; and conflict, 40–5, 246, 251, 256; and ethnographic data, 23, 38, 46–51, 282n47, 334n33; and occasion of 1 Timothy, 11, 17, 19, 33, 38, 59–60, 74, 110, 226, 239, 252; and sociological theories, 282n48
social sanction, 109–11, 195, 305n48; rebuke as, 218, 223; and shame, 110–11, 145, 181

teaching. See elders; older women; opponents
thirty: and Jesus, 117, 261; and living parents and grandparents, 7, 300n32, 340n12; and male identity, 6, 293n10; and public roles, 62, 268n11, 285nn17, 20, 286n21, 305n7, 322n38; and widowhood, 94
Timothy: and age-related relationships, 238–9; appointing leaders, 16, 221, 335n42; character of, 15–16, 181, 218, 221, 225–6; as exemplary model, 54, 71, 72–4, 78, 80–1, 92, 180, 217, 227, 235, 240, 243; as historical person, 72; and inheritance to guard, 43, 54, 71, 220–1, 238; and leadership, 74, 88; sanctioned by elders, 66, 72, 74, 88, 221, 238, 240; as a servant (*diakonos*), 238, 270n18, 335n42;

teaching of, 54, 66, 71, 237–9; as young, 3–4, 34, 53–4, 217, 221–2, 226, 238
traditional Mediterranean cultures. See modern Mediterranean cultures

univira, 96, 126–7, 170–1, 230, 310n30
urban life, 23, 35, 82–3, 92, 160, 169–70, 227, 237, 267n6

vice list, 104, 241, 337n13, 338n16
virgins: and public roles, 158, 171, 182, 322n38; and widows, 99, 132, 181, 188, 307n18, 315–16n1, 323n13
voluntary associations, 25, 66–8, 230; as analogy for Christ groups, 250–1, 256, 287n29, 288n32; with functions like kin, 82–3, 92, 214, 217

washing feet, 129–30, 310n34
wealth: of community members, 202, 242, 243; and generosity, 120, 327n38, 330n12; and intergenerational behaviour, 43, 86; and love of money, 205; of older women, 121, 124, 128, 131, 168, 171; and opponents, 56; in Roman context, 61, 239, 312n49, 332n19; and selfish gain/motives, 191, 205, 284n5, 300n29; and social standing, 27, 32, 86, 88, 109, 207; of women, 96, 159, 166, 169, 188, 229, 231, 326n30, 336n5. See also inheritance

widows, 93–197, 227–32; and assumptions about financial aid, 118–21; attracted to Christ groups, 257; contrast between real and younger, 152–3; definition of, 93–4, 97; image of, 100; as liminal, 99, 132; in modern Mediterranean (traditional), 95–6; portion of population, 269n14; power, 121–6; sexual passion, 130–3; as suspect, 159; as unlucky, 127; vulnerability of, 152, 159, 176, 177–9, 196, 231, 257, 316n7
widows with family, 36, 96, 101–3, 107–11, 156, 196, 228, 230, 232, 235–6, 239, 243
witness, 69–70, 211, 213, 220, 226, 233–4, 289n38
women's networks: ancient, 36, 169–71, 187–8; modern, 83, 129, 167, 319nn27, 29, 321nn30, 36
wrongdoing: of accusers, 211–13, 333nn24–25; and age, 241–3; contrast with noble works, 235–7; seriousness of, 220–3, 332–3n23; of younger men, 35, 218, 224

younger men, 213–20; as accusers, 213, 218, 224, 233, 235; and ambition, 74, 189, 215, 217, 256, 295n19; and challenge to leadership, 65, 222, 234, 255, 288n34; deference of, 4, 33–4, 210; as disciplined/rebuked, 35, 235; and disrespectful behaviour, 198, 211, 294n15; and envy, 214, 290n43, 334n35; as exceptional, 88–9, 294n14; as gullible, 62, 215, 217; and ideal behaviour, 83–9; and marriage, 121; on opinions given to elders, 40, 44, 85, 90; as portion of population, 256; as rebellious, 215, 219, 233, 254; and reputation, 197, 221; and resistance to control, 41, 214; and self-control, 194, 222; and stereotypes, 216, 218, 238; visible in Christ groups, 245, 251–2, 255–6, 259; in voluntary associations, 67–8. *See also* deference; older men; wrongdoing

younger widows, 148–75; and the adversary's condemnation, 154, 156, 163, 196, 240, 316n7; and children, 151, 316n4; definition, 117, 100, 131, 151–2; "denial of" (problematic translation), 118, 151, 172, 230, 307n17, 319n18; desire to remarry, 181–4, 231, 317n10; expectations to remarry, 98, 100, 127–8, 148, 160–1, 176–7, 197; and idleness, 102, 156, 160; "intercede for" (παραιτοῦ), 149, 152–3, 172–3, 197, 231; and motion away from Christ, 157–8; as not "under sixty," 151; and opponents' judgment, 156, 181, 183–4, 197; and Paul's directive desiring (βούλομαι) remarriage, 150, 156, 160–5, 163, 165, 177, 184–5, 319n18; perception of behaviour of, 56, 97, 154–8, 173, 181; and reasons for wanting remarriage; 94–6, 158; and reputation of the group, 40, 58, 98, 148, 154, 157, 176–7, 184, 197, 230–1, 316n7; as sexualized, 157–60; as vulnerable, 152, 157, 159, 171, 173, 176, 178, 231, 257, 316n7; without father, 189. *See also* middle-aged women, younger women

younger women, 91, 151, 163–4, 167, 183–4, 227, 316n7. *See also* middle-aged women; older women; purity; younger widows